Emory Upton

The Armies of Asia and Europe

Embracing official reports on the armies of Japan, China, India, Persia, Italy, Russia, Austria, Germany, France, and England, accompanied by letters descriptive of a journey from Japan to the Caucasus

Emory Upton

The Armies of Asia and Europe
Embracing official reports on the armies of Japan, China, India, Persia, Italy, Russia, Austria, Germany, France, and England, accompanied by letters descriptive of a journey from Japan to the Caucasus

ISBN/EAN: 9783744797184

Printed in Europe, USA, Canada, Australia, Japan

Cover: Foto ©ninafisch / pixelio.de

More available books at **www.hansebooks.com**

THE ARMIES OF ASIA AND EUROPE:

EMBRACING

OFFICIAL REPORTS

ON THE

ARMIES OF JAPAN, CHINA, INDIA, PERSIA, ITALY, RUSSIA, AUSTRIA, GERMANY, FRANCE, AND ENGLAND.

ACCOMPANIED BY

LETTERS DESCRIPTIVE OF A JOURNEY FROM JAPAN TO THE CAUCASUS.

BY

EMORY UPTON,

BREVET MAJOR-GENERAL UNITED STATES ARMY.

NEW YORK:
D. APPLETON AND COMPANY,
549 AND 551 BROADWAY.
1878.

LETTER OF TRANSMITTAL.

FORT MONROE, VIRGINIA, *December* 15, 1877.

To the Adjutant-General U. S. A., Washington, D. C.

SIR: I have the honor to submit, herewith, my report on the armies of Japan, China, India, Persia, Italy, Russia, Austria, Germany, France, and England.

The authority for making the military tour around the world, which enabled me to make this report, is contained in the following letter of instructions from the Hon. Secretary of War, viz.:

WAR DEPARTMENT, WASHINGTON CITY, *June* 28, 1875.

GENERAL: On or about June 30th next you will be relieved from the Military Academy.

Upon being so relieved, it is desired that you proceed to San Francisco, Cal., visiting, on the route to that city, Salt Lake City, the mines of Nevada, and the Yosemite Valley; that on or about August 1st you sail from San Francisco for Japan and China. On reaching Canton, in China, you will proceed, *via* Singapore, to Calcutta; thence up the valley of the Ganges to Peshawar, and thence to the Russian possessions at Tashkend, by the most practicable route.

Should it, however, be found impracticable to proceed to the Russian possessions from Peshawar, you will select the most feasible route that will enable you to reach Europe. Having arrived in Europe, you are required to visit the camps of instruction and military schools of Italy, Germany, Austria, Russia, France, and England, and thence return to the United States.

The professional object of this order is to enable you to examine and report upon the organization, tactics, discipline, and the manœuvres of the armies along the route mentioned, and in Germany the special examination of the schools for the instruction of officers in strategy, grand tactics, applied tactics, and the higher duties in the art of war, and the collection and compilation of such other information as might naturally be expected to be of utility to this Government.

During your absence upon this duty, which shall not exceed eighteen months, you will report, as nearly monthly as practicable, your address to the Adjutant-General; and on your return will make a full, detailed, written report to the Secretary of War upon all the subjects mentioned in this communication.

. . . .

You will report to General Sherman for further instructions, if he desires to give you any ; and you will be accompanied by Major George A. Forsyth, Ninth Cavalry, and by Captain J. P. Sanger, First Artillery, who have been detailed for that purpose.

Yours, very respectfully,

WM. W. BELKNAP,
Secretary of War.

General EMORY UPTON, WEST POINT, N. Y.

In pursuance of the orders of the Hon. Secretary of War, I reported on the 12th of July to the General of the Army at St. Louis, who gave me the following letter of instructions:

HEADQUARTERS ARMY OF THE UNITED STATES,
ST. LOUIS, MO., *July* 12, 1875.

General EMORY UPTON, *United States Army, present.*

DEAR GENERAL: I have read with pleasure the letter of instructions to you by the Secretary of War, and congratulate you and your associates on having an opportunity, such as has never in my recollection been enjoyed by any officers of the army at any former period of our history. I know that you will profit by it, and only to suggest a few thoughts will I venture to use that part of the letter of the Secretary which requires you to report to me.

You and I have already had much correspondence—mostly private—on this very contemplated tour of the world, so that I think we mutually understand each other. You know that, about four years ago, I traveled up the Mediterranean and Black Seas to Tiflis, the capital of the Russian Caucasus. Naturally I would like to have you approach Europe by that gateway. The objects of interest in Japan and China seem to me to have been well examined and reported on by modern travelers. In like manner, the armies, forts, garrisons, and camps of Europe seem to me to have been studied by American officers and authors, until we know all that seems applicable to our system of government and people; but Asia, especially India, Afghanistan, Persia, Khokand, Bokhara, Toorkistan, etc.—the lands whence came our civilization, whence came the armies of Xerxes, Genghis Khan, etc.—remain to us, in America, almost a sealed book, though we know that the reflux tide of civilization is setting back from Europe to those very lands. England and Russia are the two great powers that are now engaged in the work, and you cannot devote too much time and study to the systems of military government, by which these nations utilize the people and resources of interior Asia. I therefore advise you to spend as much time as possible in Calcutta and India; cultivate the acquaintance of the officers, civil and military; ascertain how a small force of British troops, aided by the native troops, govern 200,000,000 people; notice how they quarter, feed, and maintain their men, and transport them in peace and war; then make up your mind how to reach the Caspian Sea preferably all the way by land.

There are several routes: the one I would prefer is from Peshawar through the famed Khyber Pass to Cabul; thence to Herat, to Teheran, around the lower end of the Caspian Sea to Tabriz and Mount Ararat. From Tabriz, I know, you will have no trouble to reach Tiflis, where you meet a highly-civilized and refined people, with railroad to the Black Sea, where you will have choice of routes by steamer to Odessa or Constantinople.

Another route of equal interest would be from Peshawar across the Hindoo Koosh, to Bokhara, Khiva, and the Caspian.

Any or either of these routes will enable you to see the nomadic nations of Central Asia, who are far from being barbarous, but hold themselves as the most cultivated people on earth. Their customs, habits, laws, and rules of morality, date far behind the history of Christianity; and, I doubt not, a sojourn among them will give you much knowledge that will be useful to us, as we come to people the interior of America.

Should, however, neither of these routes be practicable, you can go by rail to Bombay, and take steamer to the Persian Gulf, and thence cross over to the Mediterranean at Smyrna, or to the Black Sea at Trebizond, whence steamers will convey you to the more agreeable and more familiar routes of Europe.

I will watch your progress with intense interest, and will be pleased to hear from you at any time at your own convenience; and, when you return, I shall welcome you back, and do all that is in my power to enable you to record your observations and publish them for our common instruction and entertainment.

With great respect, your friend,

W. T. SHERMAN, *General.*

Having been joined by Major Sanger at St. Louis, and by General Forsyth at San Francisco, we sailed on the 2d of August for Japan, where we arrived on the 26th.

Nearly all of the month of September we devoted to Japan, and thence sailed for China, where we remained till November, visiting, in the mean time, Peking, and the objects of military interest at the capital, Tientsin, Shanghai, Chekiang, and Canton.

From Hong-Kong we sailed for Ceylon and Bombay, where we arrived the 29th of November.

The interval from this time till the 11th of February, in pursuance of the instructions of the General of the Army, we spent in India, visiting nearly all of the great military stations in the valley of the Ganges, from Calcutta to Peshawar.

The study of army organization was greatly facilitated by being twice permitted to visit the camp of instruction at Delhi, which, being organized specially in honor of the visit of the Prince of Wales, was the largest ever held in India.

On arriving at Calcutta, I immediately called upon his excellency the viceroy, Lord Northbrook, to whom I had a letter of introduction from the General of the Army, which stated the object of our tour, and the routes he preferred we should take. As we were required to defer to the views of the viceroy, he informed us that, in order to cross the Himalayas, the passes of which were between 16,000 and 17,000 feet high, we would have to wait till the following summer, and that, while we might reach Kashgar, it would be altogether uncertain as to whether we would be permitted to proceed farther toward Tashkend and the Russian possessions. In consideration of the shortness of our time, which was limited to eighteen months, this route was therefore abandoned.

As to the route through the Khyber Pass to Cabul, and thence to Herat and Teheran, the viceroy informed us that the orders of the Indian Government positively prohibited British officers from attempting it, on account of the complications that might arise in case they should be killed or maltreated by any of the savage or semi-independent tribes who dwell in Afghanistan. He stated that it might be possible for us to get through; but, as the danger would be great, and particularly as the Indian Government would be censurable in permitting us to cross the frontier should any harm befall us, he preferred that we should relinquish the project.

The third route therefore only remained open. Accordingly, we left Bombay on the 11th of February, disembarked at Bushire, and taking horses proceeded, *via* Shiraz, Ispahan, Teheran, and Tabriz, to Tiflis; thence, crossing the Caucasus, we proceeded, *via* Rostoff, to Sevastopol and Constantinople.

As representatives of the Army of the United States, we

were received with great courtesy by the Governments of all of the countries we were ordered to visit, and every facility was cheerfully extended to us for the prosecution of official investigations.

From our ministers, and consuls, in Japan, China, India, Italy, Russia, Austria, France, and England, we received great kindness and every assistance necessary to complete our mission.

I have already reported that through the action of our legation at Berlin my comrades and myself were excluded from the German manœuvres, and that, as a consequence, we were prevented from witnessing the practical application of modern tactics in the army in which they have found their widest development.

In preparing my reports on the different armies, I have given in brief their organization, and then have enlarged on those features which, in my judgment, we ought to imitate. These features are:

1. The three or four battalion system for infantry regiments.

2. A system of detail, whereby our officers may serve alternately in the staff and the line.

3. A system of personal reports, by means of which the Government may be informed of the character, capacity, and qualifications, of all of its officers.

4. Examinations previous to promotion.

5. Schools for enlisted men.

6. Schools and qualifications for officers preparatory to receiving commissions.

7. Schools for officers in the art of war, and the higher branches of their profession, subsequent to receiving commissions.

Until we change our present inexpensive organization, which, with few modifications, comes down to us from the Revolution, and devote more attention to military education, the details of arms and equipments in foreign armies merit little, if any, of our attention. I have therefore excluded them from the report, in order that the more prominent objects should not be obscured.

Finding that I would not be able to collect, in the short time allowed, all of the information that might be desirable, I devolved upon General Forsyth the investigations in reference to cavalry, and upon Major Sanger the same in reference to the artillery.

Both of these officers are preparing their reports, which have been delayed in consequence of the performance of other duties.

In the hope that our united labors may prove acceptable to the Hon. Secretary of War,

I am, very respectfully, your obedient servant,

E. UPTON,
Lieutenant-Colonel 4th Artillery,
Brevet Major-General, U. S. A.

ARMY OF JAPAN.

The introduction of modern ideas into the Army of Japan dates from 1867, when the Emperor Napoleon III., at the solicitation of the Tycoon, sent out a military commission, consisting of—

    1 Captain of the staff, commandant,
    1 Captain of engineers,
    1 Captain of artillery,
    2 Lieutenants of infantry,
    1 Lieutenant of cavalry ; and
    15 Non-commissioned officers.

The commission, whose object was to instruct the Japanese troops in the tactics and regulations of the different arms of service, had scarcely begun its work, when, in consequence of the Revolution of 1868, it was recalled to France.

The primary object of the revolution was to restore to the Mikado the temporal power, which for centuries had been usurped by the Tycoons. The secondary object, scarcely less prominent, was the expulsion of foreigners, whose arrogance had become intolerable, and whose influence was regarded as subversive of the ancient principles of government.

No sooner, however, did the government of the Mikado come in contact with the foreigners than, like that of the Tycoon, it perceived the value of military organization and training. Formidable men-of-war, within cannon-range of the capital, told of the naval strength of foreign nations, while foreign troops at Yedo and Yokohama attested the superior skill and discipline of modern armies.

Anxious to establish his throne in the capital of the deposed Tycoon, the Mikado, with the consent of the clans, which had supported his cause, issued in 1871 the decree which called into existence the imperial army.

By the terms of the decree the clan of Satsuma was to raise and transfer to the Mikado 4 battalions of infantry, and 2 battalions of artillery; the clan of Chôsiu 3 battalions of infantry; the clan of Tosa 2 battalions of infantry, 2 battalions of artillery, and 2 squadrons of cavalry.

These troops, to which other clans agreed to add their contingents, were ordered to Yedo, where they were to constitute the nucleus of a national army.

To organize and discipline the army, foreign aid was again invoked.

On application of the Mikado the Emperor of France appointed a second commission, which arrived in Japan in 1872.

This commission was composed as follows:

1 Lieutenant-colonel, commandant,
2 Captains of engineers,
2 Captains of artillery,
2 Captains of infantry,
1 Lieutenant of artillery,
1 Lieutenant of infantry,
1 Lieutenant of cavalry,
1 Quartermaster Sergeant of engineers,
1 Controleur d'Armes, to superintend the manufacture of arms; and
15 Non-commissioned officers of all arms.

The object of the commission was to reorganize and instruct the army, and to found such military institutions as were necessary to place the army on a firm modern basis.

Adopting the French army as a model, the commission began its labors in July, 1872.

The first work was to cause the French regulations and tactics to be translated. In the mean time, by means of interpreters, theoretical and practical instruction was given at Yedo to

2 Regiments of the Guard,
1 Squadron of the Guard,
2 Batteries of the Guard, and
1 Battalion of engineers.

In addition, several battalions of infantry, batteries of artillery, and squadrons of cavalry, of the line of the army, were sent annually to Yedo to receive the same instruction as the guard.

The officers and non-commissioned officers were frequently assembled, and instructed in the principles of tactics and military discipline. Camps of instruction were established annually for the purpose of illustrating service in campaign, and teaching the movements of large bodies of troops. Target-practice was also taught to the infantry and artillery.

As the mission of the French officers was not to command, but to instruct, Japanese officers retained command of their battalions, batteries, and squadrons, and on the drill-ground learned through interpreters the movements they were required to execute.

MILITARY INSTITUTIONS.

The French commission has already established at Yedo the following institutions, viz.:

A Military Academy for Officers,
A School for Non-commissioned Officers,
A School for Musketry and Gymnastics,
A Veterinary School, and
A School for Practical Engineering.

It has also established an arsenal at Yedo, and a foundery at Oji; and near Yedo a depot for remounts, and a polygon or school of practice for artillery.

MILITARY ACADEMY.

The object of the Military Academy of Japan, like our own at West Point, which was adopted as a model, is to educate officers for the engineers and all arms of service.

The admissions, which are by competitive examination, number about one hundred and fifty per year, and of this number about one hundred and forty graduate.

The course of study for the engineers, artillery, and cavalry, which are regarded as special arms, is three years; for the infantry two years.

The practical instruction for the first two years is mostly limited to infantry, at the end of which time the students designated for officers of infantry go to their regiments, while the students for engineers, artillery, and cavalry, remain another year to perfect themselves in the specialties of their arms.

The course of study embraces—

  Drawing,   Physics,
  French,   Tactics,
  Mathematics,   Artillery,
     Fortification.

The system of instruction is by lecture, and subsequent interrogation, the same as pursued in all of the Continental military schools of Europe. The professors are Japanese, who have received their instruction either from French officers or professors.

The pay of the cadets, in addition to clothing and rations, is about $3.00 per month.

The buildings for the Military Academy, constructed between 1873 and 1875, consist of offices, barracks, mess-hall, riding-hall, and laboratory, inclosing a large court which is used as a drill ground. The energy of the Government and its appreciation of the value of the academy are shown by the magnitude of the buildings, and the great rapidity with which they were erected.

As an instance of the latter, a building, nearly 300 feet long, which was burned in the spring of 1875, was reconstructed and nearly ready for use by the following July.

SCHOOL FOR NON-COMMISSIONED OFFICERS.

The object of this school is to educate non-commissioned officers for all arms of service. The course is eighteen months for infantry, and two years for artillery, cavalry, and engineers.

From 300 to 500 non-commissioned officers graduate annually. On graduation they are required to serve seven years, and receive the grade of corporal, or sergeant, according to their proficiency. Those who specially excel are sent as cadets to the Military Academy to study for commissioned officers.

The course of instruction is both theoretical and practical. The theoretical embraces the common branches, and the tactics and regulations for each arm of service. For practical instruction the non-commissioned officers are organized into 2 battalions of infantry, 2 batteries of artillery, 1 squadron of cavalry, and 2 companies of engineers.

Instruction is also given to musicians, and these are trained to become instructors of buglers and trumpeters.

At reviews and manœuvres the battalions, batteries, and the squadron of non-commissioned officers exercise with the troops of the guard and line, and show by the precision of their movements the value of the training they receive.

The pay of the non-commissioned officers, in addition to clothing and rations, is about $1.50 per month.

THE SCHOOL OF MUSKETRY AND GYMNASTICS.

The object of this school is to teach precision in musketry-firing, and to increase physical training in the army. To this end one or more officers and non-commissioned officers are sent annually to the school from every regiment and corps in the service. On completing the course, they return to their corps, where they serve as instructors. The number of officers and men undergoing instruction, in 1875, was as follows:

21 Captains,
24 First-lieutenants,
26 Second-lieutenants,
8 Sergeant-majors,

30 Sergeants,
32 Corporals,
40 Trumpeters.

ORGANIZATION OF THE ARMY OF JAPAN, 1875.

WAR DEPARTMENT.

The War Department consists of—
1 Minister of War, and
2 Vice-Ministers of War.

For the rapid dispatch of business the department is divided into bureaus and sections, as follows:

1st Bureau.—Six Sections.

1st Section.—Letters and correspondence.
2d   "   Recruiting.
3d   "   General and staff officers, and military schools.
4th   "   Military Justice.
5th   "   Returns and reports.
6th   "   Translations.

2d Bureau.—Five Sections.

1st Section.—Personnel of the infantry.
2d   "   Personnel of the cavalry.
3d   "   Breeding of horses.
4th   "   Trains and transportation of supplies.
5th   "   Provost-Marshal.

3d Bureau.—Two Sections.

1st Section.—Personnel of the artillery.
2d   "   Expenses of artillery in the purchase and manufacture of guns, carriages, ammunition, and other matériel.

4th Bureau.—Two Sections.

1st Section.—Personnel of the engineers.
2d   "   Expenses of matériel.

5th Bureau.—*Nine Sections.*

1st Section.—Subsistence and fuel.
2d   "   Clothing, camp, and garrison equipage.
3d   "   Hospitals and ambulances.
4th   "   Payment of officers and men.
5th   "   Regulations of the 5th bureau.
6th   "   Correcting and auditing the expenses of the 5th bureau.
7th   "   Auditing disbursements for matériel.
8th   "   Estimating expenses for coming year, and payment of pensions.
9th   "   Total expenses of the entire War Department.

6th Bureau.

This bureau, which in 1875 was not yet organized, is intended to supervise the military affairs of the island of Yesso. Until organized, the duties will be performed by officers of the 1st bureau.

There is also a small bureau having charge of the correspondence of the Minister of War, consisting of two majors and three captains, who are detailed from both the staff and the line.

The Minister of War is a general officer; the chief of the 1st bureau may be a major or brigadier-general the chiefs of the 2d, 3d, and 4th bureaux are brigadier-generals; the chief of the 5th bureau is the Intendant-General.

The assistant chiefs of bureaux are colonels or lieutenant-colonels; the chiefs of sections are majors.

GENERAL OFFICERS.

There are—
 1 General,
 3 Major-generals,
 12 Brigadier-generals.

Of the brigadier-generals three are members of Parliament, and one is Vice-Minister of Justice.

ADJUTANT-GENERAL'S DEPARTMENT.

This department, in 1876, was not fully organized.

For the transaction of business, it is divided into seven sections.

1st Section.—Is charged with correspondence.
2d   "   Collects military, statistical, and geographical information concerning Asia.
3d   "   Same, concerning America, and Europe.
4th   "   Study and writing of military history.
5th   "   Geography.
6th   "   Topography.
7th   "   Printing, preservation, and translation of records.

ORGANIZATION OF THE ARMY.

In 1875 the army, on a footing of peace and war, was organized as presented in the following tables:

Standing Army.

ARM OF SERVICE.	NUMBER OF ORGANIZATIONS.	Peace-footing.	War-footing.	Total Peace-footing.	Total War-footing.
Infantry	14 Regiments, or 42 Battalions.	640	960	26,880	40,320
Cavalry	2 Battalions.	120	150	240	300
Artillery	9 Battalions, or 18 Batteries.	120	Mountain-Artillery. 160 / Field-Artillery. 180	2,160	2,700
Engineers	9 Companies. / 6 Companies.	120 / 60	150 / 80	1,080 / 860	1,350 / 480
Heavy coast-artillery	9 Companies.	80	100	720	900
Total				31,440	46,050

INFANTRY.

Imperial Guard.

ARM OF SERVICE.	NUMBER OF ORGANIZATIONS.	Always maintained on a War-footing.	
Infantry	2 Regiments—6 Battalions.	672	2,046
Cavalry	1 Battalion.	150	150
Artillery	1 Battalion—2 Batteries.	150	240
Engineers	1 Company. 1 Company.	150 60	150 60
Total			2,594

Total Number of Soldiers.

ARM OF SERVICE.	NUMBER OF ORGANIZATIONS.	NUMBER OF MEN.	
		Peace-footing.	War-footing.
Infantry	16 Regiments, or 46 Battalions.	29,069	45,006
Cavalry	8 Battalions.	890	440
Artillery	10 Battalions, or 20 Batteries.	2,480	2,960
Engineers	10 Companies. 7 Companies.	1,280 440	1,500 500
Heavy coast-artillery	9 Companies.	720	900
Total		84,709	49,373

The population of Japan, in 1874, was 33,008,430, giving a ratio of the army on a peace-footing to the total population, of 1,000 to 1,000,000.

INFANTRY.

How completely the army has been Europeanized may be inferred from the organization of the infantry.

A regiment consists of three battalions, of four companies each.

The field and staff is composed of—

1 Colonel, commandant.
3 Majors, commandants of battalions.
1 Captain, regimental adjutant.

3 First-lieutenants, battalion-adjutants.
1 First-lieutenant, regimental paymaster.
3 Second-lieutenants, battalion paymasters.
1 Major, regimental surgeon.
3 Captains, battalion surgeons.

In war each battalion has an additional surgeon.

The company consists of—

1 Captain,
2 First-lieutenants,
2 Second-lieutenants,
1 Sergeant-major,
1 Quartermaster-sergeant,
8 Sergeants,
16 Corporals,
1 Commissary-corporal, and
160 Privates.

In war the number of privates is increased to 240.

The artillery, cavalry, engineers, adjutant-general's department, departments of supply, medical corps, and military train, bear equally with the infantry the stamp of European or French organization.

Recognizing the duty of every citizen to bear arms in the defense of his country, military service is made obligatory.

Recruits are obtained by drafting, and, after the expiration of the term of enlistment, which is three years, pass into the reserve.

The height of the Japanese soldier is from five feet one to five feet three inches.

The ration consists principally of rice and fish, but meat is issued twice a week. Bread is also to form part of the ration; but, for want of skill in making it, the men have thus far preferred rice.

The uniform of the army is thoroughly European, and is made of white duck for summer, and of dark-blue cloth for winter.

The infantry is armed with the Snyder and Enfield rifles, sabre-bayonet.

At the arsenal at Yedo, muzzle-loading muskets were rapidly being converted into breech-loaders of the Albani pattern.

The barracks of the army are of the most substantial and imposing construction. Those of the guard at Yedo inclose a square court of many acres, all smoothly graveled. Each building accommodates an entire regiment. The companies are quartered in the upper story; the lower story is devoted to offices, mess-rooms, reading-rooms, and store-rooms. The national habit of cleanliness is encouraged by ample provision for both hot and cold baths.

The hospital, like the barracks, is modern in all of its arrangements. The guard-house is light and airy, and gives evidence that punishment is administered according to modern military law. On a visit from officers of rank all prisoners, whose offenses are not capital, are released. This privilege was extended to the sole prisoner who was in confinement on the occasion of our inspection.

The sudden transition of Japan from ancient to modern civilization, which will ever be the marvel of history, is nowhere more conspicuous than in the army. Appreciating the necessity of substituting a national force in the place of the undisciplined hordes, voluntarily furnished by the clans under the old *régime*, the Government applied for assistance to a nation renowned for the success of its arms.

In response to its appeal, officers of distinguished reputation, responsible to their Secretary of War, and not adventurers, were designated for the mission.

The zeal, the intelligence, the enterprise, and the success of the French officers were no less surprising than the wisdom of the Government in supporting them, without jealousy, in all measures for reform. Wherever we went we saw the evidence of their skill. At the review at Yedo, kindly tendered by the Minister of War, we saw four battalions of the guard, two battalions of non-commissioned officers, and two squadrons of cavalry, manœuvre with commendable precision.

At Lake Biva, and Osaka, hundreds of miles from the capital, we saw the French tactics successfully applied by Japanese officers to skirmishing, and to the schools of the battalion and regiment. In the barracks and foundery at Osaka the same neatness, order, and system, prevailed as at Yedo.

If the army bears unmistakable evidence of French organization, it bears equally the impress of French ideas in its drill and discipline. The men were badly set up, and on review and at exercises appeared to have fallen into the swinging of arms and slovenliness of marching, once so admired in the French army, but so utterly in contrast with the precision and steadiness of the English and German soldiers.

The recent modifications in tactics require increased individuality among the men, and this individuality, it has been shown by experience, can only be developed by rigid discipline and steadiness when in ranks. As Japan has military observers in America and Europe, it is to be hoped that they will call the attention of their Government to so vicious a practice, before it takes root in her military system.

In every other respect the progress of reorganization is to be admired. The fact that all of the military institutions have been established, and many buildings erected, within the space of three years, and that the same period has sufficed to inaugurate a uniform system of instruction in all corps and arms of the service, is sufficient proof of the enlightened policy which Japan, in spite of financial embarrassment, is pursuing in reference to her army.

Already she has reaped the reward of her foresight. The foundations of her government, which, in 1868, were built upon the sand, are settling down to the rock; insurrections, before ripening into rebellion, have been promptly stamped out; while her success in Formosa and Corea give evidence that Japan, no longer contented with progress at home, is destined to play an important part in the history of the world.

ARMY OF CHINA.

The Board of War, or *Ping Pu*, like the War Department in other countries, is charged with the general management of the army, and in addition has the control of the navy.

Its duty, as expressed by the Chinese, is "to aid the sovereign in protecting the people by the direction of all military affairs in the metropolis and the provinces, and to regulate the hinge of the state upon the reports received from the various departments regarding deprivation of, or appointment to, office; succession to, or creation of, hereditary military rank; postal, or courier arrangements; examinations and selections of the deserving, and accuracy of returns."

The Board of War is a civil court composed of a superintendent, who is generally one of the cabinet ministers, two presidents, and four vice-presidents. Ordinarily all of the members are civilians, the majority of them being Manchus.

The board receives reports from all officers in command of land and marine forces; from those responsible for the transport of grain, and the security of river-embankments; from those who administer the affairs of nomads and half-subdued savages; and from persons in charge of the horse and camel pastures.

To enable the board to discharge its duties, it is divided into four bureaux, or *sze*, which are further divided into sub-divisions, or sections:

1. The *Wu-siuen*, or first bureau, regulates promotion according to service, in order of succession, or in right of descent, and has 13 secretaries.

2. The *Chih-fang*, or second bureau, corresponding to the Adjutant-General's Department, regulates the distribution of rewards and punishments, the camp and field inspection of troops, and the issue of general orders, and has 17 secretaries.

3. The *Chay-ma*, or third bureau, provides for the supply and distribution of horses for the cavalry, and has 9 secretaries.

4. The *Wu-hu*, or fourth bureau, which, in addition to other duties, seems to unite the Ordnance and Quartermaster's Departments, attends to the rosters, prepares the army estimates, provides equipments and ammunition, attends to the examination of military candidates, and has 7 secretaries.

Attached to the Board of War are several other sections of great importance. One of these sections keeps the rosters for duty, promotion, and employment of the bannermen; a second has the management of the couriers and posts, and sees to the reception and transmission of dispatches and memorials; a third attends to the delivery of commissions and orders from all the governmental bureaux; another delivers all memorials addressed to the emperor, and seals and sends off the replies to these, and the letters from the Council of State.

The total force employed in the board at Peking, including under-secretaries and clerks of all grades, whose names are inscribed in the Red-Book as receiving pay, is 197, of whom about one-third are Chinese.

The board has no control over the bannermen, and other troops stationed in Peking and Yuen-ming Yuen; and, as the oversight of the troops in each province is intrusted in a great degree to the local authorities, its duties, in comparison with those of Ministers of War in Western countries, are much circumscribed.

INFANTRY.

As the guards in European countries are considered as models for other troops, so in China the condition of the army may be inferred from the organization, equipment, and discipline, of the troops at Peking.

The infantry consists as follows:

4 Battalions, of 875 officers and men each, armed with muzzle-loading rifles of Russian manufacture. These battalions are partially instructed in European tactics, 400 of their number having gone to Tientsin several years since for the purpose of receiving foreign instruction with the view of transmitting it to their comrades.

1 Battalion, or Cadet Corps, under the authority of the *Nui-rou-Fu* or Court of the Household, composed of 500 young men armed with bows, arrows, spears, and several other varieties of Chinese weapons.

1 Battalion, composed of 500 men, armed with the small matchlock.

2 Battalions, composed of 500 men each, armed with large matchlocks, called *gingals*, one to every two men. The barrel of the large matchlock is six feet long, and when fired rests near the muzzle on the shoulder of one of the men, who assumes a stooping position, supporting his hands upon his knees.

1 Corps of 1,200 men, armed with swords and shields.

1 Battalion, composed of 200 men, armed with various Chinese weapons, who constitute the body-guard of Prince Chun, or the Seventh Prince.

CAVALRY.

The cavalry consists of—

2 Divisions of 1,000 men each, armed with carbines and Chassepots, and

3 Battalions of 500 men each, armed with matchlocks.

ARTILLERY.

The artillery consists of 24 field-guns, 2 horses and 6 men being attached to each gun. The guns are of Russian manufacture, and all are small brass smooth-bores, except two, which are rifled. The artillery brigade is attached to the four battalions of infantry, armed with muzzle-loading rifles.

In addition to the above there is a force of 1,000 artillery, armed with the swivel, a small iron gun, fired from a bench, wall, or tripod, with a calibre varying from four ounces to a pound.

All guns are still discharged by means of the port-fire, blank cartridges being used for practice.

TROOPS OUTSIDE OF PEKING.

Outside of Peking, and mostly at Hai-tien, in the vicinity of the summer palace of Yuen-ming Yuen, there are two battalions of infantry, 875 men each, armed with muzzle-loading rifles of Russian manufacture.

1,600 Infantry, armed with the large matchlock.

2,000 Cavalry, armed with matchlocks and short swords.

1 Battery of field artillery, 4 guns, 125 men, foreign drilled, and

1 Howitzer battery of 4 guns, with 125 men.

The force in and around Peking, in 1874, was—

Infantry..................	10,250
Cavalry..................	5,500
Artillery..................	1,750, with 32 field-guns;
making a total of......	17,500

This force may be said to constitute the regular army stationed in and around the capital.

BANNERMEN.

In addition to the regular troops at Peking, there is an hereditary or privileged soldiery, composed of Manchus, Mongols, and enrolled Chinese, the latter being the descendants of the Chinese troops who, in 1643, joined the force of invading Manchus. All of these troops, according to their nationality, are organized into "*pah-ki*," or "eight banners." The banners are further arranged in two wings, or divisions, the first, third, fifth, and seventh banners constituting the left wing, the remaining banners the right wing.

Each banner is distinguished by a triangular flag of plain yellow, white, red, and blue, for troops in the left wing, and the same colors bordered with a narrow stripe of different color for troops in the right wing.

Out of the Manchu and Mongol banners, two special forces are selected and enrolled, one of which is named the "*Tsien-fung*," or Vanguard Division, the other "*Hu-kiun ying*," or Flank Division.

These selected corps guard the emperor's palace within the Forbidden City, and serve as his escort whenever he goes out.

The Vanguard Division, including officers, numbers about 1,500 men; the Flank Division is much larger, and has been estimated as high as 15,000.

Besides these two corps, the "*Pu-kiun ying*," or Infantry Division, corresponding to gendarmery, is detailed for the preservation of order within the capital and suburbs; the strength of this division is sometimes reckoned as high as 20,000 men.

The number of bannermen of all arms in and around the capital under pay, exclusive of the Vanguard and Flank Divisions, is estimated at 60,000.

As the city of Peking is wholly set apart from the provincial government of Chihli, and governed by military rule, with troops specially selected for its defense, the capital of the empire, with its series of double and triple walls, assumes the forms and proportions of a vast intrenched camp.

In the province of Chihli there are, exclusive of Peking, twenty-five other banner garrisons, composed mostly of infantry, numbering approximately 40,000 men.

The bannermen are seldom required to drill, and, when called out, muster with rusty swords, bows, spears, and weapons of various descriptions. Receiving but small pay, they are permitted to engage in various kinds of business and traffic.

In twelve of the provincial capitals, where bannermen are stationed, as at Wuchang, Canton, Fuchau, etc., they are assigned with their families to a special and usually fortified quarter, with a view as much as possible to isolate them from the inhabitants. But, notwithstanding the original precautions to secure purity of descent, and attachment to the dynasty, they have in the course of years associated with the people to such a degree as to adopt Chinese language, manners, and customs, and to obliterate the harsh traits of character that distinguished their warlike ancestors. As soldiers they have long since ceased to be useful, and, until reorganized and disciplined, they must remain but profitless pensioners of the Government.

The organization of the troops about Peking gives a good idea of the military system in other parts of the empire. In many of the larger cities, in addition to the hereditary bannermen, there is the *Luh ying*, or Green-Banner Division, consisting altogether of Chinese. These troops ordinarily render merely nominal service, having purchased from their officers, in consideration of their pay, the privilege of engaging in all kinds of commerce. Those who remain in service, instead of being employed as a garrison force, are used rather as a vast land and naval constabulary; couriers; grain, mint, or revenue guards; and escorts for criminals.

The troops for the defense of the distant frontiers, and for the preservation of peace in the provinces, are armed, like those at Peking, with matchlocks, bows, cutlasses, and spears.

In case brigandage or insurrection becomes too formidable to be put down by the regular troops, volunteers, called *Chwang-Yung*, or Braves, are summoned into service, and disbanded when no longer required.

STRENGTH OF THE CHINESE ARMY.

The strength of the Chinese army can never be definitely stated, a fact due to the long-established military policy of the Government, which obliges every province, if possible, to support all of the military and naval forces needed, not only for its own defense, but for the defense of the empire.

The result of this policy is that, as a measure of economy, each province, in time of peace, seeks to reduce its military forces to a minimum, relying in time of war on both regulars and volunteers to supply its deficiency.

In this manner the number of troops in service constantly varies. In 1823, however, a careful analysis of native records gave a total force of 1,263,000 men who were on the pay-rolls of the army, but of whom fully one-third, being only liable to duty, received no pay.

A subsequent investigation, deemed more reliable, fixed the cavalry force of the empire at 87,000; infantry in the field, 195,000; infantry in garrison, 320,000 : giving a total in these two arms of 602,000. It may, therefore, be assumed that the total number of troops varies from 500,000 to 1,000,000, according to the internal condition of the provinces, the governor-generals being allowed to regulate the size of their armies as they may see fit.

Even ignoring these causes of fluctuation, had the army a careful and definite organization on paper, as it pretends to have, the corruption which permits officers to give soldiers indefinite leave, and pocket their pay, would hopelessly reduce the army below the legal standard. As a consequence, when troops are ordered to move, the ranks have to be filled. Men are then called from the field and the workshop, arms are thrust into their hands, and, without knowledge or training, they are exposed to the danger and fatigues of campaigns.

The troops embarked at Shanghai for the recent Formosan expedition were largely of this class. Inveigled on board the vessels through false pretense, many of them, on learning of their destination, and the perils that awaited them, sprang over board and were drowned.

TACTICS.

The Chinese army is as backward in its tactics as in its armament. At the large seaport towns a portion of the troops, since 1860, have from time to time been drilled by Europeans, and this knowledge has been partially extended toward the interior. But, as yet, the Chinese officers have not the slightest appreciation of the amount of instruction required for troops in modern war, nor do they possess any knowledge of the method of arranging and conducting troops in battle. Having prepared their works, and posted their men so as to slaughter an enemy in an attack from the front, they regard an attack in flank as low-minded, if not cowardly.

The instruction witnessed at Peking was a mere burlesque of infantry-drill. There were about 1,200 men on the ground, outside the walls, armed with the large and small matchlock. The superior officers were comfortably seated under tents arranged along the line of battle. The troops were formed in a dense mass, or column, and at a given signal formed right and left front into line. There was no order, nor step; the men marched in twos, threes, and fours, toward the line, laughing, talking and firing their pieces in the air. On arriving in line the fire was continued to the front, in the direction of the tents occupied by the officers.

The band, with gongs, drums, cymbals, and other instruments, was posted behind the centre, and swelled the noise of arms by a continuous clangor.

On a certain signal the line faced to the rear; the band passed through the centre, when the men bearing the large matchlocks, hitherto silent, advanced, like a skirmish-line, a few yards to the front and opened fire. In front of the matchlocks was squatted a line of flagmen who, during the firing, waved their flags horizontally above the ground.

All the signals were made either by flags or by music, a feat that was not difficult, as the formation of line, and the alternate firing to the front and the rear with the small and the large matchlock, were the only movements executed.

At the conclusion of the drill ranks were broken, and the men, individually and in squads, wandered back to the city.

The artillery at the capital is drilled with as little intelligence as the infantry, its firing, through ill-judged economy, being mostly limited to blank cartridges.

The cavalry, such as was seen at the funeral of the late emperor, was mounted on pony-built horses, and was mostly armed with the bow and spear. Drill adapted to such weapons can have no relation to the instruction required for modern cavalry, and need not be described.

DISCIPLINE.

China is the only country in which the profession of arms is not honored. For ages a proverb, to the effect that, "as you would not use good iron to make a nail, so you would not use a good man to make a soldier," has hung like a millstone about the necks of the officers and soldiers of the Chinese army.

Branded as the refuse of society, the policy of the Government has been such as to condemn both officers and men to hopeless ignorance, and to drown every sentiment of magnanimity and honor. Preserving traditions antedating the introduction of fire-arms, the officers have been looked upon as trained athletes, needing only physical development to fit them for their profession. So completely does this idea dominate the Government and the army, that the sole qualifications required of officers at the competitive examinations are expertness in archery on foot and on horseback, sword-practice, and ability to lift and to swing heavy weights.

At Peking, in 1874, 135 officers, who had graduated at the triennial military competition, were subjected to a second examination by two vice-presidents before being admitted to the palace competition of the same year. Each graduate was required to exhibit his skill in horse and foot archery, sword-practice, and stone-lifting. After careful tests, 11 were declared deficient, and were debarred from entering the palace competition. Among the officers were 22 who had been turned back three years, and one six years before.

In accordance with the rule, the record of graduation of the latter, who failed on his third trial, was canceled. The result of the examination was so unsatisfactory that penalties were recommended to be inflicted upon the ministers who presided at the graduating competition.

When the successful candidates at the second examination were brought before the emperor at the palace competition, four were honored with military degrees; seven who failed in either archery, sword-practice, or stone-lifting, were turned back for three years; while one candidate, who failed in both sword-practice and stone-lifting, was turned back six years. Penalties were also pronounced against the ministers who presided at the preliminary examinations.

At the competition in archery at Canton, which we witnessed in November, 1875, the governor-general presided. The targets for archery were sixty yards off, and were six feet high by two feet wide. Each candidate was permitted to shoot six arrows, and at the beginning and end of his trial saluted the governor-general by kneeling. The tally was kept by sticks, deposited before the governor-general after each hit. Some of the candidates missed every shot, while others, more successful, entered the list for stone-lifting. Those who passed all tests successfully were commissioned lieutenants in the army.

The system of competitive examinations for the army was introduced by the present dynasty, in imitation of the time-honored system prevailing in the civil service, and the nature of competition clearly shows the relative esteem in which the military and civil services are held.

Reversing the practice of Europe, where a higher scientific and general education is required to enter the military than the civil service, the latter frequently requiring no special test, the Chinese Government simply demands an aspirant for a commission to give evidence of physical expertness and brute strength; whereas the candidate for civil honors, after spending the best years of his life in study, must show an exact knowledge of the national literature and classics. The quality of officers furnished by such a system can readily be inferred. No encouragement being given to study the art of war, tactics, artillery, engineering, fortification, or any of the sciences so intimately connected with modern war, the Chinese officer is sunk in ignorance as deep as the men, and frequently shows as little respect for law and military discipline. This ignorance, and enforced idleness, its concomitant, encourage vice, particularly the use of opium, which destroys the endurance of the soldier, and disqualifies him for the fatigues and hardships of campaign. The use of opium, which has already become formidable, bids fair, if not checked, to entirely destroy the efficiency of the army.

PUNISHMENTS.

Whenever a serious offense is committed, the governor of the province recommends to the Board of War the summary dismissal of the offender, who, if the recommendation be approved, ceases to be an officer. This power of summary dismissal, or cashiering, is applied to officers of all ranks from general to second-lieutenant, and is usually administered for such offenses as arbitrary conduct, embezzlement, indolence, incapacity, and carelessness.

In 1874, on the application of the Governor of Honan, a captain was cashiered for "undertaking litigious proceedings with an eye to promotion." A subaltern officer, belonging to the nobility, on hearing that a householder was carrying on illicit distillation, ordered the offender into his presence, and, when the accused told him that he was simply making his own spirits for the celebration of the New Year, he refused to believe him, punished him with forty blows, and let him go. For this arbitrary and illegal conduct the officer was cashiered, and stripped of his hereditary title.

HONORS.

To encourage officers to a faithful performance of their duty, various marks of imperial favor are bestowed upon them, such as brevet rank, donations of money, presentation to the emperor, and permission to officers of rank to ride on horseback within the Forbidden City.

Special acts of bravery are rewarded by permission to wear the yellow jacket.

SUPPLIES.

The supplies for the army in money, fuel, forage, arms, and clothing, are usually procured by requisitions made by the commanding officers upon the provincial treasury, the requisitions being submitted for approval to the commander of the forces and the governor, who are responsible for disbursements and expenditures. The money which is paid into the military chest passes through the hands of the commandant of the forces, and is disbursed pursuant to his orders.

In an expedition made outside the Great Wall against the Mohammedan rebels in 1874, the troops were organized into three divisions, numbering 17,000 men. Servants, coolies, and camp-followers, swelled the number to 20,000. The supplies for the expedition were collected in the provinces of Kansuh and Hunan, and thence forwarded, the cost of transportation exceeding many times the original price of the provisions. The long continuance of hostilities, the inevitable consequence of a feeble military policy, so impoverishes some provinces, that application has to be made to the Board of Revenue at Peking for the necessary funds to carry on the war. Other provinces are then called upon to contribute. The Governor of Kweichow, in 1874, acknowledged the services rendered by the different provincial governments in supplying funds for the military operations of the last *twenty years*, which finally terminated in the complete pacification of the province.

TRANSPORTATION.

In the northern part of the empire, and particularly outside the Great Wall, the two-humped Bactrian camel is principally used in transportation. One driver is assigned to a *kafila* of five or six camels, which move in single file. To conduct, the camels a wooden pin, with a broad head, is passed through the nasal cartilage of each animal, and then attached to a cord about six yards long, which is tied to the tail of the camel in front. A large bell is tied to the neck of the hindmost camel, to give notice of any break in the column.

The average load of a camel is 400 catties, or 533 pounds, and his rate of travel two miles and a half per hour.

The length of a string of five camels, carrying but 2,666 pounds, allowing six yards for each camel with his cord, is 30 yards, whereas our six-mule government wagon, frequently carrying 5,000 pounds, occupies when hitched but 14 yards. To carry the load of five such wagons, extending 78 yards, would require a caravan of camels 360 yards long.

The above figures show the enormous length of Chinese trains, when operating in mountainous regions, as compared with the compact trains employed by us in our campaigns against the Indians.

With the length of trains the difficulties and dangers of transportation directly increase. As a rule, even when the width of the road will permit, the camels will only march in single file, and when the road becomes slippery they frequently fall, never to rise.

When carefully nursed and driven, they make good beasts of burden, but when subjected to cold and wind, or to terrific heat, as in the English campaign against Afghanistan, they perish by thousands.

In the populous portions of the empire, carts drawn by mules and bullocks, the latter frequently serving as pack-animals, are used for transportation, while along the course of the great rivers, and in the seaboard provinces, innumerable junks and small boats serve the same purpose.

One of the great impediments to successful military operations in China is the want of good highways. Every river, every stream, every canal, for want of bridges, constitutes a barrier to the speedy march and concentration of troops.

Unlike the colossal power overshadowing her on the north, which found the construction of broad roads the surest means of subduing the warlike Circassians, China has thus far opposed their construction, perhaps lest they might facilitate the march of rebels upon the capital. The fact that there are no pavements or sidewalks in Peking, and that as late as October, 1875, a mule might be seen hopelessly floundering in a mud-hole within a stone's-throw of the gates of the city, is sufficient evidence of the little importance attached by the Government to a proper system of communication.

GOVERNOR-GENERALS OR VICEROYS.

The efficiency of the Chinese army largely depends upon the governor-general, governor, or highest civil authority in each province; when a governor-general and governor reside at the same capital, they coöperate in providing for all military operations within their respective jurisdictions, leaving the details of military movements to the *Tsung-ping* and *Tituh*, or general officers who serve as their subordinates.

·The governor-generals and governors recommend officers for promotion and degradation, and possess the initiative in matters of reform.

All memorials, reports, and petitions, before being forwarded to the Board of War, pass through their hands. These memorials are sometimes signed openly by officers; at other times, when fearful of the result, they resort to the round robin.

As an instance of the former, officers of all grades, from general down, if disabled by wounds, may petition to be exempted from displaying proficiency in archery on horseback.

In Yunnan, where the *Luh ying*, or Chinese infantry forces, had become inefficient and demoralized by prolonged hostilities against the Panthays, and the incorporation into their midst of the *Chwang-yung* or irregulars, the whole body of officers, on being compelled to be more active in drill, and attentive to duty, sent a round robin to the governor, requesting that, in consequence of the increased demands made upon them, certain stoppages might be removed, and that they might no longer be compelled to receive their pay in paper. The petition, supported by the governor-general, was approved.

In each province the standard of discipline is maintained by a system of triennial inspections. The governors receive orders from the Board of War when to make the inspections, charging them to "examine with sedulous care and denounce to the throne any instances of laxity among the officers in command." Frequently the orders are accompanied with the injunction that they are not to be regarded as "an idle form of words." Whenever these functionaries make their military inspections, they inquire into the general affairs of their provinces. The Governor of Cheh-kiang, in making his report of 1874, expressed himself "well satisfied with the skill in musketry-firing, shield-exercise, use of the spear, and scaling-ladder; also with the exhibition of horse and foot archery, matchlock and gingal practice." When it is considered that this province lies on the seaboard, and that its capital is less than 150 miles from Shanghai, the above report is conclusive as to the little progress modern ideas have made in the Chinese army.

While the governor-generals are practically the heads of the regular army in their respective provinces, having power to arm and equip, to increase and reduce, both the regular and irregular forces, they cannot be held responsible for the inefficiency, lack of discipline, and disorder, that everywhere prevail. There are some among them who, through contact with foreign officers, appreciate fully the value of modern arms and organization, but their plans have been opposed or disapproved at the capital, where conservatism, like a barrier, resists all progress.

Nevertheless, within the field of discretion left to them, some have sought to improve the arms and to increase the instruction of their commands.

At Tientsin, in 1875, an arsenal was nearly completed, in which Remington cartridges, and powder and shells for cannon of all calibres, were then manufactured. The best English machinery for the manufacture of Remington breech-loaders was also shortly expected. The arsenal with its different buildings, occupying an inclosure a mile square, was planned and constructed by an Englishman, and the superintendents of instruction in the different departments were likewise foreigners.

Remington rifles are also made at the arsenals at Shanghai and Nanking. At Shanghai a short musketoon for cavalry is manufactured side by side with one of the best breech-loaders in the world—a proof that the best weapon for all arms of service is not yet appreciated.

At Canton, where American arms are also manufactured, the Remington and Spencer have been enlarged to a calibre of one inch, with a barrel six feet long. On being told that the barrels were too long, the intelligent Chinese superintendent replied that he "knew it, but that the length was added to give them a formidable appearance." These enlarged breech-loaders, like the matchlock, are to be carried by two men.

The breech-loaders made at the different arsenals gradually disappear toward the centre of the empire, where they may be produced when least expected.

The troops near the seaboard still carry antiquated weapons, and, to judge by the soldiers seen at Chinkiang, are unfit to be intrusted with arms of delicate mechanism. Quartered in low, dark, dirty mud huts, liable to be washed down in the first rain, it is impossible for them to keep their arms clean. Furthermore, as little attention is paid to the care of arms as to other features of discipline and drill. The Chinese soldier, naturally brave, and in the northern part of the empire hardy and muscular, is little more than a man with a musket. No care has been taken to train him, or to give him pride in his profession; neither can such a spirit be inculcated while the officers are suffered to remain ignorant and indolent. The uniform, too, is a great obstacle to military pride. It consists of a cotton jacket, usually blue, with trousers so loose and flowing as to completely conceal the figure.

The wide discretion given to the governors inevitably tends to destroy uniformity in the army. In no two provinces are the troops armed and equipped alike, and, according to the greater or less conservatism of the governors, the troops stand still or advance.

This condition of affairs with its multitude of attendant evils cannot be improved till the Board of War becomes awakened, and the Government at Peking assumes full control of the organization, discipline, and support of the army.

GENERAL REMARKS.

The study of the military policy of China is equally interesting to the soldier and statesman.

The corruption that stands at the receipt of customs and the doors of justice, that bars the approach to officers of state, and pervades all branches of civil administration, has penetrated the army, and makes it as often an instrument of oppression as the beneficent means of preserving the peace. In China, as in other countries, corrupt officials have recognized a state of war as affording the best field for the gratification of avarice, and it is not a violent assumption that the army has been kept small and inefficient in order that prolonged hostilities might afford them the opportunity of accumulating riches.

With a civilization extending back to the remotest antiquity, the policy of China has been essentially pacific. Continually lulled into a state of false security by the absence of formidable neighbors on her borders, her army has never borne any relation to her population, or the vast extent of her territory. Sunk into a state of political and military decadence, twice she has been subjugated, and to-day she still bears the yoke of a foreign dynasty whose ancestors were despised as barbarians. Within our own time repeated rebellions have imperiled the existence of the Government, and have only been suppressed after years of devastation, cruelty, and carnage.

Insurrections, which might have been put down by a company of trained soldiers, have been permitted to spread until towns, cities, and provinces, have been overrun and desolated. In the great Taiping rebellion the Government forces, regular and irregular, were repeatedly put to flight by the unorganized hordes, who sought to throw off the imperial yoke. Ill-fed, ill-paid, ill-clothed, with neither confidence in themselves nor their officers, the Government troops struggled in vain to suppress the revolt, while many, lured by the prospect of plunder, joined the army of insurgents. Unable to cope with its adversaries, the Government, in its distress and feebleness, sought external aid, and presented the humiliating spectacle of contracting with foreign adventurers to recapture its cities. The little of military skill these strangers imported into the army soon produced its effect. One city after another was taken, until the tide of revolution began to recede, when the Government forces, with fire and sword, suppressed the revolt.

The bloody wars which for centuries have ravaged the empire have been prolonged for want of a well-organized and disciplined army. The soldiers, composed of the lowest class of society, have been held in contempt, and, when called upon to quiet disorders, have frequently met the disaffected on equal terms, and if overcome have spread fear and demoralization in their own ranks. Encouraged by first successes, civil wars have alternately revived and languished until the Government by a supreme effort has brought them to a close, only to be followed by wholesale executions and slaughter.

So harsh is the Government toward its rebellious subjects that its aim appears to be the prevention of rebellion more by the practice of cruelty than by the more sensible policy of maintaining a sufficient force to preserve peace.

In 1874 twenty-eight prisoners belonging to a body of banditti were put to death, in cold blood, because a rescue was feared; and during the Taiping rebellion repeated acts of cruelty and perfidy shocked the foreigners, and made them repent the assistance they had given.

But it is not only in the destruction of life and of property, and in the sufferings and ill-treatment of her own subjects that the wickedness and folly of the military policy of China is revealed.

Conquered by Mongols and Manchus, the present dynasty, ruling nearly 400,000,000 people, and boasting of an army of more than 500,000 men, has suffered within a few years a European army of less than 20,000 to march to its capital, and dictate the terms of peace. What England and France have done Russia, and possibly Japan, may repeat.

A glance at the map shows that the destiny of Asia is in the hands of England, Russia, Japan, and China. Two of these nations, by means of their armies and navies, are ranked among the great powers of the world. The third, abandoning an effete civilization, is rapidly founding civil and military institutions, which will enable her to play her part in modern development.

China, servile in her admiration of the wisdom of past ages, attaining the highest stage of pagan civilization centuries before her competitors sprang into existence, remains motionless, a prey to corruption and discord. Without well-organized forces, without good roads or other means of speedy concentration, her seaboard provinces, and even her capital, lie at the mercy of her enemies.

If, reversing the picture, she were to adopt the Christian civilization; were to encourage purity, justice, truth, and integrity, by recognizing as the basis of human action responsibility to divine power; if, imitating the example of Japan, she were to establish schools and academies for the education of the officers and men of her army and navy, and were to make them feel that they were honored agents for the preservation of peace at home, and to insure respect abroad—who could compute the vast resources and military strength of her people?

With reform in her civil service; with the sentiment of new national life; with liberty, a word as yet unknown in her language, beating in the hearts of her citizens; with railroads and telegraphs leading to her frontiers; with troops armed with breech-loaders, organized on modern principles, and commanded by generals skilled in the art of war—to what seas might she not carry her standards?

The realization of visions of peace and of conquest is within her grasp, but, delivered over to weakness, cruelty, ignorance, and superstition, history has yet to record whether she shall continue to be an independent nation or, like India, become the vassal of a nobler people.

ARMY OF INDIA.

The established strength of the military forces of India, in 1876, was as follows:

European army—officers, 2,986; men, 60,224: total, 63,210.

Native army—European officers and staff-corps, 3,398; natives, officers and men, 123,479: total, 126,877.

Total military strength, 190,087.

These forces were distributed in the three presidencies as follows:

BENGAL.	Numbers (per Establishment).			Total.
	European Army.		Native Army.	
	Officers.	Men.	Officers and Men.	
Artillery	303	6,087	619	7,544
Cavalry	109	2,790	12,915	15,816
Engineers and sappers	28	......	1,385	1,408
Infantry	1,054	28,364	48,350	77,779
Invalids and veterans	19	18	......	37
MISCELLANEOUS OFFICERS.				
Staff corps	1,125	......	......	1,125
General list, cavalry (including cadres)	64	......	......	64
General list, infantry (of old corps)	226	......	......	226
Unattached officers	11	......	......	11
General officers unemployed	73	......	......	73
Total	2,894	37,069	63,197	104,104

MADRAS.	Numbers (per Establishment).			Total.
	European Army.		Native Army.	
	Officers.	Men.	Officers and Men.	
Artillery	147	2,670	.....	2,817
Cavalry	56	910	1,723	2,689
Engineers and sappers	67	.....	1,439	1,506
Infantry	297	7,974	80,801	89,072
Invalids and veterans	24	144	.....	168
MISCELLANEOUS OFFICERS.				
Staff corps	659	.....	.....	659
General list, cavalry...... { including cadres	54	.....	.....	54
General list, infantry..... } of old corps	123	.....	.....	123
Unattached officers	3	.....	.....	3
General officers unemployed	44	.....	.....	44
Total	1,478	11,699	83,963	47,139

BOMBAY.	Numbers (per Establishment).			Total.
	European Army.		Native Army.	
	Officers.	Men.	Officers and Men.	
Artillery	139	2,428	177	2,744
Cavalry	28	455	3,965	4,448
Engineers and sappers	67	.....	525	592
Infantry	297	7,974	22,086	30,357
Invalids and veterans	15	.....	.....	15
MISCELLANEOUS OFFICERS.				
Staff corps	504	.....	.....	504
General list, cavalry...... { including cadres	24	.....	.....	24
General list, infantry..... } of old corps	66	.....	.....	66
Unattached officers	8	.....	.....	8
General officers unemployed	27	.....	.....	27
Total	1,170	10,857	26,753	38,780

OFFICERS OF THE INDIAN ARMY.

The transfer of the government of India from the East India Company to the crown was followed by a complete reorganization of the army.

Previous to that time the officers of artillery, cavalry, infantry, and engineers, belonged permanently to their respective arms, or corps, and received their promotion in the same manner as in the British army.

It is not necessary to state all of the reasons that led to the reorganization, but prominent among them was one developed by the mutiny, which seems to have exerted a controlling influence.

It was observed that irregular regiments, hastily equipped, and led by brave and skillful English officers, fought with a zeal and steadiness approaching, if not equaling, that of the native regiments in the regular establishment.

In all of the wars of India, the latter had gone into battle under great disadvantages.

The cadre of each infantry regiment, for example, numbered twenty-five European officers, yet, so many were detached, in consequence of the increasing demand for officers to serve in the staff, and also in civil and political positions, that companies in time of peace were frequently left in the hands of boys fresh from England, who were without the slightest military experience. Even when this did not occur, those who had staid with their regiments during the intervals of peace, and were ambitious of distinction, found themselves superseded at the opening of each campaign by officers hastily ordered back, whom years of detached service had unfitted for command.

It was impossible that such a system should not produce bad results. In India, as in every other country, where detached service is indefinite, officers sought exemption from the hardships and restraints of military discipline.

Furthermore, the history of India proved that the surest road to distinction lay in the civil service, in which officers were frequently appointed governors of millions of people.

Having grown old in such service, having enjoyed its pleasures and its honors, having forgotten their tactics and regulations, it was not unnatural that their return to military duty should have produced jealousy and confusion, and been followed by the most dangerous, if not the most criminal, of all experiments, the sending of men into action under incompetent leaders. The conduct of the irregular regiments in the mutiny, it was thought, suggested a remedy for the abuse.

If they could fight so well under three or four English officers, why should not the regular regiments do the same? Why should not each regular regiment be given seven or eight officers, instead of twenty-five, thereby leaving a surplus of seventeen or eighteen available for staff duty, and other detached service?

This idea appears to have been the germ which, in its development, led to the organization of a staff corps in each presidency, embracing not only the non-combatant, but all of the combatant officers of the old Indian army.

STAFF CORPS.

It was resolved that all the officers then in the staff, the artillery, and cavalry, should be ultimately merged into one body, to be known, in Bengal, as the "Bengal Staff Corps;" in Bombay, as the "Bombay Staff Corps;" and in Madras, as the "Madras Staff Corps."

There was to be no permanent quartermaster, commissary, or ordnance department. All of these positions in each Presidency were to be filled for a term of years by officers detached from the "staff corps," or from the British troops serving in India. The same great corps was to furnish by detail the seven combatant officers of native infantry, and eight combatant officers of native cavalry.

In organizing the staff corps, special arrangements were made, whereby, under certain conditions, officers of the Indian artillery and engineers, could enter the same corps in the Royal army.

Provision also had to be made for the young officers, who were gazetted to the Indian army after November 1, 1858, the date of transfer of the government to the crown, up to the year 1862. As these officers had never served with the native army, their names were placed on a

GENERAL LIST,

which was gradually to disappear by the process of absorption and death.

They were guaranteed promotion to the grades of major and lieutenant-colonel after a service, respectively, of twenty and twenty-six years, the same as in the staff.

Promotion to the grade of captain was secured by assignment to vacancies as they occurred in the cadres of the old native regiments.

OLD CADRE LIST.

This list embraces those officers of the old Indian army who, on the general reorganization, declined the offer to enter the staff corps.

Their names were continued on their regimental lists, the same as if the regiments had not been disbanded or reorganized, their promotion being secured as vacancies occurred in these lists the same as before the mutiny. The old cadre list will disappear only on the death of the last officer.

UNEMPLOYED LIST.

This list consists of officers of the staff corps, general list, and old cadre list, who exceed the number of appointments or places at the disposal of the Government. They draw the Indian pay of their rank, and are available for special duty, such as courts and boards.

BENGAL STAFF CORPS.

This corps, organized in 1861, may be accepted as the model of the staff corps of the other two presidencies.

To induce officers to enter it, the Bengal Army Regulations prescribe that no staff appointments, except those tenable for five years, and personal staff appointments, shall be held by an officer of the British army, unless he enter the staff corps. This prohibition does not apply to officers of Royal Engineers serving in the sappers and miners; in the public works, survey and telegraph departments; nor to officers of the Royal Artillery serving in the native batteries, and in the ordnance department.

Any officer desiring to enter the staff corps must be above the grade of sub-lieutenant, and must serve a year on probation with native troops, either as a wing or squadron subaltern. The application for transfer must be accompanied by the certificate of the commander of the regiment, stating that he has passed the examination in the native languages according to the higher standard; that he has acquired such knowledge of his drill and duty as to qualify him to command a company of troops in all situations; that he possesses a fair knowledge of the articles of war, army regulations, and the Bengal Army Regulations; that he has a general acquaintance with the organization and duties of all branches of the army serving in Bengal, and that during his service with his regiment he has been attentive to his duty, and unexceptionable in his conduct. The application must also be accompanied by the certificate of the medical officer of the regiment.

The object of probation is to test the "tact, temper, and judgment," and other qualifications of the officer, for employment with native troops.

If successful in his probation, the officer, before his final transfer, is required to pass an examination divided into two parts, as follows:

FIRST PART.

TACTICS.

Embracing the evolutions of a regiment of cavalry, or battalion of infantry, including skirmishing, duties of outposts, patrols, escorts, advanced and rear guards.

INTERIOR ECONOMY.

Of a troop, company, or detachment, embracing a knowledge of correspondence, regulations, and returns; also musketry instruction.

REGULATIONS.

Embracing the native articles of war, and the military regulations of the presidency, particularly those that apply to native corps.

REGIMENTAL ECONOMY OF NATIVE CAVALRY AND INFANTRY.

Embracing the system of keeping accounts and rosters; the mode of dealing with the offenses, complaints, and petitions of the men; a knowledge of the articles of equipment kept by the men, with the cost and mode of carrying them; the system of purchasing horses; knowledge of their defects and good qualities; also a general knowledge of shoeing, and of the diseases and injuries to which horses are subject, with the method of treatment.

SECOND PART.

This part embraces:
Military law,
Elements of tactics,
Field-fortification, and elements of permanent fortification,
Military topography and reconnaissance, and riding.

The examinations of probationers for the staff corps are held at division and district headquarters. The examining board consists of a general officer and two commandants of native regiments, or one commandant and one second in command of native regiments.

Since the 1st of January, 1875, every captain of the staff who aspires to the position of commandant, second in command, or wing-officer of a native regiment, or who, being in a native regiment, desires an appointment outside of his regiment, has been required to pass an examination in two parts.

FIRST PART.

For cavalry:
Command of a regiment singly on parade; as part of a brigade; as advance or rear guard; as outpost covering a brigade or division, and manœuvring on varied ground, adapting the movements to the accomplishment of specified purposes.

For infantry:
Riding, and the command of a regiment singly on parade; as part of a brigade; as advance or rear guard; as outposts, covering a brigade or division, and skirmishing, adapting the movements to the ground and a specified purpose.

SECOND PART.

This part embraces:
Military law,
Elements of tactics,
Field-fortification,
Elements of permanent fortification,
Military topography and reconnaissance.

Principles of combining the movements of infantry, artillery, and cavalry, for mutual support.

Representing on a map of a piece of ground, previously seen by the officer, the map being furnished the officer under examination, the disposition of a combined force of the three arms:

1. As advance and rear guard.
2. As outposts.
3. For attack and defense of a given position such as a hedge, wall, or defile.

The examination for captains, as given above, is required to qualify any officer of the staff corps to hold the positions of:

Military secretary of the viceroy, and to the commander-in-chief,
Assistant adjutant-general,
Assistant quartermaster-general,
Deputy assistant adjutant-general,
Deputy assistant quartermaster-general,
Brigade-major.

GARRISON INSTRUCTION.

To enable officers to pass the examinations specified, a system of garrison instruction has been established at different posts in the Bengal Presidency.

The course of study embraces two terms, the first of which extends from the 1st of October to the 1st of February; the second from the 1st of February to the 31st of May.

The garrison instructors are officers who have specially qualified for this position, many of them being graduates of the Staff College at Sandhurst.

The classes, usually not exceeding ten to twelve members, are composed of officers from the native and British troops at the rate of—

    2 officers from each regiment British infantry.
    1 officer   "   "   "   "   cavalry.
    1   "   "   "   "   native infantry.
    1   "   "   "   "   "   cavalry.

The subjects to which special attention is given, are:
Military law,
Field-fortification,
Field-sketching, surveying, and reconnaissances.

NATIVE LANGUAGES.

The only officers serving on staff duty in India, who are not required to show proficiency in the native languages, are:

One-half of the personal staff of the viceroy, commander-in-chief, a governor or lieutenant-governor; the staff of a station occupied exclusively by British troops; inspectors of gymnasia, and garrison instructors.

The "lower standard of examination" is required to be passed by:

One-half of the personal staff of the viceroy, commander-in-chief, governor or lieutenant-governor; assistant and deputy assistant adjutant-general for musketry and station staff.

All other staff appointments can only be held by officers who have passed the interpreter's test, or higher standard Hindostani, or an equivalent examination in other native languages.

The "lower standard" in Hindostani consists in reading fairly and translating with accuracy a given portion of two standard text-books; also ability to converse with examiners, or natives of India, on such subjects as relate to every-day life, and the performance of regimental or professional duty.

Examinations for the "lower standard" are held every two months at every large station such as Agra, Allahabad, Cawnpoor, and Lucknow. The station committee appointed for this purpose is composed of three officers who have passed the "higher standard."

The "higher standard" examination consists in reading fluently, and translating into English with readiness and accuracy, an octavo page of a standard text-book; reading fairly and translating readily and correctly Hindostani manuscripts, written in both Persian and Hindi characters; conversing with examiners or natives with fluency and sufficient correctness to be clearly intelligible.

These examinations are held annually at Simla, Landour, Murree, and Nynee Tal, and half-yearly at the headquarter stations of divisions, districts, and brigades. The committees consist of one civil, and two military officers, who have passed the higher standard.

Examinations are also held in sixteen other languages, as follows:

Arabic, Assamese, Bengali, Burmese, Canarese, Guzerathi, Mahrati, Malayalam, Ooriya, Persian, Punjabi, Pushtoo, Sanskrit, Sindhi, Tamil, and Telego.

The importance attached to a knowledge of the native and other languages is shown by the pecuniary rewards offered to the successful competitors.

To every officer who passes the "lower standard" of Hindostani an allowance of 180 rupees is given, nearly equal to $90. On passing the "higher standard" an additional allowance of 180 rupees is also given. If both standards are passed at the same time, the whole allowance of 360 rupees is paid at once.

A donation of 800 rupees ($400) is made to every candidate who passes an examination in Arabic, Pushtoo, or Sanskrit, and 500 rupees to candidates who pass an examination in any other of the sixteen languages before mentioned.

"High proficiency" examinations, a grade next above the "higher standard," are provided for eleven of the most important languages. Any officer or soldier who passes the "high proficiency" examination in Arabic or Sanskrit receives a donation of 2,000 rupees ($1,000); in the other languages 1,500 rupees.

"Degrees of Honor" are accorded for attaining the highest

proficiency in Persian, Arabic, and Sanskrit. Candidates who obtain this honor in Arabic and Sanskrit receive a donation of 5,000 rupees ($2,500), and in Persian 4,000 rupees. They are also presented with a gold medal by the presidency in which they are serving.

Abbreviations like L. S., "Lower Standard," "H. S. P., "Higher Standard Persian," are placed on the army list opposite to the names of all officers who have passed examinations.

The encouragement to learn native languages, a knowledge of which is indispensable to enter the staff corps, or to hold certain staff positions, together with the incentive offered by means of donations, degrees of honor, and medals, has resulted in the acquisition of a greater variety of languages by the Indian officers than in all probability is possessed by the officers of any other army.

TENURE OF APPOINTMENTS.

Appointments in the adjutant-general's department, including musketry branch; quartermaster-general's department; appointment as brigade-majors (corresponding to assistant adjutant-general of brigade); fort adjutants; adjutants of volunteer corps; personal staff; station staff, and garrison instructors, is open alike to officers of the Indian army and British army serving in India.

The tenure of appointment in each of the foregoing positions is five years, except on the personal staff of a governor, where it is extended to six years.

PROBATION FOR STAFF EMPLOYMENT.

Service in the judge advocate-general's department, military account department, commissariat department, stud, survey, civil and foreign departments, is open to all officers of the staff corps and Indian army.

Previous to appointment in the judge advocate-general's department, an officer must pass an examination in military law, Mutiny Act, Articles of War, Queen's Regulations, Bengal Army Regulations, and Indian Penal Code. He must also show a capacity to review the proceedings of minor courts-martial, and to conduct the proceedings of general courts-martial.

The examination is conducted by the deputy judge advocate attached to the division or district, and two selected field-officers. After passing the examination the officer must serve a year on probation in the department. If at the expiration of this period the deputy judge advocate-general, and the general commanding the division, or district, to which he is attached, make a satisfactory report of the practical qualifications of the probationer, he becomes eligible for a permanent appointment.

An applicant for the Military Account Department must be examined by a paymaster to ascertain that he has a good general knowledge of accounts and book-keeping. He must then serve a year on probation under the controller of military accounts, who assigns him to duty in the various branches of the department. If the controller at the conclusion of the year reports that the conduct of the probationer has been satisfactory, and that he gives promise of usefulness in the department, he is examined by a committee composed of the controller, military accountant, and a pay-examiner. In case the examination is satisfactory, the appointment is confirmed.

In the Commissariat Department an officer must serve a year on probation, preceded and followed by an examination. The same rule applies to the Stud Department, except that no preliminary examination is required.

In the Survey Department the same period of probation is required. The preliminary examination embraces arithmetic, algebra, geometry, trigonometry, topographical and mechanical drawing. In certain cases such as artillery officers holding certificates of qualification from the Academy at Woolwich, the preliminary examination is dispensed with. The final examination, at the close of the probation, embraces a fair knowledge of the rules of the department; the computation and mapping of a small area of territory; a knowledge of the use of all the instruments employed in the department, with the manner of adjusting them, and sufficient knowledge of astronomy to ascertain time, azimuth, and latitude.

The final application for transfer to any department of the staff corps must be accompanied by the certificate of the chief as to the conduct of the officer while on probation.

PAY.

Officers of the staff corps receive the following monthly pay:

Lieutenant-colonel,	827 rupees	14 annas,		$413.92
Major,	640 "	14 "		320.42
Captain,	374 "	1 anna 6 pice,		187.04
Lieutenant,	5 "	12 annas,		112.86

The above is the pay proper of officers employed and unemployed.

In addition, nearly every appointment in India carries with it staff pay and allowances, equal and frequently exceeding the officers' pay proper.

The pay, per annum, of the following officers, is:

Commander-in-chief,	100,000 rupees =	$50,000.00
Military secretary,	18,000 "	9,000.00
Adjutant-general,	36,000 "	18,000.00
Deputy adjutant-general,	22,560 "	11,280.00
Assistant adjutant-general,	15,725 "	7,862.50
Quartermaster-general,	30,000 "	15,000.00
Inspector-general of artillery,	28,024 "	14,012.00
General commanding division,	38,564 "	19,284.00

A colonel commanding a brigade of horse-artillery receives 1,358 rupees per month, and command allowance of 400, making $879 per month.

A lieutenant-colonel commanding a regiment of British cavalry receives 1,037 rupees per month, with a command allowance of 400 rupees = $718.50.

A lieutenant-colonel commanding a regiment of British infantry receives 1,002 rupees per month, and a command allowance of 400 rupees = $701.

The commandant of a regiment of native cavalry receives

640 rupees 14 annas per month, and a command allowance of 700 rupees = $670.

The monthly pay of a commandant of a native infantry regiment is $620.

In the Indian service great distinction is made between the pay of officers in command, and at the head of departments, and the pay of the grades next below, but the fact that a sub-lieutenant, on probation in a native regiment, receives $165 per month, is sufficient to show that the officers, if serving in the worst of climates, are, as a compensation, better paid than those of any other army in the world.

PROMOTION.

Officers of the staff corps are entitled to promotion to the grade of captain after 12 years' service, to major after 20 years, and lieutenant-colonel after 26 years.

RETIREMENT.

Officers of the staff corps who have served half of the required periods in the corps, are permitted to retire according to the following scale:

After 20 years' service in India, on £191 12s. per annum.
" 24 " " 292 "
" 28 " " 365 "
" 32 " " 456 "

After 38 years' service officers are allowed to retire with "off reckonings," which increases their pay to £1,100 per annum.

Under the old rule colonels were granted an allowance for clothing their regiments, and the difference between the allowance and the actual cost of the clothing, usually amounting to £650 per annum, was regarded as an emolument, and was termed "off reckonings." Officers entitled to "off reckonings" usually retire as soon as they become available, after which their promotion goes on to the highest grades in the service, but their pay cannot exceed £1,100.

Officers who are not entitled to "off reckonings," when retiring on full pay, are given a step in brevet rank, after which their promotion ceases, but their names are retained in the Army List in italics.

Officers who contract disability in the service, or become unfit for duty before being entitled to retire on full pay, are allowed to retire on half pay, or their names may be placed on the half-pay list. Those who subsequently recover their health may be restored to the active list at the option of the Government.

FURLOUGHS.

For the purpose of enabling officers of the Indian army to preserve their health and vigor, and to support the prolonged heat of the climate, the Government has established liberal rules for leave of absence and furlough.

Every officer in military employ in India is entitled to 60 days' "privilege-leave" each year, without loss of pay or emoluments, and at particularly unhealthy stations the period is extended to 90 days. The officers are encouraged to take this leave, as experience has proved that change of climate, of thoughts, and of scenes, gives to them an increased zeal and cheerfulness in the discharge of their duty during the remaining months of the year, more than sufficient to compensate the Government for the loss of pay during their absence.

In case of urgent private affairs, officers are allowed a "general leave" not exceeding six months, with full pay, but a loss of one-half of their staff emoluments. If this leave be taken three years in succession, certain officers may lose their staff appointments.

In addition to the privilege and general leaves, every officer of the Indian army is entitled, if the public interests permit, to two years' furlough on the completion of eight years' service in India, and an additional year for every subsequent six years' service.

During his furlough the officer retains any staff appointment he may hold at the time, and receives half pay and allowances, provided the sum does not exceed £1,000, nor fall below £250.

To secure the full advantage of his furlough an officer is granted 30 days' leave to enable him to reach the port of embarkation, and the same length of time to get back to his station on his return.

In all he is granted eight years' furlough during his service in India, and of this amount he is allowed to count as service toward retirement or pension—

<blockquote>
2 years in 20,
3   "   " 25,
4   "   " 30,
5   "   " 34,
6   "   " 38.
</blockquote>

Besides the usual leaves of absence and furloughs, provision is made for furlough without pay, and for leave on certificate of disability. Special provisions are also made for officers of the British army, and for officers of the Indian army serving in civil departments. These rules vary but slightly from those established for the staff corps.

VARIETY OF SERVICE IN INDIA.

As all of the European officers of the Indian army will ultimately belong to the staff corps, the principle of detail for staff employment, and for service with native troops, will find its widest application in India. The extent of its present application to the staff corps, general list of infantry and cavalry, old cadre list, and to officers of British troops serving in India, may be inferred in the Bengal Presidency by reference to the Bengal Army List.

The personal staff of the viceroy consists of 12 officers; 7 detailed from British troops, and 5 from the Indian army, embracing representatives from all of the lists above mentioned.

The personal staff of the commander-in-chief consists of 6 officers; 4 detailed from British troops, and 2 from the Indian army.

The secretariat of the Government of India, Military Department, is composed of 5 officers; all detailed from the staff-corps.

The Adjutant-General's Department is composed of 8 officers; 3 detailed from the British troops, and 5 from the staff corps.

The Quartermaster-General's Department is composed of 24 officers; 12 detailed from the British troops, and 12 from the Indian army.

The Judge-Advocate-General's Department is composed of 8 officers; all detailed from the staff corps, and old Bengal infantry.

Of the 8 assistant adjutant-generals of division 4 are from the British troops, and 4 from the staff corps.

Of the assistant adjutant-generals of musketry, 1 assistant and 7 deputy assistants, 6 are detailed from the British troops, and 2 from the Indian army.

The garrison instruction staff in India is composed of 27 officers, 24 of whom are detailed from officers of British troops, and 3 from the Indian army.

The brigade-majors, station-staff, and fort-adjutants, are detailed about equally from officers of British troops and the Indian army.

The ordnance and ordnance manufacturing establishments are composed of 20 officers; all detailed from the Royal Artillery.

The Accounts Branch, Military Department, is composed of civilians and 22 officers; all detailed from the Indian army.

The Army Commissariat Department is composed of 53 officers; 44 detailed from the staff corps, the remainder from other officers of the Indian army.

In addition to details in the Military Department, the civil service opens to officers in India a vast field for ambition and usefulness.

The officers of the Survey Department, embracing the Great Trigonometrical and Topographical Survey of India, are nearly all detailed from the Royal Engineers.

The officers in the Revenue Survey are nearly all from the staff corps.

The Great Public Works Department, which builds the forts, barracks, irrigation canals, roads, and railroads, is largely composed of officers of the Royal Engineers, Artillery, and staff corps.

The telegraph is likewise under military control.

Without specifying further the civil and military occupations to which officers may aspire, the variety of service required of them will best appear by quoting the remarks opposite ten consecutive names, taken at random in the grades of lieutenant-colonel, major, captain, and lieutenant, of the Bengal staff corps:

Lieutenant-Colonels.

Names.	Remarks.
....	Chief Commissioner of Mysore and Coorg.
....	Judge-Advocate-General.
....	Civil employ, Assam.
....	Civil employ, Northwestern Provinces.
....	In Europe.
....	Army Commissariat Department.
....	In Europe.
....	Civil employ, Bengal.
....	First Assistant Adjutant-General.
....	Civil employ, Punjab.

Majors.

....	Third Squadron Officer 6th Bengal Cavalry.
....	Civil employ, Punjab.
....	Topographical Survey Department.
....	Quartermaster-General's Department.
....	Second Commander Malwah Bheel Corps.
....	Civil employ, Punjab.
....	Civil employ, Central India.
....	2d Squadron Officer 14th Bengal Lancers.
....	Commandant 16th Bengal Cavalry.
....	Second in command and Wing-Officer Corps of Guides.

Captains.

....	Civil employ, Hyderabad.
....	Army Commissariat Department.
....	Second in command and Squadron Officer 18th Bengal Cavalry.

MILITARY OFFICERS AND CIVIL AUTHORITIES. 51

Names.	Remarks.
....	Second in command and Squadron Officer 8th Bengal Cavalry.
....	Officiating Brigade-Major.
....	2d Squadron Officer 5th Punjab Cavalry.
....	Quartermaster-General's Department.
....	Commandant of Cavalry and Squadron-Officer Corps of Guides.
....	Wing-Officer 89th Native Infantry.
....	Quartermaster-General's Department.

Lieutenants.

....	Quartermaster 34th Native Infantry.
....	1st Wing Subaltern 29th " "
....	" " 31st " "
....	Adjutant 45th " "
....	Civil employ, Rajpootana Agency.
....	2d Squadron Subaltern 5th Punjab Cavalry.
....	Adjutant 1st Punjab Cavalry.
....	1st Wing Subaltern 29th Native Infantry.
....	Deputy Controller Public Works Department.
....	Adjutant Erinpoora Irregulars.

RELATION OF MILITARY OFFICERS TO THE CIVIL AUTHORITIES.

In no free country is the subordination of the military to the civil authority more clearly defined than in the politico-military despotism of India. The Army Regulations prescribe that—

"The civil officer is vested with authority to call upon the military commander for the services of the troops under his command, whenever, in the judgment of such civil officer, the public interests of the Government may require such a measure; and it is the absolute duty of the military officer to whom such requisition is addressed, whoever and whatever he may be, forthwith to comply with the same. It is not competent for him to enter into any discussion upon the merits of the measure proposed, or to take any cognizance whatever of its policy, justice, or necessity.

"It is for the civil officer, and him alone, to judge of the policy, the justice, or the necessity, of the measure. For these he alone is responsible to the government he serves; and he is not called upon in duty either to justify his conclusions or to communicate his reasons to the military officer to whom he may address the requisition for troops. Although such manifestations of confidence and cordiality are always to be desired, he is only required by his strict duty to state distinctly (in writing) the service he desires to see performed and the necessity of troops for the purpose, and to afford such further information as may be necessary to enable the officer in command efficiently to perform the service he is called upon to execute.

"The civil or political officer is not authorized to interfere in any way with the formation or details of the force, the military officer being held responsible for the success of the operations to be undertaken; and it is for the latter, and for him alone, to judge in what manner the troops shall effect the object which the civil officer has indicated, and to direct the force in the execution of the service in which it is engaged.

"If, however, the military officer should consider his force inadequate for the performance of the service required, or the service itself impracticable on purely military grounds, it would be competent for him to decline to accede to the requisition. But in so doing he must be prepared to justify his refusal to the satisfaction of the government he serves, and whose interests are affected by his acts."

While the Regulations place the military officers under the civil in all political affairs, and relieve them from all responsibility when acting under the orders of the civil authorities, they also, in the interest of the Government, subordinate the civil officer to the military whenever, as in military constructions, economy can be promoted.

In relation to the Department of Public Works, which builds forts, barracks, and arsenals, and which, while strictly civil, is largely composed of military officers, the Regulations prescribe:

"Commanding officers are directly responsible to their immediate superiors, and to the Government, that the public works, buildings, etc., within the limits of their commands are properly maintained, and that these works and buildings properly provide for the wants of the troops under their orders; and it will be their duty to bring to the notice of superior authority all deficiencies that may exist in these respects from whatever cause they arise.

"Although commanding officers should avoid interfering in the details of the duties of the functionaries of the Public Works Department, they are fully competent to point out any apparent defect of arrangement, want of diligence in the prosecution of works, or the like, and to report any shortcoming, if the case shall appear to demand such a step.

"Executive engineers will comply with the requisitions and act in conformity with the wishes of commanding officers whenever they can do so without infringing departmental rules; and they are at all times to treat commanding officers with becoming respect.

"It will be the duty of an executive engineer, and of his assistant or subordinate in charge of any station or outpost, to afford the commanding officer every assistance in forming his judgment and issuing his orders on any subject relating to military works or buildings, and to lay before him, when necessary, any general or departmental orders which may bear upon such subjects.

"Before submitting to the engineer authorities any proposals, estimates, drawings, etc., connected with military works, executive engineers shall invariably submit them to the regimental or departmental officers concerned, as well as to the commanding officer of the station, and obtain their counter-signatures and opinions for transmission with the papers under dispatch.

"General officers in local command should refer all matters appertaining to the Public Works Department, in which executive engineers may differ from them, to the superintending engineer before making any reference to the commander-in-chief, the local government or administration, or the Government of India."

Could our "Regulations" prescribe with equal clearness the relations of our officers to the civil authorities, and relieve them from responsibility for the use of troops in civil affairs, it would place this duty before the country in a proper light, and would tend to disarm personal and partisan criticism.

If at the same time in purely army matters they were to require commanding officers to exercise a limited control over all disbursements for military purposes within, or in connection with, their commands, the Government might be saved millions of dollars.

As matters are now conducted, we may have, as at Fort Monroe, three separate jurisdictions at the same post, where staff officers have disbursed, and may continue to disburse, large sums of public money—and yet the commanding officer cannot offer a suggestion; nor can he apprise the Government of a useless expenditure without placing himself in the light of an informer.

All of this arises from breaking away from the established

usages of other armies, simply to gratify our natural love of personal independence, which is as strong in the army as in civil life.

NATIVE INFANTRY.

A regiment of native infantry consists of eight companies, with an established strength as follows:

Europeans.

1 Commandant.
1 Second in command and wing-officer.
1 Wing-officer.
2 Wing-subalterns.
1 Adjutant.
1 Quartermaster.
1 Medical officer.

Natives.

2 Subadars (captains) 1st class.
2 " " 2d "
4 " " 3d "
4 Jemandars (lieutenants) 1st class.
4 " " 2d "
1 Havildar (sergeant-major).
40 Havildars (sergeants).
40 Naicks (corporals).
16 Drummers.
600 Sepoys (privates).

The native infantry force in the three presidencies consists as follows:

Bengal.	45 Regiments	Bengal Infantry	Numbering in native officers and men...	48,293
	5 "	Goorkha "	European officers, 8 per regiment......	528
	6 "	Punjab "	Total	48,821
	4 "	Sikh "		
	6 "	Guide, Deolee, and other Infantry.		

NATIVE INFANTRY.

Madras: 40 Regiments	Numbering in native officers and men..	30,761
	European officers....................	320
	Total........................	31,081
Bombay: 30 Regiments	Numbering in native officers and men..	22,056
	European officers....................	240
	Total........................	22,296
Total, three presidencies..................................		102,197

The European officers attached to the native regiments are detailed from the staff corps of each presidency; the general list of officers of infantry and cavalry, and from officers of the British army serving in India, who desire to enter the staff corps.

The duties of the commandant of a native regiment are in general similar to those of the commandant of a European regiment. Three times a week he holds a "durbar," which the wing-officers, wing-subalterns, adjutant, quartermaster, and all native officers, are required to attend. At the durbar he hears reports and complaints, awards punishments, issues orders, and transacts the general business of the regiment.

Wing-officers act in the capacity of majors, and command wings or half-battalions. They are responsible to the commandant for the appearance, drill, and discipline of their wings, and at the durbars wait on him with such men as are brought up for punishment, or whose complaints and petitions are of such a nature as to be beyond the limits of their authority.

The men are paid by the native officers in their presence; they also have charge of, and are responsible for, the arms, accoutrements, ammunition, clothing, and all warlike stores, belonging to their half-battalions, for which they receive increased pay.

They are likewise required to keep themselves informed of the names, services, and characters, of the men, and to exercise all of their authority through the native officers.

Wing-subalterns assist their wing-officers generally in their duties, superintend target-practice, and such drills as they may be required to attend.

The adjutant issues all orders from the commanding officer, keeps the records, and is largely responsible for the drill and instruction of the native officers, non-commissioned officers, and men.

The quartermaster is charged with the care and preservation of stores, ammunition, equipments, and clothing, of the men. The barracks, bazaar, and camp-equipage, are also under his care, and he is responsible for their order and cleanliness.

NATIVE OFFICERS.

The native officers are commissioned by the Government of India. As a rule they are promoted from the rank of non-commissioned officers, and are of the same caste as the privates. Latterly a few educated Hindoos, and owners of land, have been appointed, with a view to elevating the standard.

As a special recognition of the native officers, one is appointed aide-de-camp on the staff of the viceroy, and another on that of the commander-in-chief. In each regiment also the senior native officer, called the subadar-major, receives an increased allowance of twenty-five rupees per month.

The native officers are required to command their companies, and are supposed to receive sufficient instruction to enable them to do so in all situations.

For the purpose of interior economy each company is divided into two half-companies, each under the command of a native officer, and each half-company is further divided into two squads.

The Bengal Army Regulations prescribe that—

"It is the imperative duty of the native officers to keep their wing and commanding officers acquainted with everything that takes place in their companies, to report all infractions of orders and discipline, and to bring to light *at once* all causes of discontent or misconduct; as it is impossible for a grievance to exist without their knowledge, if they know their duty, and are willing to act up to it."

When on detached service a native officer is allowed to command his company, but "no battalion parades should take place without the presence of a British officer."

NATIVE NON-COMMISSIONED OFFICERS.

In each regiment there is a drill-sergeant (drill-havildar) and drill-corporal (or naick), selected from their respective grades with special reference to their efficiency and qualifications, who receive a special monthly allowance of five rupees. The same allowance is granted to the pay-havildar, drum-major, and fife-major.

In each company the color-havildar, or first-sergeant, receives an extra allowance of two rupees.

Corporals are promoted from the sepoys (privates), who know how to read and write in at least one character, exception only being made in the case of sepoys who have displayed conspicuous courage.

Drill-instructors are appointed in each company from the sepoys, and, to encourage emulation among them, one is promoted annually to the grade of corporal (or naick).

The havildars and naicks are arranged in the regimental list in each grade, and, without regard to companies, are promoted to vacancies according to seniority.

If the regiment is composed of "class troops," that is of companies of different religions or castes, the lists are arranged according to caste, and vacancies are filled by seniority in each class.

To enable sepoys to qualify for promotion, a school is maintained in every regiment, attendance being voluntary. For the privilege each sepoy is required to pay his teacher two annas (six cents) monthly; naicks and havildars pay four annas.

PAY.

The following table shows, in rupees, annas, and pice—the currency of India—the monthly pay and allowances of a native regiment of infantry:

ARMY OF INDIA.

RANK.	PAY PROPER.			COMMAND AND STAFF ALLOWANCES.			TOTAL.			Equivalent in Dollars per Month.
	Rs.	As.	Ps.	Rs.	As.	Ps.	Rs.	As.	Ps.	
EUROPEAN OFFICERS.										
Commandant........................	640	14	..	600	..	..	1240	14	..	620.42
Second in command and wing-officer.	374	1	6	270	..	..	644	1	6	822.04
Wing-officers........................	374	1	6	230	..	..	604	1	6	302.04
Adjutant............................	225	12	..	250	..	..	475	12	..	237.86
Quartermaster......................	225	12	..	150	..	..	375	12	..	187.86
Wing-subaltern.....................	225	12	..	100	..	..	325	12	..	162.86
Medical officer.....................	600	..	..	...	..	..	....	..	..	300.00
NATIVE OFFICERS.										
Subadar-major	100	..	..	25	..	..	125	..	..	62.50
Subadars, first class................	100	..	..	..	..	..	100	..	..	50.00
" second class................	80	..	..	..	..	..	80	..	..	40.00
" third class.................	67	..	..	..	..	..	67	..	..	38.50
Jemandars, first class..............	35	..	..	..	..	..	35	..	..	17.50
" second class.............	30	..	..	..	..	..	30	..	..	15.00
NON-COM. OFFICERS, SEPOYS, ETC.										
Drill-havildar......................	14	..	..	5	..	..	19	..	..	9.50
Pay-havildar.......................	14	..	..	5	..	..	19	..	..	9.50
Color-havildar.....................	14	..	..	2	..	..	16	..	..	8.00
Havildar...........................	14	..	..	..	..	..	14	..	..	7.00
Drill-naick.........................	12	..	..	2	8	..	14	8	..	7.24
Naick..............................	12	..	..	..	..	..	12	..	..	6.00
Drum-major.......................	7	..	..	5	..	..	12	..	..	6.00
Fife-major.........................	7	..	..	5	..	..	12	..	..	6.00
Drummers.........................	7	..	..	..	..	..	7	..	..	3.50

The non-combatants of each regiment, consisting of hospital assistants, attendants, bheesties (or water-carriers), cooks, sweepers, schoolmasters, tindal (or head native, quartermaster's department), lascars (or tent-pitchers and laborers), bildars (or scavengers), chowdry (or headman of the bazaar), mulsooty (or clerk), and weighmen, numbering in all 45, receive on the average from 4 to 5 rupees per month. In addition to the staff allowance already stated, each wing-officer receives 85 rupees per month for the repair of arms, and for superintending the payment of the men. The quartermaster likewise receives for the repair of tents, targets, and school-sheds, and for purchase of school-books, an allowance of 49 rupees per month.

The annual pay-roll of a native regiment, according to the fixed establishment, numbering 720 combatants and 45 non-combatants, amounts to 1 lac and 38,228 rupees, or about $69,114.

In consideration of the pay stated for all of the native ranks, each man is required to provide his own rations and clothing, except one coat and one pair of trousers issued by the

Government every two years. If the cost of rations exceeds one-half of the soldier's pay per month, the Government gives him a compensation equal to the difference between one-half of his pay and the actual cost of the ration.

Arms, ammunition, camp-equipage, and medical attendance, are provided by the Government.

BAZAAR.

In consequence of requiring the native soldiers to provide their own rations and clothing, each regiment is accompanied by a native village, called a bazaar, in which are to be found tailors, shoemakers, grocers, grain-dealers, dry-goods merchants, and tradesmen of nearly every description.

The bazaar is under strict military discipline, and is managed by the quartermaster under the orders of the commanding officer.

Each inhabitant of the bazaar is required to register, showing his occupation, after which he becomes amenable to the articles of war, and to trial by court-martial. No man, having registered, can withdraw without a regular discharge. The chowdry, or headman, has to give security to the commanding officer to keep on hand transportation for five days' supply of all articles of consumption required by the troops. The prices of supplies sold in the bazaar are regulated by the commanding officer, and such reports and inspections are made as are necessary to keep him informed of its actual condition.

When the regiment moves, the bazaar follows it with all kinds of transportation, and on the arrival of the men in camp immediately provides the food and other articles required.

In case the bazaar cannot accompany the troops, the Government provides rations, which consist of wheat, flour, rice, dhall (or pulse), ghee, resembling butter, and salt.

REWARDS.

The "Order of British India" is conferred on native commissioned officers for long, faithful, and meritorious services.

The first class is composed exclusively of fifty captains (subadars or ressaldars), to whom are given the title of "Sirdar Bahadoor," and an annuity of 730 rupees. The second class, composed of fifty members, is open to all grades, and carries with it the title of "Bahadoor," and an annuity of 366 rupees.

The insignia of the order consists of a gold star, inscribed with the words, "The Order of British India." Commanding officers of native regiments are required to forward annually to the adjutant-general the names of two native officers for the bestowal of the order of the second class, if they deem them deserving of the honor. They are also authorized to recommend deserving officers for promotion from the second to the first class.

The "Order of Merit" is conferred for "personal bravery," irrespective of rank or grade. The order is divided into three classes, and carries with it an annuity. Admission to the first and second classes is restricted to members of the class next below. Admission to each class is granted by the Government of India, on application, specifying the special act of gallantry for which the reward is solicited.

Whenever an officer or soldier is recommended for the order, the commander of the division or district in which he is serving, convenes a mixed court, composed of a major, two captains, and two subadars, before which the claimant is required to appear, as also witnesses who are examined under oath, the proceedings being conducted, when practicable, by a deputy judge-advocate.

If the testimony establishes an act of conspicuous and undoubted gallantry, the court records its opinion to that effect, which is forwarded with the application to the commander-in-chief, to be laid before the Government.

The insignia of the order consists of a gold badge, in the shape of a military laureled star for the first class, and a silver badge for the second and third classes. In the centre of each star is inscribed "The Reward of Valor."

Campaign medals are likewise granted to both officers and men.

Good-conduct pay, pension for life after forty years, or in

case of disability, after fifteen years' service, and discharges with gratuity, are among the other inducements offered to the officers and soldiers of the native army to faithfully perform their duty.

PUNISHMENTS.

The Indian articles of war provide trial by court-martial for all serious offenses, and in minor offenses confer ample authority upon European officers for the enforcement of discipline in all native regiments and corps.

The extraordinary power is given to the commandant, in case of incapacity and neglect, to disrate a native officer, or to reduce him from a higher to a lower class; he can also, in promotions, advance a junior over the head of an incompetent senior. In each case, a full record, presenting the reasons for his action, has to be forwarded to the adjutant-general.

In minor offenses, not deserving courts-martial, the commandant can inflict—

1. *Imprisonment* in the guard-house, or solitary cell, for seven days, carrying with it deprivation of pay and allowances.

2. *Confinement to the lines* for any period not exceeding thirty days. The limits of confinement are within a space occupied by the barracks or huts of the regiment.

In addition to all regular duty, confinement to the lines carries with it *punishment-drill* to the extent of fifteen days, and extra fatigue. Punishment-drill also accompanies all confinements to the lines for any period not exceeding fifteen days. It is carried out by a non-commissioned officer detailed for the purpose, and is not to exceed two hours per day, or an hour at a time.

Confinement to the lines, carrying with it punishment-drill, can also be inflicted by wing-officers and the adjutant for ten days; by wing-subalterns and the quartermaster for seven days, and by native officers for three days.

Subject to such restrictions as the commandants may impose, every commander of a detachment can inflict the same punishments for minor offenses as the commander of a regiment.

The effect of these regulations is to establish a uniform system of discipline throughout the Indian army, and to subject the soldier only to such punishments as are strictly legal.

TRANSPORTATION.

All arrangements for the march and transport of troops are made by the quartermaster's department.

Whenever troops move, the officer in command is required to notify the commissariat officer of the station to which the troops are destined. He is also required to inform the civil officers, along the line of march, of the probable date of his arrival in their several districts.

The necessary carriage or transportation is usually hired by the commissariat officers, but, when it is difficult to be procured, requisition is made upon civil officers. The local governments make the necessary regulations governing the supply of transportation, and fix the rates to be paid for carts or camels, and the load each is to carry. On application to the civil officer, arrangements are usually made with chowdries, or contractors. One-half of the cost of transportation is paid before the march is begun, and the other half on its conclusion, or while in progress.

The Government only transports a given allowance of baggage. If officers and soldiers exceed this amount, they have to hire their own transportation, and are authorized to call upon civil officers for such assistance as is necessary.

The bazaars always provide their own means of transport.

The variety of transportation accompanying the march of troops in India has to be seen to be appreciated. At the manœuvres at Delhi in 1876, it consisted of the elephant, the camel, the buffalo, the ox, the horse, the mule, and the donkey, each with its pack; together with litters, carts, wagons, and wheeled vehicles of many descriptions. On the backs of the elephants and camels were carried chairs, tables, bedsteads, bath-tubs, trunks, chests, tents, and many other articles which impede the march of an army.

Accompanying the baggage were swarms of natives belonging to the bazaars, who gave to the column the appearance of a vast caravan. In no other country except India, where the enemy is unenterprising, could an army be so encumbered with camp-followers and baggage. In the expedition of 1778 sent across from the valley of the Ganges to the Bombay Presidency, to coöperate in the Mahratta War, the detachment composed of 6,600 native troops, under 103 European officers, was accompanied by 31,000 camp-followers.

The above figures cannot be accepted as showing the average proportion of troops to non-combatants, but so long as the regulations permit officers and soldiers to carry an unlimited supply of baggage, and especially so long as the Government adheres to the economical system of allowing the native troops to provide for themselves, the army in India, as has been observed, must continue to resemble "a nation emigrating, guarded by its troops."

MOVABLE COLUMNS.

To facilitate the rapid movement of troops with a view to quiet disorders and suppress insurrections, transportation for seven days' supplies of all kinds for British troops, two days' rations for native troops, forage for horses, sixty rounds of spare ammunition for infantry, and twenty for cavalry, is constantly kept on hand for movable columns, which aggregate in the Bengal Presidency 54 guns, 6 squadrons of British cavalry, 9 regiments of British infantry, 9 regiments of native cavalry, and 12 regiments of native infantry.

The stations occupied by movable columns are designated by the commander-in-chief, and also the number of troops composing them. The list of troops to compose the column at each station is published monthly and furnished to the commissariat officer, who is responsible that the transportation is on hand or within call, and that it is in a thoroughly effective condition. The columns are also frequently ordered out for exercise, in order to accustom them to move with promptness when an emergency arises.

SUPPLIES.

For the purpose of transporting troops with rapidity for long distances, railroads are now available to nearly every province in India. Experiments have also been made in shipping troops with their transportation from point to point, in order to accustom them to loading and unloading promptly and without confusion. The arrangement of cars preferred for this purpose is with end-doors, so that the cars may be loaded successively from one end of the train to the other.

As the whole railroad system, already embracing from 8,000 to 10,000 miles, will ultimately fall into the hands of the Government, there is no doubt that every recommendation of the military authorities will be adopted with a view to hasten and simplify military operations.

Whenever troops are ordered to march in India, the commanding officer notifies the civil officers of the time he will arrive at the various stages along the route within their several districts, and forwards to them requisitions for such supplies as will be required at each point. The civil authorities send a native functionary to join the troops the day before they enter the district, whose duty is to receive the instructions of the commanding officer, and to precede the corps daily, so as to insure that the supplies will be on hand and be of good quality.

The "Route-Book of India" describes the lines of march, and locates the camping-places between all of the principal cities and villages. The supplies are delivered and paid for at each camping-place. Those for the native troops are turned over by the contractors, or persons furnishing them, to the chowdry of the bazaar, through whom they are sold to the officers and men. The supplies remaining on hand at the end of the day are returned at the price fixed for them in the morning.

The native officer appointed to accompany the troops is responsible for the adjustment of the accounts, which he submits to the quartermaster at 4 P. M. daily. On the settlement of the account he is required to give to the commanding officer an acknowledgment to that effect.

INFANTRY (EUROPEAN).

The cost of supplies procured through civil officers is regulated by price-currents of all articles of fixed value. In case of imposition in reference to articles of fluctuating value the civil authorities are at once notified, who have the necessary power to redress the grievance.

BRITISH ARMY IN INDIA.

The total number of British troops in India, as has already been stated, is 66,220 men, distributed as follows:

Bengal.
- 32 Regiments of infantry.
- 6 Regiments of cavalry.
- 11 Batteries horse-artillery.
- 22 Light batteries field-artillery.
- 2 Batteries mountain-artillery.
- 2 Batteries heavy field-artillery.
- 11 Batteries garrison-artillery.

Madras.
- 9 Regiments of infantry.
- 2 Regiments of cavalry.
- 2 Batteries horse-artillery.
- 11 Light batteries field-artillery.
- 1 Heavy battery field-artillery.
- 6 Batteries garrison-artillery.

Bombay.
- 9 Regiments of infantry.
- 1 Regiment of cavalry.
- 2 Batteries horse-artillery.
- 10 Light batteries field-artillery.
- 1 Heavy battery field-artillery.
- 5 Batteries garrison-artillery.

INFANTRY (EUROPEAN).

The established strength of a regiment of British infantry in India is as follows:
- 1 Lieutenant-colonel.
- 2 Majors.
- 8 Captains.
- 16 Lieutenants and sub-lieutenants.
- 1 Paymaster.

1 Adjutant.
1 Quartermaster.
1 Surgeon-major.
2 Surgeons.

Total commissioned, 33.

1 Sergeant-major.
1 Bandmaster-sergeant.
1 Quartermaster-sergeant.
1 Paymaster-sergeant.
1 Armorer-sergeant.
1 Hospital-sergeant.
1 Sergeant-pioneer.
8 Color, or first sergeants.
32 Sergeants.
1 Sergeant instructor of musketry.
1 Orderly-room sergeant.
1 Drum-major.
16 Drummers.
40 Corporals.
780 Privates.

Total enlisted, 886.
Aggregate, 919.

The regiment is composed of eight companies, each consisting of—

1 Captain.
2 Lieutenants or sub-lieutenants.
1 Color, or first sergeant.
4 Sergeants.
2 Drummers.
5 Corporals.
97 Privates.

The term of service of British infantry is ten years, and during this period two years are passed at one of the Hill-Stations.

In the Bengal Presidency the troops change station periodically from south to north, and the reverse, the troops to go home being gradually moved toward the port of embarkation. For the purpose of transporting the troops to and from India, troop-ships, capable of carrying a whole regiment, have been built, and are commanded by officers of the navy.

RECREATION.

The cost of transporting, invaliding, and replacing invalid soldiers, is so great that, with a view to economy, every disposition is made by the Government to preserve and promote the health of the British troops. To this end occupation of mind and body is encouraged, and every amusement provided that can tend to turn or divert the thoughts of the soldier from the discomforts of the climate.

Each regiment has its canteen, libraries, reading, recreation, and refreshment rooms.

The object of the canteen is to supply the soldiers with rum, wine, and beer, which are provided by the Government, without charge for transportation, and are sold in limited quantities to the soldiers at the rate of three cents a dram for rum, and nine cents a quart for beer.

The profits from the sale, arising from the difference between the cost and the retail price, constitute the basis of the regimental canteen-fund, which is applied to the support of regimental schools, reading and refreshment rooms; to the purchase of necessaries for the soldiers' messes; to donations to widows and orphans belonging to the corps; to invalid soldiers going home; and to other purposes having the welfare of the men in view.

Each regiment of infantry has two libraries, one belonging to the regiment, the other to the state; the two numbering 1,200 volumes. The libraries and reading-rooms, in which are kept writing-materials and games for the men, are managed by a committee of non-commissioned officers and men, under the supervision of an officer. Adjoining the reading and recreation rooms is a refreshment-room, in which are sold tea, coffee, soda-water, lemonade, and other refreshments. The reading-rooms, in which are to be found, in addition to books, the newspapers and periodicals of the day, constitute, in connection with the refreshment-rooms, a club where all of the men can pass an agreeable evening, or divert themselves during the idle hours of the day.

For physical exercise, regimental workshops, racket-courts, swimming-baths, and gymnasiums, are provided. The workshop is specially fostered by the Government to enable soldiers and their children to learn profitable trades. To this end prizes are offered for first and second class workmen, and when an apprentice acquires a thorough knowledge of a trade the soldier who instructed him receives a donation of 25 rupees. The charges for work done in the regimental shops are fixed by a tariff or by the hour. The tools, in the first instance, are purchased by the canteen-fund, and afterward paid for and kept in repair by the profits of the shop. The soldiers who work in the shop are encouraged to deposit their earnings in the savings-bank of the regiment.

The object of all of the regimental institutions is to deliver the soldiers from idleness, and to give them profitable employment and recreation, and it is safe to say that in no country in the world is more done for their comfort than in India.

SUNDAYS.

The only duty required of soldiers in India on Sunday is attendance at divine service. There are no Sunday-morning inspections nor drills. Since the mutiny, the men march to church under arms. After their return from service the remainder of the day is at their own disposal.

In addition to the rest given to the soldiers on the Sabbath, a holiday every Thursday has recently been given to them for the purpose of encouraging shooting and other out-door sports.

Notwithstanding the loss of time, it is maintained that discipline is not impaired, but on the contrary is improved, through the increased cheerfulness of the men.

BARRACKS.

The barracks, hospitals, and other buildings for the accommodation of the European troops in India, are constructed by the Public Works Department.

BARRACKS.

The principles governing the construction of barracks were drawn up by Colonel Crommelin in 1863, and by direction of the Home Government were submitted to the Sanitary Commission for Bengal. The governor-general in council also directed that they should be submitted for remarks to the Governments of Bombay, Madras, Bengal, Northwest Provinces, the Punjab, and British Burmah. In addition, opinions were expressed by the viceroy and governor-general, the commander-in-chief in India, other members of the governor-general's council, and by the commander-in-chief in Bombay, and the Sanitary Commission for Bombay.

After weighing the opinions of the officers above cited, who were familiar with the climate of nearly every locality in India, the governor-general in council decided that, in the future construction of barracks, the following principles should be observed, viz.:

1. That specimen plans suitable for different localities be provided, together with a statement of the general rules and principles to be observed. These being furnished for guidance, the preparation of designs for particular barracks is to be left to the local officers who construct them.

2. That for a regiment of infantry, half-company barracks are to be provided, except in forts, where, for want of space, barracks for a whole company may be substituted.

For a regiment of cavalry a separate barrack should be provided for each troop. For a light battery of artillery there should be a separate barrack provided for each platoon. For a garrison-battery of artillery one or two barracks should be provided according as local circumstances may require.

The object of the arrangement is that in infantry and artillery not more than forty-four men, and in cavalry sixty-six men, shall sleep under one roof.

3. That four rooms be provided for a company of infantry, three for a troop of cavalry and battery of light artillery, and three for a battery of garrison-artillery, except when two barracks are allowed, in which case each is divided into two rooms.

By this arrangement not more than twenty-four nor less than sixteen men occupy the same room.

4. That double-storied barracks, in which only the upper floors are to be used as dormitories, and the lower for day-rooms and for auxiliary purposes, should be adopted *as a rule* in all parts of India.

That in places where ground is restricted three-story buildings may be adopted, the two upper floors being used as dormitories; that in forts or other places where the efficient ventilation of the lower floor is obstructed by the proximity of a rampart or hill-side, this floor should not be occupied by dwelling-rooms; that at Hill-Stations it is not obligatory to build two-story barracks, but, when it is more convenient to have them, there is no objection to using both floors as dormitories.

Without adopting any definite arrangement for the lower story, it was decided in general terms that one-half of the space should be assigned to day-rooms for the men, one-fourth as an open arcade, and one-fourth for *auxiliary purposes* such as store-rooms, sergeants' mess, regimental library and recreation-rooms; but offices, privies, cook-rooms, etc., etc., fall under the head of *subsidiary accommodation.*

5. That the *space* in barrack dormitories be arranged as follows:

On the Plains—

$7\frac{1}{2}$ running feet of wall-space per man.

90 superficial feet per man.

24 feet width of ward.

20 feet height of ceiling above floor in both stories.

1,800 cubic feet per man.

At Hill-Stations—

7 running feet of wall-space per man.

77 superficial feet per man.

22 feet width of ward.

16 to 18 feet height of ceiling on both floors.

1,232 to 1,408 cubic feet per man.

Beds are to be arranged in two rows in each ward; no bed

to be placed within nine inches of a door, nor more than two within the wall-space between two contiguous doors. In all Indian barracks, doors with large transoms take the place of windows.

6. Each barrack to be kept free from anything likely to affect the purity of the air; the barrack-room unit to consist of—
   1. The dormitory.
   2. Mess-room.
   3. The quarters of a sergeant.
   4. Water-room.
   5. Any other day-rooms that may be allowed.

Lavatories to be in detached buildings. Closet containing two close stools and two urinals permitted for each upper story dormitory for night purposes, but to be kept locked in daytime.

The sergeant's quarters are the same as authorized for married men, viz.: two rooms, one 18′ × 12′, and one 12′ × 12′. A small bath-room is provided for the sergeant's wife, who can have no suitable out-building in the vicinity of the single men's barracks to resort to.

The width of the verandas of barracks on the plains is twelve feet, in the hills ten feet.

The principles together with the plans of barracks approved by the Indian Government in 1864, have since been modified in some unimportant particulars, such as diminishing the height of ceiling in upper story from twenty to sixteen feet, reducing wards from twenty to eighteen beds, superficial area from seventy-seven to seventy-one feet per man at Hill Stations. Where good barracks existed before the new plans were adopted, they have been simply remodelled to conform to the general principles of the new system.

OUT-BUILDINGS.

The kitchen, lavatory, privy, bath-house, and laundry, are special buildings. At most of the stations swimming-baths from four to five feet deep are also provided.

BARRACKS FOR MARRIED MEN.

Each married man is allowed two rooms, one $16' \times 14'$, the other $14' \times 10'$. Barracks, one story high, surrounded by verandas, are preferred, but two-story barracks are permitted. Each barrack contains from eight to ten sets of quarters. To insure privacy, all of the partition-walls between quarters are carried to the roof; and privies for women and children are not under the same roof as those of the men. Bath-rooms are provided in detached buildings.

HOSPITALS.

As the Government does not consider general hospitals desirable in time of peace, a separate hospital, as a general rule, is provided for every regiment or detachment.

The hospitals are required to accommodate 10 per cent. of the regulation strength of regiments, and detachments exceeding 400, and 12 per cent. for detachments under 400. In unhealthy climates such as Agra, Delhi, Peshawar, the accommodation is increased to 12 per cent. for detachments above 400, and 15 per cent. for detachments below 400.

In accordance with the above proportion, a hospital must furnish beds as follows:

	Unhealthy Stations.	Healthy Stations.
Regiment of infantry,	110	92
Regiment of cavalry,	62	50
Battery of artillery,	20	18
Company of garrison-artillery,	10	10

The hospitals, like the barracks, are two-storied, and for a regiment of infantry consist of two buildings, 400 feet long.

The out-buildings consist of a privy, dead-house, guard-house, wash-house, and shed for ambulance.

Separate hospitals are provided for the women belonging to the married establishment.

The importance attached by the Government of India to a proper system of barrack and hospital accommodation of the European troops, is shown by the fact that £10,000,000, or $50,000,000, would be required for their construction.

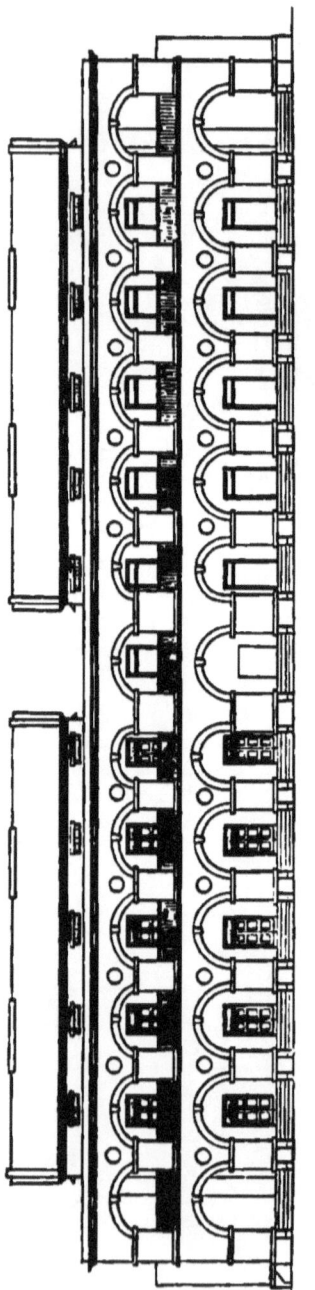

Elevation of double-storied half-company barrack, for British infantry, Saugor, India.

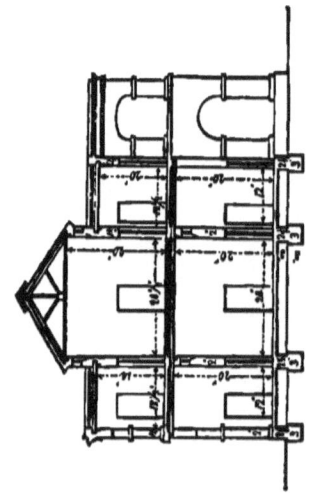

Section on line A, B.

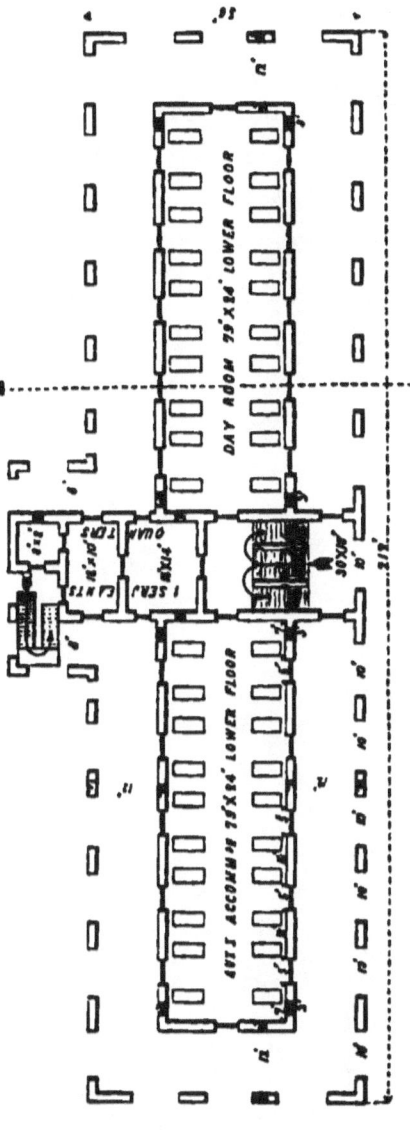

Plan of upper floor of double-storied half-company barrack, for British infantry, Saugor.

The lower floor is set apart as day-rooms and for auxiliary purposes.

Superficial feet per man in dormitories, 98'.
" " " " " day-rooms, 47½'.

The magnitude of the barracks and their imposing structure may be inferred from the accompanying plans—section and elevation of a double-storied half-company barrack for British infantry at Saugur.

The interesting features of the barracks when considered with reference to our hot climates in the South—such as Texas and Arizona—are, that they are two-storied; that each is surrounded with a broad two-story veranda; that by means of blinds the sun never strikes upon the walls of the rooms in which the men sleep; that the ventilation by flues within the walls, and by clear-story windows is perfect, and that most ample provision is made for the recreation of the men, and also for their cleanliness by providing both lavatories and swimming-baths.

To enable the men to sleep, "punkas," or large fans, are worked all night by coolies, whose labor costs a mere pittance.

As a general rule the Government does not provide barracks for the native troops, but instead gives them an allowance called "hutting-money." With this fund the troops construct their own huts, the walls of which are made of mud or adobes. The contrast between the lofty barracks of the white troops, and the huts, or "lines," of the natives is very marked; nevertheless, the latter, never having had better accommodation, do not fret under the distinction that is made.

No quarters are provided as a rule for officers in India. They have an allowance instead, and occupy "bungalows," or one-story cottages, built in the cantonment not far from the troops.

In campaign they supply their own tents. These are well adapted to the hot climate, and always consist of one tent pitched wholly within a second or larger one. The space between the two tents is from two to four feet wide, and this permits the air to circulate freely. To give additional coolness, and to soften the glare, both the inner and outer tents are lined with yellow cotton.

It is not uncommon for officers to have a double supply of tents, in which case the set not in use is sent ahead and pitched at the next camping-place, where it is ready for occupation on the arrival of the troops.

In hot weather, matting, kept wet by bheesties, or water-carriers, is hung before the doors of the tents. The circulation of the air through the interstices of the matting produces such rapid evaporation as to keep the temperature between 80° and 90°.

PAY.

The expense of the British troops serving in India is defrayed by the Indian Government.

The following table shows the monthly pay and allowances of each grade in a regiment of British infantry serving in India:

RANK.	Number.	PAY PROPER.			COMMAND, STAFF, AND HORSE ALLOWANCE.			TOTAL PER MONTH.			DOLLARS.
		R.	A.	P.	R.	A.	P.	R.	A.	P.	
Lieutenant-colonel	1	1002	4	..	480	..	..	1482	4	..	$716.12
Major	2	759	8	..	30	..	..	789	8	..	394.50
Captain	8	415	6	..	30	..	..	445	6	..	222.68
Lieutenant and sub-lieutenant	16	202	12	5	..	..	..	202	12	5	101.37
Paymaster	1	445	13	..	78	10	8	524	7	8	262.22
Adjutant	1	256	10	..	257	..	../	513	10	..	256.60
Quartermaster	1	274	14	8	85	..	..	869	14	8	184.93
Surgeon-major	1	789	8	..	..	..	..	789	8	..	894.59
Surgeon	2	317	8	..	..	..	..	317	8	..	158.74
Total	33										
Sergeant-major	1	50	9	6	..	..	..	50	9	6	25.37
Bandmaster-sergeant	1	47	14	10	..	..	..	47	14	10	23.93
Quartermaster-sergeant	1	39	14	10	..	..	..	39	14	10	19.98
Paymaster-sergeant	1	29	4	2	..	..	..	29	4	2	14.62
Armorer-sergeant	1	77	4	2	..	..	..	77	4	2	38.62
Hospital-sergeant	1	33	5	4	..	..	..	33	5	4	16.65
Sergeant-pioneer	1	29	4	2	..	..	..	29	4	2	14.62
Color-sergeant	6	37	4	2	..	..	..	37	4	2	18.62
Sergeant	32	29	4	2	..	..	..	29	4	2	14.62
Sergeant instruct. of musketry	1	45	4	2	..	..	..	45	4	2	22.62
Orderly room-sergeant	1	29	4	2	..	..	..	29	4	2	14.62
Drum-major	1	29	4	2	..	..	..	29	4	2	14.62
Drummer	16	15	14	10	..	..	..	15	14	10	7.93
Corporal	40	18	9	6	..	..	..	18	9	6	9.37
Private	780	14	9	6	..	..	..	14	9	6	7.28
Total	886										
Grand total	919										

The total annual cost of a British regiment of 919 men is $173,670. The cost of a native regiment of 720 men is $69,228. If increased to 919 men, its cost would only amount to half that of a British regiment. The total cost of the fifty regiments of British infantry in India is $9,212,458. The total cost of the sixty regiments of Bengal infantry is $4,537,343.

The gross expenditure on account of the army of India, numbering 190,000 men, for 1875–'76, was £11,930,400 = $59,652,000.

GENERAL REMARKS.

The military institutions of India present more features for our imitation than those of any army or country in Europe. From the battle of Plassy, when the vision of conquest first dawned upon the East India Company, until the final subjugation of the empire, every war was prosecuted with mixed troops. The British regulars formed a nucleus around which the native troops could rally, and furnished to them the standard of drill, discipline, and valor. The value and economy of native troops were early discovered, and nowhere in history has the wisdom of a government been so signally rewarded as in the organization of the native army. It would have been surprising if, with the material for soldiers everywhere at hand, the project of forming native corps, under European officers, had not suggested itself.

The first use of sepoys was at Bombay. Later, in 1746, they took part in the siege of Madras. Those first employed in the Madras Presidency were organized into companies, commanded by native captains and subalterns, and were organized into battalions of ten companies, commanded by British captains, with one British subaltern to each company. With this leaven of European officers, several campaigns were successfully prosecuted by the sepoys, which greatly increased their *esprit de corps* and attachment to the company's service.

In the campaigns of 1790–'91 European troops were intermixed with the natives, and with this composition, in 1757, the great Clive, with a force numbering 3,000 men, of whom less than 1,000 were English, defeated an army of 60,000 at the battle of Plassy, and changed the fate of an empire. The stupendous results of the battle, in which Clive lost but 72 killed and wounded, can only be attributed to the wisdom of distributing military talent among the native troops, and to their subsequent perfection in drill and discipline.

In 1766 the native army in Madras consisted of 10 battalions of 1,000 men each, with three European officers to each battalion; in 1770 it had expanded to 18 battalions, and 1784 it had increased to 2,000 cavalry, and 28,000 infantry. In 1796 the native troops were formed into regiments of two battalions each, with a complement of European officers nearly the same as in a British regiment. In 1876 the established strength was 1,700 cavalry and 30,000 infantry.

In Bombay the sepoys were first organized in companies under their native officers, and afterward formed into battalions under Europeans. In 1796 the force was organized into four regiments of two battalions each. In 1876 the established strength was 3,900 cavalry and 22,000 infantry.

In Bengal, the first battalions raised were composed of ten companies of 100 men each. The Europeans attached consisted of 1 captain, 1 lieutenant, 1 ensign, and 1 or 2 sergeants. This force has been expanded and contracted until it reached its present established strength of 12,800 cavalry and 48,000 infantry.

The average height of the infantry sepoys in Bombay and Madras is five feet five inches, and the minimum five feet three inches; the maximum height is five feet six inches. The Sikhs from Northern India, in the Punjab, are the tallest and finest-looking soldiers in Bengal, many of them being six feet in height. The Goorkhas, short, thick-set, muscular men from the mountains, dispute with the Sikhs the reputation of being the best fighters in Bengal, if not in India.

The religion of the native troops is mostly Hindoo and Mohammedan, but in Bombay there are also many Jews and some Christians. When Mohammedans and Hindoos serve in the same regiments the companies are arranged in classes according to their religion.

This variety of religion, and particularly of caste, is the source of much annoyance and difficulty. The men of different castes will not only not associate with each other, but will not partake of the same food unless it is prepared by one of their own order. The result is, that a company may be divided into as many messes as it has men, each of whom sweeps and washes a plot of ground about a yard or two square on which he builds his fire and cooks his food. If this ground is touched by his European officer, or a sepoy of different caste, it becomes unclean, and has to be washed and swept again.

DISCIPLINE.

The drill, discipline, movements, and appearance, of the native troops at the camp of exercise at Delhi in 1876 would compare favorably with those of many of the troops in Europe.

At the review before the Prince of Wales they marched with a precision approaching that of the English regiments, and at the subsequent manœuvres applied the German tactics with as much intelligence as the troops seen in Italy, Austria, and Russia.

The movements of the thirteen regiments of cavalry, three of which were British, were particularly dashing and brilliant. All of the evolutions, whether at the walk, trot, or gallop, were executed with a strictness and precision that would have reflected credit upon any army.

As in Europe, so in India, the value of the carbine is but little appreciated. Apparently indifferent to the brilliant achievements of the American horse, a majority of the officers still hold to the sabre as the only weapon worthy of a cavalry-man.

Whatever may be the external appearance of the native troops, whether infantry or cavalry, their value almost wholly depends on the European officers who lead them. If these fall, the natives are liable to confusion, and to wander about without direction or guidance. The value of skilled officers in conducting troops was never more conspicuously illustrated than during the mutiny. No sooner were the revolted troops left to the management of their own officers, than the utmost disorder and confusion prevailed.

These officers had all risen from the ranks, and knew nothing of the art of war except the movements of a battalion or regiment. They had been trained to be the mere medium of communication between the European officers and the men, and to assist in their drill and discipline. Above them, the sepoy knew, was the stern, inflexible British officer, and to him he looked alike for reward and punishment. When this motor and governor was removed, the native officers found themselves powerless; no system or order was maintained, the troops rushed into battle blindly, fought bravely, and when repulsed fell back disheartened and demoralized. It seems strange that, after a century's service with British troops, there could not be found a single native officer capable of planning a campaign against their oppressors. They allowed a small British and native army, composed mostly of Sikhs, to plant itself on a rocky ridge overlooking the city of Delhi, and, with the exception of one or two forays, never sought to interrupt the long line of communications from the Punjab, which was always open to their attacks. While the infantry mutineers fought with desperation, the revolted artillery gave the besieging army the most trouble and inflicted the greatest loss. So admirably was it served that since the mutiny all of the native artillery, except three or four batteries, has been disbanded.

The conduct of the native troops during the siege of Delhi was such as to gain the admiration of their British comrades: they fought side by side with them; endured all the exposure from May 30th, the beginning, to September 20th, the end of the siege, and in their lists of casualties gave unmistakable proof of their valor and fidelity.

The frequent mutinies that have broken out among the native troops cannot with justice be imputed to bad discipline, or to the inefficiency of the European officers. In most armies the causes leading to them, such as withholding pay, bad food and clothing, can by proper foresight be removed; but, when this is not the case, the vigilance of the officers and patriotism of the men are sufficient to reduce the insubordination within narrow limits, and to secure a speedy return to duty. But in India the causes are widely different, having their source in the deep religious animosities and prejudices of the races. However fair a regiment may be to look upon, it is but a smothered volcano whose flames may break forth at any moment and destroy every European within reach.

Nevertheless, if the total number of regiments in the native army be considered, it is doubtful if mutiny is more frequent in India than in other countries, and particularly in those which rely upon raw and untrained troops.

If treated with kindness, the native soldier, in battle and elsewhere, shows a devotion to his officers which cannot be excelled, and it is only when his sense of military duty is overcome by an appeal to his fanaticism that he becomes ferocious and ungovernable.

The greatest struggle England has yet had in India was with the mutiny of 1857, and this struggle was with the officers and men she had trained for her own service. No combination of races or tribes, without military organization, could for a moment have resisted her arms; and it was only through the prearranged defection of her troops that the effort to regain independence assumed form and proportion: even then the same weapons with which she had conquered the empire were successfully used in suppressing the rebellion. The little army that captured the King of Delhi and his capital, and settled for an indefinite time the foundations of the Indian Empire, was composed of but 12,000 effective men, of whom only 3,000 were British.

Like the American Indians, the different races in India have always shown more eagerness to fight each other than to fight the English, and it was by taking advantage of this disposition, and, like the ancient Romans, mingling in their quarrels, that they successively subdued them all. The same causes that led to the fall of India still exist to keep her in subjection. The troops of Madras would clamor to be led against the troops of Bengal; if the Mohammedans revolt, the Hindoos would be true, and so long as, in the order of Providence, the races keep separate in religion and feeling, so long will it be possible for England to rule.

Like all great commotions, the mutiny precipitated a reorganization of the whole native army. The authorities did not stop to discover the real causes, but attributed many of them to the army, and to the "absenteeism" of officers that had up to that time prevailed. It was therefore resolved that all of the officers in India, excepting those belonging to British regiments, should be merged into one great staff corps, and that thereafter the officers detailed with native regiments should remain with them.

The result of this change was to reduce the number of Europeans serving with each regiment of infantry from twenty-eight to eight, of which number nearly one-half are usually absent on leave, or detached service. This reduction is still the subject of much discussion, and, considering the inefficiency of the native officers when left to themselves, it may well be doubted if the Government has acted wisely.

In no department of an army is skill so much needed as in leading troops to battle, especially when they have not confidence in themselves and their company officers.

It is in this respect that England has set us an example of distributing military talent, which, had it been followed in our late war, would have saved thousands of lives and millions of treasure. But it is not in this respect alone that the Indian army is worthy of our imitation. It presents the spectacle of nearly 200,000 men conquering and keeping an empire in subjection, without a single permanent staff corps. In our army all of these corps are closed; the appointments are permanent, and no means are provided to weed out the inefficient or to encourage the aspiring. In India all the officers in the adjutant-general's department and quartermaster-general's department are changed every five years; and in the other staff departments, such as the commissariat and ordnance, in which the appointments are held more or less permanently, officers can at any time be relieved and sent to other duty. Another marked feature of all of these departments is that, after officers are detailed in them from the general staff corps, no regard is paid to seniority in selecting officers for heads of bureaux, or for any other position. In this manner, while favoritism is not absolutely excluded, a sure encouragement is given to all officers who perform their duty with zeal and efficiency. The military policy of the Government has unquestionably produced a beneficial effect in India upon the corps of officers, and has imparted to them a variety of military knowledge and experience not possessed by any other army.

At Calcutta we met a colonel who was a civil and military governor of four millions of people; at Muscat and Bushire military officers were intrusted with the diplomatic relations of India with Arabia and Persia; at the camp at Delhi the adjutant-general had previously been quartermaster-general, and was anticipating the expiration of his five years' service, which would give him the command of a brigade or a division.

All of the officers we met at Delhi and elsewhere in India gave evidence that, whether in a military or civil capacity, they had been acting in spheres of responsibility far greater than those occupied by officers of other armies, and as a consequence showed a capacity and self-confidence far above their rank. The results attained in India are worthy of our closest study, and suggest the question whether, in the impending reorganization of our army, we should not, as the first step, establish a vital and interchangeable relation between the line and the staff.

DISTRIBUTION OF TROOPS.

Unlike the armies of Europe, which are maintained in a state of ceaseless preparation to wage war and to resist conquest, the army of India rests from its labors.

The Himalayas and the deserts of Afghanistan and Beloochistan have fixed the bounds of conquest, and henceforth the army, like a huge police force, must be maintained only to preserve the peace.

The disposition maps of the three presidencies for 1874–'75 show that, instead of concentrating large bodies of troops at the great strategic points, like Bombay, Madras, Calcutta, Allahabad, Lahore, and Peshawar, the army is distributed in small garrisons, not only with a view to exhibit the military power of the Government at as many points as possible, but also to be within such distance as to crush insurrections in their beginning.

In the Bengal Presidency, extending up the valleys of the Ganges and the Jumna, the principal points occupied are Calcutta, Dinapore, Benares, Allahabad, Cawnpore, Lucknow, Agra, Bareily, Delhi, Meerut, Umbala, Meean-Meer, Lahore, Sealkote, Rawul, Pindee, and Peshawar. The garrisons at all of these points are composed of mixed troops.

At Calcutta and vicinity there are 3 regiments of British infantry, 3 of native infantry, and 3 batteries of artillery; at Allahabad there are 2 regiments of British infantry, 1 of native infantry, 2 squadrons of native cavalry, and 2 batteries of artillery; at Cawnpore, 1 regiment of British infantry, 1 of native infantry, and 1 of native cavalry; at Lucknow, 2 regiments of British infantry, 2 of native infantry, 1 of British cavalry, and 2 batteries of artillery. Four batteries of artillery are stationed at Meerut, 2 at Umbala, and 3 at Meean-Meer.

The largest garrison in India is at Peshawar, which generally consists of 2 regiments of British infantry, 4 of native infantry, 2 of native cavalry, and 3 batteries of artillery; numbering in all from 6,000 to 7,000 men.

The largest concentration of troops in any one district in India is in the Punjab, where there are from 30,000 to 35,000 men, or nearly one-half the force of the Bengal Presidency. It was through this door that Alexander, Genghis Khan, and Tamerlane, entered India, and it is the door through which many Indian officers confidently expect the Russians.

The troops in Madras are principally stationed at Trichinopoly, Bangalore, Bellary, Hyderabad, and Nagpoor, all being points within railroad communication, and lying on a line nearly bisecting the peninsula from Cape Comorin to Jubbulpore and Allahabad.

In the Bombay Presidency the principal garrisons are at Bombay and Kurrachee on the coast; Belgaum, Poonah, Ahmedabad, Rajkote, Deesa, and Hyderabad, all on a line about fifty miles from the sea; and Mhow-Neemuch, and Nusseerabad, in Rajpootana in the northeast.

Small garrisons, consisting of half-battalions, companies, and small detachments, are likewise dotted over the country wherever turbulence may be apprehended.

To prevent the wild, irresponsible tribes of Beloochistan and Afghanistan from raiding across the Indus and escaping with their plunder, a strip of territory about fifty miles wide has been acquired to the west of the river from Kurrachee to Peshawar. This territory from the mouth of the Indus to Peshawar is occupied by about 12,000 men, composing a special frontier force, under the exclusive control of the Lieutenant-Governor of the Punjab. The success that has attended this acquisition of territory suggests the similarity of our frontier on the Rio Grande.

The continued occupation of India by England must afford a subject of deep speculation to statesmen, and all the causes that may contribute to prolong her rule deserve attentive consideration.

The one great result of the mutiny was, to teach the natives how powerless they were to throw off the yoke, even when aided by the soldiers England had trained, who took with them all of their arms and munitions of war. The mutiny broke out when the Government was least prepared for it, and when the subjugation of the warlike tribes of the Punjab had scarcely been completed.

Realizing that a crisis had arrived, the aid of the men who had so recently fought to preserve their independence was invoked, and had they not responded, or had the Punjab failed as a base of supply, no one could have fixed the bounds of a movement that bade fair to expel the invaders.

Since the mutiny was crushed, the whole face of India has changed. The Suez Canal enables English troops to be landed at Bombay in fewer weeks than before it took months, while the great lines of railway permit them to be sent directly to every important part of the empire.

But, without aid from England, the railway system by itself is sufficient to enable the 60,000 British troops to hold India almost indefinitely, even against the defection of the entire native army. Starting from Bombay, one trunkline goes to Madras, and by its branches opens up all of the southern peninsula; another stretches across to Allahabad, and connects with the great line of the Ganges, already completed from Calcutta to within two hundred miles of Peshawar; a second cross-line is in process of construction from Agra in the direction of Ahmedabad, and is completed to Nusseerabad; while a third cross-line from Lahore is completed to Mooltan, and will soon be extended down the Indus to Kurrachee. As the link between Madras and Calcutta may be supplied by sea, four great lines of communication will shortly be opened from the shores of the Indian Ocean to the lines of the Ganges.

INVASION OF INDIA.

As the time has passed when the fate of India can be decided by a single battle, the lines of railway will be equally important in resisting invasion and in preserving the peace.

If an army enter by the north, the five rivers of the Punjab form as many lines of defense. If deemed preferable to lure an enemy to the southward, and allow the climate to do its fatal work, the strategic points of Lahore, Agra, and Allahabad, can be successively abandoned, and communication still be maintained with Bombay by way of Madras; while from Kurrachee an army moving *via* Mooltan could cut off retreat. Should an army descend the Indus, a pursuing army from the Ganges might drive it into the sea, or into the deserts of Beloochistan.

Thoroughly prepared to suppress insurrection and rebellion, it is only when England beholds the encroachments of Russia that she becomes alarmed for her Eastern possessions. Like a wild beast gloating over its prey, she is conscious that the actual or supposed discontent of her subjects invites foreign nations to their rescue. Napoleon thought of emancipating them, and to Russia is ascribed the inheritance of his designs. Jealous of her great Northern rival, and not considering the barren wastes which extend hundreds of miles to the north and west of her frontiers, a future invasion, like a hideous nightmare, disturbs the dreams of the Indian rulers. The recent successes of Russia in Central Asia, by means of which the frontiers of the two powers have been brought nearly into contact, have increased the alarm; while the present war between Russia and the Turks is regarded as the sure forerunner of the great conflict.

With vast possessions stretching across two continents, and with only one natural outlet to the Atlantic, Russia feels that geographically she has a right to Constantinople, and, by the force of tradition, no less than by the irresistible weight of her 70,000,000 people, she demands and ultimately will conquer a free passage to the sea.

The expulsion of the Turks from Europe, whenever it may occur, will increase the dangers of England. Availing themselves of the sympathy of their co-religionists, who revere the sultan as the successor of the Prophet, it is not impossible that the Turks should seek to indemnify themselves in Asia for their losses in Europe.

Largely outnumbering the Persians, and in every respect superior to them, the weakness of that kingdom invites subjugation; pressing onward in the footsteps of Alexander and Tamerlane, 40,000,000 Mohammedans stretch forth their hands for deliverance, and long for the restoration of the empire of the Moguls.

This may not be accomplished in one or a dozen campaigns; but, supported and encouraged by Russia, repeated invasions may involve the Indian Government in such expenditures as to induce it, in deference to an opinion already existing in England, to abandon India to her fate. But, without dwelling on the probabilities of Turkish aggrandizement, it is possible that the fate of India may be settled nearer home.

Constantly increasing, by her Eastern policy, the deadly feeling of hostility which already exists in Russia against her, the moment the former occupies Constantinople, England must seize upon Egypt. Once secure in Constantinople, the fleets of England can no longer oppose the designs of Russia. Converting the Black Sea into an inland lake, thus insuring her communications, a railroad from Trebizond across to the valley of the Euphrates, and thence on to Damascus, will place Russia on the flank of England's line of communication. Thus brought face to face, it is not impossible that these two great powers may change the face of Asia on the famous plain of Esdraelon.

While such are the dangers which confront England from the west, another danger, thus far concealed, lies nearer than Russia or Turkey. To the north and east, on the very confines of her empire, a nation of 400,000,000 is sleeping, unconscious of its strength. To awaken it, to vitalize, consolidate, and give it power, to imbue it with schemes of conquest, is but the work of a single man, like any of the great kings who have sat upon its throne. Its richest provinces lie close to British Burmah, and only railroads are needed to enable it to pour its armies like successive waves down the valley of the Brahmapootra and through the passes of the Himalayas. Lofty as are these mountains, Chinese troops have traversed them, have invaded Nepaul, and looked down upon the valley of the Ganges. What Napoleon did for the passes of the Alps, what Russia has done more recently for the communications across the Caucasus, China can do for the Himalayas. She may sacrifice army after army, but, like the barbarians who subdued Rome, or like the Tartars who knocked for a thousand years at the gates of her own empire, success eventually must crown her efforts.

The possibility of such a conflict suggests the contrast of the present condition of the two empires: China has 400,000,000 people; India has 200,000,000. China is governed by a foreign dynasty which adopted the manners and customs of its people; India is ruled by a foreign people whose mission, if not object, is to extend the blessing of Christian civilization. In China an army, nominally 1,000,000 strong, is incapable of suppressing brigandage, insurrection, and rebellion; in India peace has followed the British ensign, and an army of 200,000 men, wisely distributed, preserves absolute tranquillity.

In the language of the one, the word "liberty" is unknown; in the other, the rights of the people are protected by a "firm and impartial despotism." In the one, rulers may seize the property and sever the necks of their subjects with impunity; in the other, sacredness of person is secure.

In China, men without trial languish in prisons, cruel and unusual punishments, injustice, bribery, and corruption, prevail; in India, English law secures speedy trial, and protects life and property. In China, servile admiration of the wisdom of past ages resists progress; in India, schools, churches, railroads, steamboats, telegraphs, and just laws, are giving new life and energy to the people.

With such mighty contrasts between Asiatic and European civilization, no stranger, free from national prejudices, can visit China and India without rejoicing that England controls the destinies of 200,000,000 people; neither can he observe the great institutions which she has founded for their moral and physical amelioration without hoping that, in the interest of humanity, she may continue her sway until she has made them worthy to become a free and enlightened nation.

ARMY OF PERSIA.

The decline in military organization from India to Persia is scarcely less marked than from Japan to China.

Sandwiched between the great powers, England and Russia, and brought more intimately in contact with Europe than China, Persia has been made to feel the want of military institutions, and has made in the course of her history several efforts to adopt European models and tactics.

As early as the time of Queen Elizabeth, the artillery was organized by an Englishman. Nearly two centuries later, when the flames of war, kindled at the birth of freedom and republicanism in France, had swept over Africa and had reached the shores of Asia, Napoleon, in 1801, in the hope sooner or later of invading India, sent to the Shah a commission of seventy officers and non-commissioned officers. This commission shortly afterward was replaced by English rivals, who carried on military instruction till 1840.

Since that period the work has been successively undertaken by Austrian, Italian, and French commissions, and is still carried on by a corps of five or six instructors from Italy, France, and Denmark.

INFANTRY.

The Persian infantry consists of 76 regiments or battalions, of which—

20 contain 1,000 men each.
1 contains   900 "   each.
53 contain   800 "   each.
1 contains   400 "   each.
1   "   250 "   each.

A company of infantry consists of 1 captain, 2 subalterns, and 100 men.

The kingdom of Persia is divided into provinces, which are subdivided into districts, each one of which is supposed to furnish a regiment or *fowg*.

Nominally, the army consists of ten divisions of two brigades each, but in reality no brigades exist. A general of division is styled "Emeer Tooman," or chief of ten thousand; a general of brigade is called "Emeer Panj," or chief of five thousand.

Each regiment is usually composed of men of the same tribe, the chief of which is colonel. If a tribe occupies several districts, it furnishes as many regiments. Districts may be exempted from raising corps on condition of paying increased taxes; in like manner, when a district furnishes a regiment, its taxes are reduced.

In consequence of this policy, the northern and western provinces, settled by tribes of Turkish origin, furnish nearly all of the regiments; a few only are composed of mixed tribes, while, of the seventy-six regiments, only four are purely Persian.

Regiments are raised by conscription, the details being left in the hands of their colonels. The draft always begins with the rich, who purchase exemption, and then proceeds down the list until poverty forces its victim into the ranks.

OFFICERS.

General and field officers are appointed by the Minister of War, and their commissions bear the seal of the Shah. Company officers are appointed nominally by the Minister of War, but in reality by the colonels, particularly when they possess political influence. The officers of each regiment are required to belong to the same tribe as the men, who are usually their vassals or tenants.

Company officers are wholly ignorant of military affairs, and most of them can neither read nor write; the field-officers generally belong to wealthy families, and are better educated.

It is not lawful to purchase promotion; yet, in practice, advancement can only be secured by purchase, or by favor.

Company officers buy their promotion from the colonel, who, if sufficiently powerful, retains the bonus; if not, he divides with the Minister of War. General and field officers purchase directly from the minister. If a general officer commands several regiments, he shares in the profits from the sale of commissions to all of his field and company officers.

The price paid by general and field officers for promotion is two years', and for company officers, one year's pay.

With such a system only the greatest incompetency can prevail, and it is well understood that, without regard to qualifications, money will buy any rank in the army, together with its honors and emoluments. A practice so destructive of honor and efficiency might surprise us, did we not reflect that it once prevailed in the English army, and that even Marlborough was accused of fighting a battle in order that, through the death of his officers, he might profit by the sale of their commissions. Afterward, so regulated as to redeem the system from fraud and corruption, it continued in the English army till 1871, when it was finally abolished.

CAVALRY.

All of the Persian cavalry is irregular and unorganized. In case of a popular war, it is supposed that the tribes could furnish from 60,000 to 70,000. In the contrary case it is doubtful if it would muster 20,000.

Its arms consist of swords, guns, and horse-pistols, frequently ornamented with fanciful designs.

The Persians, like the Cossacks, are fine horsemen, and ride with short stirrups and high saddles. Firing in various attitudes, leaping barriers and ditches, simulating the rescue of a wounded comrade, standing on their saddle, and on their heads while at full speed, were some of the feats of horsemanship performed by the villagers who came out to meet us. The typical horse is short, compactly yet gracefully built, and well adapted to cavalry service. The saddle is high and long, inflexible, and equally cruel to man and beast.

ARTILLERY.

This arm of service consists of 20 battalions of 250 men each, but there are no organized batteries nor trains.

ARMS AND MATERIAL.

In the arsenals at Teheran and Tabriz a supply of muskets is kept on hand, consisting of 10,000 Chassepots, 40,000 tabatières, and from 20,000 to 30,000 arms of other descriptions.

The tabatière is a worthless, transformed muzzle-loader, captured by the Germans in 1870, and sold to the Shah when in Europe at 21 francs each. The ammunition for it is likewise worthless.

The artillery material consists of about 500 smooth-bore and 60 rifled guns, all of brass. The latter were rifled in Persia, on the Belgian system.

Ammunition is kept on hand for the smooth-bores, but none has yet been provided for the rifles.

Powder is manufactured at a mill near Teheran.

At a special audience, given without solicitation, to General Forsyth, Major Sanger, and myself, the Shah manifested great interest in American fire-arms. As a specimen, I presented to him a Smith & Wesson revolver, with which he was much pleased.

He knew of our different kinds of breech-loaders, and requested me to write to Smith & Wesson, and to the Remingtons, to send him their price-lists; and also to General Franklin, for the cost of a battery of Gatlings.

In compliance with his request, while at Teheran, I wrote to Smith & Wesson, and to General Franklin, while General

Forsyth wrote to the Remingtons, of which action I informed the War Department at the time.

At the same audience the Shah expressed his regrets that our Government was not represented at his capital, and requested me to communicate to it his desire to establish diplomatic and commercial relations with us.

CLOTHING AND CAMP-EQUIPAGE.

A supply of about 20,000 uniforms, of the zouave style, is generally kept on hand. That required for immediate use, as for the garrison at Teheran, is kept in depots with the arms, and is issued to the soldiers on occasions of ceremony, after which it is again turned in.

On service, the soldiers are supplied with tents. Barracks specially constructed are scarcely ever provided.

PAY.

The annual pay of officers is nominally as follows:

General, 1st class (Emeer Tooman)	2,000 tomans, or	$4,500
" 2d " (Emeer Panj)	1,500 "	3,450
" 3d "	1,000 "	2,250
Colonel	500 "	1,125
Major (no lieutenant-colonel)	150 to 200 "	540
Captain	80 "	181
Lieutenant	50 "	113

The maximum pay an officer is to receive is stated in his commission, but it is merely nominal. Each year a paper is made out, either by the Minister of War, or the governor of the province in which the regiment is serving, stating the sum each officer is to receive, of which amount 20 per cent. is retained.

The annual pay of non-commissioned officers and soldiers is 7 tomans, or $15.89. In addition, non-commissioned officers receive a monthly pay of 5 krans ($1.00); soldiers receive 4 krans, or 80 cents.

Each soldier is paid in hand, and, as a receipt, he attaches to the pay-roll his seal, on which his name is engraved.

In the interest of economy, regiments are usually in service one year, and on leave the next. While on leave their pay is reduced one-half, and must be provided by the district in which they were raised.

Few of the generals receive full pay, but gifts to the minister may secure an increase.

When a regiment is ordered on service, which is always outside of its district, the Government provides the soldiers with a uniform valued at 15 krans, or $3.00. Sometimes a money allowance is paid to the colonel, who then supplies the clothes.

GENERAL REMARKS.

The effect of Asiatic civilization is conspicuously illustrated in the army of Persia. As in China, corruption pervades every branch of military administration. The soldier who is too poor to escape the draft buys his time from his officers, and frequently remains at home, when he is supposed to be in ranks on the distant frontier. Even when following the colors of his regiment, by relinquishing his pay he may ply his trade, or freely engage in commercial pursuits.

Ordinarily, the soldiers are small money-lenders, and, clubbing together, establish their banks in the bazaars near the centres of business. Loaning only in small sums, and for short periods, they accept only exorbitant rates, varying from 120 to 500 per cent. per annum. Cavalry-soldiers, with equal aptitude for gain, frequently hire out their horses or donkeys, and become the carriers of the country.

So prevalent is the employment of soldiers in all trades and professions that, when, at Teheran, reviews or manœuvres are ordered, it is not uncommon to see workmen, not suspected of being soldiers, drop their tools, don their uniforms, and take their places in the ranks. The duty completed, they return their clothing and muskets to the depot, and again resume work.

All of these irregularities are well known, and are encouraged by the officers, who, in consequence of low salaries, seek, through corrupt practices, to eke out the means of support.

In no service in the world is it difficult for officers without principle to rob their government and at the same time keep their accounts with apparent exactness. To avoid the danger of false muster, the soldier who is permanently absent is replaced by a substitute, who serves at a lower price; to enable the officers to draw his pay, the soldier simply leaves in their possession his seal with his name, which the substitute attaches to the rolls.

With such relations between officers and soldiers it is impossible for discipline to survive. The substitutes only receive the instruction necessary to personate the soldiers who are absent, and so ignorant are they of arms and their use that only those that are worthless are placed in their hands.

The cost and extravagance of raw soldiers are well illustrated by the fact that, on issuing tabatières to regiments for trial, they were turned in, nearly ruined, at the end of a month.

Drill to the Persian soldier, like our old "general trainings," signifies naught but noise and display.

The tactics employed resemble the French of 1831. At the manœuvres before the Shah, the only movements executed were to advance and retire.

One movement consisted of a line of battle in double rank, from which skirmishers appeared to advance, as in our deployment by numbers. Behind the line of battle, in imitation of the German system, companies were posted at intervals in double rank. At a signal, the skirmishers fell back, the companies advanced, and, joining at the line of battle, all opened fire, the line of battle kneeling. On the left, irregular cavalry made irregular charges, scattering over the ground, raising a great dust, and firing and flourishing their pieces in the air; on the right, the artillery joined its deep tones in the combat.

At the review, the infantry walked rather than marched past. The cavalry, marching in squads of five or six, ducked their heads as a salam to the Shah.

The army of Persia has its lessons for the military observer. In India we saw an army of 190,000 men, ably commanded and well supplied, without even a permanent staff corps. In Persia there is no staff at all.

Each infantry-man provides his own food, and each cavalry-man his rations and forage. As each soldier knows he must eat, he forages at every opportunity, and transports his supplies on a horse or donkey.

Wheeled vehicles being practically unknown, and there being no wagon-routes, provisions and munitions of war have to be transported on mules, donkeys, horses, and camels. The number of animals thus accompanying an army often exceeds the number of men.

Having no commissariat, the necessity to forage carries with it cruelty and distress, and inspires so great a dread of troops, even of the shah's escort, that when he proposes a journey to a distant province, it is not uncommon for the people of the towns and villages along the route, in the hope of escaping plunder, to present him with money as an inducement to relinquish his design.

The one great distinction between ancient and modern armies is the organization of the departments of supply, which, in providing for the daily wants of the soldier, have done more to mitigate the horrors of war than all other causes combined. Without them, discipline is impossible, and an army losing its cohesion, like a swarm of locusts sweeps over a country, leaving despair and starvation behind.

Concentrating for battle, the troops may make a few wild rushes, and, if successful, continue their work of devastation and carnage; but, if repulsed and pursued, their flight must end in dispersion.

With the arms, organization, and discipline described, and with no commissariat, the influence of the army of Persia in Eastern affairs can easily be computed.

Bordered by Russia on the north, open to attack from Turkey on the west, accessible to England on the south, future events may soon prove that the capital of Persia, like that of all countries where military institutions are neglected, lies at the mercy of a few disciplined battalions.

MILITARY ORGANIZATION OF EUROPE.

The study of military organization, to be profitable, must not only embrace the objects for which armies are raised, but the means adopted to enable them to accomplish these objects.

A glance at the armies of Asia shows that the Government of Japan, adopting a new civilization, has preserved its authority and consolidated its power by the maintenance of a military force of 35,000 men, bearing the ratio of 1,000 men to every 1,000,000 inhabitants.

In China, an army varying from 500,000 to 1,000,000 men, bearing a ratio of 1,000 or 2,000 to every 1,000,000 population, through corruption and faulty organization, is unable to preserve the peace. As a consequence, insurrection and rebellion frequently deluge the country with blood.

In India, as in Japan, a well-organized army of 200,000 men, bearing the ratio of 1,000 to 1,000,000 inhabitants, preserves tranquillity throughout the empire.

The chief object of all these armies is the maintenance of order and peace within their borders.

Turning from Asia to Europe, a remarkable contrast is presented. Claiming a higher civilization, we find from 6,000,000 to 8,000,000 of young men taken from the family, the field, and the workshops, to compose armies whose object is less the preservation of internal peace and the present status of their governments, than to contend for new territory and increased power, in the ceaseless struggle for ascendency which has characterized the history of Europe for the past thousand years.

To enable these vast armies to accomplish their mission, not only are national resources exhausted, but human ingenuity is taxed to its utmost.

It is when fighting against foreign enemies that military policy and organization are put to the severest test. If they are based upon wisdom, a single victory or series of victories may secure territorial aggrandizement, and crown the nation with glory; if ignorance or fatal indifference have caused military organization to be neglected, national independence may perish in the first onset.

With the object for which they are maintained clearly in view, it is to the armies of Europe that we ought to look for the best military models; and if through remoteness from formidable neighbors, or through the difference of our institutions, we are permitted to deviate from these models, either in details or numbers, it should be only for such reasons as commend themselves to common-sense, and can be vindicated by the wisdom and experience of other nations no less than ourselves.

In treating of the principal armies of Europe I shall only give their organization in brief, and then enlarge on the means of promoting their efficiency, which must be employed by all nations, regardless of the nature of their institutions, if they hope to secure similar results.

ARMY OF ITALY.

The military forces of Italy are composed of the regular army, the militia mobile (Landwehr), and the militia territoriale (Landsturm).

The effective strength of the regular army, in July, 1875, was as follows:

ORGANIZATION.	Officers.	With the Colors.	On Furlough or Reserve.	Total.
General staff and administrative officers	1,430	.....	.....	1,430
Infantry of the line	4,860	97,458	123,841	220,799
Bersaglieri (rifles)	760	16,255	21,147	37,402
Cavalry	898	18,669	15,437	34,106
Artillery	946	20,786	27,462	48,243
Engineers	228	4,702	4,916	9,618
Sanitary corps	886	1,152	2,065	8,217
Local service	127	1,614	.....	1,614
Gendarmerie	606	20,970	.....	20,970
Military districts	1,488	15,898	10,567	25,965
Institutions, educational establishments, etc.	2,070	7,251	236	7,487
Total regular army	13,694	204,255	205,171	410,856
Ersatz reserve	1,016	14,786	166,409	181,195
Militia mobile	2,610	.....	277,265	277,265
Reserve officers	1,516	.....	.....	.....
Total	18,886	219,041	648,845	869,316

GENERAL OFFICERS.

This list consists of—
 5 Generals,
 42 Lieutenant-generals,
 83 Major-generals,

Total, 130.

ADJUTANT-GENERAL'S DEPARTMENT.

(*État-Major*).

The officers of this corps are composed of—
1. Officers actually belonging to the corps, termed "real."
2. Officers attached, termed "aggregate." These officers belong either to infantry or cavalry, and are in excess of the complement required to fill the grades of their regiments. Their number is not fixed. While on staff duty they wear the uniform of their arm with certain modifications, denoting staff employment.
3. Captains of the line temporarily employed as auxiliaries, who wear regimental uniform, with special modifications.
4. Lieutenants who are borne on the strength of their regiments.

The corps proper is composed of the first and second classes, with an organization, in 1876, as follows:

7 Colonels,[1]
30 Lieutenant-colonels and majors,
70 Captains,
20 Lieutenants.

The third class consisted of—
60 Captains.

The fourth class consisted of—
18 First and second lieutenants.

A general officer acts as chief of staff. A committee of four or five staff officers constitutes an advisory organ to the Minister of War in all important questions relating to organization, instruction, and military operations.

The duties of the staff at the War Department are arranged in bureaux, or sections, as follows:
1. Statistical section; charged with collecting statistical information relative to all foreign armies.

---

[1] Since increased to 11 colonels, 38 lieutenant-colonels and majors, 81 captains, and 25 lieutenants. The number of auxiliary officers has also been increased to 66.

2. Historical section; charged with writing military history, and collecting information relative to past military operations.
3. Railway section; charged with studying the railway systems of Europe, and their use in the movement and concentration of troops.
4. Information section; charged with collecting information in reference to foreign armies, embracing changes in arms, instruction, tactics, construction of fortifications, etc.
5. Topographical section; charged with studying the topography and maps of all of the theatres of war in which the army of Italy may be called to operate.
6. Topographical Institute; charged with the construction and completion of the map of Italy, and with the construction of maps of other countries.

There is also a bureau in the War Department charged with the direction of military education, details for camps of instruction, and compilation of regulations for the army.

At the division and territorial corps headquarters the staff officers are specially charged with orders relating to the discipline and instruction of the troops.

ADMINISTRATIVE CORPS.

In general terms, the administration is divided into two separate corps, one called the "Commissariato Militaire," the other "Contabile Militaire."

The Commissariat Corps consists of—
 8 Colonels,
 12 Lieutenant-colonels,
 24 Majors,
 98 Captains,
 98 First-lieutenants, and
 50 Second-lieutenants.
  Total, 290.[1]

[1] Since increased to 301.

The officers of this corps, in time of peace, audit the accounts of the contabile, or accountant corps. In time of war they make the great contracts for provisions and forage, are responsible for the provision-trains, and for the delivery of supplies to the accountant officers.

The Corps Contabile (Accountant) consists of—

7 Lieutenant-colonels,
52 Majors,
424 Captains,
590 First-lieutenants, and
295 Second-lieutenants.
    Total, 1,368.

This corps pays the officers and soldiers, provides the clothing, arms, and accoutrements; and in time of war receives and distributes rations and forage. Four officers of the corps are assigned to duty with each regiment, and are under the orders of the colonel.

In time of peace all of the ration except bread, which is made in government bakeries under charge of accountant officers, is supplied by contractors, who are paid by the regimental accountant officers every ten days. In time of war field-bakeries accompany the troops.

INFANTRY.

A company of infantry consists as follows:

Peace-footing.	War-footing.
1 Captain,	1 Captain,
3 Lieutenants,	4 Lieutenants,
1 First-sergeant,	1 First-sergeant,
4 Sergeants,	8 Sergeants,
2 Lance-sergeants, or Corporals (Maggiore),	4 Lance-sergeants,
1 Corporal (clerk),	1 Corporal (clerk),
6 Corporals,	16 Corporals,
6 Lance-corporals,	16 Lance-corporals,
2 Trumpeters,	4 Trumpeters,
2 Trumpeters (apprentices),	

Peace-footing.	War-footing.
2 Pioneers,	5 Pioneers,
1 Pioneer (apprentice),	
73 Privates.	145 Privates.
Total, 104.	Total, 205.

A battalion consists of four companies, with a staff and non-commissioned staff, as follows:

Peace-footing.	War-footing.
1 Lieutenant-colonel or major, commandant,	1 Lieutenant-colonel or major, commandant,
1 Lieutenant, adjutant,	1 Lieutenant, adjutant,
	2 Surgeons (lieutenants),
1 Sergeant-major,	1 Sergeant-major,
1 Corporal (clerk),	1 Corporal (clerk),
1 Corporal (trumpeter),	1 Corporal (trumpeter),
1 Corporal (pioneer),	2 Corporals (pioneers),
1 Wagoner.	3 Wagoners,
	4 soldiers (officers' servants).
Total, 7.	Total, 16.
Total 4 companies, 416.	Total 4 companies, 820.
Total battalion, 423.	Total battalion, 836.

A regiment consists of three battalions and a depot. The staff and non-commissioned staff of a regiment is composed as follows:

Peace-footing.	War-footing.
1 Colonel,	1 Colonel,
1 Captain (adjutant),	1 Captain (adjutant),
1 Surgeon (captain),	1 Surgeon (captain),
2 Surgeons (lieutenants),	1 Accountant officer (lieutenant),
3 Sergeant-majors,	3 Sergeant-majors,
1 Chief musician,	1 Chief musician,
1 Sergeant of pioneers,	1 Sergeant of pioneers,
1 Chief armorer,	1 Chief armorer,
1 Sergeant (band),	1 Sergeant (band),
1 Sergeant-trumpeter.	1 Sergeant-trumpeter,

Peace-footing.
2 Corporals (clerks),
1 Corporal (band),

16 Musicians,
10 Musicians (pupils),
2 Armorers (apprentices),

2 Vivandières.
   Total, 46.

War-footing.
2 Corporals (clerks),
1 Corporal (band),
1 Corporal (commissary clerk),
26 Musicians,

2 Armorers (apprentices),
4 Wagoners,
5 soldiers (officers' servants),
2 Vivandières.
   Total, 55.

The depot consists as follows:

Peace-footing.
1 Major,
1 Accountant director (captain),
1 Paymaster (subaltern),
1 Registrar (subaltern),
1 Accountant officer (subaltern),
5 Accountant (commissariat) sergeants,
5 Accountant corporals,
1 Captain,
1 First-sergeant,
4 Sergeants,
1 Corporal (clerk),
6 Corporals,
1 Trumpeter,
1 Trumpeter (pupil),
30 Privates.
   Total, 60.

War-footing.
The depot in time of war is not fixed, but varies according to the necessities of the service.

In war the men unfit for field-service are transferred to the depot-companies, which guard the barracks, and have charge of the books, records, and papers, of their regiments.

In case of mobilization they usually go to district headquarters, where they receive and train men belonging to their regiments, and also aid in the general instruction of the men called to arms.

The total strength of a regiment is as follows:

Peace-footing.

Regimental staff and non-commissioned staff	46
3 Battalions	1,269
Depot	60
Total	1,375

War-footing.

Regimental staff and non-commissioned staff	55
3 Battalions	2,508
Total	2,563

BERSAGLIERI.

The bersaglieri, or riflemen, consist of ten regiments, of four battalions each, organized the same as infantry. The strength of a regiment on the peace-footing is 1,798 officers and men; the war-footing is 3,399. In peace each regiment is united for instruction and administrative service, but in war it is intended to attach a battalion to each division or brigade, to act specially as skirmishers and sharp-shooters.

The infantry of the standing army consists in time of peace and war of 80 regiments (240 battalions), with 10 additional regiments of bersaglieri (40 battalions).

The strength of the infantry regiments is as follows:

Peace-footing.

80 regiments	110,000
Bersaglieri	17,980
Total peace-footing . . .	127,980

War-footing.

80 regiments	205,040
Bersaglieri	33,990
Total war-footing	239,030

BRIGADE.

A brigade of infantry consists of—
2 regiments (6 battalions).

DIVISION.

A division consists of—
The division staff,
2 Infantry brigades (12 battalions),
1 Artillery brigade (3 batteries),
2 Squadrons of cavalry,
1 Division artillery park,
1 Sanitary section,
1 Subsistence section.

CORPS.

An army corps consists of—
The corps staff,
2 Divisions of infantry (24 battalions),
1 Regiment bersaglieri (4 battalions),
1 Brigade of cavalry (2 regiments or 8 squadrons),
1 Artillery brigade,
1 Brigade of engineers (2 companies),
1 Engineer park and brigade train, and
The supply-trains.

ARMY.

An army consists of—
The army staff,
2 or 3 corps,
The army intendance, or supply department.

TERRITORIAL COMMANDS.

For purposes of command and military administration, Italy is divided into 7[1] general or corps, 16 divisional, and 63 district, commands.

[1] By the law of March 22, 1877, the territorial commands have been increased to 10; divisional commands to 20; and military districts to 88. In addition, 20

The corps commands and the divisional commands, embracing one or more provinces, are held by general officers. The districts which generally coincide with provinces are commanded by colonels or field officers.

MILITARY DISTRICTS.

All of the details of recruiting and mobilizing the regular army, of organizing, mobilizing, and training the militia mobile, are carried out in the eighty-eight military districts.

To this end the personnel of each district consists of a staff and non-commissioned staff, and from four to five permanent companies, which are concentrated at the district headquarters. There is also at the headquarters a depot of arms (provided there is no artillery-depot in the same city) and also a depot of equipment and clothing, where the clothing is made for all of the soldiers furnished by the district.

The organization of the district of Rome may be taken as a representative of the others. It consists of five permanent companies, with staff, company, and non-commissioned officers as follows:

1 Colonel,
1 Lieutenant-colonel,
1 Major,
9 Captains,
19 Lieutenants, and
15 Clerks.

All of the above officers are detailed from the regular army, and are in excess of the regimental complements.

One hundred and seventy-six permanent companies are distributed among the eighty-eight military districts. The privates composing them are mostly such men of the regular army as have been found unable to endure the hardships of campaign.

The names of all the men of the regular army on leave and in the different categories are on the books, or rolls, of these companies. On reporting at the district headquarters when

superior commands of military districts have been newly created, 8 of which are to be commanded by major-generals, and 12 by colonels.

mobilization is ordered, each man receives from the captain of the company to which his name is attached his arms and equipments, and, while waiting to be forwarded, he is drilled and instructed by the officers and non-commissioned officers of the company.

According to the law of March 22, 1877, the eighty-eight military districts are to be divided into three classes, with the following staff and non-commissioned staff:

GRADE AND EMPLOYMENT.	STAFF AND NON-COMMISSIONED STAFF OF DISTRICT.		
	1st Class.	2d Class.	3d Class.
Commandants (colonels or lieutenant-colonels)	1	1	1
Lieutenant-colonels or majors	1	1	1
Senior adjutant (captain)	1	1	1
Junior adjutants (first-lieutenants)	3	2	1
Surgeon (captain)	1	1	1
Chief administrative officer (major)	1	1	
Director of accounts (captain)	1	1	1
Clothing-officer (lieutenant)	1	1	1
Registrar (lieutenant)	1	1	1
Commissariat or administrative officers disposable in addition to above	5	4	3
Total commissioned	16	14	11
Sergeant-majors	2	2	2
Commissary and quartermaster sergeants	2	2	2
Chief armorer	1	1	1
Lance-sergeants			1
Commissary corporals	2	2	1
Corporals (clerks)	1	1	1
Corporal trumpeter	1	1	1
Soldiers (first class)	1	1	1
Armorers (apprentices)	3	3	2
Total non-commissioned	15	13	12
Total commissioned and non-commissioned	30	27	23

The cadre of each permanent company consists of:
  1 Captain,
  1 Lieutenant,
  1 First-sergeant,
  3 Sergeants,
  1 Lance-sergeant,
  4 Corporals,
  1 Corporal (clerk),
  1 Trumpeter,
  24 Privates.
      Total, 37.

From these figures it appears that a district of the first class, with five permanent companies, has a personnel of 26 officers and 178 men; but this is not all, for, in excess of the cadres, there are distributed among the 88 districts for special duty—such as clerks and bakers—another force of 134 non-commissioned officers and 2,585 men, making a total of more than 11,000 officers and men, who simply constitute the machinery for recruiting and mobilizing the Italian army.

RECRUITMENT.

The recruitment of all the great armies of Europe is conducted on the same principles.

All men who are physically qualified are held to owe the state military service between certain ages, and must perform the service unless for special reasons they are exempted by law.

In Italy the period of military service is nineteen years, and extends from the beginning of the twenty-first to the end of the thirty-ninth year.

About 140,000 men annually become liable to military duty, and are divided into three categories:

FIRST CATEGORY.

This category, which is regulated by Parliament, is composed of about 65,000 men, who are drafted into the regular army, where they serve in the infantry, artillery, and engineers, for three, and in the cavalry for five, years. Those in the infantry, artillery, and engineers, after serving three years are sent on furlough, and for the next five years are liable at any time to be recalled to the colors. These men, in connection with troops of the second category, enable the army when mobilized to pass from the peace to the war footing. Taking 127,000 as the peace-footing of the infantry, one-third of that number, 42,333, will represent the number of men annually drafted into that arm of the service; and the same number, diminished by deaths and discharges, will represent the number of trained soldiers who, on leave of absence, annually return to their homes to be called back to the ranks in time of war. As there are five classes on leave, the maximum number available to fill up the ranks cannot exceed 211,000.

In case of general or partial mobilization, the classes are recalled, beginning with the last one sent on leave.

After a service of eight years in the regular army—three with the colors, and five on leave—the men pass into the second category, and their names are transferred at district headquarters to the companies of militia mobile, in which they serve another five years. They then pass into the third category for seven years, and, on the completion of nineteen years' service, are exempt from further military duty.

The men of the first category are those who in the draft draw numbers from one up to the number denoting the quotas to be furnished by their municipalities, and also such men of the second category as having drawn numbers immediately above the latter are required to replace the men in the first category entitled to exemption.

SECOND CATEGORY.

The number of men in this category is annually fixed by Parliament, and varies from 20,000 to 35,000. In the draft it is composed of the men who draw consecutive numbers next above those who enter the first category.

ERSATZ RESERVE.

The men of the second category belong to the regular army for five years, and constitute what is called the Ersatz reserve, or "troops of complement."

The object of this reserve, in connection with the men of the first category on leave, is to raise the army to a war-footing, and in addition provide a reserve to fill the vacancies that may occur after the opening of the campaign.

The men of the second category are arranged in classes, and on entering the service repair to district headquarters, where for forty days they are drilled and instructed by the officers and non-commissioned officers of the permanent companies. They draw caps, shoes, linen coats, trousers, arms, and equipments, from the district depot, which are turned in at the completion of the course of instruction. Before being dismissed on leave, they are assigned to the various regiments and corps of the regular army, and their names are also attached to the rolls of the permanent companies. The Ersatz reserve in 1876 consisted of 171,758 men, of whom 164,412 belonged to the infantry.

In case of mobilization the men at once repair to district headquarters, report to the permanent companies to which their names are attached, draw arms and equipments, and receive drill and instruction until they can be forwarded to their regiments.

After serving five years in the Ersatz reserve, the men of the second category are transferred for four years to the militia mobile. They are then transferred for ten years to the third category, which completes their military service.

THIRD CATEGORY.

After deducting 65,000 men for the first category, and 20,000 to 30,000 for the second category, the remainder of the contingent of 140,000 men, amounting to from 45,000 to 55,000 men, are assigned to the third category, as are also all of the men of the first and second categories, who, for reasons other than physical, are exempted from service in the army and Ersatz reserve.

To ascertain the number of men who annually enter the third category, there must be added to the above numbers from 50,000 to 60,000, representing the men of the first and second categories who have completed their fourth year in the militia mobile.

The men of this category are neither organized, uniformed, nor instructed.

DETAILS OF RECRUITMENT.

The mayor of every municipality submits annually to the prefect of the province a list embracing the names of all the young men who have completed their twentieth year, and have become liable to military duty. On the receipt of these lists the total number liable to military duty in the province is forwarded by the prefect to the Minister of War, who publishes tables showing the number of men each province will have to furnish for the different categories.

When the prefect receives from the Minister of War the number of men required for the first category he convenes the provincial council, and in its presence assigns the quota to be furnished by each municipality. On a day appointed by the prefect, the draft takes place in each municipality in the presence of the mayor and municipal council.

As many numbers are placed in a wheel as there are men liable to military duty. The men having drawn numbers within the quota required for the first category, repair, between certain days named by the Minister of War, to the capital of the province, where they present themselves to the recruiting commission for examination.

The commission, nominated annually for each province, is composed of the prefect or sub-prefect, two provincial councilors (delegates in the provincial government from the municipalities), two army officers, one government commissary, one officer of gendarmes, and one army surgeon.

The men of each municipality are examined separately in the presence of the mayor, who is required to answer questions in the interest of both the individual and the state.

The commission usually meets in October, or November, for the examination of the first category, and remains in session about five or six days.

The men who are found to be physically disqualified are forever free from military service. Those who are exempted for family reasons, such as only son of a father over sixty years of age, mother a widow, etc., are placed in the third category.

The commission, having examined and assigned the men required for the first category, assembles a second time, and having received notification from the prefect of the quota required from each municipality for the second category, it resumes the examination, beginning with the lowest number that escaped the first category. As before, the physically disqualified are relieved from further military duty, while those exempted for family reasons are placed in the third category.

All of the men not examined for the first and second categories are assigned to the third.

The men of the first category having been notified of their acceptance, are allowed to return to their homes for a month or two, until called under arms, when they repair to district headquarters, where, after a physical examination, they are assigned to infantry, cavalry, artillery, or engineers, according to tables furnished by the Minister of War.

The men are not allowed to choose their arm of service, but are assigned according to physical and other qualifications.

If any fail to pass the examination, the prefects are notified and the recruitment commission selects from their municipalities men from the second category to replace them.

MILITIA MOBILE.

The militia mobile constitutes an army in the second line, and is intended to reënforce and support the regular army in time of war.

It is still in process of organization, but in 1876 there could have been mobilized 108 battalions of infantry and 15 battalions of bersaglieri.

The future cadre, exclusive of the island of Sardinia, is to consist of—

120 Battalions (480 companies) of infantry.
20 " (80 ") of bersaglieri.
10 Brigades (30 batteries) of artillery.
10 Companies artillery-train.
20 " foot artillery.
10 " engineers and sappers.

The cadre for the island of Sardinia embraces—

9 Battalions (36 companies) of infantry.
1 Battalion (2 ") of bersaglieri.
1 Squadron of cavalry.
1 Brigade (2 batteries) of artillery.
2 Platoons of engineers.

In addition to the troops of the militia mobile, staff and administrative departments are to be organized on the same principles as in the army.

In consequence of the difference of population in the military districts, the battalions in time of peace cannot be organized uniformly, some having two and three, while others have five and six companies each, but in war they will be equalized by transfers within the same superior district and divisional commands, so that in each of the latter there may be formed two regiments of infantry of three battalions of four companies each.

The cadre of the field and staff of the two regiments organized within each superior district, which in its geographical limits coincides with the divisional command, is organized at the headquarters of the superior district. It also devolves upon the superior district commandants to keep themselves informed of the number and strength of the companies in each military district, and to notify the district commandants which companies will be transferred to equalize battalions.

The cadres of the companies and battalions are organized by the district commandants as rapidly as officers and non-commissioned officers become available for assignment.

The company and battalion organization is the same as in the regular army. From what has already been said under the head of recruitment, the militia mobile is composed of men of the first category who have served eight years in the regular army, and of men of the second category who have served five years in the Ersatz reserve.

The number of men who enter the infantry and bersaglieri annually from the class first mentioned may be estimated at 42,000; those from the Ersatz reserve at 20,000. As service in the militia mobile is for four years, the force of infantry and bersaglieri may be estimated at 248,000 men. Of this number more than two-thirds have served three years in the ranks of the regular army, while the other third has had at least forty days' training in the Ersatz reserve.

The preponderance of trained over the untrained soldiers is

so great that only a few skillful officers are required to convert the militia mobile into an active, efficient force.

OFFICERS OF THE MILITIA MOBILE.

The officers of the militia mobile consist of former officers of the regular army not over fifty years of age; of sergeants promoted, who have served twelve years in the regular army, and of one year's volunteers, who have passed a qualifying examination as officers of complement. The total number now available is between 2,000 and 3,000. The captains and subalterns are assigned to companies by the district commandants. Battalion and regimental commanders are specially selected by the Minister of War, and usually from the field-officers of the regular army.

In case of a mobilization of the militia mobile, the district of Rome is expected to furnish arms and equipments for 28 companies of infantry and 2 of bersaglieri.

The number of officers available for these companies in 1876, and whose names were borne on the Army Register, below those of the regular officers serving in the district, was 1 captain, 2 first-lieutenants, and 6 second-lieutenants.

This deficiency of officers, amounting in the entire militia mobile to more than 500 captains and 400 lieutenants, is engaging the serious attention of the Minister of War, who hopes to remedy the evil by designating as captains, officers of complement in the regular army, and also officers in reserve, corresponding to our retired list.

MILITIA TERRITORIALE.

This militia is composed of the men assigned to the third category in each annual contingent, and of all the men of the first and second categories from the completion of their service in the militia mobile till the end of their thirty-ninth year.

It has no organization, but can be called out by classes the same as the Ersatz reserve. Practically, the men receive no instruction, nor are they uniformed. In case of war they would be distinguished by a band around the arm.

VOLUNTEERING.

Volunteering is encouraged for the purpose of mitigating the hardships of military service, and of permitting it to interfere as little as possible with trades, professions, and business pursuits. Its general principles are the same in nearly all Continental armies.

In Italy any boy who can read and write can present himself at the age of seventeen, serve till twenty, then go on leave five years, afterward serve four years in the militia mobile, seven years in the third category (militia territoriale), and thus complete his military service at the age of thirty-six. Volunteers of this class are allowed to choose their regiments, and may in consequence sometimes serve the three years with the colors in their own towns.

A second class of volunteers consists of those men of the annual contingent who aspire to be sergeants, and who, after agreeing to serve eight years with the colors, are sent to the battalions, batteries, and squadrons of instruction, where they pursue a course of study for two years.

VOLUNTEERS FOR ONE YEAR.

The third, and by far the most important class, consists of the volunteers for one year.

The conditions for admission to this class are, that they must volunteer before becoming liable to military duty; pass a prescribed examination in reading, writing, composition, Italian language, grammar, arithmetic, and geography; and furthermore pay to the Government the sum of 1,200 francs in the infantry and artillery and 1,600 francs in the cavalry.

Those who comply with the requirements are given a certificate, and are permitted to choose for their service any year between seventeen and twenty-six. On becoming twenty years old they attend the draft and are assigned to a category, but are exempted from service therein on showing their certificates.

After completing their service of one year they are for seven years liable to service in the regular army, but on the payment of 600[1] francs they may at once pass into the second category, and thence into the third, where they complete their service at thirty-nine years of age.

The volunteers for one year are, as a rule, young men who wish to pursue a university course, learn a difficult trade, or who may wish to assume the management of great business and commercial enterprises.

Those who prefer the engineers, artillery, and cavalry, are permitted to choose their regiments, where they receive special instruction. Those who choose the infantry repair to district headquarters, where they are organized into a volunteer company, commanded by officers of the regular army, who are specially selected by the Minister of War. These officers, who are usually graduates of the War Academy, are detailed for a period extending from two to six years.

The volunteers are enrolled the 1st of October of each year, and, in connection with their military training they pursue a course of study embracing grammar, arithmetic, geography, regulations, tactics, administration, and elementary fortification.

At the end of the year all are examined by a commission appointed by the general commanding the division, pursuant to a programme prescribed by the Minister of War. Those who fail to pass the examination are sent to their regiments, provided that at the draft they came within the first category; those who pass the qualifying examination for corporal and sergeant, and pay the sum exempting them from the first category, enter the militia mobile as non-commissioned officers.[2]

OFFICERS OF COMPLEMENT.

The volunteers who pass the qualifying examination for officers are denominated "officers of complement," and are assigned to companies in regular regiments, where they serve for three months. During this period they are allowed five francs

---

[1] This exemption from service in the first category is to be discontinued after 1877.

[2] After 1877 the volunteers for one year in infantry are to be instructed in their regiments the same as the volunteers in the cavalry and artillery.

a day, and transportation to and from their regiments. At its expiration they go home on leave, where they remain out of the line of promotion until the Government recalls them to the colors.

They may, however, be called back temporarily to their regiments, or they may be required at district headquarters, to aid in the instruction of the second category, and the militia mobile.

SCHOOLS.

Every army in Europe, in all of its grades, is a training-school for war, and intelligence and education are insisted upon as essential alike to officers and men.

Having explained the method of procuring the personnel of the Italian army, the next thing in importance is to describe the institutions and training establishments, considered indispensable in the transformation of the recruit into the soldier, to whom in the hour of battle must be confided the happiness and destiny of his people. The benefit of these institutions is not confined to the army. The education they impart, the principles of obedience and respect for law which they encourage, are carried back to the people by the soldier, who has become the better qualified to enjoy the liberty and rights of a citizen.

SCHOOLS FOR THE MEN.

The first school for the enlisted men is, in its largest sense, the school of the soldier, in which, during the three years' service with the colors, they learn every duty that may devolve upon a soldier. Joining their regiments as recruits about the 1st of January, the course of military instruction progresses regularly through the school of the soldier, the school of the company, skirmishing, school of the battalion, and the evolutions of a regiment, brigade, division, and corps.

A stated period in each year is given to the schools of the company, battalion, and regiment, during which the new recruits learn new principles, while the old soldiers review the instruction of the year previous.

In addition to the tactics, the men receive the most thorough practical instruction in reconnaissance, outpost and scouting duty; musketry-practice at different ranges, with both fixed and movable targets; marches; skirmishing, and manœuvres, specially adapted to the ground ; as also the manner of intrenching and taking advantage of cover under fire.

The evolutions of brigades, divisions, and corps, take place at camps of instruction, ordered by the Minister of War, where both officers and men become accustomed to the movements of large bodies of troops.

They likewise become accustomed to the sound of battle, and learn to adapt themselves to every movement in the presence of the enemy except actual firing.

After three years' instruction in these schools, the once raw recruit goes back to his home a trained and disciplined soldier, ready at the first signal of danger to return to the ranks.

THEORETICAL SCHOOLS.

The advance in military science has eradicated from every army in Europe the idea formerly held that the best soldier was a mere machine, with no aim but to execute blindly the orders of his superior officer. To-day the modifications in tactics require every soldier to be endowed with intelligence, in order that he may assume responsibility, and act with judgment, in cases where no officer or non-commissioned officer may be present to guide him.

To this end theoretical schools are established in each regiment, battalion, and company.

The lieutenant-colonel, or second in command, of every regiment superintends and visits all of the schools, and reports the progress made to the colonel.

Battalion and company commanders are responsible for the schools within their commands, all of which are maintained from the funds of the regiment.

ALPHABETICAL SCHOOLS.

In the Italian army as many as sixty per cent. of the recruits from some districts are unable to read or write. All soldiers are therefore compelled to attend the alphabetical schools, in which are taught reading, writing, and arithmetic. This school in each company is superintended by a lieutenant, with non-commissioned officers for instructors.

CORPORALS' SCHOOLS.

Candidates for the grade of corporal must attend the corporals' school in each battalion, where they are taught grammar, arithmetic, army regulations, code of punishments, patrol and guard duty.

The course of study begins October 15th, and ends March 15th, and is superintended by a captain, with other officers and non-commissioned officers as assistants.

SERGEANTS' SCHOOL.

This school is regimental, and must be attended by all corporals who aspire to the grade of sergeant. The course of study is five months, the same as for corporals, and embraces grammar, geography, arithmetic, army regulations, and the use of maps. The school is superintended by an officer, with non-commissioned officers as assistants.

ADMINISTRATIVE SCHOOL.

This school is superintended by an accountant officer, and is attended by all non-commissioned officers and soldiers who seek employment in the "Corps of Comptabilité."

HIGHER SCHOOL FOR NON-COMMISSIONED OFFICERS.

The object of this school is to prepare intelligent and deserving sergeants, who aspire to the grade of officer, for admission to the military schools at Modena and Parma.

The school in each regiment is usually superintended by a graduate of the Academy of War. The course of study lasts from eight to nine months, and embraces grammar, geography, arithmetic, elements of geometry, and the use of maps.

REWARDS OF INTELLIGENCE.

Soldiers who learn to read and write well, who are good marksmen, and perform satisfactorily all of their military duties, are sometimes sent home six months before the expiration of their three years' service. On the contrary, those who neglect to learn to read and write are detained with the colors after the discharge of the class to which they belong. They are examined every two months, and are discharged as soon as they pass a satisfactory examination. At the end of six months all are discharged. The number detained is about six per cent. Those who are discharged as hopelessly ignorant number about three per cent.

The effect of the encouragement of education on one hand, and the punishment for the neglect of it on the other, has given an impetus to the schools in every village of the kingdom. In this respect the army confers a great benefit on the country, not only by educating the 65,000 recruits who annually join it, but in a far greater degree by inspiring every father with the desire to educate his sons, in order to diminish the length of their military service, and at the same time enable them to serve with better hopes of promotion.

BATTALIONS OF INSTRUCTION.

The battalions of instruction are specially designed to educate and train sergeants for the army. They constitute, in fact, military schools for non-commissioned officers.

The first was established in 1871, at Maddaloni; the second at Asti in 1872; the third at Senigallia in 1873.

They all owe their vitality to the recent inducements held out by the Government to attain the grade of non-commissioned officer, and to the guarantee of employment, after honorable discharge, either in the administration of the War Department, or on the lines of state railroads.

The conditions of admission are to be able to read and write, and an engagement to serve eight years with the colors.

The candidates consist—1. Of volunteers between the ages

of seventeen and twenty-six; 2. Of such soldiers of the first category who, being required to serve three years, possess the necessary qualifications, and express a willingness to serve eight years as non-commissioned officers; 3. Of soldiers who at any time during their term of service desire to become non-commissioned officers.

The enrollment for each battalion begins the first of January, and terminates the last of February each year, the number of candidates being limited to 400.

The course of theoretical and practical instruction embraces two years, and is divided into four quarters, of six months each.

During the first quarter the pupils receive the same practical instruction as a soldier in a regiment; during the second they apply this instruction practically to the ground; during the third they become the instructors of the new class, and thus learn to command and instruct as well as to obey; during the fourth they make a general review, and thus complete the instruction deemed necessary to qualify them for the grade of sergeant.

The military subjects taught the first year of the course are: School of the soldier, with and without arms; elementary gymnastics; gymnastics with arms; school of the company; construction, mounting and dismounting of arms; estimating distances; aiming drill; target-practice; reconnaissance; garrison duty; theory of regulations and penal code.

Those taught in the second year are: School of the guides; sabre-exercise; practical performance of all of the duties of corporal and sergeant in garrison and camp; reading and application of maps; transportation of wounded, and construction of field-intrenchments.

The studies pursued are Italian language, embracing letters, reports on military subjects, compositions on modern military history, reports descriptive of ground and positions; arithmetic, through the rule of three; first principles of geometry; geography, embracing all of the continents, particularly Europe and the kingdom of Italy; reading of maps, embracing the conventional signs; reconnaissance of ground with the aid of maps, and military organization.

The students, according to their proficiency, are arranged in three classes, viz., inferior, middle, and superior.

The superior class, in addition to the prescribed programme, receives instruction in company accounts, and also in hygiene.

Each battalion is organized into four companies, with the usual complement of commissioned officers, who serve as instructors and superintendents of instruction.

At the end of every six months the students are classified according to merit.

Two grades of corporal, corresponding to lance-corporal and corporal, exist in each battalion. The number in the first grade is unlimited, that of the second grade is fixed at 80.

At the end of the first six months all of the students who have shown the required proficiency, and whose conduct has been good, are promoted lance-corporals. Those who fail to obtain the grade at this examination are promoted according to their progress during the second six months. Those who fail at the end of their first year to become lance-corporals are sent to the regiments as private soldiers.

At the end of the first year the most deserving lance-corporals are promoted to corporal, and at the end of eighteen months all of both grades who are qualified are promoted to sergeants.

At the end of the course the names of the students who have merited the grade of sergeant are reported to the Minister of War, who assigns them to their regiments. The corporals who fail to qualify as sergeants are assigned to regiments as corporals.

The three battalions of instruction for the infantry supply sergeants to the infantry and bersaglieri.

The engineers, artillery, and cavalry, have companies, batteries, and squadrons of instruction, corresponding to battalions of instruction for the infantry.

NON-COMMISSIONED OFFICERS.

It is not alone in the system of schools provided for their special education and training that the Italian Government manifests its care in forming an efficient body of non-commissioned officers.

Accepting the theory, now universally adopted in Europe, that a good non-commissioned officer can no more be improvised than an officer, it imposes as the first condition of becoming a sergeant that the candidate shall subscribe to an agreement (*ferma permanente*) to serve eight years with the colors. It furthermore imposes another condition that the candidate cannot be promoted to this grade till he shall have served in the ranks from two to three years, which, however, are included in the eight years' engagement.

So tenacious is the Government in adhering to these conditions that it prefers to keep open hundreds of vacancies rather than permit unworthy occupants to fill them; and, as an evidence that this policy has been adopted after mature reflection, it only needs to be stated that, in order not to cripple the companies by the temporary want of sergeants, a new grade has been created called "corporal-major," corresponding in our army to the grade of lance-sergeant.

These corporals receive increased pay, and many of them possess all of the qualifications for the grade of sergeant except a willingness to sign an engagement for eight years.

The difficulty of securing competent men for the grade of sergeant has led the Government to offer special inducements as an encouragement both to aspire to the grade and to continue in it so long as the incumbent is qualified for duty.

To appreciate these inducements it is necessary to state that, according to the military budget, the pay of a sergeant-major of infantry is 2 francs per day, a first-sergeant 1 franc 45 centimes, and a sergeant 1 franc 15 centimes. To this pay the sum of 150 francs per annum is added the moment a sergeant receives his promotion.

Having educated the sergeants at great expense, and still

further increased their efficiency by a long system of practical training, the next inducement is offered as a means of encouraging reënlistment, and to this end they are allowed in the infantry to reëngage three times, with an increase of 150 francs per annum for each reënlistment. The advantage of increased pay for the first reënlistment, by way of anticipation, is granted to the sergeant at the commencement of his seventh year of service.

It thus appears that an aspirant to the rank of sergeant, in addition to the pay proper of the grade, is assured an increase of 150 francs from the moment of his promotion; 300 francs from the beginning of his seventh to the end of his eleventh year of service; 450 francs from the beginning of the twelfth to the end of his fourteenth year of service; and 600 francs from this time to the end of his seventeenth year of service. After the seventeenth year of service a sergeant is permitted to reënlist up to forty-five years of age, but with no further increase of pay.

Substantial as the foregoing inducements may appear, still others are added. The sergeant who is discharged after seventeen years' faithful service is granted an annuity of 360 francs, which is equal to four-fifths of the premium allowed for three reënlistments, and this annuity, at the option of the sergeant, can be capitalized, and received in hand on quitting the army.

The sergeants who remain in service up to the age of forty-five on their discharge receive a pension varying from 415 to 725 francs per annum, which includes the amounts to which they were entitled on completing their third reënlistment.

The expenses for increased pay, premiums for reënlistment, annuities, and pensions for non-commissioned officers, are not charged in the military budget, but are defrayed out of the military chest, into which between 4,000,000 and 5,000,000 francs are paid annually by the volunteers of one year, who average between 3,000 and 4,000.

But the care of the Italian Government for its faithful non-commissioned officers does not end with their discharge from the service. Those who have served twelve years with the colors are, as a rule, furnished with employment either on lines of state railways or in the various offices and bureaux appertaining to the War Department, which, in 1874, gave positions to more than 1,000.

The total number of sergeants required by the law of organization for the different arms of service is as follows:

Infantry	6,480
Bersaglieri (rifles)	1,000
Alpine battalions	120
Cavalry	1,000
Artillery	1,431
Engineers	292
Total	10,323

This number is recruited by the annual graduation of about 1,200 sergeants from the various battalions, batteries, and squadrons of instruction; by the promotion within the regiments on an average of about 400 sergeants per year after completing the prescribed course of instruction; and by the annual reënlistment of nearly 300—amounting in all to 1,900 per annum. This number multiplied by six gives 11,400 as the total number of sergeants available to fill the 10,323 vacancies, giving a surplus of 1,177 available to fill vacancies created by death and discharge.

After receiving their promotion the sergeants are given special privileges, and as far as possible are encouraged to separate themselves from the men, in order not to destroy their authority by constant intercourse and familiarity. They sleep in separate rooms; are not required to return to quarters till taps; are confined by themselves when punished; have a special mess, and also a reading-room properly lighted and heated, and provided with books, papers, and periodicals.

To pass from the peace to the war footing, nearly 4,000 sergeants are required in addition to 10,323 already in the army. This deficiency, it is expected, will be made up by the one-year volunteers, who already supply annually for the reserve 400 non-commissioned officers, making available in the eight classes 3,200. The remaining 800 will probably be supplied from the same source, as the recent modifications in army laws, it is believed, will produce increased volunteering.

The foregoing description of sergeants in the Italian army applies with very few modifications to all of the armies on the Continent, and should impress us with the conviction that, if in future wars we would increase the chances of victory, and diminish the waste of human life, we should devote our attention to the education of our non-commissioned no less than the commissioned officers of our army.

SCHOOLS FOR OFFICERS IN EUROPE.

The systems of education for military officers, adopted by all the great powers, are substantially the same, and are based upon the principle that different degrees of instruction are required for the different arms of service.

In pursuance of this principle, officers of artillery and engineers are educated at one academy, while officers of infantry and cavalry are educated at another.

Inferior schools, more or less military in their organization, prepare cadets for admission to the academies or schools from which they pass as commissioned officers into the army. On the Continent instruction is imparted by lecture, more or less in connection with text-books. The lectures on all subjects in the course of study are generally delivered to the entire class, the members of which take notes. If not provided with text-books, these notes supply the student with all the information he can get on the subject, and with these he must show himself familiar at subsequent recitations called "interrogations."

The interrogations take place usually the day after or second day after the lecture, and are conducted by the professor, or assistant professors, according to the size of the class, which is divided for the purpose into sections.

Frequently the classes are so large that interrogations cannot take place more than once a week, and often once in two weeks. Under such circumstances the cadets are notified when they will be interrogated, and are also informed on what portions of the subject they must be prepared.

When complete text-books are provided, the subjects in each lesson are also explained by the professor. The students as before take notes, and afterward are interrogated both upon the notes and the lesson as given in the text.

This system of instruction involves great loss of time, and in thoroughness cannot be compared with the American system of recitations from text-books, especially when confined to small sections as at the Military Academy.

The instructors at all foreign military schools are both military and civil. The former usually teach mathematics and the sciences, the latter languages and history.

The lecture-rooms are prepared for entire classes, but sometimes, when these exceed a hundred members, they are divided into two sections.

The students sleep in large dormitories, which they are not permitted to visit between reveille and tattoo.

The studying is done in large halls, arranged for each class, which is under the supervision of an officer, who is always present to preserve order and give assistance.

The military schools of each country are under the supervision of the Minister of War, but the general control is assigned to an officer styled the Superintendent or Director of Military Education.

This officer presides over a bureau of the War Department, to which are referred all matters pertaining to military schools and military education.

Cadets who seek admission to the academies and schools, whence they graduate as officers of the army, are usually prepared at inferior schools termed military colleges, military gymnasia, or, as in Germany, the cadet corps.

From these schools the cadets pass according to their ability to the academies for artillery and engineers, or to the schools for infantry and cavalry.

On graduating from these higher schools the officers of infantry go directly to their regiments; the officers of cavalry go to a special school of application for cavalry, where they usually remain a year, while the officers of artillery and engineers go for two years to a school of application for artillery and engineers.

The highest military schools are the War Academies, specially designed to qualify officers who have been in the army not less than three or four years for high command, and the performance of duty on the staff.

All of the foregoing schools are supplemented by the great manœuvres, where officers and soldiers of all grades learn practically the duties required in the presence of the enemy.

MILITARY SCHOOLS OF ITALY.

As a general rule, the expenses of military education are defrayed by the parents, and usually amount to 900 lire or $180 per year, which is paid in quarterly installments. If unable to meet the payments, the cadet must quit the school and return to civil life.

In the case of sons of deserving public men and officers, and also as a reward for success in study, the state sometimes assumes one-half of the expense, while in the case of officers killed in battle it pays the entire expense of education.

MILITARY COLLEGES.

The lowest military schools are termed Military Colleges, and are three in number: one at Naples, one at Florence, and one at Milan.

The field and staff of each college consists of one field-officer as commandant, one field-officer as second-commandant, one adjutant, and two accountant-officers.

The cadets are organized into three companies, to each of which are assigned one captain and three lieutenants from the army, who serve as instructors in both the military and academical departments. Each company is composed of men of the same class, except the sergeants and corporals, who are chosen from the two higher classes.

Cadets are admitted from thirteen to sixteen years of age, and for admission are examined in arithmetic, grammar, and writing. These examinations are held at Milan, Florence, and Naples, before commissions composed of professors and instructors of the colleges, and also at Palermo and Turin before local commissions appointed for the same purpose. The total number of cadets received at each college approximates 230.

The course of study is three years, as follows:

First Year.—Arithmetic, plane geometry, Greek and Roman history, geography, Italian and French languages, drawing, and writing.

Second Year.—Algebra, plane and solid geometry, history of the middle ages, geography, Italian and French languages.

Third Year.—Algebra, geometry, plane trigonometry, modern history, geography, Italian and French languages, natural history, geometrical and landscape drawing.

The maximum mark for a recitation is 20, the minimum 0.

The examinations are conducted by sub-committees, with a common president, who is a general officer appointed by the general of division within whose territory the college is located.

The sub-committees for the first and second classes are composed of three members chosen from the instructors, one of whom is the instructor of the subject upon which the cadets are to be examined.

The sub-committee of the third or graduating class is composed of a field-officer, one officer named by the general of division, and the professor of the subject upon which the cadets are to be examined.

All cadets of the first and second classes who receive 10 out of 20 marks in each subject at the examination are advanced to the class next above. Cadets of the third class who receive 14 out of 20 marks in mathematics, and 10 in every other subject, are permitted to pursue a special course in mathematics with a view to admission to the military academy for engineers and artillery at Turin. At the end of the year they are examined by a special commission appointed by the Minister of War, composed of a general and two professors of the academy who visit the military school at Modena in addition to the three military colleges. The students who at this examination receive 10 out of 20 marks in the special course, and in all of the other subjects, are eligible for appointment to the military academy.

The other members of the third class who do not compete for appointments to the academy at Turin, and who receive 10 out of 20 marks in all subjects, are eligible for appointment to the military school at Modena for cavalry and infantry, where they enter the second year's course. Such cadets as do not desire to pursue a military career are allowed at the completion of the course to return to civil life. Cadets who fail to pass the examination are allowed to repeat the course once.

The military instruction at the colleges is entirely practical, and limited to the schools of the soldier, company, and battalion. Gymnastics, dancing, and swimming, complete all of the practical exercises.

Each year, in the month of September, the cadets make excursions under their officers to different parts of the country, where they attend to military exercises, and study ground and fortifications.

The discipline at all these colleges is paternal in its nature. The officers are constantly in contact with the cadets. They superintend them at recitations, recreations, at meals and gymnastics, and an officer of service is always present with them in the hall of study and in the dormitory.

Coming to the college at a tender age, they learn obedience and subordination without compulsion; but, if refractory, discipline is enforced by the commandant, according to a known scale of punishment. Confinement in light prison and dismissal are the severest punishments inflicted.

The generals of division where the colleges are located can examine into the discipline, but cannot interfere with the course of study, for which the commandant is responsible to the Minister of War.

At the conclusion of the examinations the general who presides over the committees makes his report as to the condition of the college to the Minister of War. This report is shown to the commandant, who is authorized to make explanations.

MILITARY SCHOOL OF MODENA.

The object of this school is to prepare cadets to receive commissions in the infantry and cavalry.

The examinations for admission are competitive, and are held, as in the case of military colleges, before commissions appointed by the Minister of War, which convene at Turin, Milan, Modena, Florence, Naples, and Palermo.

It is intended that the number of admissions annually shall approach 300, but in 1875 the total number of cadets did not exceed 566. Competition is open to the cadets at the military colleges, to civil students, and to soldiers, several of whom were in the school in 1876.

Candidates must be between the ages of fifteen and twenty-two, and on entering the second year of the course are required to engage for eight years' service with the colors.

Cadets who complete the third year's course at the military colleges, which coincides with the first year's course at Modena, enter at once on the second year's course. All others pursue the full course of three years.

The officers of the school consist of a general, as commandant; one field-officer, second in command; one field-officer, director of studies; two adjutants; three accountant-officers; five captains, commandants of cadet companies; 15 lieutenants, assigned to the cadet companies; 12 captains and 5 lieutenants, instructors; 14 civil professors; in addition, there are instructors of riding, fencing, and gymnastics—making the total personnel, military and civil, 77.

The course of instruction is three years, as follows:

First Year.—Algebra, geometry, plane trigonometry, geography, modern history, Italian and French languages, natural history, line and landscape drawing.

Second Year.—Military art, topography, elements of physics, chemistry and mineralogy, study of arms, French and Italian literature, geometrical and topographical drawing.

Third Year.—Military history, military geography, fortification, Italian and French literature, military law and administration, topographical drawing, also drawing of fortifications.

The annual examination takes place in July. Cadets who fail are allowed a reëxamination in September, when, if they fail, they are turned back. If they fail a second time, they are sent to a regiment of the line to complete their eight years' service.

In consequence of the great demand for officers, 400 being required annually, from 96 to 97 per cent. of the cadets are allowed to graduate.

The military organization is in five companies, with one captain and three lieutenants from the army as officers. The duties of these officers have heretofore been exclusively military, but it is contemplated to make them instructors in other branches of study.

The military exercises are limited to infantry tactics, riding in the third year (school of the trooper), and gymnastics.

The cadets encamp from 20 to 30 days each year, during which period they devote their time to military exercises, study of ground, and reconnaissances.

If there be vacancies, the cadets on graduation are commissioned as officers, otherwise, until vacancies occur, they rank as sergeants. The officers assigned to the cavalry go to the cavalry school at Pinerolo, those assigned to the infantry join their regiments.

Attached to the military school at Modena is a special school for 250 non-commissioned officers, selected from the best sergeants of the army, who, on completing a course of instruction for two years, are commissioned as officers in all arms of service. These sergeants are qualified for admission either in the school for non-commissioned officers in their regiments, or else at the battalions of instruction already described.

The course of study is two years, as follows:

First Year.—Italian language, history of Italy, arithmetic, geography, linear drawing, physics, natural history, matériel of artillery.

Second Year.—Italian language, topography, fortification, military art, military law and administration, study and treatment of the horse (for cavalry and artillery), use of artillery, and construction of batteries (for the artillery).

The military and gymnastic exercises correspond to those for the cadets in the higher school.

MILITARY ACADEMY AT TURIN.

The object of this academy is to educate officers for the artillery and engineers.

The examinations are competitive, and are conducted, as already stated, by a commission appointed by the Minister of War, which visits the military school at Modena and the military colleges at Naples, Florence, and Milan.

Competition is open to all, but preference is given to cadets who have completed the third year's course at the military colleges, or the first year's course at the military school at Modena, which are identical.

The number of admissions annually is 90. Age at date of admission must be below twenty-three.

The officers of the academy consist of a general as commandant; 1 colonel, as second commandant and director of studies; 1 lieutenant-colonel, as director of interior economy and military instruction; 1 secretary; 1 adjutant; 2 accountant-officers; 9 officers for practical instruction; 23 military and civil professors and assistant professors; 1 riding-master, besides the necessary instructors for fencing and gymnastics.

The course of study is three years:

First Year.—Higher algebra, analytical geometry and elements of calculus, mechanics, surveying, Italian and French languages, geometrical and topographical drawing.

Second Year.—Analytical geometry, differential calculus, descriptive geometry, fortification, chemistry, Italian and French literature, military drawing (fortification), and topographical drawing.

Third Year.—Mechanics, descriptive geometry, organic

chemistry, military art, military history, military law and administration, elements of architecture.

The total number of cadets varies, rarely ever exceeding 250. On graduating the cadets receive commissions as second-lieutenants in the artillery and engineers, which commissions are antedated one year, in order to place the graduates on the same footing as regards promotion as the cadets of the school at Modena, who graduate a year before them.

SCHOOL OF APPLICATION FOR ARTILLERY AND ENGINEERS.

As soon as the cadets graduate at the Military Academy they go as second-lieutenants to the school of application.

The course of instruction is two years, as follows:

First Year.—Applied mechanics, matériel of artillery, permanent fortification, attack and defense of fortified places, military geography, military bridges, architecture, and art of construction.

Second Year.—Ballistics, matériel of artillery, permanent fortification, art of construction, military history, employment of artillery in war, manufacture of artillery matériel, drawing, architecture, and geodesy.

The officers of the school consist of a general as commandant; 1 lieutenant-colonel, as second commandant; 1 captain, as adjutant; 1 first-lieutenant, as assistant adjutant; 2 lieutenants, at the disposition of the commandant; 6 captains, military professors; 4 lieutenants, assistant professors; 2 civil professors; 5 captains, directors of practical instruction, 1 captain, riding-master, and 1 fencing-master. The school is also furnished with 44 men and 60 horses by the Normal School for Cavalry at Pinerolo.

On graduating from the school of application the officers are appointed first-lieutenants; those who fail are sent to the cavalry and infantry.

NORMAL SCHOOL OF INFANTRY AT PARMA.

There are several distinct courses of instruction pursued at the Normal School.

The first is for such lieutenants of infantry and cavalry as wish to compete at the examination for admission to the War School at Turin. The course is four months, and embraces arithmetic, geography, algebra, plane and solid geometry; trigonometry, mediæval and modern history; Italian and French literature.

The examinations in arithmetic, algebra, geometry, and trigonometry, are oral, and are conducted by a commission composed of two superior officers and one professor of the Normal School.

The examinations in the other subjects are written, and the papers are sent to the War School at Turin, where they are examined by a commission composed of the commandant, second commandant, and a professor of the War School.

To be eligible for admission, the competitor must obtain the medium mark of 10 out of 20.

The second course lasts three months, and is repeated twice a year for the benefit of the first and second lieutenants of infantry who wish to prepare for examination previous to their promotion.

Each course is pursued by about one hundred officers at a time, and embraces the theoretical and ballistical principles of portable fire-arms; construction and repair of fire-arms; recharging metallic cartridges; field fortification, and target-practice, with both fixed and movable targets.

The third course lasts forty days, and embraces the same subjects as the second course. It is pursued by the officers of infantry and cavalry of the lowest class at the War School, at the end of their first year, one-half of the class attending at a time.

The fourth course is for the education of non-commissioned officers who aspire to be officers in the Accountant Department or Department of Comptabilité. The course lasts two years, as follows:

First Year.—Arithmetic, Italian language, military law, theoretical and practical book-keeping, theory of the construction of fire-arms, and practical repair of fire-arms.

Second Year.—Continuation of the first year's course, together with the method of provisioning troops.

The examination for admission of non-commissioned officers to the schools at Modena and Parma is competitive, two or three sergeants being permitted to compete from each regiment. Before being permitted to present themselves before the commission named by the Minister of War, the sergeants from each regiment must compete with the other sergeants of the regiment who seek the same privilege.

The number of competitors for both schools is approximately 300, of whom about 200 succeed. Of this number about 120 to 125 go to the school at Modena, the remainder to Parma.

The Government establishes no arbitrary rule fixing the proportion of officers to be promoted from the ranks, but by means of these schools encourages every good soldier in the army to aspire to a commission.

The officers of the school consist of a colonel as commandant, 1 lieutenant-colonel or major as second commandant, 1 adjutant, 1 surgeon, 1 major of comptabilité director of the course of comptabilité, 3 lieutenants of comptabilité, 9 officers (captains and lieutenants) practical instructors, and 16 military and civil professors.

NORMAL SCHOOL FOR CAVALRY AT PINEROLO.

The principal object of this school is to carry on the education of second-lieutenants of cavalry who join it immediately after graduating at Modena.

The course of instruction is ten months, being mostly devoted to riding and practical duties required of cavalry.

A second course of instruction is provided for officers who desire to become first-class instructors in riding, and a third course of two months for the preparation of senior lieutenants to pass their examination for promotion.

SCHOOL OF WAR AT TURIN.

The object of this school is to train officers for that branch of the staff corresponding in our army to the Adjutant-General's Department.

The officers of the War School consist of a general as commandant; 1 colonel or lieutenant-colonel as second commandant; 3 staff officers, and 23 military instructors and professors. The military instructors are mostly officers of the General Staff.

Admission to the school is by competitive examination for officers of infantry and cavalry; and without examination for officers of artillery and engineers, who have graduated at the military academy and school of application for the artillery and engineers.

The conditions of admission for officers of infantry and cavalry are two years' service with troops, and ability to pass an examination in the subjects mentioned in the first course at the Normal School at Parma, which is specially designed to prepare them for admission to the War School. The number of competitors is usually about 100, of whom 50 to 60 are admitted.

The course of study for these officers is three years. At the end of their first year they are joined by about six officers of artillery, and two of engineers, taken in the order of class-rank, after graduating at the school of application.

Failure to pass the annual examinations reduces the graduating class to about fifty, of whom eight or ten, after returning to their regiments or corps, are summoned to Rome for duty with the General Staff.

The course of study embraces:

First Year.—Topographical drawing, field fortification, study of fire-arms, elementary mathematics (arithmetic and algebra), descriptive geometry, Italian and French languages, and, at the option of the student, one of the four following subjects: English and German languages, political economy, and physics.

Second Year.—Field topography, permanent fortification, military art, military history, mathematics, Italian and French literature, and, at the student's option, one of the four following subjects: English and German languages, law, and chemistry.

Third Year.—Practical geodesy, military art, military administration, military geography, military history, French, English, and German languages, general history, geology, and mineralogy.

The practical course of study merits special attention.

At the end of the first year one-half of the students are sent into the country to make maps for forty days, the other half go to the normal school of infantry at Parma, where they take a course of target-practice, study ballistics as applicable to small-arms, also the construction of small-arms. They also receive practical instruction in repairing arms, and in constructing and refilling cartridges. At the end of the forty days each half exchanges duty with the other for the same length of time, which completes the practical course for the first year.

At the end of the second year the entire class goes into the country for a period of fifteen days, and plays the game of Kriegsspiel. To accomplish this, two corps d'armée are supposed to be operating against each other. A professor takes command of each corps, and the students are placed in command of the supposed divisions, brigades, regiments, battalions, and batteries.

Before the operations begin a reconnaissance is made on each side, and in all the subsequent movements the students are required to show on the ground where they would post their commands, and explain in detail all the dispositions they would make in the various attacks and counter-attacks.

After the game is over, the ground is visited with a view to ascertain the correctness or faultiness of the various movements.

After the expiration of the fifteen days the same period is employed in studying military positions on the frontier, and their occupation by troops. In posting the troops they are required to designate the exact positions they would give to battalions, regiments, brigades, divisions, or corps, according to the command they might hold. They also make maps showing the position of the troops, and the offensive and defensive dispositions they would make in consequence of supposed movements made by the enemy.

After the expiration of the thirty days they return to Turin, and are specially examined in the practical duties they have performed.

After the examination the class visits some of the principal fortresses of Italy, to study practically the art of fortification. After inspecting and criticising the fortress, the officers study the ground, and are required to trace on maps the positions they would assign to batteries, approaches, and parallels, in case they were directing a siege. Fifteen days are allotted to the above duty, followed by an examination in regard to all of the fortresses visited.

At the conclusion of this examination, the infantry and cavalry officers of the class go for a month to Casale, for a course in practical engineering, where they learn the construction of trenches, parallels, epaulements, temporary bridges, as also the method of destroying and repairing railroads. The officers of artillery and engineers of the class during this time are employed with the next higher class in making maps in the country.

At the end of the third year, the officers in the vicinity of Turin study logistics as applicable to ground; the marching and camping of corps and other large bodies of troops; embarkation and disembarkation of troops; routes for marching, and also the means employed to make them practicable. This duty occupies two months, and is followed by graduation when the officers, before returning to duty with their regiments, are sent to the grand manœuvres to serve on the staff of the corps, division, and brigade commanders.

To encourage officers to pursue the course of study at the School of War, all of the lieutenants of infantry and cavalry who complete the course successfully, and are not called to the staff, are entitled to promotion as soon as they arrive in the upper third of the grade to which they belong at the date of graduation. For example, there being 2,717 first-lieutenants of infantry, each graduate of the War School, on reaching the number 905 on the general list, would be entitled to the first vacancy of captain, and would pass over the heads of 904 officers.

The object of this advancement is to enable trained men to arrive early at the higher commands of the army.

PRINCIPLE OF DETAIL FOR STAFF DUTY IN THE ARMY OF ITALY.

The utility of diffusing staff knowledge and experience in the army, and the advantage to be gained by encouraging officers of the line to fit themselves for staff employment, as well as high command, are fully recognized in the constitution of the Italian Staff. Three of the four classes of which it is composed are exclusively detailed from the line, and all above the grade of lieutenant are in excess of the regimental complements.

All of the adjutant-generals of brigade or brigade-adjutants are captains detailed from the line, in excess of the regimental complement. To be eligible for appointment they must be graduates of the School of War.

Aides-de-camp must be graduates of the School of War, and are borne on the strength of their regiments. Only aides-de-camp attached to the royal household, Minister of War, and to generals commanding armies and corps, perform personal service. The others assist the brigade-adjutants in their duties, and, in case of necessity, replace them.

All subaltern officers return to regimental duty after *two years*' detached service, and cannot again be detailed till the expiration of another two years.

The principle of encouraging line officers to excel in professional knowledge is strikingly acknowledged in the laws regulating promotion in the staff proper.

The lieutenants of the staff, twenty (20) in number, must be graduates of the highest proficiency from the War School; must subsequently have served a year with troops; and have passed the test of probation for staff duty at Rome.

Of the captains, seventy (70) in number, two-thirds are appointed from the lieutenants of the staff, and one-third from the captains of the army at large, who are graduates of the War School and possess the required qualifications.

An officer, therefore, who fails to receive the appointment

of lieutenant has still the hope, if he distinguishes himself with troops, of obtaining a captaincy in the staff at a later day.

The majors of the staff are selected from captains of the staff who are previously promoted majors in the line, where they serve with infantry or cavalry for two years; from majors of the line who, having graduated at the War School, are proposed for admission to the staff, and from the most distinguished majors of artillery and engineers, who need not of necessity have graduated at the War School.

The colonels and lieutenant-colonels are appointed from the grade next below, but they may be transferred to the line, and be required to command battalions and regiments.

The promotion to major shows that an officer who has been both lieutenant and captain in the staff has no certainty that he will receive the next higher grade. He must first go into the line as major, and there he must remain unless summoned back to the staff. The same rule applies to lieutenant-colonels and colonels.

The staff officers know that on going to the line their connection with the staff is severed, and that the Government is left free to call them back or keep them with the troops.

The officers of the line, to the grade of major included, know that staff preferment is open to them.

This constant interchange from the staff to the line, and from the line to the staff, draws to the staff the highest talent and skill in the army; prevents the staff officers from becoming slaves to routine; enlightens them as to the wants of the troops; gives them a thorough knowledge of the instruction, drill, and discipline of the troops; and, by holding the command of companies, battalions, and regiments, qualifies them for all the higher grades of the army. The army, too, in its turn profits by all the talent of the staff, whose officers, returning periodically to the command of the troops, become instructors in the grades where their influence will most surely be felt.

In addition to the variety of experience secured to officers by transfers from the staff to the line and the reverse, there are many other positions open to officers of the line—such as commandants of military districts, commandants, professors, and instructors, at military academies, schools, and colleges—all of which are filled by detail.

The number of these different positions, and the care taken by the Government to avoid crippling the regiments by depriving them of their complement of officers, are shown by the following table, in which the first column represents the number of officers required to fill each grade in the 80 regiments of infantry and 10 regiments of bersaglieri, and the second column the number of officers actually in service according to the most recent legislation:

GRADES.	Officers for 90 Regiments.	Officers actually in Service.
Colonels	90	140
Lieutenant-colonels and majors (one to command each battalion and depot)	460	493
Captains (including 90 regimental adjutants and 90 on duty at depots)	1,260	1,744
First-lieutenants (including 290 battalion-adjutants)	2,520	2,750
Second-lieutenants	1,120	1,377
Total	5,450	6,504

Of the number 493, 136 are lieutenant-colonels and 357 are majors.

The difference between 6,504 and 5,450, which is 1,054, gives the number of supernumerary officers of infantry available for the different varieties of detached service.

These supernumeraries are distributed among the several regiments, to which they return on the completion of their tour of duty, while the ratio which they bear to the total number of officers in the regiments shows conclusively that every efficient officer in the course of his career may hope to increase his experience by military employment outside of his own arm of service.

PROMOTION.

With the exception of graduates of universities or institutions of technology, who must pass a special qualifying examination, and also one-year volunteers, no officer is commissioned in the Italian army without graduating at one or more of the established military schools.

Promotion in infantry, cavalry, artillery, and engineers, is lineal in each arm or corps. As appears from the preceding table, the list of officers in each arm embraces, in addition to the number necessary to fill the regiments to their complement, the number of officers required for detached service on the staff, at military schools, military districts, etc.

No officer can be promoted to the grade next above without passing a prescribed examination.

The examining committees are appointed by the Minister of War, and for the grade of colonel are composed of general officers; for the grades of captain to lieutenant-colonel inclusive, they are presided over by a general officer; for the grade of sub-lieutenant by a field-officer.

The examination for promotion to the grade of captain in infantry takes place at Parma, where the officers pursue a special course of study. The examination for the grade of major takes place in the territorial divisions, and is oral, written, and practical. The written examination embraces tactical and military themes, while the practical applies to the drill and movements of a battalion, or a higher body of troops. The test for lieutenant-colonel consists in commanding satisfactorily a battalion and regiment.

About 200 lieutenants and 60 captains are ordered at the same time for examination. If a lieutenant fails to pass three successive examinations he must remain in the same grade for twenty-five years, when, if he be forty-eight years of age, the Government can retire him on full pension. If he becomes forty-eight years of age before having served twenty-five years, he can ask to be retired with as many twenty-fifths of the full pension as he has served years.

For example, if allowed to retire after twenty years' service, he would receive four-fifths of the full pension.

A lieutenant may waive an examination the first and second year after failure, but he must submit to three examinations in six years.

The same rules apply to the examinations of captains for promotion to major, the limit being fifty-two years of age and thirty years' service. For example, if a captain fails in his examination, and after twenty-five years' service reaches the age of fifty-two, the Government can retire him on five-sixths of the full pension. The examination of captains is most severe, and in 1876 about five per cent. failed.

The limits for promotion from major to lieutenant-colonel are fifty-six years of age and thirty years' service; lieutenant-colonel, sixty years of age and thirty years' service.

Generals can be retired without regard to age or length of service, and the Government can prolong at pleasure the service of any officer beyond the prescribed age.

In all regiments and corps about one-third of the vacancies is reserved for the sergeants who have been trained at the military schools for the grade of officers.

In time of peace four-fifths of the promotions in infantry and cavalry to grade of first-lieutenants are by seniority, and one-fifth by selection; in time of war, two-thirds are promoted by seniority, the other third by selection.

Graduation from the War School entitles a lieutenant to promotion as soon as he arrives in the upper third of his grade.

To the grade of captain two-thirds are promoted in time of peace by seniority, the other third by selection; in time of war, one-half are promoted by seniority, the other half by selection.

Promotion to major in time of peace is half by seniority and half by selection; in time of war it is all by selection.

All promotions above the grade of major are by selection, the candidates being required to pass practical examinations.

Promotion by selection is based upon the fact that it is impossible for the Government to give all officers the same education. In the interest of the state, therefore, the intelligent and efficient are promoted over the heads of the ignorant and indolent; while, by the provision that all promotions above the grade of major shall be by selection, worthless officers are wholly debarred from attaining high commands.

In the consolidation and organization of the present army

the Government from time to time has found it necessary to discharge officers who were known to be ignorant and worthless.

The first purification took place in 1861, after the army of Piedmont was consolidated with the armies of Lombardy, Parma, Modena, Emilia, and Naples. In the latter army, which contained more than 100,000 men, there were a large number of the Garibaldi volunteers with little or no education. On failing to pass a prescribed examination, many officers were discharged with six months' pay.

In 1870 the army was again purified. Colonels of regiments and generals were required to report to the Minister of War the names of all officers disqualified for service either through ill health or inefficiency. These officers were invited to retire from the service with a pension proportioned to their length of service. A lieutenant, for instance, of fifteen years' service, was offered fifteen twenty-fifths of the full pension; a captain of twenty years' service was offered twenty thirtieths of the full pension. Such officers as refused to apply for retirement were ordered before a commission for examination.

The action of the Government in giving proportional pensions was based upon the consideration that officers who had given to the Government the years from twenty to forty, in which civilians lay the foundations of their fortunes, could not with justice be turned adrift to begin, with advancing years, occupations for which their previous life had unfitted them.

ARMY OF RUSSIA.

Since the adoption of the principle of obligatory military service in 1870, the Russian army has been in a state of transition.

When the organization is completed, the military forces will be divided into the regular and irregular army, the former of which embraces the field, reserve, depot, and local troops.

The following table represents approximately the proposed strength of the field-army on a peace and war footing:

REGULAR ARMY.

	No. of Battalions.	Officers.	Combatants.	Non-Combatants.
INFANTRY, PEACE-FOOTING.				
European Russia	528	10,771	313,925	24,291
Caucasus	116	1,918	55,487	5,852
Asiatic Russia	4	90	1,908	293
Total	648	12,779	371,820	30,436
INFANTRY, WAR-FOOTING.				
European Russia	528	13,565	537,421	80,824
Caucasus	116	2,380	113,055	7,127
Asiatic Russia	4	106	8,316	326
Total	648	16,060	658,792	88,277

REGULAR ARMY.

	No. of Squadr'ns.	Officers.	Combatants.	Non-Combatants.
CAVALRY, PEACE-FOOTING.				
European Russia...............	888	2,569	85,171	8,924
Caucasus.......................	16	140	2,916	611
Total........................	840	2,669	85,087	9,585
CAVALRY, WAR-FOOTING.				
European Russia...............	841	2,946	85,296	8,949
Caucasus.......................	16	140	2,856	566
Total........................	857	2,528	88,060	9,888

	Batteries.	No. of Guns.	Officers.	Combatants.	Non-Combatants.
FIELD-ARTILLERY, PEACE-FOOTING.					
European Russia...............	246	984	1,602	40,548	7,985
Caucasus.......................	42	168	278	7,068	1,598
Asiatic Russia................	11	50	75	1,715	440
Total........................	299	1,202	1,950	49,578	9,888
FIELD-ARTILLERY, WAR-FOOTING.					
European Russia...............	246	1,964	1,602	89,985	10,165
Caucasus.......................	42	836	278	10,567	2,118
Asiatic Russia................	11	88	75	2,544	649
Total........................	299	2,872	1,950	76,086	12,935
HORSE-ARTILLERY, ALL IN EUROPE.					
Peace-footing..................	84	202	221	4,087	1,894
War-footing....................	84	204	204	7,466	1,852

	No. of Battalions.	Officers.	Combatants.	Non-Combatants.
ENGINEERS.				
Peace-footing..................	19½	488	11,692	1,780
War-footing....................	15½	488	18,190	2,268
TOTAL				
Peace-footing..................	....	19,102	496,469	52,672
War-footing....................	....	21,220	615,544	64,945

The reserve troops are composed of trained soldiers, and, like the landwehr of Germany, are intended to reënforce the active army, and to form an army in the second line.

Scarcely any cadres exist for the reserve in time of peace, but ultimately, in time of war, it is intended to form 164 battalions of infantry, with an approximate strength of 3,500 officers, 170,000 combatants, and 13,000 non-combatants.

The depot troops in time of war are intended to fill vacancies in the field-army, and to train recruits. Except in the artillery and cavalry, no cadres exist in time of peace. In time of war it is intended to form 199 battalions of infantry, with an approximate strength, in infantry, cavalry, and artillery, of 6,650 officers, 270,000 combatants, and 40,000 non-combatants.

Local troops are intended for garrison and local defense, but can be utilized for field-service. The proposed organization of these troops consists of 132 battalions in time of peace, capable in time of war of an expansion to 245 battalions, with an approximate strength of 11,900 officers and 360,000 men.

The total war-strength of the regular army of European Russia, embracing reserve, depot, and local troops, is estimated at 38,000 officers, 1,350,000 combatants, and 140,000 non-combatants; in the Caucasus, 4,900 officers, 216,000 combatants, and 19,000 non-combatants; in Asia, 1,050 officers, 35,000 combatants, and 4,000 non-combatants — making the total war-strength of the empire 43,950 officers, 1,601,000 combatants, and 163,000 non-combatants.

The above figures cannot be attained until the plan of reorganization is completed.

The present strength available for war purposes can only be deduced from the war-footing of the troops composing the active army, together with the troops that have passed from the active army into the reserve. This number depends upon the annual contingent called to perform military duty, which varies from 150,000 to 180,000. The period of military service being six years in the active army and nine years in the reserve, if it be assumed that of the annual contingent 100,000 should complete the six years' service, the nine classes of the reserve would amount to 900,000 men. Of this number, 300,000 would be required to raise the active army from the peace to the war footing, leaving 600,000 men available for organization as reserve, depot, and local troops. In consequence of the great difficulty of procuring officers, and want of time to organize the troops of the second line, it is probable that for the immediate future the reserve will only be available by calling out the men by classes to fill the vacancies in the active army.

INFANTRY.

IRREGULAR ARMY.

This consists of the Cossacks, all of whom owe military service, and who constitute the irregular-cavalry force, with an approximate peace-footing of 35,000 men, and a war-footing of 140,000 men.

INFANTRY.

The infantry of the line is maintained on four different footings, viz.:

War, increased peace, peace, and cadre.

The organization of a company, according to the four footings, is as follows:

RANK.	War-footing.	Increased Peace-footing.	Peace-footing.	Cadres.
Captain	1	1	1	1
Lieutenants	8	2	2	2
Sergeants	6	6	6	4
Junior sergeants	12	8	4	4
Corporals	20	19	16	14
Privates	160	119	84	50
Buglers	3	2	2	2
Drummers	8	2	2	2
Non-combatants	7	6	6	6
Total	215	165	123	85

The footing of increased peace and cadre are not usually adopted. The regiments of the three divisions of the guard, and the six divisions of the Army of the Caucasus, have four battalions, of four companies each. All other regiments have three battalions of five companies each, but ultimately they will be organized like those of the guard.

The field and staff of a regiment consists of—

1 Commandant,
1 Field-officer, superintendent of interior economy,
3 or 4 Field-officers, one for each battalion,
1 Regimental adjutant,
1 Regimental quartermaster,
1 Regimental paymaster,
1 Instructor of arms,
1 Surgeon,

1 Officer in charge of non-combatants,
3 or 4 Battalion surgeons,
3 or 4 Battalion adjutants,
1 Chaplain.

In the guards the commandants of regiments have the rank of major-generals, and commandants of battalions the grade of colonel. In all other regiments they have respectively the grades of colonel and major.

The strength of a regiment of four battalions is as follows:

REGIMENT.	Officers.	Combatants.	Non-Combatants.
Peace-footing	64	1,897	192
War-footing	80	4,057	233

The non-combatant class embraces the administrative officers, surgeons, chaplains, clerks, artificers, drivers, and officers' servants, one being allowed to each.

BRIGADE.

An infantry brigade consists of two regiments with six or eight battalions, according to the organization of the regiments.

DIVISION.

An infantry division consists of two brigades (12 or 16 battalions), and a brigade of artillery of four to six batteries.

The chief of staff of the division is a colonel or lieutenant-colonel of the general staff, and is assisted by two captains of the staff, who attend to all the administrative and routine work.

CORPS.

A corps d'armée consists of two divisions of infantry, one division of cavalry, with the proper complement of artillery and engineers.

The cavalry division consists of two brigades of two regiments of four squadrons each, also two batteries of horse-artillery.

The Russian army is divided into fourteen territorial commands, corresponding to the same number of provincial governments.

The recruitment of the army is carried out by the various local governments, and the recruits are trained and equipped by the reserve, or local troops, in the same manner as in the military districts in Italy.

The term of service is fifteen years, beginning with the twenty-second year. Of this period six years are spent with the colors, and nine years in the reserve. The annual contingent varies from 150,000 to 180,000 men, and constitutes about twenty-five per cent. of the number of young men who annually become liable to military service.

As an encouragement to intelligence, the battalion and regimental schools are established the same as in other armies, and a further inducement is offered in a reduction of the term of active service.

To secure a body of reliable non-commissioned officers the Government has recently offered special advantages to all sergeants who will reënlist. Not only are they guaranteed employment in the civil and military departments of the Government after their discharge, but pensions are likewise granted. A sergeant of ten years' service on going into reserve receives 250 rubles, or $200. Those who have served three reënlistments, or twenty years, receive in hand 1,000 rubles ($800), or, if they prefer, an annual pension of 96 rubles ($76).

SCHOOLS FOR OFFICERS.

The means of providing an efficient body of officers for the immense army has long since engaged the attention of the Government, and has led to the establishment of a greater number of military schools than exists in any other country of Europe.

By far the largest portion of officers is composed of non-commissioned officers promoted after pursuing a special course of military instruction. For this purpose there are 14 schools for non-commissioned officers of infantry, one in each provincial government; one for the Cossacks of the Don at Novo Tcherkask; one for the Cossacks of the Caucasus at Stavropol; one for the Cossacks of Orenburg at Orenburg; one for the cavalry at Twer, and another at Elizabethgrad.

The course of instruction at the infantry schools is two years, and embraces—

First year:
    Religion,
    Russian language,
    Mathematics,
    Principles of physics and chemistry,
    Military drawing,
    Geography,
    History.

Second year:
    Infantry tactics,
    Applied tactics,
    Military topography,
    Fortification,
    Theory of fire-arms,
    Military administration,
    Military law,
    Military hygiene,
    Method of teaching soldiers to read and write.

The practical course embraces drill, gymnastics, and fencing. The students are also required to pursue a practical course with their regiments, to which they return during the summer vacation of three months.

The number of scholars at the different infantry schools varies from 200 to 400; the total number is 3,800, of whom about 1,800 graduate annually, and return to the army as commissioned officers.

MILITARY GYMNASIA.

These schools, numbering thirteen, correspond to the military colleges of Italy, and are intended to prepare cadets for the higher schools for infantry, cavalry, artillery, and engineers.

INFANTRY SCHOOLS.

The course of study is seven years, and is open to boys from the age of ten to seventeen.

Cadets named by the Minister of War, mostly sons of civil and military officers, receive a free education, while the sons of civilians are educated at the expense of their parents.

The course of instruction embraces—

    Religion,
    Grammar,
    Geography,
    Arithmetic,
    Algebra,
    Geometry,
    Trigonometry,
    History,
    Physics,
    Chemistry,
    Drawing,
    Russian,
    French and German languages,
    Singing,
    Dancing,
    Gymnastics,
    Fencing,
    Swimming.

Only the senior class is instructed in the use of arms.

The military instruction of the other classes is limited to marching and gymnastics. All the cadets wear uniform, and are subject to mild military discipline. On graduation, those who pass the examination can enter the higher military schools; those who dislike a military career are free to return to civil life.

INFANTRY SCHOOLS.

For the special education of officers of infantry there are three schools, known as the Paul and Constantine Schools of War, at St. Petersburg, and the Alexander School of War at Moscow.

Admission to these schools is open to such civil students as can pass a qualifying examination, and to the cadets who pass the final examination at the military gymnasia. The expenses of education are paid by the state, and also by parents. The number of cadets in each school is 300.

The course of instruction lasts two years, and embraces—
Religion,
Russian,
German and French languages,
History,
Natural philosophy,
Chemistry,
Tactics,
Theory of arms,
Military geography,
Topographical and mechanical drawing,
Military law and administration,
Dancing,
Gymnastics,
Fencing,
Swimming.

Music and singing are also taught, but are not obligatory. Riding is taught only the second year.

The cadets are organized into a battalion of four companies, and annually take part in all the great manœuvres near St. Petersburg and Moscow.

From 400 to 450 officers enter the army annually from these three schools with the grade of second-lieutenant. Those who are best qualified are assigned to the guard, others to the field-artillery, but the great majority enter the regiments of the line.

CAVALRY SCHOOL.

The Nicholas War School for cavalry at St. Petersburg corresponds to those just explained for infantry. All of the expenses of education are borne by the parents. The number of cadets is 150. The course of instruction is two years, the subjects being the same as in the infantry schools, with addition of hippology.

The cadets are organized into a squadron, and take part in the manœuvres.

About 75 cadets graduate annually and enter the cavalry of the guard, and the line as second-lieutenants, or cornets. The graduating ceremonies of the two infantry schools, and the cavalry school at St. Petersburg, take place in the field on the last day of the manœuvres, when the Emperor in person welcomes the young graduates into the army.

FINLAND CADET CORPS.

The school for this corps is a combination of the military gymnasium and the infantry schools already described. The course is seven years, the last two years being devoted to military subjects. The number of cadets is 100, all of whom are natives of Finland. The graduates, about 12 each year, are assigned to the infantry.

CORPS OF PAGES.

This school has the same organization as the Finland Cadet Corps. The cadets are sons of the nobility, and officers of the court. The number of cadets is 150, of whom about 20 graduate annually, and are assigned to the infantry, cavalry, and artillery of the guard.

ARTILLERY SCHOOL.

This school is denominated the Michael Artillery War School, and is located at St. Petersburg.

Candidates for admission must be above sixteen years of age, and must pass a qualifying examination, or else have graduated at a military gymnasium.

The number of cadets is from 125 to 150. The course of instruction at the artillery school is three years, and embraces—

    Religion,
    History,
    Analytical geometry,

Calculus,
Elementary mechanics,
Natural philosophy,
Chemistry,
Tactics,
Science of artillery,
Artillery administration,
Fortification,
Military geography,
Military law,
Landscape and artillery drawing,
Russian, French, and German languages.

The practical instruction embraces—
Riding,
Fencing,
Gymnastics,
Swimming.

MICHAEL ARTILLERY ACADEMY AT ST. PETERSBURG.

This is a school of application for officers of artillery who must have served two years with their regiments, and must pass a qualifying examination for admission.

The course of instruction is two years, and embraces—
Ballistics,
Technology,
History of artillery,
Artillery administration,
Higher mathematics,
Analytical and applied mechanics,
Natural philosophy,
Chemistry,
Geometrical drawing.

SCHOOLS FOR ENGINEERS.

The Nicholas War School for engineers, and Nicholas War Academy, or school of application for engineers, are both located at St. Petersburg. The course of instruction in each is almost identical with the corresponding school for the artillery, except that in the academy more attention is paid to fortification, architecture, and military constructions.

NICHOLAS STAFF ACADEMY.

The object of this academy, which is located at St. Petersburg, is to train officers for the general staff.

The conditions of admission are to be below the rank of major, to have had four years' service with troops, and to be able to pass a competitive examination in mathematics, including plane trigonometry, tactics of the three arms, theory of arms in use in the service, history, geography, fortification, Russian, and German or French languages.

The course of study is two years, and embraces the following subjects, classified as principal and secondary, according to their importance:

The principal subjects are—
    Tactics,
    Strategy,
    Military history,
    Military administration,
    Military statistics,
    Geodesy,
    Cartography,
    Topographical drawing.

The secondary subjects are—
    Russian, French, and German languages,
    History,
    International law,
    Artillery,
    Fortification,
    Riding.

All of the principal subjects, except tactics, extend through the course.

The students are classified according to merit, and those most distinguished are admitted to the staff corps.

Attached to the academy is a geodetical division for the

education of officers for the topographical corps. The principal subjects of this course are astronomy, physical geography, geodesy, and cartography.

Special inducements in way of medals, employment, and promotion, are offered to officers who graduate at the artillery, engineer, and staff academies; and, as a mark of distinction, they are permitted to wear on their breasts a badge to denote that they have completed the course of instruction.

OTHER SCHOOLS.

In addition to the schools already described, there is a medical academy for the education of military surgeons; a veterinary academy for the education of veterinary surgeons; a military law-school to train officers for the department of military law; a riding-school for the training of riding-masters; also a school for the education of hospital-stewards and apprentices.

PROMOTION.

Promotion in the infantry and cavalry to the rank of captain is by seniority. Instead of having a general list for the entire infantry or cavalry of the army, a general list is prepared in each infantry and cavalry division, and promotions are made as vacancies occur in the divisional lists.

Promotion to the grades of major, lieutenant-colonel, and colonel, is entirely by selection based on reports from the generals of brigade and division. This promotion by selection enables the Government at all times to have at its disposal vacancies in the line to be filled by officers of the staff, guard, engineers, and other corps, who desire to serve with the troops of the line.

In the artillery and engineers, promotion is by seniority to the grade of lieutenant-colonel. Above that grade, promotion is by selection.

In the artillery, separate lists for promotion by seniority are made out for the field-artillery of the guard and the field-artillery of the line, also for the horse-artillery of the guard and the horse-artillery of the line.

In the engineers, separate lists are made for the sappers, pontoniers, park-detachments, etc.

In the general staff (adjutant-general's department), up to the grade of captain, officers receive a grade every two years. A captain after three years' service in his rank, and who has commanded a battalion of the line with success, is promoted to the grade of lieutenant-colonel.

The object of rapid promotion in the staff is to enable highly-educated officers to arrive at the grade of general while still in the possession of mental and bodily vigor.

The officers of the guard, who are better educated than officers of the line, are also given advantages for promotion with the same object. To this end they rank with the next grade above them in the line, and can at any time be transferred with increased rank.

DISCIPLINE.

For the purpose of enforcing discipline, all officers and non-commissioned officers are permitted to inflict punishment for all minor offenses. Serious offenses are punished by the sentence of regimental and district courts-martial.

The power confided to the several grades for the punishment of minor offenses is as follows:

Corporal.—Reprimand, twenty-four hours' confinement to barracks, and one extra tour of police or fatigue duty.

Sergeant.—Reprimand, forty-eight hours' confinement to barracks, two extra tours of police or fatigue duty, twenty-four hours' confinement in guard-house.

Company Officer.—Reprimand, eight days' confinement to barracks, three extra tours of police or fatigue duty, four days' confinement to guard-house, two days' solitary confinement.

Officer commanding a Company, Squadron, or Half-battery.—Reprimand, two months' confinement to barracks, four extra tours of police or fatigue duty, eight days' confinement to guard-house, five days' solitary confinement on bread-and-water, fifteen lashes to men on punishment-list.

Officer commanding a Battalion or Battery.—Reprimand,

three months' confinement to barracks, six extra tours of police or fatigue duty, fourteen days' confinement to guard-room, eight days' solitary confinement on bread-and-water, twenty-five lashes to men on punishment-list.

Officers commanding a Regiment. — Reprimand, three months' confinement to barracks, eight tours of police or fatigue duty, one month's confinement to guard-room, two weeks' solitary confinement on bread-and-water, temporary reduction to the ranks, name placed on punishment-list, fifty lashes.

Punishments inflicted by non-commissioned officers must at once be reported to the company commanders.

Non-commissioned officers can be permanently or temporarily reduced to the ranks, and can be punished to the same extent as men not on the punishment-list.

Company, battalion, regimental, and higher commanders, can inflict punishment upon officers for minor offenses. These punishments are reprimands, extra tours of duty, confinement to quarters or within main guard, suspension from command of a company or battalion. An officer can likewise be reported as unworthy of promotion.

The care which the Russian Government has taken to educate its officers, and to form a reliable body of non-commissioned officers, in connection with the long term of service and stolid temperament of its soldiers, has enabled the army, despite the introduction of breech-loaders, to preserve the steadiness in battle which made it so famous in the days of Napoleon.

The success, too, with which military operations have been planned and executed during the present conflict, and the great saving of life as compared with the previous wars against Turkey, offered indisputable proof of the wisdom and humanity of maintaining a proper military organization in time of peace.

ARMY OF AUSTRIA.

The following tables present the armed strength of Austria on the peace and war footings.[1]

Peace-footing.

REGULAR ARMY.	Battalions.	Companies.	Squadrons.	Batteries.	Depot of Battalions, Companies, etc.	Officers.	Men.
Staff and administrative corps	....	....	....	....	....	1,692	1,757
Guards	....	....	....	....	....	114	540
80 Regiments of infantry	400	....	....	....	80	6,880	141,440
1 Regiment of rifles	7	....	....	....	1	151	8,612
33 Battalions of rifles	33	....	....	....	33	698	16,995
41 Regiments of cavalry	....	....	246	....	41	1,772	42,971
13 Regiments of field-artillery	....	....	....	169	39	1,027	19,900
12 Battalions of fortress-artillery	....	60	....	5	12	256	7,422
2 Regiments of engineers	....	56	....	....	10	244	5,054
1 Regiment of pioneers	....	25	....	....	....	129	2,922
Trains	....	....	36	....	40	906	2,845
Sanitary troops	....	....	....	....	....	69	2,404
Military establishments, schools, etc.	....	....	....	....	....	1,451	9,729
Total	440	141	282	174	256	14,666	257,091
LANDWEHR.							
81 Battalions of infantry and rifles	....	....	....	....	81	509	1,699
Tyrolese riflemen	....	....	....	....	11	62	370
Cavalry	....	....	....	....	....	1	......
Total	....	....	....	....	92	572	1,990
HUNGARIAN LANDWEHR.							
Guard of the crown	....	....	....	....	....	2	84
Infantry	....	....	....	....	93	379	5,740
Cavalry	....	....	....	....	20	80	1,590
Total	....	....	....	....	113	461	7,314
Gendarmerie	....	....	....	....	....	148	13,908
Total peace-footing	440	141	282	174	461	15,847	240,311

[1] By the law of the 5th of December, 1868, the strength of the regular army, navy, and reserve, for the next ten years, was fixed on the war-footing at 800,000 men, of which number Austria proper was to furnish 457,012, and Hungary 342,988.

War-footing.

REGULAR ARMY.	Battalions.	Companies.	Squadrons.	Batteries.	Depot of Battalions, Companies, etc.	Officers.	Men.
Staff and administrative corps	....	....	....	....	......	8,008	10,460
Guards	....	....	....	....	......	116	540
160 Regiments of infantry	480	....	....	....	80	10,640	475,040
1 Regiment of rifles	8½	....	....	....	1	218	10,037
41¼ Battalions of rifles [1]	41¼	....	....	....	33	990	47,223
41 Regiments of cavalry	....	....	287	....	41	2,214	56,457
13 Regiments of field-artillery	....	....	....	195	13	1,334	59,842
12 Regiments of fortress-artillery	....	72	....	10	......	526	13,388
2 Regiments of engineers	....	56	....	....	10	855	16,248
1 Regiment of pioneers	....	25	....	....	5	202	7,856
Train	....	....	72	....	42	991	80,047
Sanitary troops	....	....	....	....	......	262	18,738
Military establishments, schools, etc	....	....	....	....	......	2,618	17,616
Total	530	153	359	205	225	23,504	753,992
Landwehr	81	....	....	....	81	2,266	92,206
Tyrolese rifles	20	....	2	....	11	500	22,100
Cavalry	....	....	25	....	25	150	4,320
Total	101	....	27	....	117	2,916	118,626
HUNGARIAN LANDWEHR.							
Guard of the crown	....	....	....	....	......	2	58
Infantry	92	....	....	....	92	2,626	118,856
Cavalry	....	....	40	....	20	400	8,620
Total	92	....	40	....	112	3,028	127,284
Gendarmerie	....	....	....	....	......	148	13,903
Grand total	728	153	426	205	454	29,596	1,013,755

INFANTRY.

The Austrian infantry is organized into regiments composed of five field battalions of four companies each, and one depot battalion of five companies.

In case of war, the six battalions are organized into two regiments of three battalions each, the fifth company of the depot battalion remaining as a common depot for both regiments.

The first, second, and third battalions constitute the field regiment; the fourth, fifth, and depot or complementary battalion form the reserve regiment.

The field regiment is commanded by the colonel, the reserve regiment by the lieutenant-colonel.

In time of peace the cadre of the depot battalion consists only of 6 officers and 15 men, but the names of all of the officers who, in the event of war, would be assigned to each of the companies of the reserve regiment, including the depot

[1] Can be increased to 60 battalions if necessary.

INFANTRY. 163

battalion, are kept on a list at the War Department, where the lists are revised twice a year.

The organization of a company is as follows:

COMPANY.	PEACE-FOOTING.		WAR-FOOTING.	
	1st, 2d, and 3d Battalions.	4th and 5th Battalions.	Each of 4 Battalions.	Depot Company.
Captain...........................	1	1	1	1
Lieutenants.......................	2	2	3	3
Cadet or officers' substitute.....	1	..	1	..
First-sergeant....................	1	1	1	1
Sergeants.........................	4	4	4	4
Corporals.........................	5	5	12	12
Lance-corporals...................	5	5	12	12
Privates..........................	70	50	150	150
Pay-sergeant......................	1	1	1	1
Drummer...........................	1	1	2	2
Bugler............................	1	1	2	2
Pioneers..........................	..	..	4	..
Hospital attendants...............	..	..	3	..
Officers' servants................	3	3	4	4
Total.........................	95	74	256	229

The cadet is a non-commissioned officer, specially educated, who is eligible for appointment as lieutenant.

The strength of each of the first, second, and third battalions, on the peace and war footing, is as follows:

BATTALION.	PEACE-FOOTING.		WAR-FOOTING.	
	Officers.	Men.	Officers.	Men.
FIELD AND STAFF.				
Battalion commander...............	1	....	1	....
Battalion-adjutant................	1	....	1	....
Drummer...........................	....	1	....	1
Bugler............................	....	1	....	1
Armorer...........................	....	....	....	1
Staff-sergeant....................	....	....	....	1
Officers' servants................	....	2	....	2
FOUR COMPANIES.				
Captains..........................	4	....	4	....
Lieutenants.......................	8	....	12	....
Cadets............................	....	4	....	4
First-sergeants...................	....	4	....	4
Sergeants.........................	....	16	....	16
Corporals.........................	....	20	....	48
Lance-corporals...................	....	20	....	72
Privates..........................	....	280	....	720
Pay-sergeants.....................	....	4	....	4
Drummers..........................	....	4	....	8
Buglers...........................	....	4	....	16
Pioneers..........................	....	....	....	12
Hospital attendants...............	....	....	....	16
Officers' servants................	....	12	....	16
Total.........................	14	372	18	904
Total officers and men............	386		950	

The field, staff, and non-commissioned staff, appropriate to the three battalions which constitute the field-regiment, are as follows:

FIELD REGIMENT.	PEACE-FOOTING.		WAR-FOOTING.	
	Officers.	Men.	Officers.	Men.
Colonel....................................	1	....	1	....
Regimental adjutant.....................	1	....	1	....
Commissary...............................	1	....	1	....
Regimental surgeon.....................	1	....	1	....
Senior surgeons.........................	2	....	2	....
Assistant-surgeons.....................	2	....	3	....
Paymaster (captain)...................	1	....	1	....
Paymaster (lieutenant)................	1	....	....	....
Clerk......................................	....	1	....	1
Sergeant-major...........................	....	1	....	1
Drum-major................................	....	1	....	1
Corporals..................................	....	4	....	4
Lance-corporals..........................	....	5	....	5
Privates...................................	....	36	....	36
Armorers..................................	....	2	....	3
Staff-sergeants..........................	....	2	....	....
Drivers (wagoners)....................	....	....	....	32
Hospital-attendants...................	....	....	....	6
Officers' servants.....................	....	9	....	10
Total.................................	10	61	10	99
Total of three battalions............	42	1,116	54	2,802
Total of field regiment..............	52	1,177	64	2,901

(Corporals, Lance-corporals, Privates marked as "Band.")

The strength of each of the fourth, fifth, and depot battalions on the peace and war footing, is as follows:

RESERVE REGIMENT.	FOURTH AND FIFTH BATTALIONS.				DEPOT BATTALION.			
	PEACE-FOOTING.		WAR-FOOTING.		CADRE, PEACE-FOOTING.		FIVE COMPANIES, WAR-FOOTING.	
	Officers.	Men.	Officers.	Men.	Officers.	Men.	Officers.	Men.
Battalion commander....	1	....	1	....	....	....	1	....
" adjutant........	1	....	1	....	....	....	1	....
District recruiting officer.	....	....	....	....	1	....	....	....
Paymaster................	....	....	....	....	1	....	?	....
Surgeon..................	....	....	....	....	1	....	1	....
Clerks...................	....	....	....	....	....	3	....	3
Drummers................	....	1	....	1	....	....	....	....
Buglers..................	....	....	....	1	....	....	....	....
Armorers................	....	....	....	1	....	1	....	1
Staff-sergeants.........	....	....	....	1	....	....	....	1
Officers' servants.....	....	2	....	2	....	3	....	5

INFANTRY.

RESERVE REGIMENT.	FOURTH AND FIFTH BATTALIONS.				DEPOT BATTALION.			
	PEACE-FOOTING.		WAR-FOOTING.		PEACE-FOOTING.		WAR-FOOTING.	
	Officers.	Men.	Officers.	Men.	Officers.	Men.	Officers.	Men.
FOUR COMPANIES.								
Captains...............	4	....	4	....	1	....	5	....
Lieutenants............	8	....	12	....	2	....	15	....
Cadets.................	....	4	....	4	....	....	....	5
First-sergeants........	....	4	....	4	....	5	....	20
Sergeants..............	....	16	....	16	....	....	....	60
Corporals..............	....	20	....	64	....	....	....	90
Lance-corporals........	....	20	....	72	....	....	....	90
Privates...............	....	200	....	720	....	....	....	900[1]
Pay-sergeants..........	....	4	....	4	....	5	....	5
Drummers...............	....	4	....	8	....	....	....	10
Buglers................	....	4	....	8	....	....	....	10
Pioneers...............	....	....	....	16	....	....	....	....
Hospital attendants....	....	....	....	12	....	5	....	....
Officers' servants.....	....	12	....	16	....	....	....	20
Total.................	14	287	19	984	6	15	25	1,180

The field, staff, and non-commissioned staff appropriate to the fourth, fifth, and sixth (or depot) battalions, which constitute the reserve regiment, are as follows:

RESERVE REGIMENT.	PEACE-FOOTING.		WAR-FOOTING.	
	Officers.	Men.	Officers.	Men.
Commandant, colonel, or lieutenant-colonel.........	1	....	1	....
Regimental adjutant..............................	....	....	1	....
Commissary.......................................	....	....	1	....
Surgeon..	1	....	2	....
Assistant-surgeons...............................	1	....	2	....
Paymaster (lieutenant)...........................	....	....	1	....
Clerks...	....	....	....	1
Staff-sergeants..................................	....	1	....	2
Drivers (wagoners)...............................	....	....	....	21
Hospital attendants..............................	....	....	....	4
Officers' servants...............................	....	8	....	8
Total of 4th and 5th battalions..................	28	574	86	1,904
Total depot.....................................	6	15	25	1,180
Total reserve regiment...........................	37	598	90	3,084
Total infantry regiment (5 battalions and depot)..	69	1,940	....	....
Same (6 battalions and depot)....................	....	....	155	5,985

In the reserve regiment, in time of peace, the battalion-adjutant, and commissariat officer, are detailed from the subalterns of the regiment.

The total number of non-combatant enlisted men in each

---

[1] Number of privates in the depot company can be increased from 190 to 300, giving a total of 1,250 enlisted men in the five companies.

battalion, on a war-footing, is 70. The total number in the entire regiment, including both field and reserve regiments, and depot, is 540, nearly equal to one-twelfth of the entire strength.

The number of colonels and lieutenant-colonels in the Austrian infantry exceeds 120 in each grade, enabling not only each of the 80 regiments to be commanded by a colonel, but also one-half of the reserve regiments. The lieutenant-colonels command either reserve regiments or battalions; the remaining battalions are commanded by majors. The commander of the depot cadre is a captain.

The organization of the rifle battalions and companies varies but slightly from the infantry.

BRIGADE OF INFANTRY.

The brigade of infantry in the field consists of the brigade staff, and two regiments of three battalions each, numbering approximately 6,100 officers and men.

DIVISION OF INFANTRY.

This is the highest tactical unit maintained in time of peace, and consists of the division staff, 2 brigades of infantry (12 battalions), 2 battalions of rifles, 2 to 4 squadrons of cavalry, 3 batteries of artillery, 1 company of engineers, 1 squadron of the military train, 1 division of ammunition-train, and 1 division of sanitary troops (ambulance corps), numbering in all between 15,000 and 16,000 men.

ARMY CORPS.

The army corps consists of the corps staff, 3 divisions of infantry, 1 cavalry brigade or division, 3 to 6 batteries of reserve artillery, 1 company of pioneers, 2 sections of bridge-train, supply and sanitary departments, numbering approximately 50,000 officers and men.

RECRUITMENT OF THE ARMY.

All men are liable to military duty between the ages of twenty and thirty-six.

The period of military service is fixed at twelve years; three with the colors, seven in the reserve, and two in the Landwehr.

The country is divided into 31 divisional, 73 brigade, and 81 district commands, one regiment of infantry being located in each district. The commander of each reserve regiment is the commander of the recruiting district. The depot cadre remains always at the headquarters of the district, and is responsible for all of the records relating to men in reserve and on furlough.

Efficient non-commissioned officers, on the expiration of their service with the colors, are usually assigned to the depot cadre, which, in war, is responsible for the equipment and training of the reserve.

In time of war, four of the five companies comprising the depot cadre may be organized into a sixth battalion, which constitutes the third battalion of the reserve regiment.

The annual contingent drafted into the active army is approximately 95,000 men. The strength of the active army on the peace-footing being 257,000, if it be assumed that one-third of that number, 85,000, go annually into reserve, the seven classes in reserve would number 595,000 or 100,000 more than would be required to raise the army to the war standard of 753,000.

The men of the annual contingent assigned to each regiment are distributed among the five battalions, where they receive all of their training. In order that the men in reserve shall not forget their instruction, they are called out for drill three times during the seven years, for a period usually not exceeding four weeks. If practicable, they join the company and battalion to which they would return in time of war, otherwise they are drilled in the battalions of the reserve regiments.

ERSATZ RESERVE.

The ersatz reserve, in time of war, is intended to fill such vacancies in the regular army as cannot be filled by the general reserve. Its strength is limited to 95,000, or the equivalent of one annual contingent. It is composed of men between the ages of twenty and thirty, arranged in ten classes. The men of each class, usually numbering 9,500, are the men of the annual contingent in excess of the actual number required to raise the army to the peace-footing.

LANDWEHR.

This force consists mostly of men who have completed ten years' service in the active army and in reserve; ten years' service in the ersatz reserve; and such men as, escaping the annual contingent, are at once assigned to it for the twelve years during which they are liable to military service. The organization is by battalions, which in peace exist only in cadre. Each battalion is assigned to a special district, which is subdivided into company districts.

The battalion cadre, which is maintained on full pay in Austria proper, consists of—

 1 Major or Captain, commandant,
 1 Regimental officer who keeps the rolls, returns, etc.,
 3 Officers as instructors,
 1 Cadet,
 1 First-sergeant,
 2 Sergeants,
 4 Corporals,
 4 Lance-corporals,
 12 Privates (drill-instructors),
 2 Armorers,
 2 Musicians.

The cadre in Hungary consists of—

 1 Field-officer as commandant,
 1 Administrative officer,
 1 Surgeon,
 1 Armorer,
 4 First-sergeants, one to each company,
 11 Non-commissioned officers and men.

All rolls and records relative to the Landwehr in each battalion district are kept at the battalion or depot headquarters.

The first-sergeants reside within their respective company

districts, and constitute the medium of communication between the battalion commander and the men.

The non-commissioned officers of the Landwehr are men promoted from the ranks of the Landwehr, or non-commissioned officers transferred from the regular army at the expiration of their service.

The officers of the Landwehr are composed of officers transferred from the regular army; of officers in reserve who have completed their service in the army; and of officers promoted within the Landwehr after passing a qualifying examination.

The list of the officers of each Landwehr battalion is revised twice a year at the war-office at Vienna.

The men of the Landwehr are required to attend one muster a year. The recruits who annually join receive eight weeks' training at the battalion headquarters, before being sent on furlough.

There is also a company drill of a fortnight each year after the harvest, and every two years there is battalion instruction for three weeks, during which time the battalions must take part in the army manœuvres. Several of these battalions were present at the manœuvres of 1870, and gave evidence of the practical instruction they had received. In time of war, the Landwehr, exclusive of the cadres left in depot, would number 193 battalions of 4 companies each, organized as in the active army.

REGIMENTAL SCHOOLS.

Captains of companies, batteries, and squadrons, are responsible for the theoretical and practical instruction of their men. The instruction begins with the school of the soldier, to which the months of October and November are devoted. The alphabetical and theoretical schools begin the 1st of December, and terminate the 30th of June. Within the same period is carried on practical military instruction in all of the duties of a soldier, embracing garrison duty, and drill in skirmishing, and school of the company. The months of July, August, and September, are devoted to the schools of the battalion and evolutions of the regiment and larger bodies of troops.

The alphabetical school for the men who cannot read and write, and the schools for non-commissioned officers, are substantially the same as in the army of Italy.

SCHOOLS FOR ONE-YEAR VOLUNTEERS.

The one-year volunteers are composed of young men of education who desire to engage in professional and business pursuits, who, in consideration of volunteering, are permitted to serve but one year with the colors, and are then sent into reserve. They perform during this year all of the duties of a soldier, and in each regiment attend a special school where they pursue a course of study, embracing—

Military correspondence and reports,
Military topography and surveying,
Pioneer service,
Fortification,
Study of arms,
Tactics and field-service,
Military administration,
Army organization,
Army regulations.

According to the examination they pass in the theoretical course and the practical duties of the year, they are appointed lieutenants or non-commissioned officers of reserve.

Of the former there are now nearly three thousand available as officers in the regular army, or Landwehr, according to the necessities of the Government.

DIVISIONAL PREPARATORY SCHOOLS.

The object of these schools is to enable meritorious non-commissioned officers and privates to prepare for admission to the cadet schools. Boys above fourteen years of age who can pass a prescribed examination are also admitted with the same object.

One of these schools is established in each of the 31 divisions, and is superintended by a field-officer, who is assisted by two or three subalterns as instructors.

The admissions to the school are at the rate of 8 candidates from each field regiment, 4 from each reserve regiment, 4 from every rifle battalion, and 6 from each cavalry regiment. Candidates from each regiment are selected on the principle of competition.

The course of study is two years, and embraces—
    Writing,
    German language,
    Some other language or dialect of the empire,
    Military correspondence,
    Mathematics,
    Geography,
    History,
    Theory of ground and military plan drawing,
    Penmanship,
    Pioneer-service,
    Theory of arms,
    Field-service,
    Tactics,
    Army regulations.

The practical exercises consist of drill, target-practice, fencing, gymnastics, and surveying.

CADET SCHOOLS.

The object of these schools is to prepare meritorious non-commissioned officers and soldiers for the rank of cadet, from which grade they are eligible for appointment as lieutenants.

There are 13 schools of infantry, 6 of which are open to candidates from the cavalry. The artillery, engineers, and pioneers, have each a separate school.

Admission is open to such non-commissioned officers, soldiers, and students, as have passed through the divisional schools, or who can pass a prescribed entrance examination.

Each school is superintended by a field-officer, who is assisted by two subalterns as instructors.

The course of study is two years, and embraces—
    Algebra,
    Geometry,

Trigonometry,
Geography,
History,
Natural and experimental philosophy,
Military topography and surveying,
Theory of ground,
Military organization and administration,
Military correspondence and reports,
Tactics of all arms,
Military history,
Field and permanent fortification,
Theory of arms,
Regulations for field-service and outpost-duty,
Army regulations.

The practical exercises consist of drill, riding (in the schools to which cavalry candidates are admitted), distance-drills, target-practice, fencing, gymnastics, and swimming.

OFFICERS' SCHOOLS.

As in Italy and Russia, the system of education for officers embraces preparatory schools, academies from which cadets graduate as officers, and post-graduate schools to which officers are admitted after a service of two or three years in the army.

MILITARY COLLEGE, ST. POLTEN.

The object of this school is to prepare candidates to enter the Military Academy at Wiener-Neustadt.

The commandant of the school is a field-officer, who is assisted by a corps of professors and instructors, composed mostly of regimental officers; a total personnel, commissioned and non-commissioned, numbering 84. The number of students is limited to 200.

The course of study, which is two years, corresponds to the course pursued by the fifth and sixth classes in the upper gymnasia or classical schools, and the *real* gymnasia or mixed classical and technical schools.

The subjects taught are:

Religion,
Arithmetic,
Geography,
Grammar,
Writing,
Algebra,
Geometry,

History,
German,
French,
Latin,
Natural history,
Drawing.

The practical instruction consists of drill, gymnastics, fencing, dancing, and swimming.

MILITARY TECHNICAL SCHOOL.

The object of this school, which is located at Weiszkirchen, is to prepare candidates to enter the Military Technical Academy, also the artillery cadet school.

The entrance examination corresponds to the last year's course in a lower gymnasium or middle classical school.

The commandant of the school is a field-officer of artillery, who is assisted by a corps of military and civil professors, the total personnel numbering 172.

The course of study is three years, and embraces—

Religion,
Geography,
Algebra,
Geometry,
Trigonometry,
Surveying,
Analytical geometry,
Philosophy,
Chemistry,
History,
Natural history,
German,
French,
Bohemian or Hungarian languages,
Army regulations,
Military correspondence,
Artillery tactics,

Science of artillery,
Writing and stenography,
Drawing,
Veterinary instruction.

The practical subjects are fencing, gymnastics, and swimming.

On graduation, the students are classified according to merit as "excellent," "good," and "satisfactory." As many of the first class as there are vacancies for are transferred according to rank to the Military Technical Academy. The remainder of the class and all those marked "good" are transferred as non-commissioned officers of artillery, and, after a year's service, are eligible for appointment to the artillery cadet school. Those classified "satisfactory" are appointed gunners.

MILITARY ACADEMY.

The object of this academy, which is located at Wiener-Neustadt, is to educate officers for the infantry, rifles, cavalry, and pioneers.

Admission to the college is open to graduates from the military college at St. Polten, and such candidates as can pass an examination corresponding to the course of study of the sixth class at an upper gymnasium, with the addition of mathematics, to include progression and equations of the second degree.

The number of students is limited to 400, but only 300 were present in 1876.

The expenses of education are partly borne by the state and partly by the student, who pays $100 (500 francs) for each of the first three years, and $120 for the fourth. A certain number of students, usually sons of officers, are educated free, others are charged half tuition.

The commandant of the academy is a major-general. The corps of military professors and instructors consists of 6 field-officers, 34 captains and lieutenants, the total personnel, commissioned and non-commissioned, numbering 273. The professors of languages, political economy, chemistry, and the instructors of religion, are civilians.

The students are organized into four companies, each of

which is commanded by a captain of the army, who is responsible for the administration, while another officer is assigned as the military instructor. Students are given no military rank in the companies, but at drill officiate temporarily as officers and non-commissioned officers. Each class is divided into two sections, of about forty students each, which have their separate class-rooms and dormitories. Each two classes have a separate dining-room.

The course of study is four years, and embraces—
    Religion,
    German poetry and literature,
    Latin,
    French,
    Bohemian (or Hungarian) languages,
    Political and physical geography,
    General history,
    Philosophy,
    Higher mathematics,
    Practical geometry,
    Analytical geometry,
    Spherical astronomy and geodesy,
    Physics and chemistry,
    Mechanics,
    Military and topographical drawing,
    Reconnaissance and study of ground,
    Political economy,
    Austrian Constitution,
    Military and international law,
    Organization of European armies,
    Military administration of Austrian army,
    Military correspondence and reports,
    History of the art of war,
    Tactics and elements of strategy,
    Infantry tactics,
    Cavalry tactics,
    Theory and construction of arms,
    Pioneer service,

>   Field and permanent fortification, including attack and defense of fortresses,
>   Free-hand drawing,
>   Hippology.

The practical exercises embrace riding, fencing, gymnastics, dancing, and swimming.

MILITARY TECHNICAL ACADEMY, VIENNA.

This academy educates officers for the artillery and engineers. Admission is open to graduates from the military technical school, and to candidates who can pass an examination corresponding to the highest class in the *real* or upper technical school. The number of students is limited to 280.

The commandant is a major-general. The corps of military professors embraces 5 field-officers and 36 captains and lieutenants; the total personnel numbering 237. Civil professors are also employed in various departments.

The course of study is four years. The subjects for the first two years, which are common both to the artillery and engineers, are—

>   German, rhetoric, and poetry,
>   French,
>   Geography,
>   History,
>   Higher mathematics,
>   Practical geometry,
>   Analytical geometry,
>   Chemistry,
>   Natural and experimental philosophy,
>   Technical and analytical mechanics,
>   Engineering,
>   International law,
>   Military law,
>   Military correspondence and reports,
>   Army organization,
>   Pioneer-service,
>   Field-service and tactics,

Army regulations,
Topographical drawing and study of ground.

The special course for artillery in the third and fourth years is—
Mechanical technology,
General architecture,
Science of artillery,
Fortification,
Attack of fortresses,
Hippology.

The course for engineering is—
Spherical astronomy and geodesy,
Civil engineering,
Architectural and ornamental drawing,
History of architecture,
Science of arms,
Fortification and mining.

The practical exercises embrace riding, fencing, gymnastics, swimming, dancing, infantry and artillery drill, target-practice, surveying with the plane table, mapping, sketching, and the construction of batteries and field-works.

SCHOOLS OF APPLICATION.

The artillery and engineers have each an advanced course corresponding to the schools of applications in other countries.

Candidates must be below the rank of captain, and must have served two years in the army.

Admission to these courses, which is not limited to officers of artillery and engineers, is by competitive examination in the following subjects:
French,
Higher mathematics,
Geometry,
Mechanics,
Military correspondence,
Topographical drawing and study of ground,

Science of arms,
Fortification,
General architecture.

The last subject is only required for admission to the engineer course.

The subjects taught in the advanced artillery course are—
Technical mechanics and machinery,
Science of artillery,
Equipment of field, garrison, and siege artillery,
Technology with reference to the science of artillery,
Attack and defense of fortresses,
Artillery tactics,
Reconnaissance and sketching,
Strategy,

As voluntary subjects officers are permitted to study—
French,
English,
Political economy,
Statistics.

The advanced engineer course consists of—

Fortification, combined with attack and defense of fortified places,
Science of artillery in reference to fortification,
Technical mechanics and machinery,
Ornamental architecture,
Technology in reference to science of engineering.
Principles of building, railway-engineering, and road-making.

As a reward for a successful prosecution of this course, lieutenants of artillery and engineers who receive the certificate "excellent" are at once promoted to first-lieutenant. Officers of other arms who receive the same certificate, or the certificate of "good," are qualified for promotion out of turn.

The advantages of the advanced course in both artillery and engineering are given to extra students who are willing to pay their own expenses.

WAR SCHOOL.

The object of this school is to qualify officers for high command, and also for employment in the staff.

The chief of the general staff is the president of the school, and is assisted by a general officer or colonel as commandant.

The professors are part military and part civil, the former being officers of the general staff.

The number of students admitted annually is approximately 40. Candidates for admission must be lieutenants or captains who have served three years in the army, and have been favorably reported upon as regards character, zeal, and ability, by the commanding officers of their regiments.

Admission is by competition in the following subjects:

Mathematics, to include spherical trigonometry and conic sections,
Practical geometry,
Mechanics, physics, and chemistry,
Geography,
History,
German literature,
French,
Field-service,
Tactics of all arms,
Pioneer-service,
Theory of arms,
Fortification,
Army organization,
Theory of ground and topographical drawing.

Without passing the competitive examination, permission is granted to officers to attend the lectures as extra students. They are classified at the final examination, but cannot claim admission to the staff corps.

The course of study is two years, and embraces the following subjects:

Army organization,
Tactics of the three arms,

Strategy as illustrated by campaigns,
Military geography,
Theory of ground, topography, and military surveying,
Military reconnaissances and reports,
Duties of general staff in the field,
Study of arms,
Fortification,
International law,
Natural sciences,
Political economy,
German literature,
History of civilization (voluntary),
French,
Riding.

Instruction has heretofore been imparted by lecture, but in 1876 it was intended to experiment with text-books and recitations.

The studies are pursued between October 15th and June 30th. The months of July, August, and September, are devoted to surveying, sketching, reconnaissances, and military tours to different parts of the empire.

The final examination is open to not only the regular and extra students, but to any officer not above the rank of captain who thinks he can pass successfully.

All who pass are classified as "excellent," "very good," "good," and "unsatisfactory."

Only those who are classified as "excellent" or "very good," and who have shown aptitude for staff duty, are eligible for staff employment.

Officers who can pass the examination direct are required to take a course of reconnaissance with the class of the following year before being detailed for staff duty.

CENTRAL INFANTRY SCHOOL.

This school, located at Vienna, is intended to prepare captains for promotion to the grade of field-officer. There is no entrance examination. The number of students is fixed by the

Minister of War. The course is eleven months, beginning November 1st, and embraces—

 Army organization,
 Tactics of the three arms,
 Principles of strategy illustrated by campaigns,
 Study of arms,
 Theory of ground and reports of positions,
 Military surveying and sketching,
 Pioneer-service,
 Fortification,
 Field telegraphy,
 Hippology,
 Riding,
 Natural sciences (voluntary),
 Fencing (voluntary).

The final examination in these subjects must be passed, either direct or after completing the course, by all captains who aspire to promotion to the rank of major, unless they have previously passed the final examination at the War School or at the advanced artillery and engineer courses.

The officers after examination are classified as "excellent," "very good," "good," and "unsatisfactory."

As a reward for diligence, officers who can pass the theoretical and also a practical test with the certificate of "excellent" are eligible for promotion out of turn. They are also permitted to enter the second year's course at the War School as extra students.

The certificate "good" entitles an officer to promotion by seniority if favorably reported upon by his commanding officer. Officers who fail to pass the examination are overslaughed on arriving at the head of the list.

A corresponding central school is established for the cavalry.

DISCIPLINE.

In the case of offenses beneath the cognizance of courts-martial, summary punishments can be inflicted upon all grades of officers and men.

The punishment for the different grades is as follows:

Officers.—Reprimands, and arrest with confinement to rooms or station for thirty days.

Cadets and Sergeant-Majors.—Reprimands; arrest with confinement to rooms or barracks, up to thirty days; withdrawal of permission to be absent after retreat for thirty days; obligation to return to quarters or camp at a fixed hour before retreat, up to thirty days; reduction to ranks for sergeant-majors in accordance with previous " warning."

Other Non-commissioned Officers and Privates.—Reprimands; obligations to return to barracks or camp at a fixed hour before retreat; withdrawal from sergeants of permission to be absent after retreat, up to thirty days; withdrawal of control of pay, with enforced daily payment for thirty days; daily attendance, up to eight times, in full dress at the " morning report" (with horse in mounted corps), applied only to corporals and privates; extra fatigue duty, up to thirty days; putting in irons for six hours; tying up for two hours, so that the delinquent can neither sit nor lie down, applicable to privates in case of degrading offenses; arrest with confinement to barracks, quarters, or camp; strict arrest, up to thirty days; solitary confinement, up to twenty-one days; confinement in dark cell, up to fifteen days; reduction after a prescribed "warning."

"Warning" is only given by a regimental or corresponding commander, and only in cases of repeated offenses, such as drunkenness, neglect of duty, etc. Power to punish is limited to commanders of units like regiments, battalions, companies.

Strict arrest implies confinement in the guard-room, under lock and key; it also involves bread and water three days in a week, and confinement six hours daily in irons, with an interval every three days of one day.

A regimental commander can inflict all of the punishments enumerated up to the full extent; a battalion commander can reprimand officers and men of all grades, and inflict the same punishments as a company commander; a company commander can inflict upon non-commissioned officers and men all of the punishments enumerated up to their full extent, except reduction, also strict arrest and solitary confinement, which he can only administer to two-thirds of the legal extent; a subaltern in command of a detachment has the same power as a captain, but is required to report all cases of punishment to his company commander; a non-commissioned officer in command of a detachment can inflict confinement to barracks, or camp, and strict arrest for two days, reporting all punishments immediately on the completion of the detached duty to his commanding officer.

General officers, besides the power to inflict punishment on officers of all grades below them, have the same power as colonels to inflict minor punishments on enlisted men.

PROMOTION.

The Austrian law of promotion is based upon the difference in professional attainments and efficiency known to exist between officers in all grades of the army. This difference is due in part to the manner in which officers originally qualify for the army, but more largely to the system of post-graduate education, which enables every intelligent, zealous, and efficient officer to prosecute a course of professional study with a special view to fit himself for promotion and high command.

Promotion in the infantry, cavalry, and artillery, is by arm, the names of all of the field and company officers in each arm being on a general list.

Promotion is both by seniority or "in turn," and by selection "out of turn."

To the grade of captain, inclusive, five-sixths are promoted by seniority, the other sixth by selection; to all of the grades of field-officers three-fourths are promoted by seniority, the other fourth by selection.

The first condition of promotion both by seniority and selection is the possession by the officer of a "certificate of qualification," embracing his entire history since his entrance to the army. The qualification list of each officer is drawn up at regimental headquarters, and is made out in duplicate—one copy being retained, the other forwarded to the Minister of War.

The qualifications of each officer are determined by a board of officers of the grade next above, the board being presided over by a superior officer. Subalterns are reported upon by captains and field-officers; captains by field-officers; field-officers by generals of brigades and divisions. The qualification-list of each officer is drawn up on six different pages, and is subdivided into headings, each of which is supported by remarks.

The qualification-list is prepared as follows:

First Page.

HEADINGS. REMARKS.

1. Regiment.
2. Name.
3. Rank and seniority.
4. Date of birth.
5. Religion.
6. Condition and education prior to admission to service. — The employment previous to entering the service is here stated, with mention of certificate obtained at any civil or military school the officer may have attended.
7. Date of entrance to the army, and mode of entrance.
8. Civil or military educational establishments, from which the officer may have graduated since entering the army. — Remarks show the result—i. e., the certificate—he may have procured as "excellent," "very good," or "unsatisfactory."
9. Private circumstances. — Whether married or single; also financial condition.
10. Decorations. — Naming all orders, medals, etc., received.

Second Page.

HEADINGS. — **REMARKS.**

1. Dates of promotion and transfer. — If promoted for distinguished conduct in battle, the fact is to be specially stated.

2. Total period of service.

Third Page.

1. Official employment. — The remarks show every position the officer has ever held, and the duties he has performed.

Fourth Page.

1. Campaigns and service in the field. — Remarks state all of the campaigns, actions, and battles participated in, wounds received, and rewards bestowed.

Fifth Page.

1. Other special services. — Showing service not connected with war, rewards received, etc.

Sixth Page.

1. Date. — Year to which report refers.
2. Rank. — Held at date of report.
3. Linguistic acquirements. — State all of the languages and dialects in the empire spoken or written by the officer with fluency.

HEADINGS.	REMARKS.
4. General adaptation and fitness for position he holds.	Remarks enter into detail as to fitness or unfitness, manner in which he performs duties, points in which he excels or in which he is deficient, positions he is specially qualified to hold, as "adjutant," "quartermaster," "instructor," "duty at depots," etc.
5. Qualification for duties outside of the sphere of present employment.	Remarks show officer's talents and inclinations; also whether he has performed the duties referred to.
6. Zeal.	Showing whether officer is devoted to his profession, and whether zeal is attributable to love of profession, or other motives.
7. Conduct:	Showing personal qualities, moral tone.
Before the enemy.	Personal bravery, presence of mind, endurance, determination, quickness to perceive advantages, etc.
On duty.	Toward superior officers, toward subordinates; manner, whether severe, kind, or engaging; ideas of discipline; readiness to assume responsibility; ability to maintain discipline; influence over officers and men, and whether or not he possesses confidence of officers and men.

HEADINGS.	REMARKS.
Socially.	Character and standing among his comrades; company he keeps.
8. Health and fitness for service.	Physique, ability to perform various duties, eyesight, sick-leaves, etc.
9. General remarks.	Such as may be necessary to be stated, but have not been referred to under previous headings.
10. Qualifications for promotion.	The remarks state whether the officer is "qualified," "not qualified," or "not as yet qualified."
11. General observations of the reporting-officers.	Each member of the board, beginning with the junior, here records his remarks or opinions.

When the report is received by the Minister of War, any remark reflecting on conduct or zeal is communicated to the officer, but remarks as to want of ability are not transmitted.

A special recommendation in favor of these reports is that while they enable the Government to know who are the efficient officers, every officer has the right, upon application, to look at his record, and thus, if reported against, be able to redeem himself by future good conduct.

As a condition precedent to the promotion of a cadet, the consent of the officers of the regiment must be procured as to his social worth and character. His military qualifications are determined by a period of probation as a cadet.

Promotion by seniority to the grades of first-lieutenant and captain depends upon the certificate of qualification, and upon a theoretical qualification which is satisfied by the possession of a certificate of the academy, college, or cadet school, through which the officer has passed. Promotion by seniority to the grade of major in the infantry and cavalry depends upon the certificate of qualification, and a certificate that the officer has passed the final examination at the central course of instruction with the classification of "good." If he fails to pass this examination, either direct or after pursuing the regular course at the school, he is passed over in promotion on arriving at the head of the list.

The certificate "good" obtained at the War School, or at the advanced course of artillery and engineers, exempts captains of all arms from further theoretical examination.

Promotion by seniority to the grades of lieutenant-colonel, colonel, and major-general, is based upon the qualification-list and practical qualifications as attested by the officer's success in command. The practical test for promotion to major-general is ability to handle a brigade composed of the three arms.

Promotion by selection is based entirely upon efficiency, and a superior degree of military education.

The certificate of "excellent" at a cadet school entitles a cadet to promotion out of turn, provided his military qualifications are satisfactory.

Lieutenants and sub-lieutenants are entitled to promotion out of turn provided they have obtained the certificate "very good" at either the War School, or at the advanced artillery and engineer course, and the certificate of qualification be satisfactory. The certificate "excellent" entitles a lieutenant to immediate promotion.

For promotion to the grades of major and lieutenant-colonel, the one-fourth of the vacancies given to selection is divided into two categories—one-third being assigned to the first category, the remaining two-thirds to the second category.

To entitle an officer to promotion in the first category, his certificate of qualification must be satisfactory; he must possess the certificate "excellent" at the central cavalry or infantry school, or the certificate "very good" at the War School, or advanced course of artillery and engineers; he must also receive the certificate "excellent" at a practical test, consisting of handling a mixed force of all arms, such as might be assigned to a field-officer holding a detached command.

To be entitled to promotion in the second category, an officer—in addition to the qualifications required in the first category—must pass, before a board of officers appointed by the Minister of War, a searching and extended examination in strategy, technical duties of the general staff in war, tactics, fortification, artillery, army organization, and military administration. A further practical test, before a board of officers, is required, consisting of handling a brigade composed of three battalions of infantry, three squadrons of cavalry, and a half-battery of artillery.

Promotion to the grade of colonel is by both seniority and selection; to major-general by seniority, and to all grades above by selection.

In all cases of promotion by selection, the officers of the same grade who possess the required qualifications for promotion to the grade next above are arranged on a special list according to seniority, and not according to their classification in the examination-lists at the schools from which they may have graduated.

In war any officer may be promoted by selection for distinguished conduct, and he may be further rewarded by the presentation of a medal.

DETAIL IN THE AUSTRIAN ARMY.

The entire general staff of the Austrian army, numbering 2 generals, 16 colonels, 21 lieutenant-colonels, 43 majors, 121 captains, 118 first-lieutenants, and 26 auxiliary officers, instead of constituting a corps by itself, is composed of officers of all arms of service, who are in excess of the regimental complements. The officers are promoted in their respective arms, and in the staff take rank according to seniority. The conditions for admission to the different grades of the staff are as follows:

A first-lieutenant must be above twenty-five years of age; must have served three years with his regiment; and must also have graduated at the War School, or taken the advanced course of artillery and engineers with the certificate of "excellent;" or else have passed the examination for promotion by selection. Previous to appointment their fitness is tested by the performance of staff duty at brigade and division headquarters, and they may also be required to serve a year on probation in the military geographical institute.

Captains as a rule are selected from those who have previously served as lieutenants on the staff, or from those who have qualified for promotion by selection in the second category. If there still be vacancies, captains may be selected who have qualified for promotion in the first category.

Majors are selected from those who have previously served as captains on the staff, or who have qualified for promotion by selection in the second category.

Lieutenant-colonels and colonels are selected from the best-qualified field-officers who have previously served on the staff.

In order that officers of the staff shall not forget the habit of command, captains are required while holding that grade to command for two years a company, battery, or squadron; and colonels are similarly required to command a regiment for at least three years.

The constitution of the Austrian general staff shows that, while composed of officers of all arms, there is a constant interchange between the staff and line. The lieutenant who, by the nature of his appointment, is qualified for promotion by selection, as soon as promoted returns to his arm, where he must remain unless summoned back as a captain.

In the same manner captains, majors, and lieutenant-colonels, leave the staff by promotion, and cannot return to it unless appointed anew.

In this manner indifferent officers can be removed without loss of pride, and good officers can be selected to fill their places.

The effect of the staff arrangement, and promotion by selection, is to enable intelligent and efficient officers to obtain while young the highest grades in the army, in which, at any moment, they may be called upon to influence the destiny of the nation.

ARMY OF GERMANY.

The troops of the German Empire are divided into three classes, as follows:

1. Field-troops intended to form the armies in the field.
2. Depot-troops composed of recruits from the reserve, and Landwehr, destined to fill vacancies in the field-troops.
3. Garrison-troops embracing the Landwehr, foot-artillery regiments, reserve cavalry regiments, reserve pioneers, and rifle-companies, intended to garrison the populous cities, and, in case of necessity, to reënforce the army in the field.

The following tables represent the armed strength of the empire.

Peace-footing.

TROOPS.	Regiments.	Battalions.	Squadrons.	Batteries.	Guns.	Officers.	Men.
Staff officers	....	....	....	....	......	2,189	2
Infantry	148	443	....	....	......	8,608	255,411
Riflemen	....	26	....	....	......	582	14,545
Landwehr cadre	....	293	....	....	......	305	4,760
Total infantry	148	762	....	....	......	9,490	274,716
Cavalry	96	....	465	....	......	2,857	64,668
Field-artillery	36	....	....	300	1,216	1,629	30,720
Garrison-artillery	....	29	....	....	......	682	15,156
Total artillery	....	29	....	300	1,216	2,311	45,876
Pioneers	....	20	....	....	......	400	10,874
Train	....	18	....	....	......	213	5,050
Railway battalion	....	....	....	....	......	51	1,988
Surgeons	....	....	....	....	......	1,481	......
Paymasters	....	....	....	....	......	709	......
Veterinary-surgeons	....	....	....	....	......	......	621
Armorers	....	....	....	....	......	......	624
Saddlers	....	....	....	....	......	......	98
Total	277	850	465	300	1,216	19,800	402,999

192 ARMY OF GERMANY.

Of the enlisted men, 48,280, exclusive of lance-corporals, are non-commissioned officers; 12,493 are musicians; 3,187 are hospital attendants; and 9,446 are tradesmen employed to make shoes, clothing, etc.

War-footing.

FIELD-ARMY.	Regiments.	Battalions.	Companies.	Squadrons.	Batteries.	Guns.	Officers.	Men.
Staff officers............	....	....	....	....	....	....	863	5,170
Infantry.................	148	448	....	....	....	....	10,190	455,620
Riflemen................	....	20	....	....	....	....	572	26,676
Cavalry.................	93	....	....	372	....	....	2,144	59,814
Artillery...............	36	....	....	....	300	1,800	2,286	78,120
Pioneers................	....	....	54	....	....	....	565	20,917
Trains.................	....	....	....	....	....	....	785	38,451
Administrative departments.........	....	....	....	....	....	....	216	2,826
Total field-army...	277	469	54	372	300	1,800	17,021	687,594
DEPOT-TROOPS.								
Staff officers..........	....	....	....	....	....	....	875	1,836
Infantry.................	....	148	....	....	....	....	2,812	179,524
Rifles.................	....	....	26	....	....	....	104	8,008
Cavalry.................	....	....	....	93	....	....	465	23,994
Artillery...............	....	....	....	....	71	426	840	13,261
Pioneers................	....	....	20	....	....	....	90	4,950
Train..................	....	....	87	....	....	....	240	11,522
Total..............	....	148	68	93	71	426	4,426	243,095
GARRISON-TROOPS.								
Various brigade and division headquarters..	....	....	....	....	....	....	850	10,000
Infantry.................	....	293	....	....	....	....	6,424	250,244
Rifles.................	....	....	26	....	....	....	104	6,500
Cavalry.................	....	....	....	144	....	....	823	22,968
		Foot-artillery.			Field-artillery.			
Artillery...............	....	58	....	....	54	324	1,870	54,852
Pioneers................	....	....	49	....	....	....	531	8,588
Total.............	....	351	74	144	54	324	10,107	353,102
Surgeons................	....	....	....	....	....	....	4,853	......
Paymasters..............	....	....	....	....	....	....	1,672	......
Veterinary surgeons...	....	....	....	....	....	....	....	838
Armorers................	....	....	....	....	....	....	....	1,057
Saddlers................	....	....	....	....	....	....	....	711
Employés...............	....	....	....	....	....	....	....	16,032
Grand total.......	277	968	211	609	425	2,550	38,479	1,302,429

INFANTRY.

The infantry of the German Empire consists, in time of peace, of 148 regiments of three battalions each, except one, which has but two battalions.

INFANTRY.

The organization of a company on the peace and war footing is as follows:

RANK.	PEACE-FOOTING.		WAR-FOOTING.	
	Officers.	Men.	Officers.	Men.
Captain...	1	....	1	....
First-lieutenant.................................	1	....	1	....
Second-lieutenant...............................	2	....	2	....
Sergeant-major..................................	....	1	....	1
Fähnrich..	....	1	....	1
Vice-sergeant-major.............................	....	1	....	1
Sergeants.......................................	....	4	....	4
Corporals.......................................	....	7	....	13
Lance-corporals.................................	....	13	....	24
Drummers.......................................	....	2	....	2
Buglers...	....	2	....	2
Privates..	....	106	....	201
Total combatants............................	4	137	5	249
Hospital-attendants.............................	....	1	....	1
Tradesmen......................................	....	3	....	....
Train-soldiers..................................	....	....	....	2
Total non-combatants........................	....	4	....	3
Total officers and men......................	145		257	

The strength of a battalion is as follows:

RANK.	PEACE-FOOTING.		WAR-FOOTING.	
	Officers.	Men.	Officers.	Men.
Battalion commander.............................	1	....	1	....
Adjutant.......................................	1	....	1	....
Non-commissioned officers......................	..	2	..	1
Drum-major.....................................	..	1	..	1
Staff-surgeon...................................	..	....	1	....
Assistant-surgeon...............................	..	....	1	....
Paymaster......................................	1	....	1	....
Paymaster-assistant.............................	1	....	1	....
Armorer..	..	1	..	1
Hospital attendants.............................	..	4	..	4
Tradesmen......................................	..	12	..	....
Train-soldiers..................................	..	....	..	20
FOUR COMPANIES.				
Captains..	4	....	4	....
First-lieutenants................................	4	....	4	....
Second-lieutenants..............................	8	....	12	....
Sergeant-majors.................................	..	4	..	4
Fähnriche......................................	..	4	..	4
Vice-sergeant-majors............................	..	4	..	4
Sergeants.......................................	..	16	..	16
Corporals.......................................	..	28	..	52
Lance-corporals.................................	..	52	..	96
Drummers.......................................	..	8	..	12
Buglers...	..	8	..	12
Privates..	..	425 [1]	..	796
Total..	20	567	26	1,023

[1] One company has 105 privates.

The field, staff, and non-commissioned staff of the regiment are as follows:

RANK.	PEACE-FOOTING.		WAR-FOOTING.	
	Officers.	Men.	Officers.	Men.
Colonel...	1	....	1	....
Lieutenant-colonel...	1	....	1	....
Adjutant...	1	....	1	....
Sergeant-major...	...	1	..	1
Musicians...	...	10	..	10
Senior staff-surgeon...	1	....	1	....
Staff-surgeons...	2	....	..	....
Assistant-surgeons...	3	....	..	....
Train-soldiers...	...	....	..	7
Total...	9	11	4	18
Three battalions...	60	1,701	78	8,069
Total regiment...	69	1,712	82	8,087

BRIGADE OF INFANTRY.

The brigade of infantry in time of peace consists of the staff, 2 regiments of infantry (6 battalions), and 2 regiments of Landwehr. In war it consists of the staff and 2 regiments, or 6 battalions, numbering 6,366.

In addition to the field staff, the brigade in time of war leaves behind a brigade district staff, consisting of a major-general, or colonel, and two officers as assistants. This staff assumes control of all depot and garrison troops of infantry, and is responsible for calling out, training, equipping, and forwarding men to the brigade in the field. The brigade staff communicates with the men to be called out through the headquarters of the Landwehr battalions, and the sergeant-majors of the Landwehr company districts.

DIVISION OF INFANTRY.

A division in time of peace consists of 2 brigades of infantry and 1 brigade of cavalry.

In war it consists of the staff, 2 brigades of infantry, 1 regiment of cavalry (4 squadrons), and 1 division of artillery (4 batteries). There is also attached to the division either 1 battalion of rifles, or 1 company of pioneers.

The staff consists of 1 general, 1 field-officer or captain of the general staff, 2 captains or lieutenants as adjutants, 2 judge-advocates, and 2 chaplains. Total division 14,500.

ARMY CORPS.

An army corps in the field consists of—
I.—The staff, embracing—
    1 General, or lieutenant-general as commander,
    2 Field-officers of the general staff, one of whom is chief of staff,
    2 Captains of the general staff,
    4 Adjutants, captains, or lieutenants,
    3 Engineer officers,
    1 Major-general, or colonel of artillery,
    2 Lieutenants, or adjutants, who constitute the artillery brigade staff,
    1 Field-officer, and 1 lieutenant as adjutant, who constitute the train staff.
II.—Two divisions of infantry—
    In all, 25 battalions, 8 squadrons, 48 guns, and 1 company of pioneers; numbering 29,000.
III.—One division of cavalry (16 squadrons), composed of—
    2 Brigades of 2 regiments each, and
    1 to 2 batteries of artillery;
    Numbering in all, 3,000 men.
IV.—Reserve artillery (42 to 48 guns), composed of—
    2 Divisions of field, and
    1 Division of horse artillery; numbering 1,300 men.
V.—Intendance, commissariat-trains, bridge-trains (1 to each division and 1 for the corps), 3 columns sanitary troops; numbering in all, 2,571 men.

The total of an army corps approximates 41,600 men.

The field-troops of Germany, consisting of 18 corps, in time of war are organized into armies of from 2 to 4 corps each.

MILITARY TERRITORIAL DIVISIONS.

Corresponding to the military organization, the territory of Germany is divided into 17 corps districts, each of which is divided into 2 division and 4 brigade districts. Each brigade district is divided into Landwehr battalion districts, which are further subdivided into Landwehr company districts.

The guard-corps selects its recruits from the entire empire.

Each of the other corps is permanently assigned to a district from which it is exclusively recruited both in time of peace and war.

RECRUITMENT.

The work of recruitment is conducted by two commissions, called the *Ersatz-Commission* and the *Ober-Ersatz-Commission.*

An Ersatz-Commission is appointed for each of the 275 Landwehr districts, and is composed of both military and civil officers, the commander of the Landwehr district being one of the members.

This commission meets in the early part of the year, and before it must appear every man of the district who is liable to military duty. After examining all the men physically, hearing all petitions, and deciding such cases as come up for postponement, the commission prepares a list of all who are qualified for service. Such cases as the Ersatz-Commission cannot dispose of, it refers to the Ober-Ersatz-Commission.

This latter commission is appointed for each brigade district, and is composed of the brigade commander, an administrative officer of high rank, and also a civil officer. The Ober-Ersatz-Commission meets in each Landwehr district, usually in the summer, and before it must appear all the men not put back by the Ersatz-Commission. After another examination and further revision of the cases submitted by the Ersatz-Commission for postponement, a final list is made out by the commission, which then proceeds to drafting, causing each man on the list to cast lots. Those who draw the lowest figures are assigned to the annual contingent, and are turned over by the president of the commission to the Landwehr commanders for distribution to the various arms of service.

The persons exempted from drawing lots are volunteers for one, or three years; volunteers for non-commissioned officers' schools; foresters' apprentices, provided with required certificates; those physically disqualified, and also those morally unworthy, or disqualified through crime.

Postponement of entry to service for one or two years is granted to men who are the sole support of indigent families, or of parents or grandparents unable to work; to only sons of landed proprietors, lessees, and tradesmen, where the son is their indispensable assistant; proprietors or tenants of land upon the cultivation of which their livelihood depends, and in the superintendence of which they cannot be replaced; proprietors of large factories who cannot be replaced in the management of business by others; persons intending to pursue a professional career or learn a trade; those who reside permanently abroad.

In addition to the cases of postponement stated above, the chief Ersatz authorities of any state can postpone, or exempt, from service any person who can present a valid reason, though such reason be not mentioned in the recruiting regulations.

Persons whose entry to service has been postponed, if not called up at the end of the second year, are passed into the Ersatz reserve, whence, in case of war, they are liable to be summoned to fill vacancies in the active army.

The annual contingent for the entire army approximates 140,000 men, and is distributed at the rate of 190 recruits to each regiment of infantry; 36 to each squadron of cavalry; 30 to each battery of artillery; 165 to each battalion of foot or fortress artillery; 160 to each battalion of pioneers; and 175 to each battalion of the train.

The term of service is twelve years, of which three are with the colors, four in the reserve, and five in the Landwehr.

The men of the reserve and Landwehr are arranged in registers, according to annual classes.

RESERVE.

The reserve is composed of four classes of men, who have completed their service of three years with the colors. The total number depends upon the proportion of each annual contingent of 140,000, who complete the three years' service, and may be estimated at above 500,000, of which number about 300,000 would be required to raise the field-army to a war-footing. Such men as are not required to complete the war-footing are available for the organization of garrison-troops.

During the four years a man is in the reserve, he may be summoned back to the ranks twice for the purpose of attending the annual manœuvres for a period not exceeding eight weeks each time. He must also attend muster twice a year—once in the spring and once in the autumn.

In time of war the reserves are called back to the colors by classes, beginning with the youngest.

OFFICERS OF RESERVE.

These officers are provided to fill to the complement the number of officers required to raise each regiment and field organization to the war-footing. They consist of such officers as have left the regular army before the completion of seven years' service; men of the furlough-list who have distinguished themselves before the enemy; fähnrichs who have been discharged with a certificate of qualification as officers of reserve; one-year volunteers with the same certificate; also men of the furlough-list, who, after their discharge, procure a like certificate.

All men of the reserve, who hold the certificate of qualification for officers of reserve, are required to serve eight weeks with a regiment of the line in order to learn their new duties. They must also, before being appointed, be accepted by the officers of the regiment to which they are assigned. On completing the total of seven years with the colors and in reserve, the officers are transferred to the Landwehr to complete the remainder of their twelve years' service. This arrangement enables the Government to confide all of its troops, who may be called to meet the enemy, to the leadership of officers who have been specially educated, and who are familiar with the duties of field-service.

ERSATZ RESERVE.

The Ersatz reserve is intended to supplement the reserve already described, and, in connection with it, to replace casualties in the field-troops. It is composed of two classes, in the first of which a man serves five years, when he is transferred to the second class, where he continues to serve till the end of his thirty-first year.

The number of men in the first class is supposed to be equal to the number required to raise the army from the peace to the war footing. The class is composed of the men who have drawn high numbers at the conscription, also such as have had their entry to service postponed, or whose physical defects do not entitle them to complete exemption from service. The second class is composed of men transferred annually from the first class, and also of those who have not been assigned to the first class in consequence of physical defects, or who were in excess of its requirements.

In case of war, the men of the first class are first summoned to fill vacancies and to compose depot-troops, after which the second class can be called upon for the same service.

FURLOUGH-LIST.

To encourage faithful and intelligent performance of duty, and also in the interest of economy, about 30,000 men, after having served two years with the colors, are sent on furlough, subject to recall, to complete their term of service. If not recalled, they pass into reserve, the same as men who have completed the regular three years.

DEPOT-TROOPS.

In time of war each regiment of infantry, artillery, and cavalry, each rifle, pioneer, and train battalion, organizes a depot for the purpose of clothing, training, arming, equipping, and forwarding recruits to the troops in the field. The depots also supply the troops with the equipments and clothing needed during the campaign.

The depot of each regiment of infantry constitutes a battalion designated the "Depot Battalion (such) Regiment of Infantry."

The battalion is organized as follows:

STAFF.	Officers.	Men.	Officers.	Men.
Field-officer	1	....	....	....
Adjutant	1	....	....	....
Surgeons	2	....	....	....
Paymaster	1	....	....	....
Sergeant-major	..	1	....	....
Drum-major	..	1	....	....
FOUR COMPANIES.			**EACH COMPANY.**	
Officers	16	....	4	....
Non-commissioned officers	..	80	....	20
Lance-corporals	..	96	....	24
Buglers	..	16	....	4
Privates	..	804	....	201
TRADESMEN'S DIVISION.				
Officers	1	....	....	....
Non-commissioned officers	..	10	....	....
Tradesmen	..	200	....	....
Total	22	1,208	4	249

The officers for the depot battalion are taken partly from officers of the regiment, and partly from officers on the half-pay and the retired lists. A portion of the non-commissioned officers are also detailed from the regiment.

When mobilization is ordered, 400 recruits are immediately called to the depot, where their training is begun under the experienced officers and non-commissioned officers appointed to receive them. The recruits consist of men from the reserves, Ersatz reserve, and later the youngest classes of the Landwehr.

As soon as the regiment in the field is reduced one-tenth of its strength by casualties, requisition is made upon the depot for the number of men necessary to fill the vacancies. These men completely armed and equipped are at once forwarded under officers and non-commissioned officers from the depot, who immediately return to it unless required to remain with the regiment.

The depot battalions (numbering 148) never take the field; they may, however, be required to replace garrison or Landwehr troops, ordered into the field or on active service.

When all the depots of the different arms of service are raised to their complement, they number 4,426 officers and 243,095 men.

LANDWEHR.

As already stated, the Landwehr is composed of men who have finished their term of service with the colors and in reserve.

In time of peace it is organized into Landwehr battalion districts, with a cadre usually consisting of a field-officer, an adjutant, and three non-commissioned officers and men.

The rolls of all men in reserve, Ersatz reserve, as also in the Landwehr, are kept at the district headquarters.

A sergeant-major, corresponding to a first-sergeant, resides in each Landwehr company district, and serves as a medium of communication with the men at their homes.

During the five years a man is in the Landwehr, he may be called out twice for company or battalion drill, for a period not exceeding eight to fourteen days at a time.

In time of war each regiment of infantry, in addition to its three field battalions, forms two battalions of Landwehr, to which it assigns a certain quota of officers and non-commissioned officers. The total number of Landwehr battalions is 293. These battalions can at once be raised to the complement of 22 officers and 1,002 men, or if the emergency does not demand the war strength each battalion may be increased to 14 officers and 402 men, called the first augmentation, or to 18 officers and 602 men, called the second augmentation. The battalions being raised to the war strength, may be organized into regiments, brigades, divisions, and corps, and sent to reënforce the army in the field.

OFFICERS OF LANDWEHR.

The officers of the Landwehr consist of officers who have completed their period of service in the regular army and are still able to perform duty; officers transferred from the reserve; men of the Landwehr who have been distinguished in the field; men who have received certificates qualifying them as officers of reserve, but who have never been promoted; also sergeant-majors and non-commissioned officers discharged from the regular army with a recommendation for promotion in the Landwehr.

In all cases, before an officer can be appointed in the Landwehr, he must be accepted by the other officers of the battalion.

In case the casualties in the regular army require it, officers of the Landwehr can be transferred to fill the vacancies.

OBLIGATIONS OF RESERVE SOLDIERS.

All men of the reserve, Landwehr, Ersatz reserve, and furlough-list, on returning to their homes must report in person to the sergeant-major of the company Landwehr district in which they reside.

Men of the reserve, and Landwehr, are permitted to settle in any part of the empire, but in case of a transfer of residence they must report to the sergeant-majors of the districts they leave, and also of the districts to which they remove. These changes must be reported within fourteen days of their occurrence, also any change of residence within the company district must be reported within the same period. Failure to report, which may be done in person, or in writing, is punishable with a fine of $1.50 to $4.00, or imprisonment from three to eight days.

Intention to remove for short periods to distant parts of the empire must be reported to the sergeant-major, and in time of the manœuvres his permission must first be procured. In all cases the address must be left so that orders may be promptly transmitted.

Soldiers who desire to reside abroad, and to enter upon

business pursuits in foreign countries, must first procure a furlough, of two years, which may afterward be prolonged by the corps commander till liability to service expires.

Whether in foreign countries, or in different parts of the empire, it is the duty of all members of the reserve, or Landwehr, when mobilization is ordered, to immediately return to their homes and report to the Landwehr authorities.

LANDSTURM.

This force practically embraces all able-bodied men capable of bearing arms not already in service. It is divided into two classes: the first of which is composed of all men between the ages of eighteen and forty-two who are not in the army, the reserve, or the Landwehr; the second class embraces all above the age of forty-two.

The first class may be organized into 293 battalions on the same basis as the Landwehr, making an aggregate force of 175,000 men. The second class has no organization.

SCHOOLS FOR ENLISTED MEN.

The perfection of the German military system lies less in the military organization than in the exactness with which men of every grade, in every branch of service, are trained for the efficient performance of their duties.

To this end, the same as in all of the other great Continental armies, the chief school for the private soldier is practical service with the colors for a period of three years. It is the graduates of this school who constitute the reserve proper, and who in time of war return to the ranks with the experience of trained soldiers. They also constitute by far the largest proportion of the Landwehr, which can be called out as a second army to reënforce the army in the field. The Government does not satisfy itself with training them simply to obey orders, to be good marksmen, to drill with precision, and adapt themselves with intelligence to a variety of service in the presence of the enemy, but requires of them a general educational training, such as is required in every other walk of life, as the only sure basis of success.

For this purpose there are schools in each battalion, in which are taught reading, writing, spelling, and arithmetic. Candidates for promotion to non-commissioned officers are, in addition, taught to make such reports and returns as may be required of non-commissioned officers. In reference to the training of this grade the Government shows special solicitude. The largest proportion of non-commissioned officers is composed of men who have completed three years' service with the colors and reëngage for another term.

PREPARATORY SCHOOLS.

Preparatory schools are established for the sons of non-commissioned officers and privates of the army, navy, Landwehr, and invalid list, at Annaberg, Erfurt, Spandau, Stralsund, and Struppen.

Boys are admitted to these schools between the ages of ten and twelve, and are discharged at the age of fourteen. The subjects taught are principally the common branches.

NON-COMMISSIONED OFFICERS' SCHOOLS.

These schools are specially established for the training of non-commissioned officers of the infantry. The four schools at Potsdam, Jülich, Bieberich, and Weissenfels, have each 496 pupils, with a staff and non-commissioned staff composed of 19 officers and 63 men.

The pupils are organized into a battalion of four companies. The fifth school, at Ettingen, has 248 pupils organized in two companies, with a staff and non-commissioned staff composed of 11 officers and 34 non-commissioned officers. A sixth school is to be established at Marienwerder.

Admission to these schools is open to boys who have passed through the preparatory schools, and to volunteers between the ages of sixteen and twenty. Candidates must be of good moral character, and be able to read, write, and perform the four ground-rules of arithmetic.

They must also engage to serve four years in the army after completing the course of study, which lasts three years.

The course embraces the common branches, tactics, regulations, reports and returns, and such other subjects as are necessary to qualify the pupils for the position of clerk, sergeant-major, first-sergeant, and the other grades of non-commissioned officers.

The military duties embrace all of the practical instruction in the different schools of the soldier, company, and battalion, required to qualify non-commissioned officers to command and to act as military instructors.

Schools like the above are also established in Saxony and Würtemberg for their respective contingents.

The artillery has its own special non-commissioned officers' schools, in the higher of which are taught mathematics, physics, German, science of artillery, fortification, plan and fortification drawing.

ONE-YEAR VOLUNTEERS.

The one-year volunteers are composed of young men of education whose liability to military service in time of peace is limited to one year, with a view to interfere as little as possible with their professional and business pursuits.

To be eligible as volunteers they must be able to provide their food, lodging, and uniform, at their own expense. They must also present to an examining committee either a certificate from a German gymnasium that the candidate is qualified for admission to the university; that he is in one of the two senior classes of a gymnasium or real school (*Realschule*); the upper class of pro-gymnasium or first-class grammar-school; that he has passed the final examination at a real school of the second class; or that he has been one year at the cadet school at Berlin or Dresden.

If the candidate cannot present one of the above certificates he must pass an equivalent examination before the committee, which is composed of two field-officers, the civil president of the Ober-Ersatz-Commission in the district to which the candidate belongs, a civil member, and a director and instructor, or two instructors of a gymnasium, real school, or higher school.

The certificate from either of the schools mentioned involves a previous course of study of six to seven years, embracing mathematics, physics, languages, and the classics.

Candidates are permitted to volunteer between the ages of seventeen and twenty, and in time of peace select any year to serve between seventeen and twenty-three. In case of war they must present themselves immediately to the Ersatz-Commissions of their districts for service with the army. If accepted, volunteers are permitted to choose their arm of service, not more than four being assigned to any one company. They pursue a special course of instruction, and are not required to sleep in barracks, nor to mess with the men. At the end of the year they undergo an examination, when those who possess the necessary qualifications are discharged with officers' certificates, and thus become available as officers of reserve. If not appointed officers of reserve, they become available, in case of war, as non-commissioned officers.

The number of volunteers averages from 4,000 to 4,200 annually, of which number about 45 per cent. receive officers' certificates. Of those who served in the Austro-Prussian War as high as 56 per cent. received the officers' certificate.

The value of this system was proved at the beginning of the Franco-German War in 1870, when the number of volunteers, at the disposition of the Government, who had qualified as officers of reserve, was, for the—

Infantry	5,143
Rifles	65
Cavalry	740
Artillery	597
Engineers	121
Train	76
Total	6,742

This number embraced only those volunteers whose term of

service (six years) in the reserve had not yet expired. Those whose service had expired were still available for the subsequent five years as officers of Landwehr.

OFFICERS.

With the exception of a very few of the most meritorious cadets, called "Selecta," who are commissioned as officers on graduating from the cadet school at Berlin, all others, previous to being commissioned, must serve for a period of at least five or six months in the ranks.

In this respect, the German system differs from that of all other Continental countries, in which officers of all arms of service are for the most part commissioned directly upon graduating from the various military schools and academies.

Persons who aspire to the position of officers in the German service are termed "Avantageurs," and must be nominated either by the colonel of a regiment, or else have completed satisfactorily the second year's course at the cadet school at Berlin.

Those nominated by the colonels constitute about 60 per cent. of all the officers of the army; the remaining 40 per cent. come from the cadet school.

The first requirement of a candidate is a good general education, as to which the Government may be satisfied, either by the production of a certificate from a gymnasium, or a real school, showing that the candidate is qualified for admission to a university, or by passing what is called the "Fähnrich's Examination" before the Supreme Military Examination Committee.

In the case of those nominated by the colonels, applications to pass the examination must be made to the examination committee through the colonel of the regiment in which the candidate desires to serve, and the examination may be passed either before or after entering the service. The application to pass the examination must be accompanied by a certificate from a gymnasium or real school that the candidate is qualified to enter the senior class at one of these institutions.

The fähnrich's examination embraces the following subjects:

> German language and literature,
> Latin,
> French,
> Arithmetic,
> Geography, physical and political,
> Algebra,
> Geometry,
> Plane trigonometry,
> Ancient and modern history,
> Free-hand and geometrical drawing,

And any other subjects which the candidates may have studied.

PORTÉPÉE-FÄHNRICH.

Candidates who have passed the fähnrich's examination, have served at least five months in the ranks, and possess a service certificate from the colonel, showing that the candidate possesses the necessary mental and physical qualifications, that his conduct has been good, and that he is proficient in the duties of a private soldier and non-commissioned officer, are eligible for promotion to the grade of "portépée-fähnrich" or "ensign designate." After serving five months in this grade, they are sent to a war school to pursue a course of professional study.

WAR SCHOOLS.

There are ten of these schools, eight of which are in Prussia, one in Bavaria, and one in Würtemberg.

The staff of each generally consists of a field-officer, as commandant, an adjutant, a paymaster, 8 to 12 captains as instructors in studies, and 6 to 8 officers charged with discipline and instruction in riding, gymnastics, and other exercises. The average number of scholars at each school is about 30.

The course of study, which is purely professional, is from nine to ten months, and embraces—

Tactics,
Science of arms,
Munitions of war,
Fortification,
Topography,
Surveying,
Military regulations,
Military correspondence.

The practical exercises consist principally of—
Drill,
Riding,
Fencing,
Gymnastics.

At the conclusion of the course, an examination is held, when those who pass it successfully are recommended for promotion to the grade of officer. Those who fail are allowed a second examination after a period of three, six, or twelve months. While waiting for promotion, the candidate still holds the grade of fähnrich.

The only persons exempted from pursuing the course at a war school, in addition to the "Selecta," are the members of the "Ober-Prima" class at the cadet school, and students who have completed one year's study at the North-German University. The latter, after a service of six months, are authorized to be appointed fähnrichs, and may present themselves at the officers' examination. If successful, they are placed on the same footing as the fähnrichs who have studied at the war schools.

CADET SCHOOLS.

It has already been stated that about 60 per cent. of the German officers enter the service through the nomination of regimental commanders. The object of the cadet schools is to prepare the remaining 40 per cent. for the grade of fähnrich, preliminary to further service in the regiments and at the war schools.

These schools consist of six preparatory schools at Potsdam,

Culm, Wahlstadt, Bensberg, Ploen, and Oranienstein, and a central or finishing school at Berlin.

The pupils at all of these schools constitute the cadet corps. The cadets are divided into two classes, paying cadets and king's cadets. The former pay $195 per annum, except the sons of poor officers, who pay $112. The king's cadets pay from $22 to $60 per annum. The king's cadets are usually the sons of officers, and distinguished non-commissioned officers, who have died in service, also sons of civilians who have performed meritorious service to the state, involving personal danger.

The number of paying cadets varies with the number of king's cadets to whom preference is given. Pensioners are admitted according to priority of application. The total number of cadets is between 1,900 and 2,000.

The cadet corps is commanded by a major-general. The preparatory schools are commanded by field-officers, who are assisted by a proper number of captains and subalterns as instructors. Boys are admitted to the preparatory schools between the ages of ten and fifteen.

The course of study is four years, and embraces—

    Latin,
    German,
    French,
    Writing,
    Arithmetic,
    Elementary algebra and geometry,
    Ancient and modern history,
    Bible history,
    Natural philosophy,
    Drawing.

The military instruction is exclusively practical, and consists of drill, gymnastics, and bayonet-exercise.

The cadets at each school are organized into two companies. The discipline is mild and paternal, being adapted to the tender age of the cadets, who rarely show signs of insubordination.

CENTRAL SCHOOL AT BERLIN.

On completing the course at the preparatory schools cadets are transferred to the Central Cadet School (house), Berlin, where they remain two years.

The course of study embraces—

    Algebra,
    Geometry,
    Trigonometry,
    Surveying,
    Science of arms,
    Tactics,
    Fortification,
    Drawing.

The final examination takes place in March, when those of the first class who are qualified, and desire to go to their regiments, are given a certificate qualifying them for the position of fähnrich. They must then serve in their regiments at least five months before going to a war school, where they are placed in all respects on the same footing as the "Avantageurs" or "fähnrichs" nominated by the colonels.

Those of the first class who possess special merit, and have distinguished themselves in the studies, are termed "Selecta," and are permitted to remain a third year to pursue a professional course almost identical with that described for the war schools. If, at the end of the course, they pass the prescribed officers' examination, they are recommended at once for commissions. Those who fail must enter the regiments as fähnrichs, and subsequently go through the war schools.

Those members of the first class who have not yet attained the age of seventeen, or are not sufficiently developed in physique to become fähnrichs, are permitted to continue their studies, and constitute a class called "Ober-Prima," or higher first. If, at the end of the course, they pass the prescribed officers' examination, they are sent to regiment as fähnrichs, and, after six months' service in that grade, can be recommended for promotion as officers.

In addition to all of the military qualifications before described, all candidates for commissioned officers, except the few cadets termed "Selecta," must possess the social qualifications deemed essential for every officer, and these qualifications are determined by a vote of the officers of the regiment in which the candidate desires to serve. If the vote be adverse the candidate cannot be commissioned. Colonels generally satisfy themselves as to the sentiment of the officers before giving the Avantageurs their nomination. The right to veto a nomination is also given to officers of Landwehr battalions.

As to the relative advantage of the two methods pursued in preparing candidates for the grade of Fähnrich opinion in Germany seems divided, but the balance appears to be in favor of the nomination by colonels.

It is certain that the six to seven years' course pursued at the cadet schools is so elementary in its nature that it cannot be deemed superior, if equal, to the course of the same length pursued at the gymnasia or real schools. Furthermore, the military discipline in these schools, which begins with boys from ten years of age upward, is so mild as to give the cadets but little idea of the stern duties required of a soldier.

On the other hand, the Avantageurs, who are nominated by the colonels, must be at least seventeen years of age, at which period the mind is peculiarly receptive. Well prepared at the gymnasia, they readily acquire, in the ten months' service in ranks, and as fähnrichs, the military proficiency of the cadets, and, as a rule, pursue with greater zeal the course at the war schools. The last fact is partly due to the natural feeling of cadets that they have become old soldiers, and that further instruction is superfluous.

It cannot be denied that the military and theoretical qualifications required of candidates for appointment as officers are not so high as in some other European countries, yet this inequality is soon made to disappear by the subsequent course of training and discipline they receive. In a military sense they only begin to go to school when they receive their commissions. Annually they see nearly 150,000 ignorant recruits received into the army who, within three years, are to be converted into trained soldiers and sent home in reserve.

Every year they must go progressively through the schools of the soldier, the company, battalion, and regiment, and review not only their own duties, but they must teach the soldier how to act intelligently, in every situation in the presence of the enemy.

In the evolutions of brigades and divisions they see all the methods that may be adopted to attack or repel an attack of the enemy, and in the great manœuvres they are permitted to study the principles of strategy and grand tactics, and to witness their practical application.

The German officer is proud, not that he belongs to a particular arm of service, but because he is a member of the "Officers' Corps," in which he knows that advancement is sure if he proves himself worthy and efficient.

The effect of giving officers the right of veto in the case of aspirants who are deficient in honor and social qualities, has made the corps of officers the most exclusive in the world, and, in the general acceptation of the term, has proved an insurmountable barrier to promotion from the ranks. In theory, such promotion for distinguished gallantry exists, but in practice the non-commissioned officers promoted are as a rule induced to quit the service by offers of civil employment.

Repressive of military enthusiasm as this policy must appear, the Germans claim that their recent triumphs in three wars show that, so far as they are concerned, all they have lost by exclusiveness has been more than counterbalanced by the high general attainments of their officers, and the feeling of professional pride which makes them prefer death to dishonor.

WAR ACADEMY, BERLIN.

The object of the War Academy is to educate officers for the staff and to hold high commands.

Admission to it is by competitive examination, held annually in each army corps before a committee composed of the chief of staff as president, and several other field-officers or captains.

The examination is written, and embraces—
Geography,
Algebra,
Geometry,
Trigonometry,
History,
Military administration,
French.

A series of themes is also proposed, from which one may be selected by each candidate. The object of these themes, or compositions, is to enable the candidate to show his literary and scientific acquirements. These compositions are prepared at leisure, and submitted to the committee on the day appointed for examination.

The general knowledge of the military art is tested by writing a theme treating of the movements and dispositions to be adopted by detachments of mixed troops in conducting certain offensive or defensive operations with a given object in view.

The conditions stated in the theme of 1876 were as follows:

The evening of July 1st a colonel, with a detachment of two battalions of infantry, two squadrons of cavalry, and a battery of artillery, arrives to the north of Mariendorf. His object is to give the feeble garrison of Berlin, consisting of one brigade, time to prepare for defense by disputing as long as possible the enemy who is advancing by Gross-Machnow and Königs-Wusterhausen, his advanced guards being established along the line of the Marienfeld-Buckow road. Another detachment guards the road from Britz.

The candidate is required in his theme to state the orders the colonel would give for the 2d of July, his intentions and ulterior views, and also indicate on a map the various positions that would be occupied by the troops.

The time allowed in the preparation of the theme is three hours.

Applications to compete must receive the approval of the colonels of regiments, and are addressed to the general commanding the corps to which the regiment of the candidate belongs, or within whose territory the officer may be serving.

The application must be accompanied by a copy of the report of the officer's character and services, from which it must appear that he has had practical service and has shown himself possessed of aptitude for it; that he has a genuine desire to increase his professional knowledge; and that he is in sufficiently good health to denote long service; and that he possesses sufficient character and firmness to indicate that the freedom he will enjoy at Berlin will not be injurious to him. The other conditions relate to the officer's financial affairs, which must be above reproach.

On a day designated the candidates assemble at corps headquarters, when each submits to the examining committee a sketch of his personal history, written in French and German, stating in what manner he qualified for the examination of Fähnrich; he also submits a sketch certified to have been executed by himself, which is intended to show his knowledge of drawing.

The time to be given to each subject is fixed by the committee of studies at the War Academy at Berlin, and the examination is conducted in the presence of one or more members of the examining committee. No books are allowed to be consulted during the examination except a table of logarithms in mathematics, and a dictionary in French.

As soon as each candidate finishes a subject he submits his paper to the officer in charge, who indorses upon it the time occupied in writing it. On the conclusion of the examination, the committee makes a report showing the names of all the competitors, the time required by each in his examination in the different subjects, the names of the competitors who have submitted the compositions already referred to, as also those who have failed to do so, and adds such further remarks as it may deem advisable. This report, accompanied by all of the papers submitted by each candidate to the committee, together with his written examination in each subject, is forwarded to the War Academy at Berlin, where an examination by the committee of studies determines who are the successful candidates. The course of study is three years, beginning each year the 1st of October and ending the 1st of July. During the months of July, August, and September, the students return to their regiments.

The total number of officers present in 1876 was 300.

The supervision of the Academy is vested in the chief of the general staff. The commandant is a general officer. The corps of professors is composed of officers and civilians. The officers are nearly all members of the general staff, who teach mostly professional subjects. The civil professors teach the languages, higher mathematics, and the sciences.

The method of instruction is wholly by lecture, and subsequently by interrogation.

In subjects like military history or applied tactics, a student, when interrogated, is subject to correction by either his instructor or any of the students. If he makes any mistake or commits an error in posting troops, his fellow-students are quick to point it out and to apply the remedy.

The object of the instruction is less to acquire positive knowledge than to develop the habit of thinking, so as to insure action from foresight rather than impulse.

The following table shows the subjects taught, and the number of lessons per week:

Obligatory Studies.

	SUBJECTS.	Year.	No. of Lessons per Week.
1	Tactics...	1st year.	4
2	Applied tactics..	2d "	4
3	History of wars (military history).......................	1st "	2
	" "	2d "	4
	" "	3d "	6
4	Artillery..	1st "	3
5	Field-fortification......................................	1st "	2
6	Permanent fortification..................................	2d "	2
7	Attack and defense of fortresses.........................	3d "	2
8	Topography...	2d "	1
9	Duties of the general staff..............................	3d "	3
10	Military geography.......................................	2d "	4
11	Military administration..................................	2d "	1
12	Military hygiene...	3d "	1
13	Mathematics..	1st "	9

Optional Studies.

	SUBJECTS.	Year.	No. of Lessons per Week.
1	Higher mathematics..	2d year.	6
		3d "	6
2	Geodesy...	3d "	6
3	Ancient history and history of the middle ages...........	1st "	4
4	History of literature.....................................	2d "	4
5	Modern and contemporary history..........................	2d "	4
6	Geography (general)......................................	1st "	4
7	Physical geography.......................................	1st "	2
8	Chemistry..	2d "	4
9	Experimental philosophy..................................	2d "	4
10	French..	1st "	6
	"	2d "	6
	"	3d "	4
11	Russian...	1st "	4
	"	2d "	4
	"	3d "	4

Of the optional studies students are required to select one or more, which then become obligatory.

The number of lessons per week is not invariable, and may be changed slightly when necessary.

An examination of the obligatory studies shows the importance attached to the study of professional subjects after officers enter the service.

Ever mindful of the national reputation, and anxious to achieve success with the least loss of life, the German Government specially provides that all officers who may hold high command, or who as staff officers may be responsible for the guidance and movements of troops in battle, shall learn the principles of war in time of peace. To this end, during the first year, four hours per week are given to theoretical tactics or the movements of troops as laid down in drill-books for the different arms of service. The second year four hours per week are given to applied tactics, or the art of posting and manœuvring troops according to the configuration of the ground.

To the history of wars, which embraces all of the details and stratogical principles of the great campaigns of history, together with the tactical principles applied to battles, more than twice as much time is devoted as to any other subject.

In addition, the third year, three hours per week are devoted to learning the duties of the general staff in reference to plans of campaigns, the movements of troops, and the orders to be given from day to day as the war progresses.

Military geography is also carefully studied with a view to knowing all of the lines of communications, strategic points, and lines of defense, of various countries. At small expense the German Government educates annually a hundred officers in the duties pertaining to high command, and every nation in Europe has vindicated her wisdom by adopting as far as practicable the methods she has pursued.

At the end of the three years' course the officers return to their regiments without examination, but the record of each is forwarded to the chief of staff, with a view to calling the most proficient officers of the class to the general staff.

GENERAL STAFF.

The first condition for admission to the general staff is that an officer shall be a graduate of the War Academy. After returning to their regiments, ten or twelve of the most proficient of each class are transferred for a period of six months to another arm of service. If they acquit themselves well, they are at the expiration of this term summoned to Berlin, where, on probation, they are assigned to general staff duty. At the end of this term they are again sent back to their regiments, shortly after which those who are regarded as qualified are named captains of the staff, and are sent into the army to serve three years as staff officers. They are then sent back to the line and required to command a company, battery, or squadron, before being promoted to the grade of major. Only the grades of field-officer and above are permanent, the promotions in these grades being by seniority.

In order, however, to preserve the habit of command, and to keep them in sympathy with the troops, staff officers before each promotion are required to return to the line, and to hold for a year a command corresponding to their rank.

The system of staff selection and promotion is specially designed to increase professional knowledge and to enable the Government to call the most highly-educated officers to the highest posts in the army.

The most rapid step in promotion is to the grade of major, to attain which an officer, from what has been said, must have served three years in the line, three at the War Academy, six months in an arm differing from his own, two years on probation at Berlin, and three years on the staff in the army; making a total of at least eleven and a half years.

Once in the general staff, the promotion goes on by seniority to the grade of colonel, and afterward by selection to the grades of general.

While the selection of generals is not limited to the staff, one of the best tests of the system of German military education lies in the fact that, at the outbreak of the Franco-German War, every general in the Prussian army was a graduate of the War Academy.

The staff system does not necessarily exclude favoritism, which may be shown in the first instance in the admission of a candidate to the War Academy, and again in selecting the ten or twelve of each class who are called on probation to Berlin; but it reduces the evils of favoritism, if they exist, to the minimum, by requiring of the officers so advanced a thorough professional training.

The operations of the general staff are entirely independent of the Minister of War, and are directed by the chief of staff.

The general staff is divided into the "Haupt-État," or main branch, and "Neben-État," or accessory branch.

The main branch is again divided into the "great general staff in Berlin" and the "general staff with the troops."

The general duties of the great general staff are to collect information regarding the organization, tactics, and armament of foreign armies, the present and projected lines of railway, and other lines of communication in foreign countries; to prepare plans of campaign, and to arrange all of the details for the mobilization, movements, and concentration of troops in different theatres of war, either within or exterior to the empire.

The duties are transacted in bureaux and sections, as follows:

1. The Central Bureau is charged with all matters relating to the personnel of the staff—the survey, War Academy, and the Railway Regiment. It is presided over by the first adjutant of the chief of staff, who has the rank of colonel, and is assisted by a captain and eight other officers.

2. The three sections and the Intelligence Bureau:

The *First Section* collects all information in reference to the organization, tactics, armament, and mobilization, of the armies of Norway and Sweden, Russia, Turkey, Austria, Denmark, Greece, and Asia. It likewise collects geographical information, and notes any changes in the fortifications and lines of communication of any of the above countries.

The *Second Section* collects the same information in reference to Germany, Italy, and Switzerland.

The *Third Section* does the same in reference to France, England, Belgium, Holland, Spain, Portugal, and America.

The information collected by these sections is mostly procured by the military *attachés* at foreign courts. It is systematically arranged, and, in order that it may be of benefit to the army, summaries of the armed strength of the different nations are from time to time distributed by the sections to all officers of the general staff.

Each section is presided over by a field-officer as chief, who is assisted by ten or eleven other officers, and a registrar.

The "Intelligence Bureau" keeps always in readiness the most recent information relative to foreign armies, and probable theatres of war, which is prepared by the three sections. It is presided over by a field-officer, who is assisted by a registrar.

3. The *Railway Section* is charged with everything pertaining to the transport of troops and military stores by rail. The officers of this section work out all the details of moving troops by rail, the time required to transport them, and the lines to be used in concentrating armies for war. To this end they are required to know the capacity of the different lines of railway

both at home and abroad, and to keep themselves posted as to all new lines of railway, and also their strategic value.

The duties of this section are considered so important, in view of their influence in effecting the speedy concentration of armies, that all officers of the general staff are required to serve in it. The chief of the section is a field-officer, who is assisted by twenty-six officers and a registrar.

The accessory branch, or Neben-État, is charged mostly with scientific duties, and is entirely separate, as regards promotion, from the general staff. The officers composing it are borne either as supernumeraries of the general staff, or, if detailed from the line, they are borne as supernumeraries in their regiments. Officers of this branch are not necessarily graduates of the War Academy.

The accessory branch is divided into five sections, with duties as follows:

1. The *Section of Military History* collects and arranges all information bearing on military history, and prepares descriptions of present and past campaigns. It is presided over by a chief, who is assisted by fourteen officers.

2. The *Geographical Statistical Section* collects all geographical and statistical knowledge relating to foreign countries and theatres of war, prepares reports showing their resources, circulates among the officers of the general staff all statistical and geographical information, and corrects to date military maps of Germany and foreign countries.

A field-officer presides over the section, who is assisted by two captains of the accessory branch and three attached officers.

3. The *Trigonometrical Section* is charged with the triangulation of Prussia.

4. The *Topographical Section* is charged with the topographical survey of Prussia.

5. The *Cartographical Section* is charged with the preparation and correction of maps to date, and supplies maps to the army.

The total number of officers of both branches doing duty at Berlin is seventy-four.

The duties of the general staff with the troops are to attend to the distribution and quartering of troops; to study the lines of march at home and abroad; to regulate the marches; to assist in drawing up plans for manœuvres; the examination of lines of communication; collection of political intelligence and all information procurable relating to neighboring armies; matters not technical, relating to artillery and engineers; armament and provisioning of fortresses; collection of geographical and topographical information; preparation of plans of campaign, and generally collection and arrangement of such information as may be of value to their commanders in conducting the operations of their troops.

To enable officers of the general staff to concentrate their attention upon the higher duties of their position, and to relieve them from the drudgery of mere routine and office work, officers called *adjutants* are specially detailed from the line for a period of from three to four years. If these officers are captains, they are replaced in their regiments, and become supernumerary; if first-lieutenants, the number of second-lieutenants is increased to fill the vacancies.

The general duties of the adjutants are to issue the daily orders; to regulate details for guards; issue paroles and countersigns; to prepare morning returns and reports; to attend to promotions, applications for leave, transfers, rewards and punishments, recruiting, and requisitions for men from the reserve; to transact business connected with the Landwehr and the organization of new levies; and also such other details as pertain to keeping the command supplied with all of the matériel and munitions of war.

It will be observed that all of the foregoing duties are of a mere routine character, demanding no special professional training in the officers who perform them; yet it is only within the last few years that in foreign armies they have been carefully separated from duties of the general staff officer, who gives all of his attention to the direction and movements of troops.

The organization of the main branch of the general staff is as follows:

1 Chief of staff—field-marshal,
19 Chiefs of section, and chiefs of staff of army corps, usually of the grade of colonel,
59 Field-officers,
32 Captains.

The accessory branch is composed of—
1 Chief of survey, ranking as a brigade commander,
5 Chiefs of sections, usually colonels,
8 Field-officers,
22 Captains.

As a means of providing officers for staff duty in time of war there are annually attached to the great general staff from forty to fifty officers from the line who have either passed through the War Academy, or are otherwise qualified for the detail.

At the end of the year's probation they pass an examination, and if qualified are recommended for staff employment on the occurrence of vacancies.

In time of war the officers of the great general staff repair to the field, where they are assigned to the staffs of the several armies.

The officers of the accessory branch remain at Berlin.

PROMOTION.

Promotions are made both by selection and by seniority, no precise limit being fixed. The Emperor is free to advance or retard the promotion of an officer according to his pleasure.

Promotions are based upon the personal reports of all officers, which are forwarded every two years for the grades below field-officer, and annually for the grades of field-officers and above. Colonels make the reports in regard to the officers of their regiments, and when they are adverse they are supposed to notify the officers concerned. General officers make reports upon the field-officers.

The reports state in detail the character, capacity, and qualifications of the officers, and are transmitted to a chief of bureau at Berlin, where, after being arranged, an abstract is made out for the Emperor, showing what officers merit special promotion, officers who are not qualified for advancement, and also the officers who are qualified for staff duty, adjutant, aide-de-camp, and other detached service.

Promotion to the grade of captain is by regiment in the infantry, artillery, and cavalry; by battalion in the rifles; and by corps in the engineers.

Promotion to major in the infantry is regimental, but subject to many exceptions; in the rifles, artillery, cavalry, engineers, and train, it takes place by arm.

The promotion to the grades of lieutenant-colonel, and colonel, is mostly by seniority and by arm.

The object of promotion by selection is to hasten the advancement of all capable and deserving officers to the responsible grades of the army. Officers passed over once or twice usually retire from the service.

PUNISHMENTS.

As in all other foreign armies, discipline is largely maintained by confiding to officers in command of regiments, battalions, companies, and detachments, the power to administer summary punishment for minor offenses. These punishments consist usually of arrests, confinements, extra duty, and deprivation of control of pay.

Serious offenses are punished by sentence of court-martial.

ARMY OF FRANCE.

The French army was established on its present basis by the laws of March 13, and December 15, 1875.

The term "cadre," as used in the law, and as applied to a regiment, signifies all of the officers, hospital stewards, musicians, clerks, armorers, tailors, shoemakers, etc., belonging to the regiment. It constitutes, in fact, the framework of the regiment, which, to be completed, requires only the addition of the private soldiers who fill up the ranks.

The following table represents the strength of the army on the peace-footing:

ARM.	Regiments.	Battalions.	Depot Companies.	Officers and Men.
Infantry	144	576	288	286,804
Chasseurs à pied	....	30	30	18,240
Zouaves	4	16	4	10,820
Algerian rifles	3	12	3	6,505
Foreign Legion	....	4	....	2,509
Light infantry (African)	....	3	....	4,148
Five companies of discipline	....	....	....	1,560
Total	151	641	325	261,601

CAVALRY.	Regiments.	Field Squadrons.	Depot Squadrons.	Officers and Men.
Cuirassiers	12	48	12	}58,160
Dragoons	26	104	26	
Light cavalry	32	128	32	
Chasseurs d'Afrique	4	16	8	4,148
Spahis	3	12	6	3,477
Volunteer scouts	One to each corps raised only in time of war.			
Remount cavalry	8 companies			2,904
Total	77	308	84	68,617

ARTILLERY.	Regiments.	Foot Batteries.	Mounted Batteries.	Horse Batteries.	Companies.	Depot Batteries.	Officers and Men.
Special staff of artillery.....	....	....	....	....	....	....	1,395
Divisional artillery..........	19	57	152	....	....	38	27,939
Corps artillery..............	19	....	152	57	....	38	27,803
Artillery pontoniers.........	2	....	....	....	28	....	8,012
Workmen (mechanics).....	....	....	....	....	10	....	1,860
Artificers...................	....	....	....	....	8	....	815
Train.......................	....	....	....	....	57	....	5,142
Musicians...................	....	....	....	....	....	....	760
Total...............	40	57	304	57	93	76	67,726

ENGINEERS.	Regiments.	Battalions.	Companies.	Depot Companies.	Officers and Men.
Special staff of engineers.............	....	....	....	....	1,354
Sappers and miners...................	4	20	24	4	10,960
Total...................	4	20	24	4	12,314

TRAINS.	Squadrons.	Companies.	Officers and Men.
Military train.................................	20	60	5,743
Same, Algeria................................	....	12	3,649
Total................................	20	72	9,392

STAFF, ADMINISTRATIVE DEPARTMENTS, ETC.	Officers and Men.
General officers; staff and administrative departments corresponding to our adjutant-general's, quartermaster's, commissary, and medical departments; military schools; recruiting service, remount depots, etc............................	23,657
Gendarmerie...	27,014
Grand total.................................	400,821

INFANTRY.

The influence of the Franco-German War in producing modifications in military organization is nowhere more perceptible than in the French infantry.

Previous to the war it was divided into infantry of the guard, and infantry of the line.

The infantry of the guard was composed of—

7 Regiments of 3 battalions of 6 companies each, with 3 companies as regimental depot.

1 Battalion of chasseurs à pied (rifles) of 10 companies.

1 Regiment of zouaves of 2 battalions of 6 companies each, with a depot of 2 companies—numbering in all 24 battalions and 171 companies.

The infantry of the line was composed of—

100 Regiments of 3 field and 1 depot battalion of 6 companies each (2,400 companies).

20 Battalions of chasseurs of 8 companies each (160 companies).

8 Regiments of zouaves of 3 field and 1 depot battalion, with 27 companies to each regiment (81 companies).

3 Battalions of light infantry (African) of 5 companies each (15 companies).

3 Regiments of tirailleurs (rifles) of 4 battalions of 7 companies each (84 companies).

1 Regiment of "sapeurs pompier" of 2 battalions of 6 com-companies each (12 companies).

1 Foreign Legion of 4 battalions of 8 companies each (32 companies).

7 Companies of discipline.

Grand total, 477 battalions, 2,962 companies.

Subsequent to the war the guard was suppressed, and, by the laws of March 13, and December 15, 1875, the infantry was made to consist of—

144 Regiments of the line of 4 battalions of 4 companies each, with 2 companies as regimental depot.

30 Battalions of chasseurs à pied of 4 companies each, with 1 company as battalion depot.

4 Regiments of zouaves of 4 battalions of 4 companies each, with 2 companies as regimental depot.

3 Regiments of tirailleurs (Algerian) of 4 battalions of 4 companies each, with 1 company as regimental depot.

1 Foreign Legion of 4 battalions of 4 companies.

3 Battalions of African light infantry, the number of companies in each being fixed by the Minister of War.

5 Companies of discipline.

The principal change effected by the recent laws was the conversion of the depot battalions of the line and other regiments into a fourth field battalion, and the substitution of four companies for six in the composition of a battalion.

The total number of battalions under the present organization is 641, total number of companies 2,904, being an increase of 104 battalions, and a decrease of 58 companies.

The cadre of a company and depot company is as follows:

CADRE OF COMPANY, AND DEPOT COMPANY.	Company.	Depot Company.
Captain.	1	1
First-lieutenant.	1	1
Second-lieutenant.	1	1
Total officers.	3	3
First-sergeant.	1	1
Commissary-sergeant.	1	1
Sergeants.	4	4
Corporals.	8	8
Drummers and trumpeters.	2	2
Total men.	16	16
Total cadre.	19	19
Privates.	66	66
Total depot company.	85	85

In the strength of each company are included 1 shoemaker, 1 tailor, and 2 pioneers.

In time of war the cadre of the active companies is increased by 1 lieutenant (officer of complement), 4 sergeants, 1 commissary-corporal, 8 corporals, and 2 musicians.

The cadre of a battalion, exclusive of field, staff, and non-commissioned staff, is as follows:

Officers.	12
Non-commissioned officers and musicians.	64
Total cadre.	76
Privates.	264
Total battalion.	340

The cadre of a regiment is as follows:

Colonel.	1
Lieutenant-colonel.	1
Majors, battalion commanders.	4
Major, chief of administration.	1

INFANTRY.

Surgeon, first class............................	1
Captains, adjutants...........................	4
Captain, paymaster...........................	1
Clothing-officer................................	1
Lieutenant, assistant paymaster................	1
Ensign..	1
Surgeon, second class.........................	1
Assistant surgeon.............................	1
Chief musician................................	1
Total......................................	19

Non-commissioned staff, and non-combatants—

Sergeant-majors...............................	4
Drum-major...................................	1
Corporals, drummers, or trumpeters............	4
Sapper-corporal...............................	1
Sappers.......................................	12
Assistant chief musician.......................	1
Musicians.....................................	38
Quartermaster-sergeant........................	1
Chief armorer.................................	1
Fencing-master (sergeant).....................	1

Sergeants,
{
1 Paymaster's clerk,
1 Assistant paymaster's clerk,
1 Storekeeper (clothing),
1 Commissary-sergeant,
} 4

Corporals,
{
1 Paymaster's clerk,
2 Clerks to clothing and ordnance officer,
1 Assistant fencing-master,
1 Hospital steward,
1 Train-conductor,
1 Master-armorer,
1 Master-tailor,
1 Master-shoemaker,
} 9

Privates, {
1 Colonel's clerk,
1 Administrative officer's clerk,
1 Paymaster's clerk,
1 Assistant paymaster's clerk,
1 Clerk to clothing-officer,
4 Armorers,
3 Tailors,
3 Shoemakers,
1 Conductor of led horses,
} 16

1 Driver to each one-horse carriage, or pack-mule. —

Total................................... 93

Total field, staff, non-commissioned staff, etc. 112

FOUR BATTALIONS.

Officers....................................... 48
Sergeants, corporals, and musicians............. 256

Total cadre............................. 304
Privates....................................... 1,056

Total of four battalions................... 1,360

DEPOT, TWO COMPANIES.

Officers....................................... 6
Sergeants, corporals, and musicians 32

Total cadre............................. 38
Privates...................................... 132

Total depot 170

TOTAL REGIMENTAL CADRE.

Officers....................................... 73
Non-commissioned officers, etc.................. 381

Total................................... 454

Privates...................................... 1,188

Total regiment.......................... 1,642

The organization of the battalions of chasseurs, as also that of the regiments of zouaves, tirailleurs, the Foreign Legion, and the battalions of African light infantry, which compose the nineteenth corps serving in Algeria, varies so slightly from the organization of the infantry of the line, that it need not be stated.

The laws establish only the cadres in peace and war, and the number of privates below which the army in time of peace shall not be reduced.

The number of privates in time of war is not prescribed, but each infantry company may be increased in its effective to 4 officers, and 250 or more men.

The active army in time of war may be raised as high as 880,000 men.

BRIGADE.

The brigade of infantry is composed of the staff, and 2 regiments of infantry, numbering 8 battalions.

DIVISION.

A division of infantry consists of the staff, and 2 brigades of infantry (16 battalions).

ARMY CORPS.

An army corps consists of—
1. Staff, and administrative services.
2. 2 Divisions of infantry (32 battalions), and a battalion of chasseurs, which is attached to one of the brigades.
3. 1 Brigade of cavalry (2 regiments of 4 field-squadrons each).
4. 1 Brigade of artillery, composed of 2 regiments, the first of which consists of 3 foot, 8 mounted, and 2 depot batteries; the second of 8 mounted, 3 horse, and 2 depot batteries. In addition, 3 companies of artillery-train.
5. 1 Battalion of engineers.

6. 1 Company of volunteer scouts (raised only in time of war).

7. 1 Squadron (3 companies) military train.

TERRITORIAL COMMANDS.

The territory of France, for the purpose of recruiting and mobilization, is divided into 18 regions, corresponding to the 18 army corps.

Algeria constitutes a region by itself, corresponding to the nineteenth corps.

The regions are again divided into eight or more "subdivisions."

Each region, in case of mobilization, is required to provide the men necessary to raise the army corps within its limits to the war-footing, and to supply all needful transportation, equipments, and munitions of war.

Each subdivision is required to supply the men needed to raise a regiment of infantry to the war-footing, and also to raise one regiment of three battalions of the army territoriale. It also supplies its proportion of the personnel of the artillery, and other special arms, maintained within the region.

RECRUITMENT.

The law of obligatory service obtains in France the same as in other Continental countries.

The period of service is—

Five years in the regular army; four years in the reserve of the regular army; five years in the army territoriale; six years in the reserve of the army territoriale — making a total of twenty years.

The details of recruitment are much the same as in Italy and Austria.

In each subdivision there is a permanent bureau of recruitment, usually superintended by a retired officer of the army, who, during the time so employed, receives full pay.

The bureau is composed of:

1 Field-officer, or captain, as commandant.

1 Captain, ⎫
1 Lieutenant, ⎪
3 Sergeants, ⎬ Department of recruiting and mobilization.
1 Corporal, ⎭

1 Captain,   ⎫
1 Lieutenant, ⎬ Administrative personnel of troops of the
1 Sergeant, ⎭   army territoriale.

The bureaux of subdivisions are under the control of the generals of brigade and division within their several regions.

The annual contingent, approximating 140,000 to 150,000 men, is divided into the "first" and "second portions," which vary with the financial condition of the country. The "first portion" consists of about 85,000 men, who are required to serve five years with the colors; but, in practice, are sent into reserve after the expiration of four years, giving them five years in reserve instead of four. The "second portion," which consists of the remainder of the contingent after the deduction of the first portion, is required to serve in the ranks only the time necessary to acquire instruction in the practical duties of the soldier, and this period has been fixed from six to twelve months. After its expiration, the men go into reserve for the remainder of nine years.

The relative strength of the "first" and "second portions" is fixed by the Minister of War, according to the state of finances. In 1868, when the annual contingent was habitually 100,000 men, 68,500 were assigned to the infantry. Of this number, 44,000 constituted the first portion, and 24,500 the second portion.

In 1872 the annual contingent was 146,000. Of this number, 101,519 were assigned to the infantry, 52,272 constituting the first portion, and the remainder 49,247 the second.

In 1874 the contingent was 142,168, of which number 68 per cent. constituted the first, and 32 per cent. the second portion.

Deducting 9,000 non-combatants, the "first portion" in 1874 numbered 85,500 men, and was distributed to the various arms as follows: infantry, 52,700; cavalry, 14,360; artillery,

12,550; engineers, 900; military train, 2,240; administrative corps, 2,850.

The "second portion," numbering 48,278, was distributed to the infantry, 37,498; artillery, 6,556; trains of artillery, 2,023; military train, 2,207.

In addition to the annual contingent, composed of men drafted into the army, from 10,000 to 11,000 young men, on the German principle, are allowed to volunteer for one year, and the contingent is further increased by from 12,000 to 15,000 men, who voluntarily enlist for five years.

Assuming the average annual strength of the "first portion" to be 85,200, and the "second portion" 48,000, the average strength of the army in time of peace may be estimated as follows:

First portion (four classes)	340,000
Second portion (one class)	48,000
Volunteers for one year	10,000
Volunteers for five years (four classes)	48,000
Foreign and Algerian troops	13,600
Officers, employés, etc.	28,000
	487,600

Deducting 10 per cent. for losses by death and disability, the reserve will be composed approximately as follows:

First portion, five classes, of 74,250 each	371,250
Second portion, eight classes, of 43,200 each	345,600
Volunteers of one year, eight classes	90,000
	806,850

Of this number, nearly one-half are soldiers who have been trained four years, while the remainder have been drilled from six to twelve months.

The infantry on the peace-footing numbers, as has been stated, 281,000, with the companies increased to 250 men each; the war-footing numbers 643,750.

The armed strength on a war-footing is estimated as follows:

ARMY TERRITORIALE.

Regular army in the field . . .	880,000
Battalions, batteries, etc., of the regular army remaining in France . .	50,000
Depot troops (companies estimated at 500 each)	220,000
Army territoriale	560,000
Depot troops, army territoriale . .	20,000
	1,730,000

ARMY TERRITORIALE.

As soon as the men complete nine years' service in the army, and reserve, they are transferred for five years to the army territoriale, and after its expiration are transferred for six years to the reserve of the army territoriale, when their liability to military duty ceases.

The army territoriale embraces troops of all arms, and is organized substantially on the same basis as the regular army.

Each subdivision of the 18 regions furnishes 1 regiment of infantry, composed of 3 battalions of 4 companies each, with 1 company as depot.

The subdivision of Aix furnishes two regiments of infantry instead of one.

The cadre of the staff, and non-commissioned staff of the regiments, also the cadres of the battalions and companies, are identical with the corresponding cadres in the regular army, except that each regiment is commanded by a lieutenant-colonel.

The troops of the other arms are furnished by region.

When the organization is completed, the troops of the army territoriale will consist of—

145 Regiments of infantry.
18 Regiments of artillery (one to each region).
18 Battalions of engineers (one to each region, the number of companies not being fixed).
18 Squadrons of military train.
72 Squadrons of cavalry.

The number of cavalry to be raised in each region depends upon the number of horses within its limits. The figure 72 is based upon the supposition that, on the average, each region will furnish four squadrons.

The law also authorizes squadrons of volunteer cavalry to be raised, to be composed partly of volunteers, and partly of soldiers of the army territoriale, provided the men mount and equip themselves at their own expense.

The rolls of the army territoriale are kept at the bureaux of the various subdivisions, and all of the business connected with its recruitment and mobilization is transacted by the officers and men composing the bureaux.

OFFICERS OF RESERVE.

The officers of reserve are mostly nominated from—

1. General officers, retired, who request employment.

2. Officers of the army, and marines, retired after twenty-five years' service, up to the time they would have completed thirty years' service; also such officers retired after thirty years' service as request employment.

3. Officers of marines, unemployed, who desire to serve in the reserve.

4. Such officers of the army, and marines, as having resigned, are within the age when men are liable to nine years' service in the army and reserve; also such as having passed this age request to be employed.

5. Former pupils of the Polytechnic School.

6. Volunteers of one year, and officers of the late garde nationale.

7. Former non-commissioned officers of the army who have not yet completed their period in reserve, and have been recommended by their chiefs of corps as capable of becoming officers had they remained in the army.

8. Former non-commissioned officers of the national guard, still subject to duty in the reserve, who possess the required qualifications.

Officers of reserve are assigned to regiments by the Minister of War, and receive pay only when called to attend manœuvres, and when otherwise actively employed.

On completing the period within which they are liable to service in the reserve, they may be continued in the reserve on their application, approved by the Minister of War. If they possess the desired qualifications, they may also continue in reserve on their own application after the expiration of twenty years' service.

OFFICERS OF THE ARMY TERRITORIALE.

Like the reserve, the officers of the army territoriale are selected partly from the officers of the army and marines who have retired or have resigned, also from the officers of reserve, all of whom pass into the army territoriale after completing the nine years' service to which they are liable, unless still retained in reserve.

Other officers are appointed from former non-commissioned officers of the army, who have completed their nine years' service, and can pass a prescribed examination.

The army register shows the names and rank of all officers thus far appointed.

The grades of commandants of regiments and battalions, by far the most important, have been filled, but a large proportion of the captaincies, most of the first-lieutenancies, and nearly all of the second-lieutenancies, are still vacant.

Field-officers, after completing the twenty years' service, if possessing the necessary qualifications, may be retained on their own application till they reach the age of sixty-five; other officers may be retained till they reach the age of sixty.

GENERAL OFFICERS.

The number on the active list consists of—

 Major-generals.......................... 100
 Brigadier-generals....................... 200

The number of marshals is not fixed.

STAFF.

The present organization of the "état-major," or adjutant-general's department, is as follows:

Colonels............................	40	
Lieutenant-colonels.................	40	
Majors.............................	120	400
Captains...........................	200	
Captains (archivistes)...............	24	

The French staff presents a striking contrast with that of the other great Continental powers. Originally, it was the model on which all of them were based, but, having stood still while others have advanced, it remains the only one in which the principles of detail, and service with troops, are not recognized.

In 1833 an effort was made to distribute the staff between the infantry and cavalry, in which arms the officers were to receive their promotion, but the opposition was so great that the project was abandoned.

Again, in 1862, the Minister of War appointed a commission with a view to dissolving the staff, and distributing two-thirds of its officers to the infantry and one-third to the cavalry, but his purpose was never accomplished.

As a consequence, with the exception of the four years' service prior to nomination as captain, an officer of the French staff never sees service with the troops of the line, and thus, confined to the atmosphere of his own corps, his principal conception of efficiency is the rapid transaction of official business, to the exclusion of the higher duties of his profession.

In Germany, Italy, Austria, and Russia, officers continually transfer from the line to the staff and the reverse, and, except in Germany, when once sent back to the line may never be recalled.

The staff is thus composed of the ablest officers of the army, who ultimately arrive at the grade of general with an experience rounded by service in every grade of the line and the staff from lieutenant to colonel.

MILITARY SCHOOLS.

According to the law of March, 1875, the military schools maintained at the expense of the state consist of the—

Prytanée Militaire, at La Flèche,
Polytechnic School, at Paris,
Special Military School, at St.-Cyr,
School of Application for Artillery and Engineers, at Fontainebleau,
School of Application for the Staff, at Paris,
School of Application for Cavalry, at Saumur,
School of Medicine and Pharmacy, at Paris,
Administrative School, at Vincennes,
Military gymnasia and musketry schools,
Regimental schools in different arms of the service,
Schools for non-commissioned officers,
Schools for children of soldiers, and
Academy of War, in the process of organization.

THE PRYTANÉE MILITAIRE.

This is a mere preparatory school, conducted on the same principles as the military gymnasia in other countries.

Admission is open to boys between the ages of ten and eighteen, preference being given to sons of officers, and to sons of non-commissioned officers whose service to the country merits recognition.

The expenses of education are borne in some cases wholly by the parents; in other cases, such as orphans, or having had a father killed in battle, tuition is either free, or reduced one-half.

In consideration of the education received, no obligation is incurred to continue a military career, but special encouragment is given to the pupils to prepare themselves to pass the competitive examination for admission to the Polytechnic School, and to the school at St.-Cyr.

The course of instruction embraces—
Arithmetic,
Algebra,
Geometry,
Descriptive geometry,
Trigonometry,

Geography,
Physics and chemistry,
French grammar and literature,
Latin,
German,
History,
Drawing.

SPECIAL MILITARY SCHOOL, AT ST.-CYR.

The object of this school is to educate cadets for commissions in the infantry, cavalry, marines, and the staff.

Admission is exclusively by competitive examination, open to all candidates between the ages of seventeen and twenty. In the cases of non-commissioned officers and soldiers, the age may be extended to twenty-five.

The examinations for admission, which are held annually in the different departments, are both oral and written, and embrace the following subjects:

Arithmetic,
Algebra,
Geometry,
Descriptive geometry,
Plane trigonometry,
Mechanics and physics (simply descriptive),
Chemistry,
Political and physical geography,
History,
German.

To be admitted to the examination, a candidate must produce his diploma as a Bachelor of Science[1] or Letters, or an equivalent certificate, and he must also undergo a preliminary examination, embracing a French and Latin composition; solution of mathematical problems, involving the use of logarithms; solution of a problem in descriptive geometry; drawing from a model, and also rectilinear drawing.

The expense of education is paid by the cadets, at the rate

---

[1] Equivalent to a diploma from the public schools, or *lycées*.

of 1,500 francs per annum. In addition, the uniform and outfit cost from 600 to 700 francs.

Cadets whose parents are in indigent circumstances, and who can establish the fact, are educated free, while others are granted a reduction of one-half the usual charges.

The number of cadets present in 1876 was 750.

The organization of the cadets is in 2 battalions of 4 companies each.

The course of study is two years, and embraces—

    Topography,
    Fortification,
    Artillery,
    Military administration,
    Military art and history,
    Military geography,
    French literature,
    German,
    Hygiene, and
    Drawing.

Theoretical instruction is also given in musketry-practice, regulations for infantry and cavalry, and equitation.

At the end of the first year the cadets make their choice of arms of service, after which the candidates for the cavalry are quartered by themselves.

The practical instruction during the course is limited mostly to infantry-drill, to include the school of the battalion and regiment, and to cavalry-drill, school of the trooper. The first year riding is taught twice a week; the second year the cavalry rides daily, and the infantry three times per week.

Artillery instruction is limited to twenty-six lessons or lectures, and to the manual of field and siege guns.

The staff of the school in 1876 consisted as follows:

Commandant.

1 General of brigade.

Second Commandant.

1 Colonel of infantry.

Instructors of Infantry.

1 Major,
8 Captains.

Instructor of Musketry.

1 Captain.

Instructors of Cavalry.

1 Major,
2 Captains,
6 Lieutenants.

Director of Studies.

1 Major.

Sub-directors of Studies.

2 Captains.

Examiners for Admission.

2 Colonels,
2 Civilians.

Mathematics.

1 Professor (civilian).

Artillery.

1 Professor (major),
2 Assistant professors (captains).

Topography.

1 Professor (captain),
2 Assistant professors (1 captain and 1 lieutenant).

Military History.

1 Professor (captain),
2 Assistant professors (lieutenants).

Military Law and Administration.

1 Professor (captain),
2 Assistant professors (lieutenants).

Fortification.

1 Professor (major),
4 Assistant professors (2 captains and 2 lieutenants).

Military Geography and Statistics.

1 Professor,
4 Assistant professors (1 captain and 3 lieutenants).

Military Literature.

1 Professor (civilian),
1 Assistant professor (civilian).

German.

2 Professors (1 civilian and 1 captain),
2 Assistant professors (civilians).

Drawing.

3 Professors (civilians).

In addition to the above there is a chief administrative officer, a paymaster, an assistant paymaster, a commissary, three adjutants, a librarian, a chaplain, three surgeons, and a veterinary surgeon.

The method of instruction, by means of lectures and interrogations, is the same as described for the Polytechnic.

POLYTECHNIC SCHOOL.

The fame of this school is due entirely to its scientific nature, the military instruction and discipline being of so elementary a character as scarcely to deserve notice.

The object of the school is to train pupils for the following branches of the public service, viz.:

Artillery, military and naval.
Engineers, military and naval.
Navy, and Corps of Hydrographical Engineers.
Navy commissariat.

Civil engineers for bridges, roads, and mines.
Staff of the army.
Manufacture of powder and saltpetre.
Telegraphs.

Other departments requiring a high scientific training are also open to the graduates of the school.

The organization of the school is military, and, while pursuing the course, the students are considered as belonging to the active army.

The military staff of the school consists of—

1 Commandant,
1 Second commandant,
6 Captains.

The commandant and second commandant are chosen alternately from the artillery and engineers. If the former is from the artillery, the latter must belong to the engineers, and the reverse.

The Educational Staff, consisting of examiners for admission, examiners of pupils, professors, and assistant professors, is largely composed of eminent civilians, many of whom are members of the Academy of Sciences.

The Council of Improvement is composed of the—

Commandant,
Second commandant,
Director of studies,
3 Professors of the school,
2 Examiners of pupils.

The other members in 1876 consisted of—

1 Delegate from the Academy of Sciences,
3 Delegates from the War Department,
2 " " Navy "
1 Delegate " Department of Mines,
1 " " " Roads and Bridges,
1 " " Astronomical section of the Institute,
1 " " Tobacco Department.

The Council of Improvement is charged with the initiative in all matters of improvement, and regulates the course of study, subject to the approval of the Minister of War, in such a manner as to promote the efficiency of all branches of the public service, whose officers are supplied by the graduates of the school.

Admission is exclusively by competitive examination, open to all candidates between the ages of sixteen and twenty. The age may be extended in the case of non-commissioned officers and soldiers to twenty-five; but such as avail themselves of this extension on graduation can only be assigned to the military service.

The annual expense of each pupil is 1,000 francs; the cost of the uniform and outfit is 600 francs.

Pupils who are in indigent circumstances are educated free; while for others, in reduced circumstances, the cost of education is reduced one-half.

The examination for admission is both written and oral, and is conducted annually in the different departments on the same principles as for the school at St.-Cyr.

To be admitted to the preliminary examination, each candidate must be either a Bachelor of Science, or Letters, or possess an equivalent certificate.

The subjects of examination are—
- Arithmetic,
- Algebra,
- Geometry,
- Trigonometry,
- Descriptive geometry,
- Analytical geometry,
- Physics,
- Chemistry,
- French,
- German,
- Drawing.

The course of study is two years, and embraces—
- Descriptive geometry,
- Stereotomy,
- Differential and integral calculus,

Mechanics (solids and fluids),
Physics,
Optics,
Acoustics,
Chemistry,
Astronomy,
Geodesy,
Architecture,
Topography,
Military art and fortification (19 lessons),
History,
French literature,
German,
Drawing—landscape, rectilinear, and mechanical.

The practical military instruction the first year is continued six days in the week, an hour and a half being allowed for each exercise, until the pupils know the School of the Soldier, and the principal movements in the School of the Company.

The second year there is at least one drill a week in the School of the Company.

The two classes are also united from time to time for exercise in the School of the Battalion. They are also conducted once or twice a year outside of Paris for target-practice, and to execute the firings.

While the pupils wear a uniform, attend roll-calls, and are under a military *régime*, it is manifest, from the little time devoted to military subjects, both practical and theoretical, that the institution cannot be regarded as a military school. It is rather a mathematical or scientific school, whose fame has been acquired through the extraordinary inducements offered by the Government to its graduates.

Thoroughness of education has been secured by the severe nature of the competitive examinations for admission, and afterward by competition among the graduates for choice of corps on leaving the school.

The method of instruction pursued at the Polytechnic has been imitated in nearly all of the schools of Europe. Instruction is imparted by lecture, and the regulations prescribe that each lesson or lecture shall be followed by questioning one or more of the pupils from a quarter to half an hour—the lecture and questioning not to exceed an hour and a half. The pupils are required to take notes, and after the lecture return to halls of study, where, during the day, they pass all of their time, except when at lecture, recreation, or meals. These halls accommodate from eight to ten pupils, and are provided with a table, blackboard, and other articles necessary to prosecute one's studies. On returning to the halls, the pupils study the subject of the lecture, which is usually delivered by the professor to the entire class, and if necessary are assisted by additional explanations from the assistant professors, who are called *répétiteurs*.

These officers, in addition to giving the pupils assistance, question them from time to time on the various subjects, giving them a mark denoting their proficiency.

The pupils are also required to submit compositions, or written exercises on each subject, and at the conclusion of the series of lessons they are given a general questioning on the entire course.

The marks given after each questioning, as also for each written exercise, drawing, and examination, are used to determine the relative proficiency of the class.

SCHOOL OF APPLICATION FOR ARTILLERY AND ENGINEERS.

At the conclusion of the course at the Polytechnic School the graduates who are assigned to the artillery and engineers are commissioned second-lieutenants, and sent to the School of Application, at Fontainebleau, where they remain two years.

The course of study is pursued in the same manner as at the Polytechnic, and embraces—

    Topography,
    Geodesy,
    Field-fortification,

Permanent fortification,
Military art and administration,
Artillery,
Architecture and theory of construction.

The professors and instructors, with the exception of a few civilians, are officers of artillery and engineers.

On completing the course of instruction, the officers are assigned to their corps according to the order of merit determined at the final examination.

As the course of study at the School of Application is pursued subsequent to receiving commissions as lieutenants, it will be observed that, however high may be the intellectual qualifications of officers of artillery and engineers, they can have but a vague idea of the value and importance of military discipline, and this fact is due to the little attention paid to discipline and military instruction at the Polytechnic School.

The same defect exists at St.-Cyr, where the course of two years is too short to train a cadet in the principles of exact obedience and discipline, and to this defect in the two great military schools of France must be largely attributed the want of respect, obedience, and discipline, which was charged against the army during the Franco-German War.

STAFF SCHOOL, PARIS.

The object of this school is to train officers for the staff, which is exclusively recruited from its graduates.

The number of officers admitted varies from 25 to 50. Of this number 3 are reserved for graduates of the Polytechnic; the remainder are selected by competitive examination, open to the graduates of St.-Cyr, and to lieutenants of the line.

The course of study is two years, and embraces—
Topography,
Geodesy,
Astronomy,
Geography and statistics,

Descriptive geometry,
Artillery,
Military art and history,
Military administration,
Fortification,
Tactics, cavalry and infantry,
Drawing,
Hippology, and
Riding.

At the conclusion of the course, the graduates are assigned two years to infantry, and two years to the cavalry, after which they are appointed permanently in the staff, with the rank of captain, and return no more to the line.

Those of each class, generally ten to twelve, who are in excess of the number of vacancies, remain in the line, but are eligible for transfer with officers of the staff when a transfer can be arranged.

ACADEMY OF WAR.

This academy, in 1876, was in the process of organization, its object being the same as that of the celebrated War Academy of Berlin.

Admission to it is by competitive examination.

The effect of the academy will probably be an entire abandonment of the present staff system, and a rearrangement of it, whereby officers may continually pass from the line to the staff, and the reverse.

By means of remaining a closed corps, the staff of France has fallen behind that of other armies, as was shown in the late war, when many of the officers, who were familiar only with office labor and routine, were found incapable of rendering valuable assistance in manœuvring and directing armies.

With the exception of conservatism in reference to the staff, the army, since its late reverses, has made immense strides in organization, instruction, and discipline, and already gives evidence that in a future struggle it may regain its former prestige.

ARMY OF ENGLAND.

The English army, from which we inherit our military organization, laws, and customs, is so nearly like our own that only its main features need be stated.

Its strength is as follows:

ARM.	Officers.	Men.	Total.
Infantry	5,124	123,500	129,624
Cavalry	873	16,402	17,275
Artillery	1,450	83,474	84,924
Engineers	824	4,886	5,710
Colonial troops	124	2,357	2,481
Staff corps, and departments	1,614	5,196	6,810
Reserve, officers and men	....	......	82,500
Total	....	......	228,624

The infantry is composed of the guard, the line, and the rifles.

The guard is composed of 3 regiments, named the Grenadier Guards, of 3 battalions; the Coldstream Guards, of 2 battalions, and Scots Fusilier Guards, of 2 battalions. Total, 7 battalions.

The infantry of the line consists of 109 regiments, of which the first twenty-five contain 2 battalions each; the Sixtieth Regiment, called rifles, contains 4 battalions; the other regiments contain but one battalion each. Total battalions, 137.

The rifle-brigade is composed of 4 battalions.

The colonial or West India troops (colored) consist of two regiments of one battalion each.

BRIGADE OF INFANTRY.

Total number of battalions, 150.

All of the battalions have eight companies, except the two battalions of West India troops, which have nine.

The minimum strength of the battalions on home service is 604 officers and men; the average strength in 1876 was 886; the established strength in India is 919; in the other colonies it varies from 689 to 917.

The war-strength of a battalion of eight companies is as follows:

RANK.	Officers.	Men.
Colonel (honorary).........................	....	....
Lieutenant-colonel........................	1	....
Majors....................................	2	....
Captains..................................	9	....
Lieutenants and sub-lieutenants...........	16	....
Paymaster.................................	1	....
Adjutant..................................	1	....
Quartermaster.............................	1	....
Surgeon...................................	1	....
Sergeant-major............................	....	1
Band-sergeant.............................	....	1
Quartermaster-sergeant....................	....	1
Drum-major................................	....	1
Paymaster-sergeant........................	....	1
Armorer-sergeant..........................	....	1
Regimental transport-sergeant.............	....	1
Sergeant-cook.............................	....	1
Pioneer-sergeant..........................	....	1
First-sergeants...........................	....	8
Sergeants.................................	....	32
Orderly-room clerk........................	....	1
Drummers..................................	....	16
Corporals.................................	....	40
Pioneers and artificers...................	....	13
Band......................................	....	20
Privates..................................	....	902
Drivers...................................	....	25
Total.....................................	31	1,066
Total officers and men....................	1,097	

BRIGADE OF INFANTRY.

The brigade of infantry in time of war consists of the

BRIGADE.	Officers.	Non-commissioned Officers and Men.	Total.
Staff....................................	3	1	4
8 Regiments (8 battalions)................	98	8,193	8,291
Control department (supply)...............	1	26	27
Chaplains.................................	1	1	2
Total.....................................	93	8,221	8,324

DIVISION OF INFANTRY.

A division of infantry consists of the

DIVISION.	Officers.	Non-commissioned Officers and Men.	Total.
Staff	10	6	16
2 Brigades of infantry (6 battalions)	196	6,452	6,648
1 Battalion of rifles	31	1,066	1,097
1 Regiment of cavalry	27	623	650
3 Batteries of field-artillery	21	547	568
1 Company of engineers	6	186	192
1 Troop of military police (provost-guard)	2	73	75
INFANTRY AND ARTILLERY (RESERVE).			
Ammunition-column	6	206	212
Control department (quartermaster and commissary departments)	10	113	123
Veterinary department	2	21	23
Chaplains	2	2	4
Total	313	9,295	9,608

ARMY CORPS.

An army corps consists as follows:

CORPS.	Officers.	Non-commissioned Officers and Men.	Total.
Staff	19	12	31
3 Divisions of infantry	939	27,885	28,824
1 Brigade of cavalry (8 regiments)	96	2,072	2,168
ARTILLERY (RESERVE).			
Regimental staff	4	2	6
3 Batteries of horse-artillery	21	516	537
2 Batteries of field-artillery	14	882	896
3 Divisions of reserve ammunition-train	18	516	534
ENGINEERS.			
Regimental staff	2	1	3
1 Company and field-park	7	209	216
1 Pontoon-troop	9	313	322
½ Telegraph-troop	6	143	149
1 Troop of military police	2	73	75
Control department	27	277	304
Medical department			
Veterinary department	45	393	438
Chaplains	3	3	6
Bakery-train	2	{ 218 52 }	272
Butchery-train			
Total	1,214	83,067	84,281

RECRUITMENT.

The basis of the English system rests on voluntary enlistment, carrying with it in time of war the payment of large bounties.

The term of service is twelve years, with reënlistment to twenty-one years, which entitles the soldier to life-pension.

RESERVE.

With a view to supply a body of trained soldiers from which to fill up the army in time of war, soldiers, after serving three years in the ranks, are permitted to go into reserve, where, in consideration of being liable to military duty, they receive sixpence a day; in case they are called back to the colors, they also acquire a right to pension. The ultimate strength of the reserve is estimated at 80,000 men.

MILITIA.

The militia is intended for local defense, but it can be ordered anywhere within the limits of the United Kingdom, and is also available as garrison-troops for the fortresses of the Mediterranean. It consists of about 120,000 men, voted annually by Parliament, and is organized into artillery and infantry. Enlistment is voluntary, and for the period of six years. The officers are commissioned by the Queen, and all of the details of recruitment and instruction are confided to the generals commanding military districts.

For the purpose of instruction the militia can be called out from three to four weeks annually, and the period can be extended to eight weeks. Regular officers can also be assigned to the militia as instructors, and the soldiers in reserve may be attached to it whenever called out for manœuvre.

MILITIA RESERVE.

This force, which is liable to army service in case of emergency, numbers about 30,000 men, or one-fourth of the militia, and is voted annually by Parliament. The term of enlistment is for six years, for which a bounty is granted of £1 per annum.

VOLUNTEERS.

Next to the regular army the volunteers constitute the principal bulwark in case of invasion.

They consist of approximately 180,000 men, organized as infantry, and garrison artillery. The officers of volunteers are commissioned by the lieutenants of counties, subject to the approval of the Queen. The men receive their arms from the Government, and are recruited and instructed under the direction of the commanders of military districts.

Unless granted leave, the members must be present at each annual inspection. Recruits, on joining, attend thirty drills, and afterward, as a minimum, they must attend nine drills annually.

In case of invasion, the volunteers are mobilized, and held for permanent service.

YEOMAN CAVALRY.

This force consists approximately of 13,000 men, each one of whom furnishes his own horse.

The force is equipped as light cavalry, drills eight days per year, and is subject to be called out in cases of riot and insurrection. When called out, the pay for each man, with his horse, is sevenpence a day.

TERRITORIAL DIVISIONS.

Following the example of Continental nations, the army has recently been organized into eight army corps, which are assigned to as many territorial districts. These districts are divided into 70 sub-districts, of which there are 54 in England and Wales, 8 in Scotland, and 8 in Ireland.

Each sub-district is the recruiting-ground of a brigade, composed of 2 battalions of infantry of the line, 2 battalions of militia, and such volunteers as belong within the district. The two battalions, or regiments, when the latter contain but one battalion each, alternate in foreign service, and are said to be "linked."

The regiment which is abroad has its depot at the headquarters of the home district, where the recruits are received, and thoroughly trained before being forwarded.

The depot is commanded by a captain, who is under the orders of the colonel of the regiment. All officers serving at the depot are detailed for a period of two years.

The division into sub-districts; the linking of regiments; the establishment of regimental depots; and the association of militia and volunteers in the same brigade with the troops of the line, is an approach to both the German and Austrian regimental systems, in which the field regiment, the depot, and the Landwehr battalions, are practically united under one commander.

STAFF.

All duty in the Adjutant-General's and Quartermaster-General's Departments of the English army is performed by officers detailed from the line.

To equalize the details, no regiment of cavalry is required to furnish at the same time more than one captain and one lieutenant, and no infantry regiment more than two captains and two lieutenants.

As a general rule, the tenure of staff appointments is limited to five years; and, in case of appointment on the staff of general officers and governors of colonies, an officer, after having served the prescribed period, must serve two years with his regiment before being eligible to a second appointment.

All officers on the staff, when their regiments are ordered to India, or on active service, are required to vacate their appointments.

With the exception of officers of engineers, whose service prior to 1870 exceeds seven years, and of all officers who have proved their ability on the staff in the field, no officer can be appointed on the staff as deputy assistant adjutant-general, deputy quartermaster-general, or brigade-major (assistant adjutant-general of brigade), without having passed the final examination at the Staff College at Sandhurst.

The names of all such graduates are borne on a special list in the army register.

The principles of staff duty in the English army, which find their widest application in India, have already been stated, in the description of the Indian army.

CONFIDENTIAL REPORTS.

General officers are required to make annual inspections of the troops under their command, and to report upon the character and qualifications of all their subordinate officers.

These reports are termed "confidential," but they are relieved from the dangers of secrecy by the requirement of the regulation that, when a report is adverse to an officer, he shall be informed as to its nature.

The reports are signed by both the commander of the regiment to which the officer belongs, and by the inspecting officer, and are then forwarded through the intermediate commanders to the military secretary of the Commander-in-Chief.

The object of the reports is to guide the Commander-in-Chief in the selection of officers for promotion to higher grades in the service, and for employment on the general staff.

ROYAL MILITARY COLLEGE, SANDHURST.

The object of this college is to afford a "special military education" to candidates for commissions in the cavalry and infantry.

In future, the course of study prescribed at this college must be pursued by all candidates for commissions in the infantry and cavalry, except lieutenants of militia, and non-commissioned officers recommended for promotion.

The number of cadets admitted to the college varies according to the requirements of the service.

Cadets are admitted on the 10th of February, and the 1st of September of each year.

Admission is granted to these classes of candidates as follows:

1. To successful candidates at a competitive examination on general subjects, held before the Civil-Service Commissioners.

2. University candidates, and to graduates in arts at Oxford, Cambridge, Dublin, and other universities, who must pass a competitive examination.

3. To "Queen's Cadets," "Honorary Queen's Cadets," "Indian Cadets," and "Pages of Honor."

Candidates admitted by competition are given a preliminary examination before the Civil-Service Commissioners in—

1. Mathematics, including arithmetic through interest and proportion, and geometry through the first book of Euclid.
2. French, German, or some other modern language.
3. Writing English correctly and legibly from dictation.
4. Elements of geometrical drawing.
5. Geography.

Candidates who pass this examination successfully are immediately admitted to the "further examination" in—

1. Mathematics, embracing algebra through quadratic equations and logarithms, geometry, plane trigonometry, and mensuration.
2. English composition, tested by writing an essay, letter, or *précis;* English literature, limited to specified authors; and English history, within fixed periods.
3. Latin.
4. Greek.
5. French, examination partly colloquial.
6. German, examination partly colloquial.
7. Experimental sciences, viz., chemistry and heat, or electricity and magnetism, examination allowed by choice in one to the exclusion of the other.
8. General and physical geography, and geology.
9. Free-hand drawing.

Exclusive of drawing, candidates cannot be examined in more than four, nor in less than two, of the above subjects.

The proficiency of each candidate is denoted by marks, given in all of the subjects of the "further examination" in which he is examined, to which are added the marks procured in drawing at the preliminary examination. The candidates are then classified according to these marks, when those nearest the head of the list, corresponding to the number of vacancies, are declared successful. The age of candidates at date of competition must be between seventeen and twenty-one.

University candidates, at the preliminary examination, are examined only in geometrical drawing. The "further examination" is the same as for other candidates by competition, already described. The age of university candidates must be between seventeen and twenty-two. The number of cadetships given to this class is fixed for each examination, and is filled by the competitors who receive the highest marks.

The Queen's Cadets are sons of officers of the army, navy, and marines, who have fallen in battle, died of wounds, or of disease contracted in the service abroad, and whose families have been left in reduced circumstances. The cadets are appointed by the Secretary of State, on the recommendation of the commander-in-chief, or First Lord of the Admiralty.

Honorary Queen's Cadets are sons of officers of the army, navy, and marines, killed in action; or who have died of wounds within six months of the time they were received; or who have died of disease contracted through privation or exposure in the field, in the presence of the enemy, within six months from the time the illness was contracted.

Indian Cadets are sons of officers of the Indian military and civil service, or of the East India Company, who are nominated by the Secretary of State for India in council.

These three classes of cadets are the only ones admitted to Sandhurst without competition, but they must pass the preliminary examination already described, and in the "further examination" must obtain such an aggregate of marks as to satisfy the Civil-Service Commissioners of their general proficiency.

This examination is dispensed with in case a candidate can produce a "University Certificate."

Sons of officers admitted to Sandhurst pay annually from £20 to £80, except Queen's Cadets, whose tuition is free.

Sons of private citizens pay £125 per year.

COURSE OF INSTRUCTION.

The following subjects are taught in the course of instruction, viz.:

1. Queen's regulations, orders for the army, regimental interior economy, accounts, and correspondence.
2. Military law.
3. Elements of tactics.
4. Field fortification, and elements of permanent fortification.
5. Military topography and reconnaissance.
6. Infantry and field-artillery drill, riding, and gymnastics.

The course of instruction lasts but one year, and is divided into two terms, one of which extends from the 10th of February to the 15th of July; the other from the 1st of September to the 20th of December.

The periods between the terms, and a fortnight at Easter, are allowed as vacations.

For the purpose of discipline and instruction, cadets are arranged in divisions of twenty-five each.

The method of instruction is principally by lecture, supplemented by text-books.

The practical instruction consists of riding, School of the Trooper, with sword-exercise; infantry drill, and field-battery drill with drag-ropes.

An examination is held at the end of each term.

The first examination is probationary, and cadets who fail lose a term. Cadets who pass the second examination are arranged according to merit, and are entitled to commissions as second-lieutenants in the cavalry, or infantry.

The Commander-in-Chief is the president of the college. The management of the college is vested in a governor, usually general officer, who is responsible to the Secretary of War, through the Commander-in-Chief.

The college is inspected each year by a board of visitors, appointed by the Secretary of State for War. The members of the board do not hold permanent appointments, but all of the members are never changed at the same time. The report of the board is submitted to Parliament.

The professors and instructors are all officers detailed from the army.

The English system of education for officers of infantry and cavalry resembles the German, in requiring, first, a good general education; and, second, a course of purely military instruction. It differs from the German in not requiring from six months to a year's service in the ranks previous to pursuing the military course.

From 1873 to 1876 the Government tried the experiment of appointing the second-lieutenants of cavalry and infantry previous to pursuing the course of instruction at Sandhurst; but the fact that the students already held their commissions, proved so detrimental to study and discipline, that the scheme was abandoned, and, since 1876, the same system has been pursued, except as to the nature and duration of the course, as was pursued prior to 1870.

ROYAL MILITARY ACADEMY, WOOLWICH.

The object of this academy is to prepare candidates for commissions in the artillery, and engineers.

Admission is by competitive examinations, held semi-annually, by the Civil-Service Commissioners.

Candidates must be between the ages of sixteen and eighteen.

The examination, like that for Sandhurst, is divided into the "preliminary" and "further examination."

The preliminary examination consists of—

1. Mathematics, embracing arithmetic, and the use of common logarithms; algebra, including the binomial theorem; geometry, to the sixth book of Euclid; plane trigonometry, including the solution of triangles.
2. French, German, or some other modern language.
3. Writing English correctly from dictation.
4. Elements of geometrical drawing.
5. Geography.

The candidates who pass in the foregoing subjects are admitted to the further examination, which consists of—

1. Mathematics, embracing theory of equations; analytical geometry, conic sections, solid geometry, differential and integral calculus, statics, and dynamics.

2. English literature and history.

3. Classics, embracing both Latin and Greek, or one separately.

4. French (examination partly colloquial).

5. German (examination partly colloquial).

6. Any one of the following languages, viz.: Italian, Russian, Spanish, or Hindostani.

7. Experimental sciences, viz.: Chemistry and heat, electricity and magnetism.

8. General and physical geography, and geology.

9. Free-hand drawing.

Exclusive of drawing, candidates cannot be examined in more than four, nor less than two, of the above subjects; but optional examination is further permitted, embracing nearly all of analytical geometry, differential and integral calculus, and also statics and dynamics.

The number of admissions depends upon the number of vacancies.

Sons of officers pay tuition at rates varying from £20 to £80 per annum.

Sons of private citizens pay £125, or $625.

COURSE OF INSTRUCTION.

The course of instruction lasts two years and a half, and embraces the following subjects:

1. Mathematics, including a thorough knowledge of plane trigonometry; practical mechanics, with the application of mathematics to machinery.

2. Field and permanent fortification, so far as suitable for officers qualifying for the artillery.

3. Artillery, so far as suitable for cadets qualifying for the engineers.

4. Military drawing, with field sketching and reconnaissance.

5. Military history and geography.

6. French and German, at the student's choice.

7. Elementary chemistry and physics.
8. Drill and exercises.

In addition to the foregoing subjects, which are obligatory, cadets are permitted to study any of the following subjects, viz.:

1. Higher mathematics.
2. Higher portions of fortification.
3. German, French, Italian, Russian, Spanish, or Hindostani.
4. Free-hand figure and landscape drawing.
5. Higher chemistry.
6. Latin.
7. Greek.

The practical instruction consists of gymnastics, riding (School of the Trooper), infantry (School of the Soldier, Company, and Battalion), artillery, field, siege, and mortar drill; also mechanical manœuvres.

The cadets constitute one company under the command of a captain, and are arranged in five classes, according to the date of their admissions.

The examinations are conducted by examiners independent of the academy.

Cadets who fail at any two of the five examinations are dismissed.

To be entitled to a commission a cadet must receive one-half of the maximum marks allotted in the obligatory course to mathematics, mechanics, fortification, and artillery; and one-half of the aggregate marks allotted to all of the subjects of the obligatory course.

The Commander-in-Chief is president of the Military Academy, but the immediate management is confided to a military officer styled the governor, who is responsible to the Secretary of War through the Commander-in-Chief.

The academy is annually inspected by a board of visitors, the same as the college at Sandhurst.

Appointment as professors and inspectors is open to officers of all ranks. The tenure of appointment, which carries with it increased pay, is limited to six years, with power of reappointment. Professors may also be selected from civil life, but in no case can the tenure of office continue after the incumbent is fifty-five years of age unless recommended by the governor of the academy, approved by the Secretary of State.

STAFF COLLEGE (AT SANDHURST).

The special object of this college is to educate officers for employment on the staff.

The total number of students is 40, the admission being determined by competitive examination.

The number of vacancies each year is 20, of which number 3 are allowed to officers of artillery, and 2 to engineers, provided they are among the 20 candidates highest on the list.

On admission, unmarried officers pay an entrance-fee of £3, and married officers £1 10s. as a contribution to the mess-funds, in excess of their regular quarterly subscription; they also pay £3 as entrance-subscription to the college library, after which no further payments are required while at the college.

To be eligible for admission, an officer must possess the following qualifications:

1. Service of not less than five years previous to examination, exclusive of leaves of absence in excess of the annual privilege-leaves, which are granted to all officers.

2. A certificate from his commanding officer that the candidate is in every respect a thoroughly good regimental officer.

3. A confidential report, in answer to specific questions regarding the character, habits, and disposition of the candidate, and his general qualifications for employment on the staff, to be made by a board of officers consisting of the commanding officer and the two next senior officers of the candidate's regiment.

4. A certificate that the candidate, if not a captain, has qualified for promotion to that rank.

5. A medical certificate of good health, and fitness for active duties on the staff.

If practicable, the candidate must also serve a month on the staff of a general officer, who is required to make a confidential report as to his general fitness for the staff.

The following are the subjects at the competitive examination, with the relative value of each indicated by marks, viz.:

	MARKS.
1. Mathematics, embracing arithmetic, algebra, geometry, trigonometry, and elementary mechanics	900
2. Military history and geography	900
3. French	300
4. German	300
5. Hindostani	300
6. Fortification	600
7. Military drawing	300
8. Geology	300
9. Chemistry (heat, electricity, and magnetism)	300

Of the above subjects, arithmetic, algebra (to include equations of the first degree), geometry (to include the fourth book of Euclid), one of the three languages, and elementary field fortifications, are obligatory. The remaining subjects are optional.

The minimum qualifying mark is 250 out of 400 allotted to obligatory mathematics; 150 out of 300 in French; 100 out of 300 in German and Hindostani; and 50 out of 150 allotted to a simple paper on field-fortification.

Examinations for the United Kingdom take place under the direction of the Director-General of Military Education, in the month of June. In the colonies the same printed questions as are used in London are answered, in writing, before a board of officers, who certify that the candidate has received no assistance from books or otherwise. These papers are then forwarded to London, where the officer's merits are determined.

The course of study lasts two years, and embraces the following subjects, viz.:

Obligatory.

Mathematics, including mensuration; mode of determining heights and distances by ground problems, and trigonometrical calculations; use of sextant, and elementary mechanics.

Fortification and field-engineering.

Artillery.

Topographical drawing, military surveying, sketching, and road-making.

Reconnaissance.

Military art, history, and geography.

Military administration and law.

French, German, or Hindostani.

Riding.

Voluntary.

The two languages not selected as obligatory.

Geology, exclusive of mineralogy.

Experimental sciences.

Photography.

Military telegraphy.

Each year's course is divided into two terms, viz., from the 1st of February to the 15th of July, and from the 1st of September to the 15th of December. The remaining periods constitute vacations.

Examinations are held at the end of every term. The summer examinations are held by the professors of the college; the winter examinations are held by examiners independent of the college.

Confidential reports are also made to the Commander-in-Chief, after each of the examinations, as to the qualifications of each officer for staff employment.

The examination at the end of the second term is probationary. Officers who fail to receive 55 per cent. of the marks allotted to the subjects, and also those who are reported upon as unlikely to make efficient staff officers, are required to withdraw.

At the final examination the obligatory subjects count as follows:

1. Fortification, field-engineering, and artillery   6
2. Military drawing and surveying   2½
3. Reconnaissance   4½
4. Military art, history, and geography   6
5. { Military administration   4
    { Military law   2
6. French, German, or Hindostani   4
7. Mathematics   3

At the final examination, the officers who have passed are arranged on a list, according to the order of seniority of their regiments, special mention being made of those who have won honors.

Officers may be permitted to pass the final examination, and thus qualify for staff duty, without pursuing the course at the college. They must, however, pass a portion of the months of October and November at the college, in order to be examined in reconnaissance, and to be tested in the practical subjects of instruction at the college.

After having passed the final examination, officers are either—

1. Attached for three months during the following summer to the staff of a general officer, at a camp of instruction at which the three arms of the service are present. At the end of this period the general makes a confidential report as to the character and abilities of the officers, and also states the departments of the staff for which they appear to be best qualified; or—

2. Attached during the following summer drill-season to another arm of service than their own, with a view to acquire a knowledge of their organization, economy, and tactics. At the end of the season the commanding officers make a special report as to their efficiency.

Officers of infantry and cavalry attend artillery instruction at Woolwich, or some other station, for a period of two months. Officers of cavalry are attached to the infantry two months.

Officers of engineers and infantry are attached to cavalry two months. Officers of artillery (horse-artillery excepted) are attached one month.

After completing the practical instruction, the officers return to their regiments, and are then eligible for appointment as—

Deputy assistant adjutant-generals,
Deputy assistant quartermaster-generals,
Brigade-majors (adjutant-generals),
Garrison instructors,
Assistant military secretaries, and
Aides-de-camp to general officers.

EXAMINATIONS FOR PROMOTION.

Examinations for promotion to the grades of captain and major are required in all arms of service.

The examination in infantry for promotion to captain embraces the following subjects, viz.:

1. Evolutions of a regiment, including skirmishing, outposts, patrols, escorts, advance and rear guards.
2. Charge of a company or detachment in every position in which it may be placed, musketry instruction, orderly-room work, requisitions, returns, accounts, and correspondence.
3. Queen's regulations and orders for the army.
4. Military law.
5. Elements of tactics.
6. Field fortification, and elements of permanent fortification.
7. Military topography.

Graduates of Sandhurst are exempted from examination in the last four subjects.

Examination for promotion to the rank of major in infantry embraces, in the field—

1. Riding.
2. Command of a regiment—
    Singly on parade,
    As part of a brigade,
    As advance or rear guard,

>   As outposts covering a brigade or division,
>   Skirmishing, with movements adapted to a specified purpose.

The theoretical examination, on paper and *viva voce*, embraces—

1. Representing on a sketch, or map, of a piece of ground previously seen by the officer (the map being furnished to the officer), the disposition of a combined force of the three arms, as—

>   Advance or rear guard,
>   On outpost,
>   For attack and defense of a given position, such as a defile, a wood, or bridge.

2. Principles of combining the movements of infantry, artillery, and cavalry, for mutual support.

3. The forms for demanding, and sources of supply of, ammunition, fuel, and forage.

4. System of regimental orderly-room work, and correspondence.

Graduates of the staff college are exempted from the theoretical examination.

The practical examination is conducted by the general commanding, or by an officer whom he may select.

The theoretical examination is conducted by a board of three officers, one of whom is of the same arm of service as the candidate for promotion.

AGGRESSIVE POWER OF ENGLAND.

The adherence of England to a military system, inherited from the last century, can only be explained by her insular position, and the security from invasion afforded by a powerful navy.

The salient defect of her system is the non-expansive organization of the regular army; and this defect, in view of European complications, becomes the more apparent when it is considered that nearly one-half of the regiments, batteries, and squadrons, exceeding 90,000 men, are employed in India and the colonies.

Of the 150 battalions of infantry only 77 are serving in the

United Kingdom, and, were these raised to the war-footing, their total strength would but little exceed 80,000.

Adding to this number 20,000, drawn from the Mediterranean and India, the force of British infantry, available for aggressive purposes, would approximate 100,000 men, and in this number would be included the greater part of the reserve recently created.

In contrast with this force, the infantry of the great Continental powers, organized on the expansive principle, can be raised, in round numbers, to the following war-footing, viz.:

Austria	545,000
France	700,000
Germany	495,000
Russia	674,000

Furthermore, as the result of obligatory military service, behind this immense force of infantry, which is supported by artillery and cavalry in the highest state of drill and discipline, there stand in readiness trained reserves, and armies of the second line, largely outnumbering the total military force which England can bring into the field.

With such disparity of strength, should England assail any of her formidable neighbors, we may safely anticipate that the war will be followed either by the speedy reorganization of her army, or by the total abandonment of the policy of armed intervention in foreign affairs.

INFANTRY TACTICS.

The successive improvements that have been made in firearms during the last hundred years have been followed by a gradual diminution of the depth of tactical formations, until to-day the "open order," or the formation as skirmishers, is the only one adopted under the fire of the enemy.

The advantages of this order were first brought to light in the War of the Revolution, and since that time its use has steadily increased in all of our wars.

Transplanted to Europe by the French officers who served in our armies, it became prominent in the wars of the French Revolution, and has since been adopted in all European armies.

In the most recent development of the "open order" the company, composed of 250 men, is recognized as the "fighting unit;" while the battalion, composed of four companies, is regarded as the "tactical unit"—that is, the smallest body of men that can be safely employed independently.

By combining in each battalion the movements of four "fighting units," each one of which is divided into three or more smaller subdivisions, the modern system of fighting has devolved upon the battalion and company commanders the tactical skill heretofore required of brigade and regimental commanders, and has further devolved increased responsibility on every subordinate rank to the private soldier.

The adoption of breech-loaders has not changed the principles of strategy and grand tactics, nor has it diminished the number of lines in which armies are drawn up to give and receive battle. It has simply demonstrated the impossibility of attacking positions in battalion columns, and, as a consequence, has necessitated a division of the troops into smaller fractions, which under fire can be moved with the greatest rapidity and least exposure, thereby insuring the least loss of life.

The open or skirmish order has, therefore, been adopted, and is employed by the first line whenever troops approach the zone covered by the enemy's fire.

The battalion being the tactical unit, the general principles of the open order are, that the skirmishers shall only occupy a front equal to the front of the battalion in line, and that the battalion shall be divided into two parts, one of which constitutes the "fighting line," the other the "reserve."

The fighting line is generally composed of two companies, each of which is posted in two or three lines, the first being the skirmishers, the second and third lines the supports.

The reserve is composed of the remaining two companies formed as a half-battalion column, or as two company columns, and is posted in rear of the supports.

The arrangement of the "fighting line" and the "reserve" will be best understood by describing the formation and use of the German and French company columns.

GERMAN COMPANY COLUMN.

The company is formed in three ranks; the tallest men are in the front rank; "the most adroit and best shots are selected for the third rank, because the special duties of this rank require these qualities;" the distance between ranks is two feet.

The company is divided into divisions (or platoons). If the divisions consist of twenty or more files, they are divided into subdivisions (or half-platoons); the subdivisions are again divided into sections of not less than four, nor more than six files.

If the company be of full strength, it will have a front of 72 files; each division will contain 36 files; each subdivision 18 files; and each section 6 files.

INFANTRY TACTICS.

The battalion consists of four companies, which are numbered from right to left. The eight subdivisions into which the battalion is divided are also numbered from right to left, and preserve their numerical designations throughout manœuvres.

FORMATION OF THE COMPANY COLUMN.

(Plate 1.) The company column is formed in the following manner:

Plate 1.

The battalion being in line, at the commands 1. "Form company column"—2. "March," the third rank of each even division of the right wing faces about, marches twelve paces to the rear, halts, and faces to the front; the first and second ranks of the uneven divisions face to the left, and place themselves six paces in rear of the first and second ranks of the even division; the third rank of the uneven subdivisions faces to the left, and, filing in front of the third rank of the even division, forms with it a third division in double rank. The movement is executed in the uncadenced step. The column when formed consists practically of three platoons in double rank.

In the left wing the movement is similarly executed; the even subdivisions ploying in rear of the uneven subdivisions.

Each division of the column is commanded by a lieutenant, who stands on the right of the front rank, and is provided with its proper quota of file-closers. The third division of each column is called the "shooting subdivision."

(Plate 2.) The battalion being ployed into company columns consists of two company columns side by side at the centre, called a half-battalion column, and of two detached company columns; the interval between the flanks of the half-battalion column and the flank-company columns is twenty-four yards, or equal to the front of a division.

GERMAN COMPANY COLUMN. 273

Plate 2.

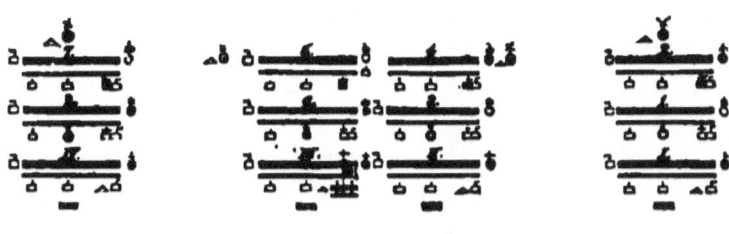

- 𝟖 Battalion-commander.
- 𝟖 Adjutant.
- 𝟖 Captain.
- 𝟖 First-lieutenant.
- 𝟖 First second-lieutenant.
- 𝟖 Second second-lieutenant.
- 𝟖 Third second-lieutenant.
- 𝟖 Sergeant-major.
- 𝟖 Portépée-fähnrich.
- 𝟖 Right guide.
- 𝟖 Left guide.
- 𝟖 File-closer.
- 𝟖 Color.
- ▬ Musicians.
- ▲ Bugler.
- ••• Skirmishers.

Plate 3.

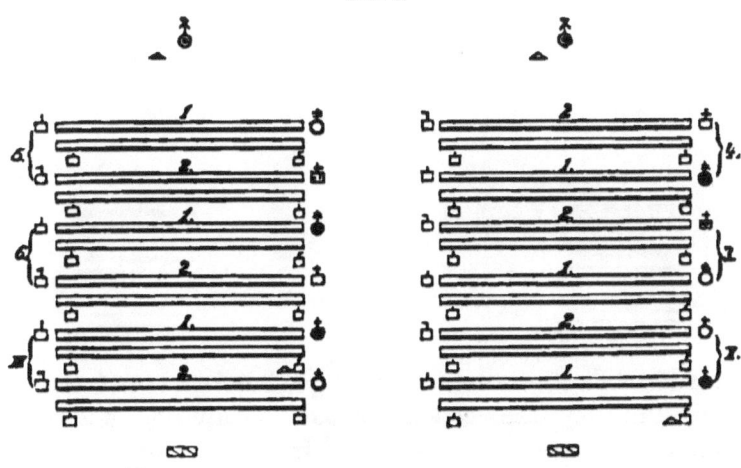

274 INFANTRY TACTICS.

(Plate 3.) The tactics provide for reducing the front of each company column to half subdivisions, giving each column six half subdivisions, and also for breaking into columns of sections—a formation which resembles our column of fours.

The company column is formed in line to the front by means inverse to those used in the ployment; the third rank resuming its proper place.

DEPLOYMENT OF THE COMPANY COLUMN AS SKIRMISHERS.

(Plate 4.) The German method of deployment as skirmishers is a successive movement usually beginning with a section,

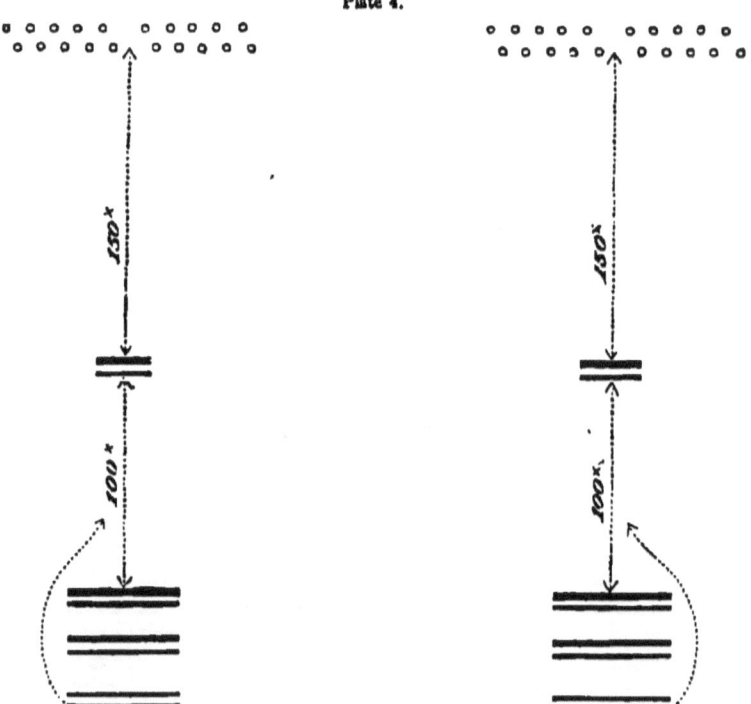

Plate 4.

or a half subdivision of the shooting subdivision. At the signal "Skirmish," the section or half subdivision designated moves by the flank until disengaged from the column, and then moves to the front, the files obliquing to the right and left till they gain an interval, usually not exceeding six paces; the rear-rank man of each file, at his option, remains in rear of his file-leader, or places himself on his right or left. The remaining part of the shooting division follows the skirmish-line at a distance of 100 to 150 yards, and acts as a support; the first and second divisions of the company column follow in rear of the support at a suitable distance, usually 100 yards.

If necessary to reënforce the skirmish-line, the portion of the shooting subdivision acting as a support is sent forward, either by sections or all at once, the men taking the open order or retaining the close order according to circumstances.

If the entire shooting division be deployed at once, the remaining two divisions in column, or in line, act as a support, and, in case of need, send forward successive sections to strengthen the line, until the entire company becomes absorbed.

The difficulty of manœuvring skirmishers with a prescribed interval is so great that it is not even attempted; the skirmishers, on the contrary, are encouraged whenever practicable to assemble in sections, or "swarms," so as to avail themselves of every opportunity for cover, only, however, to relinquish it, and again extend, on moving to the front. The greatest latitude is given to officers in command of supports, and to non-commissioned officers in charge of sections, in ordering men to and from cover.

The usual method of attack is by a series of "rushes" from cover to cover, until the enemy exhausts his ammunition, or becomes demoralized, when a final rush with a shout is supposed to gain the victory.

DEPLOYMENT OF A BATTALION.

(Plate 5.) When a battalion is to be deployed as skirmishers, it is usually broken into four company columns, as previously explained. The shooting divisions of the first and fourth companies are deployed as skirmishers, covering the front of the battalion. The remaining portions of the first and fourth companies, called *front body*, or "Vortreffen," are posted as supports to their shooting subdivisions. The second and third companies are held in reserve as a half-battalion column, or

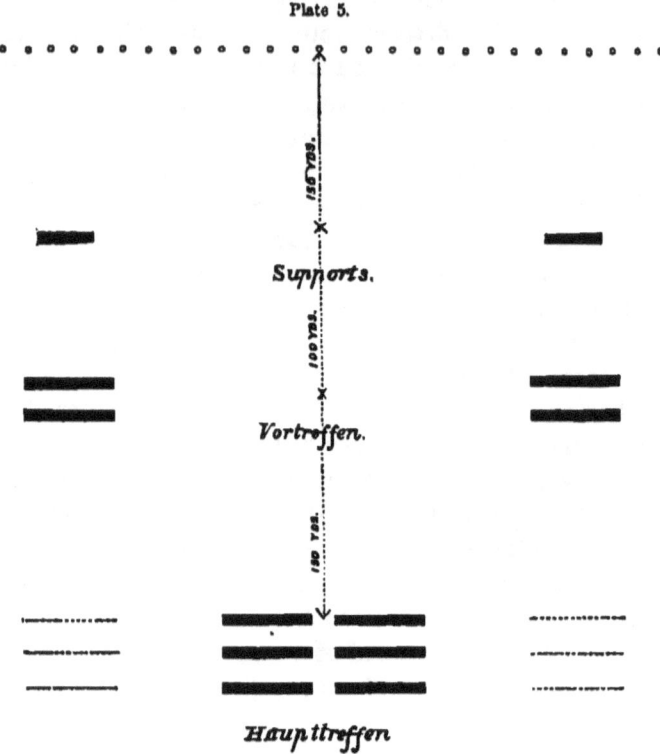

Plate 5.

they may be posted with an interval of 80 or 100 yards between them. These companies constitute the *main body*, or "Haupttreffen." The distance from the skirmishers to the nearest supports is about 150 yards; from the supports to the "Vortreffen," or the subdivisions of the first and fourth company columns, 100 yards; from the "Vortreffen" to the "Haupttreffen," 150 yards; making a total distance of 400 yards. These distances, however, are entirely dependent upon circumstances, and are usually regulated by the battalion and company commanders.

FORMATION OF THE BRIGADE.

The brigade consists of two regiments of three battalions each, and for battle is preferably formed in three lines; the battalions of each regiment being one in rear of the other. The first battalion is deployed as already explained. The second battalion is generally divided into two half-battalion columns, with an interval between them of about 250 yards, and is posted at the same distance from the main body of the first battalion. The third battalion is formed in "column of attack," double column on the centre, and is posted about 250 yards from the second line, opposite its centre.

Another formation of the brigade is in two lines: in this case the battalions of the first line are deployed as before, while those of the second line are either held in line, or in line of company columns.

The method of attack by means of the company column, when considered in its relations to the battalion and brigade, is as follows:

The shooting subdivisions of the first and fourth companies of the first battalion press forward from cover to cover, lying down when necessary, and by means of their fire drawing that of the enemy. Their fire is continually increased by sending additional sections to their support. If the enemy show signs of giving way, the supports move forward, give their fire, and then all make a rush.

If, however, the enemy resist, and continue a strong fire, the first and fourth companies will ordinarily become wholly engaged before approaching within 300 or 400 yards of the enemy. The second and third companies in the mean time will continue to approach, and, when near the line, will deploy in close order and join in the action, firing if necessary over the skirmishers, who lie down in front. The first battalion has now become entirely engaged. If sufficiently strong to continue the action, it gains ground by fits and starts until it arrives within 150 or 200 yards of the enemy, when the whole line breaks into loud cheers, and rushes forward with the bayonet. If the charge be repulsed, the second battalion, in half-battalion columns, sometimes in four-company columns, moves forward; the first line falls back, the officers making every effort to rally their men in the intervals and on the flanks of the

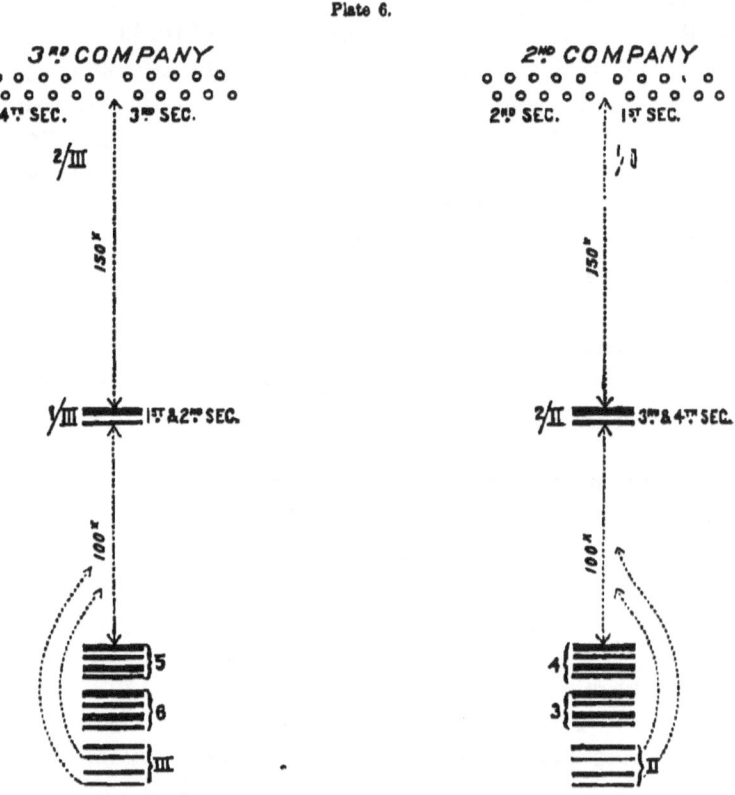

Plate 6.

second line; both lines then move forward so as to give the enemy as little time as possible to profit by his advantage. If the first line cannot be rallied in the intervals of the second, it re-forms in rear of the third.

If the first line, when wholly engaged, be not able to take the enemy's position, the second line is moved to its support, the company columns, if possible, being directed toward the flanks of the skirmish-line, from which position they open a flank or an oblique fire.

In reënforcing the skirmish-line, the German tactics pre-

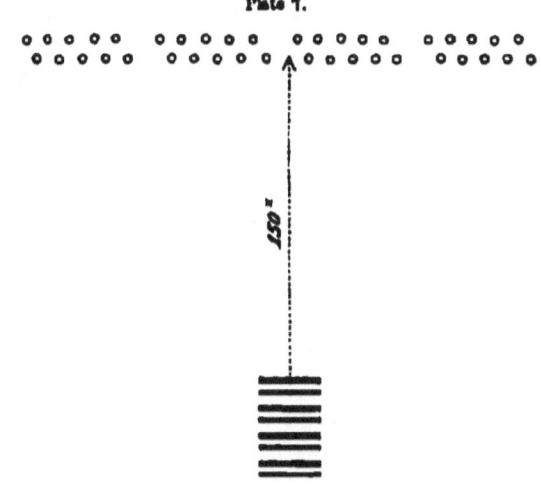

Plate 7.

scribe that, when practicable, it shall be done by extending the flank; when this cannot be done the reënforcement arrives from the rear, and mingles with the line. If, therefore, the company

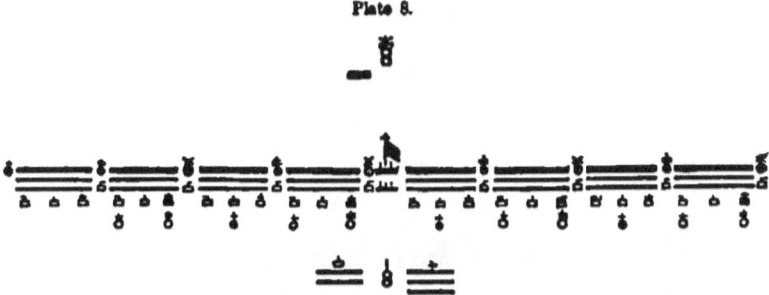

Plate 8.

columns of the second line cannot form on the flanks of the first line, they move forward, the skirmishers of the first line forming in the intervals; the two lines united then make a rush upon the enemy, and open fire as soon as his position is carried.

The first line, if repulsed before the second arrives at its support, forms in the intervals as before.

The combinations which may be made with the company columns are almost infinite, notwithstanding the German tactics favor but few movements, and these as simple as possible.

The formation of the third rank into shooting divisions necessitates many tactical movements in the School of the Battalion with a view to separating the shooting divisions from the remaining divisions of the battalion.

The following plates represent the principal formations of a company and battalion, both in the close and open order. The shooting divisions are denominated by Roman letters, the other divisions are denominated by figures.

Plate 6 represents the second and third companies deployed as skirmishers from column of subdivisions, or half-platoons.

Plate 7 represents all of the shooting division of a company deployed from column of subdivisions. The "Vortreffen" in this case is 150 yards from the skirmishers.

Plate 8 represents a battalion in line.

Plate 9 represents a battalion in line with the shooting division of each company formed in rear of the right division of the company in the right wing, and left division of the left wing. The two shooting divisions of each wing may likewise be formed in rear of its outer flank.

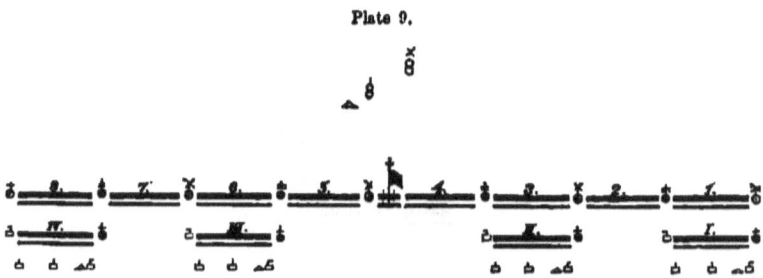

Plate 9.

Plate 10 represents a "column of attack," which is formed like our "double column" by ploying the right wing in column of divisions (platoons) in rear of its left division; the left wing is similarly ployed in rear of its right division. The distance from the front rank of one division to the file-closers of the division in front is two paces. The column of attack has

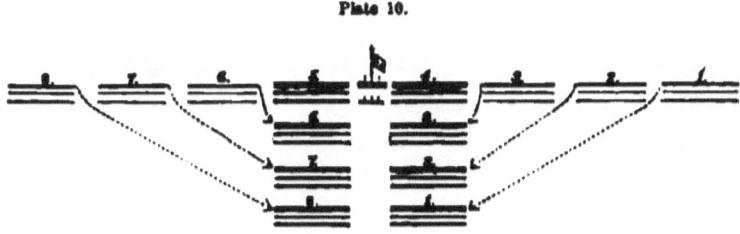

Plate 10.

ceased to be of special significance, as it is never used under fire.

Plate 11 represents the column of attack formed with

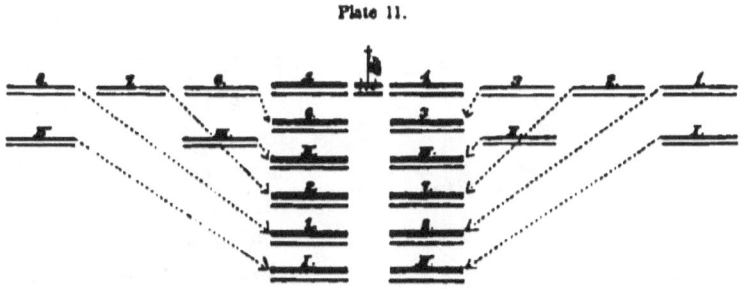

Plate 11.

each company in company column. The two shooting divisions of each wing may likewise be formed at the rear of the column; they may also be formed at the head of the column, or one division of each wing may be formed at the head, and the other at the rear.

The other column formations are:

1. Column of divisions, subdivisions, and sections, at full distance, formed by wheeling by divisions, subdivisions, and sections, to the right or left. Column of subdivisions, and sections, may also be formed by breaking from column of divisions, and subdivisions.

2. Close column of divisions, which may be formed by wheeling by divisions and closing to the distance of six paces, or directly by ployment, as indicated in Plate 12.

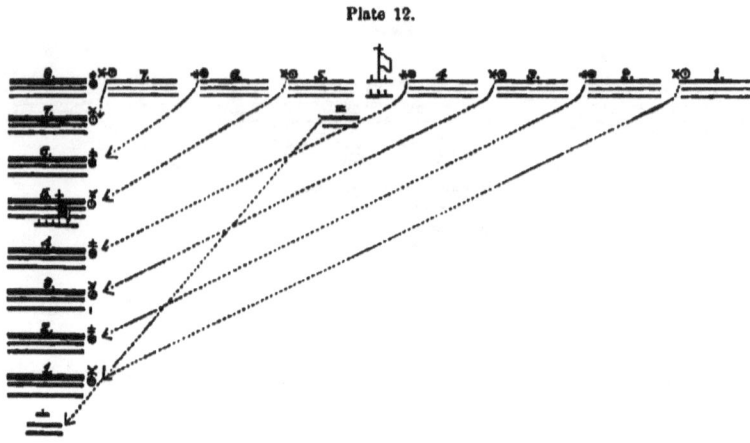

Plate 12.

Plate 13 represents the formation of column of attack from close column of divisions, right in front. The movement is executed on the fourth division, which stands fast; the three divisions in front face to the right, move forward a short distance, change direction twice to the right, and, when the head of each arrives opposite its place in rear of the fourth, it executes on the right into line; the four divisions in rear face to the left, march by the left flank till the rear of each arrives four paces beyond the left flank of the fourth

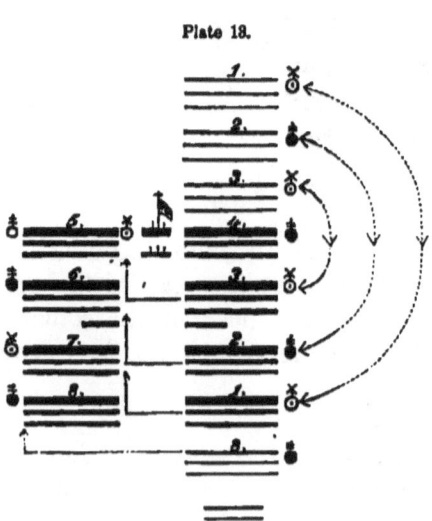

Plate 13.

GERMAN BATTALION FORMATIONS.

division, then march by the right flank, and halt when the fifth division arrives abreast of the fourth.

If the left be in front, the movement is executed on the fifth division by inverse means.

Plate 14 represents the formation of close column of divisions, right in front, from column of attack. The fourth division stands fast; all of the other divisions face to the right; the first, second, and third divisions move

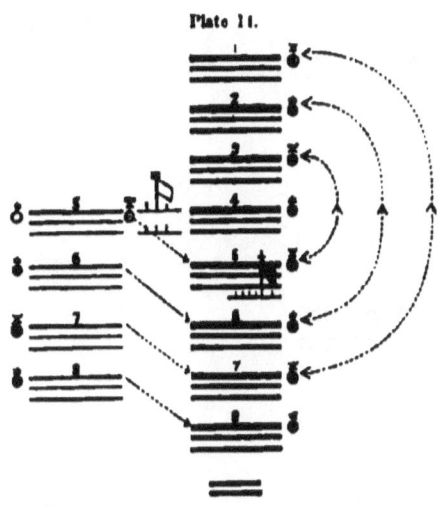

Plate 14.

forward a short distance, change direction twice to the left, and, when the right of each arrives in front of the fourth, it exe-

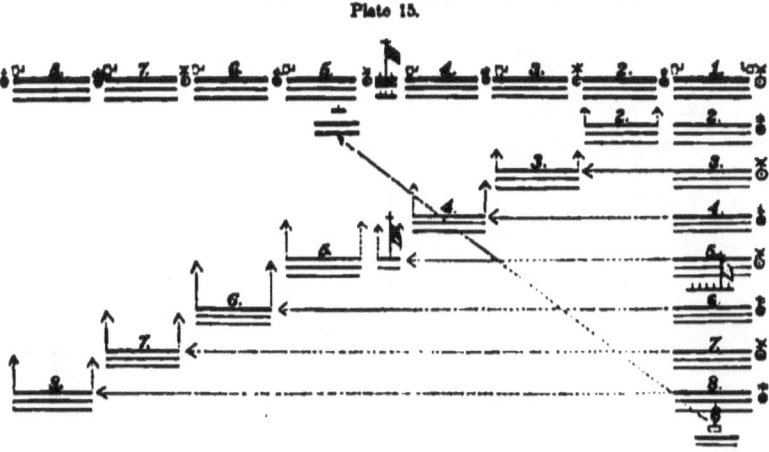

Plate 15.

cutes on the right into line; the fifth, sixth, seventh, and eighth divisions, incline to the right, move to their position

in rear of the fourth, when they halt and face to the front.

Plate 16.

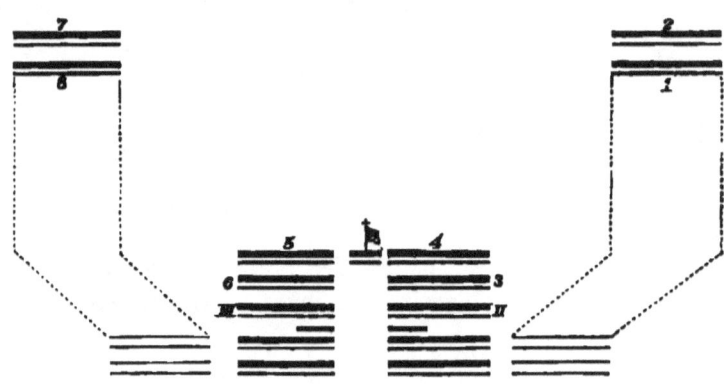

Plate 17.

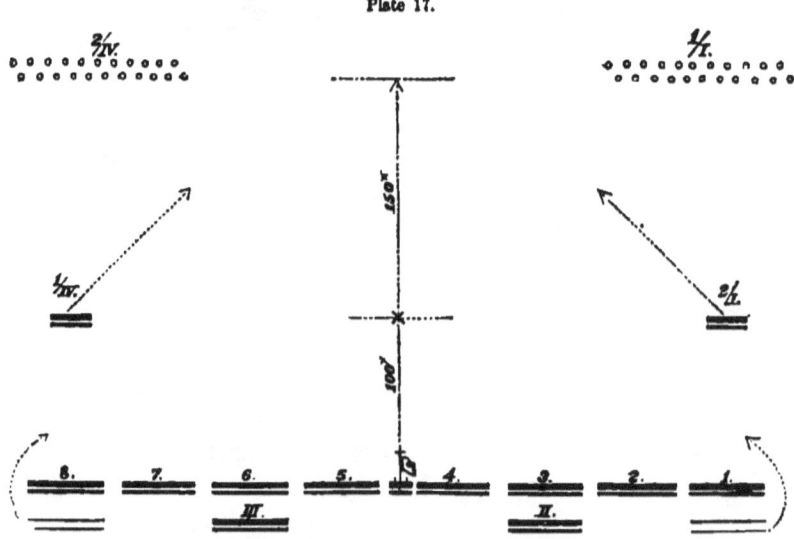

RIFLE ("JÄGER") BATTALIONS.

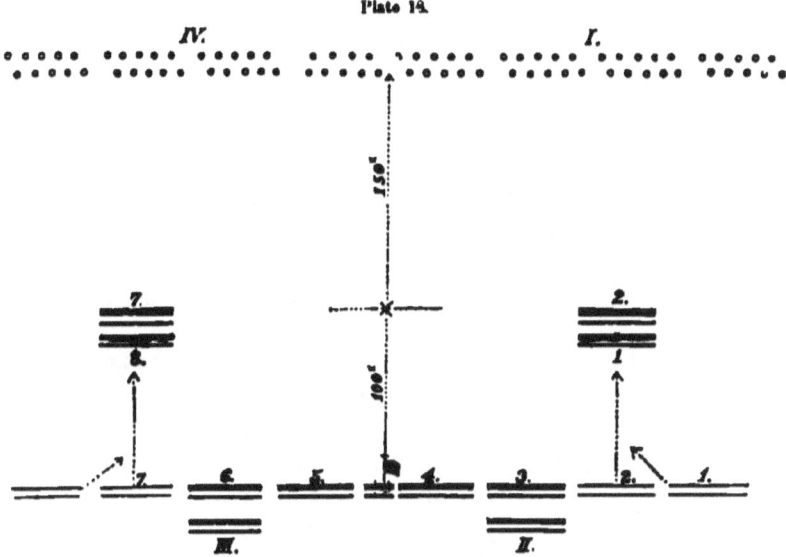

Plate 14.

The movement is executed on the fifth division left in front by inverse means.

Plate 15 shows the deployment of a close column of divisions.

Plate 16 represents skirmishers deployed from the column of attack formed of company columns.

Plate 17 represents a battalion in line, covered by deploying the shooting divisions of the first and fourth companies as skirmishers.

Plate 18 represents the deployment of skirmishers from line of battle.

RIFLE ("JÄGER") BATTALIONS.

All of the foregoing plates illustrate the movements of a company, and battalion, formed in three ranks, which is the normal formation of the

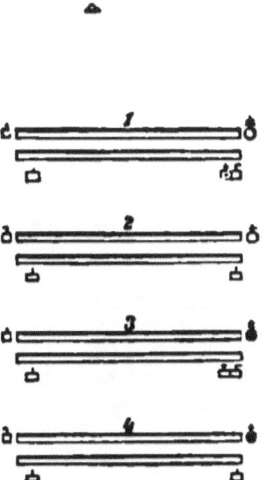

Plate 19.

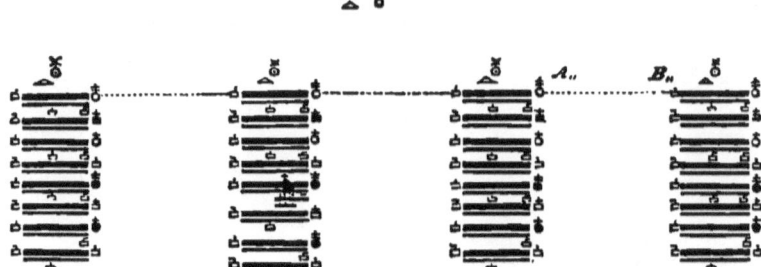

Plate 20.

infantry of the line. The formation of the rifle battalions is in two ranks.

Plate 21.

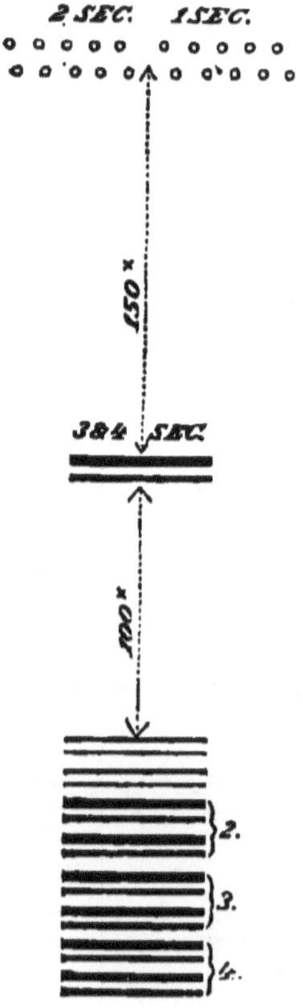

Each company, if it contains less than sixty-four files, is divided into two divisions and four subdivisions. The subdivisions are further divided into sections of not less than four nor more than six files. If the company consist of sixty-four, or more files, it is divided into four divisions, which are further divided into subdivisions and sections as before.

The company column is habitually formed of four divisions, or four subdivisions, according as the company contains more or less than sixty-four files.

In the rifles the company column, whether formed in divisions, or subdivisions, is always formed right in front.

Plate 19 represents a rifle-company of two divisions formed in company column of subdivisions.

Plate 20 represents a rifle-battalion formed in line of company columns of subdivisions.

FRENCH COMPANY COLUMN.

Plate 21 shows the deployment of a company column of subdivisions as skirmishers.

FRENCH COMPANY COLUMN.

The French battalions, like the German, are composed of four companies.

Each company is formed in two ranks, and is normally divided into four sections—the first two of which constitute the first platoon, the last two the second platoon.

Each section is divided into two squads in time of peace, and four squads in time of war, giving the company eight or sixteen squads according as it is on the peace or war footing.

The company column is always formed on the second section

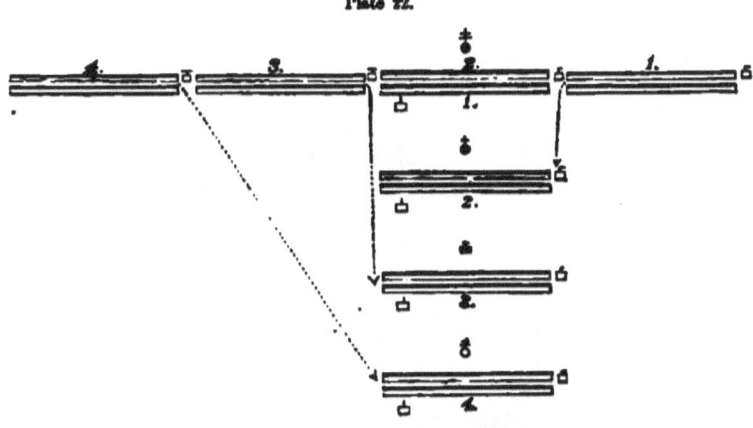

Plate 22.

Battalion-commander.	First sergeant.
Adjutant.	Right guide.
Sergeant-major.	Left guide.
Captain.	File-closer.
First-lieutenant.	Color.
Second-lieutenant.	Musicians.
Reserve lieutenant.	Skirmishers.

from the right, which stands fast; the distance between sections is six paces.

Plate 22 represents the formation of the company column from line.

Plate 23 represents its deployment.

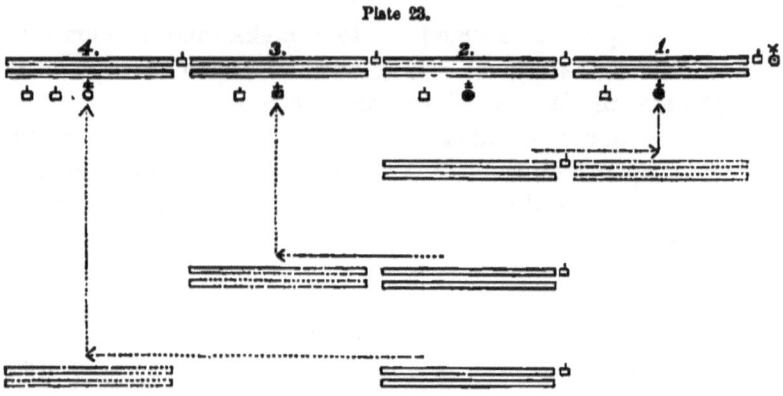

Plate 23.

Plate 24 represents the ployment of a company into a platoon column; the distance between guides is six paces.

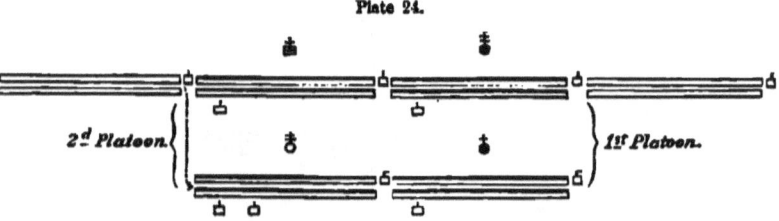

Plate 24.

Plate 25 represents the formation of the company column from the platoon column.

Plate 26 represents the formation of the platoon column from the company column.

Plate 27 represents a battalion in line.

Plate 28 represents the battalion in line of company columns, with an interval of twenty-four paces between the flanks of companies.

FRENCH COMPANY COLUMN. 283

Plate 25.

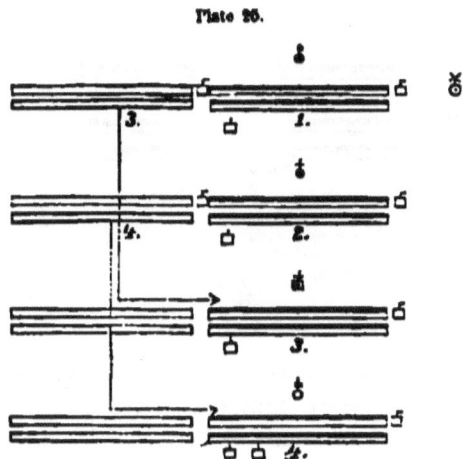

Plate 26.

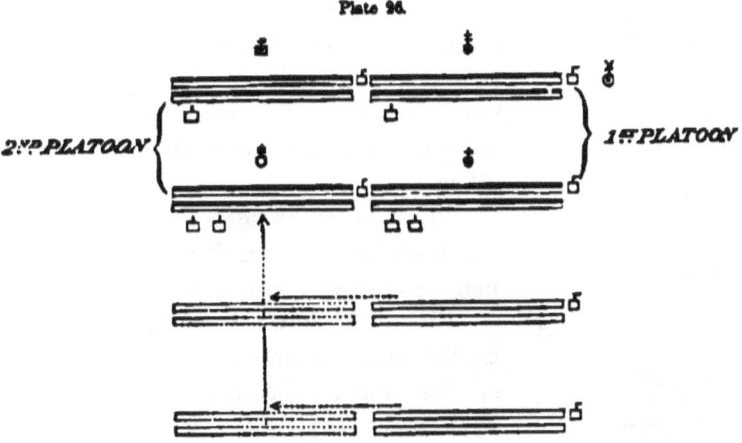

Plate 27.

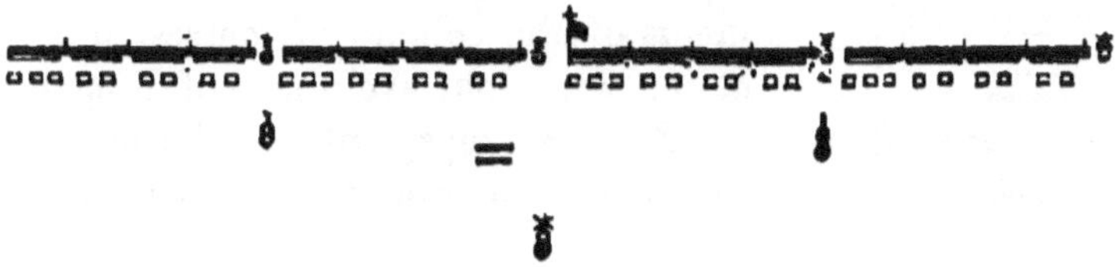

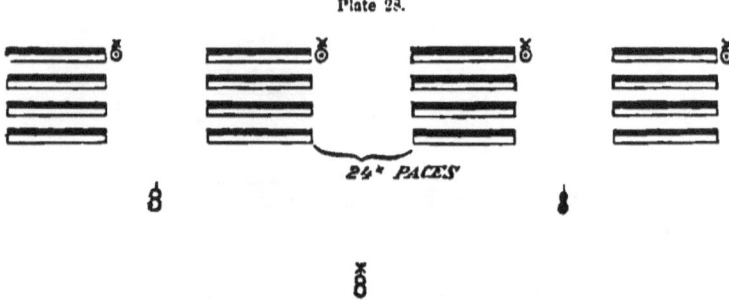

Plate 28.

Plate 29.

Plate 29 shows the "battalion column" (*colonne de bataillon*), composed of the four companies in company columns, with the distance between companies equal to the front of a section increased by six paces.

Plate 30 represents the battalion in double column, formed by placing the two wings in column side by side; the two companies of each wing are in company columns, one in rear of the other.

Plate 31 represents the formation of the battalion column from line of company columns by ployment.

Plate 32 shows the same formation by the simultaneous change of direction of the company columns by the right flank.

It will be observed that the battalion movements involving the company column are almost identical with the movements of the column of masses, and line of masses, in our evolutions of brigade.

Plate 33 represents the formation of the double column from line of company columns.

FRENCH COMPANY COLUMN.

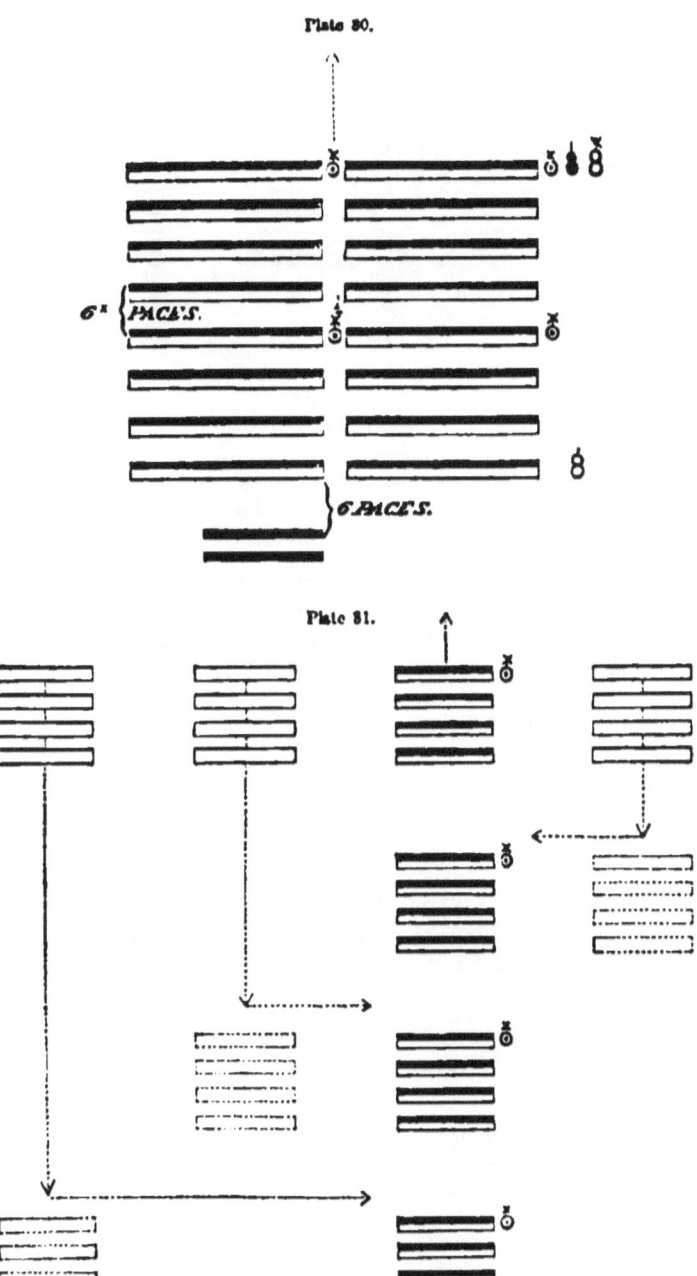

Plate 30.

Plate 31.

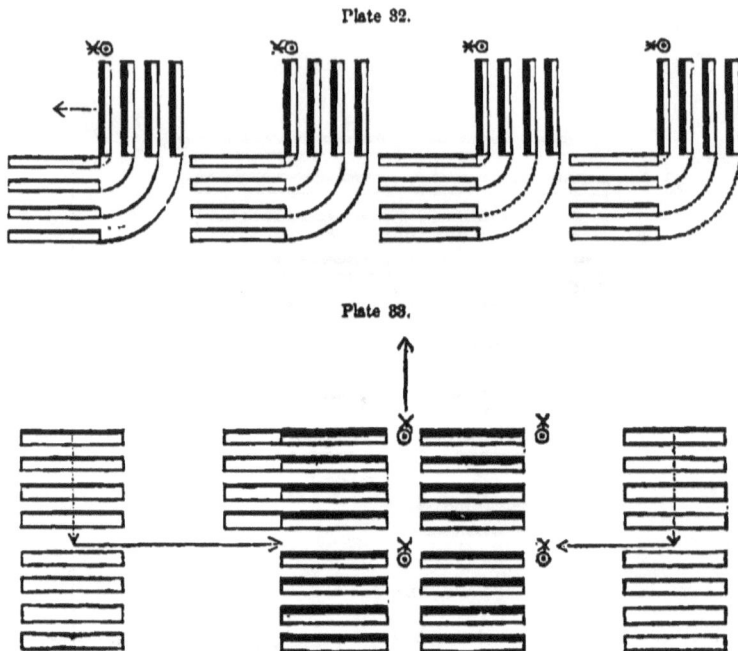

Plate 32.

Plate 33.

Plate 34 shows the same formation from the battalion column.

SKIRMISHING.

The habitual formation of the company preparatory to skirmishing is in company column; but skirmishers may be deployed from line, from the platoon column, or from any other formation.

The "formation de combat" or "fighting order" is in three echelons, or lines, as follows:

    1. Skirmishers.   2. Reënforcements.
    3. Support.

One section, composed of 2 squads (4 on the war-footing), constitutes the skirmish-line (*chaine*); another section, the reën-

DEPLOYMENT OF A COMPANY AS SKIRMISHERS. 293

forcement (*renfort*); and the remaining two sections, the supports (*soutien*). The two sections composing the skirmish-line and the reënforcement belong to the same platoon, both of which remain under the command of the chief of platoon. The supports are composed of the two sections of the remaining platoon, and are commanded by its chief.

DEPLOYMENT OF THE COMPANY AS SKIRMISHERS.

The distance from the skirmishers to the reënforcement is 150 yards, and from the reënforcement to the supports a maximum not exceeding 350 yards (metres).

DEPLOYMENT AS SKIRMISHERS.

The squad is always the unit in the skirmish-line.

To deploy a section, its chief commands:

On such squad deploy.

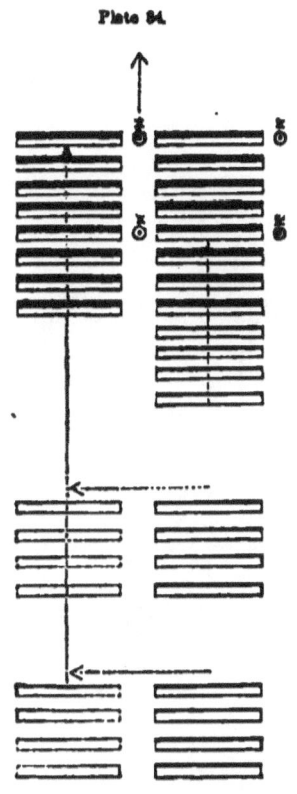

Plate 34.

Plate 35.—The squad designated, conducted by its corporal as chief, marches in the direction indicated, or upon the position that is to be occupied; the other squads, conducted by their corporals, move obliquely, or by the flank, till opposite their intervals, when they march forward.

Each squad detaches two videttes, who precede it to reconnoitre the ground over which it is to move. The distance taken between squads is such that when they are deployed there may be a distance of 6 paces between files, and 3 between skirmishers.

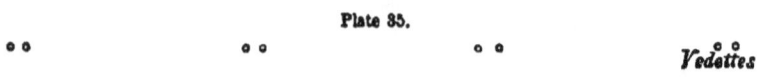

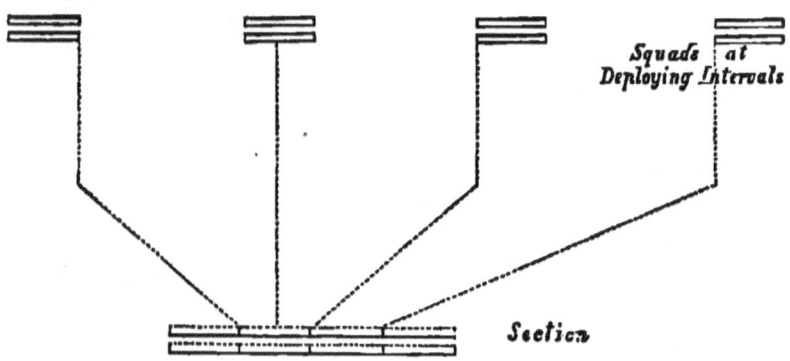

To deploy the squads, the chief of section commands:

As skirmishers.

Each squad deploys on the centre file which moves forward; the other files gain the interval of six paces by obliquing to the right and left; the rear-rank man of each file places himself on the left of the front-rank man as soon as his interval is gained.

A single squad habitually deploys on its centre file, but may be deployed on the file on either flank. It may also be deployed by the flank.

If, instead of deploying the section into squads with intervals, the chief desires to deploy it at once as skirmishers, he commands:

On such squad, as skirmishers.

DEPLOYMENT OF A COMPANY AS SKIRMISHERS. 295

Each squad then deploys as soon as it moves opposite the left or right of the squad which precedes it.

Whenever a company is to be deployed the captain instructs the chiefs of platoon, and section, as to the object to be attained, and details as far as practicable the movements to be executed; he then gives to the chiefs of platoon the order to begin the movement.

Being in company column the chief of the leading platoon causes the leading section to deploy in squads with intervals;

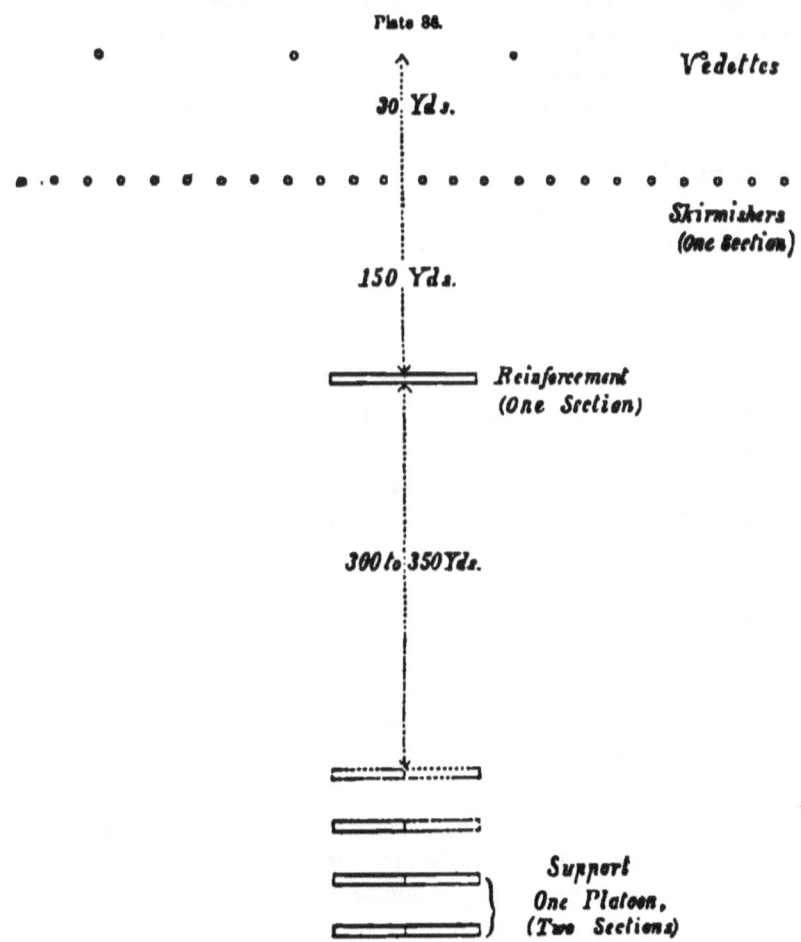

Plate 34.

the rear section follows the leading one at a distance of 150 yards; the chief of the rear platoon posts his two sections not exceeding 350 yards to the rear of the reënforcement of the skirmishers.

Plate 36 represents the company in the normal order of combat.

Great stress is laid in the tactics on keeping the squads and sections as distinct from each other as possible, in order that the men may be under the command of their proper chiefs.

The commands are general, and are given either by voice, or are transmitted by men specially selected for the purpose.

These commands are such as:

"Such section as skirmishers, reënforcement, or support."

"Such a squad or such section prolong the skirmish-line to the right."

"Such section reënforce the right of the line."

"Such section form an offensive or defensive crotchet on the right or the left."

METHOD OF ATTACK.

The company being in the order of combat, with videttes in front of each squad, advances till the fire of the enemy begins to impede the march, when the squads deploy; the videttes, chosen from the best shots of the company, open fire, and the advance is continued without further change till the opposition of the enemy becomes too strong, when the skirmishers move forward to the line of videttes and commence a slow and deliberate fire. The skirmishers now gain ground by rushing forward from one cover to another, either all at once or by successive squads, the fire of those in rear protecting those in front. In each position the fire is resumed, and is discontinued only to run forward to another position still nearer to the enemy.

In the mean time the reënforcement and the supports follow the movements of the skirmishers, concealing themselves as far as possible, and profiting by every opportunity to get cover. In advancing, they are permitted to move squad by squad, file by file, or even man by man. They thus approach the skirmishers, who are strengthened by squads sent forward from the reënforcement whenever it is necessary to increase the fire. Should the enemy attempt to turn the flank of the skirmish-line, the supports are employed to repel the attack.

If the fire of the enemy continue too strong for the skirmishers to advance, they are gradually strengthened by the remaining squads of the reënforcement, and even by squads from the supports, which have now arrived at the position formerly occupied by the reënforcement. The fire is now increased, but, should the enemy still resist, the remainder of the supports advance in closed ranks, the skirmishers fix bayonets, the drums beat the charge, and all make a rush for the enemy's position. If unable to reach it at a single bound, the line continues to approach by successive rushes made by the whole line, or by fractions, until, overcome by its fire, the enemy retires before a final charge with the bayonet.

METHOD OF DEFENSE.

On the defensive, the "order of combat" is substantially the same as on the offensive, except that the distances from the skirmishers to the reënforcement and the supports are diminished.

In proportion as the enemy approaches and increases his fire, the skirmish-line is strengthened by squads from the reënforcement. If the enemy threaten a flank, a portion of the supports is deployed to repel the attack. The supports can also be employed, if the opportunity offers, to attack the enemy in flank.

If the enemy continue to advance, the instant he moves to the assault, after having opened a severe fire on the line, the supports move forward, join the skirmishers, and assist in repelling the attack.

DEPLOYMENT OF A BATTALION AS SKIRMISHERS.

Plate 37.—A battalion of the first line, when fighting in connection with battalions on its right and left, is required to cover only its own front and one-half of the intervals between it and the adjoining battalions. This space for a battalion of 800 men is estimated at from 300 to 350 metres.

When approaching an enemy outside of his field of fire, a battalion may march in any column, or formation, prescribed in the tactics; but, when it arrives at 2,000 yards from his artillery, it immediately forms in the "order of combat." The battalion

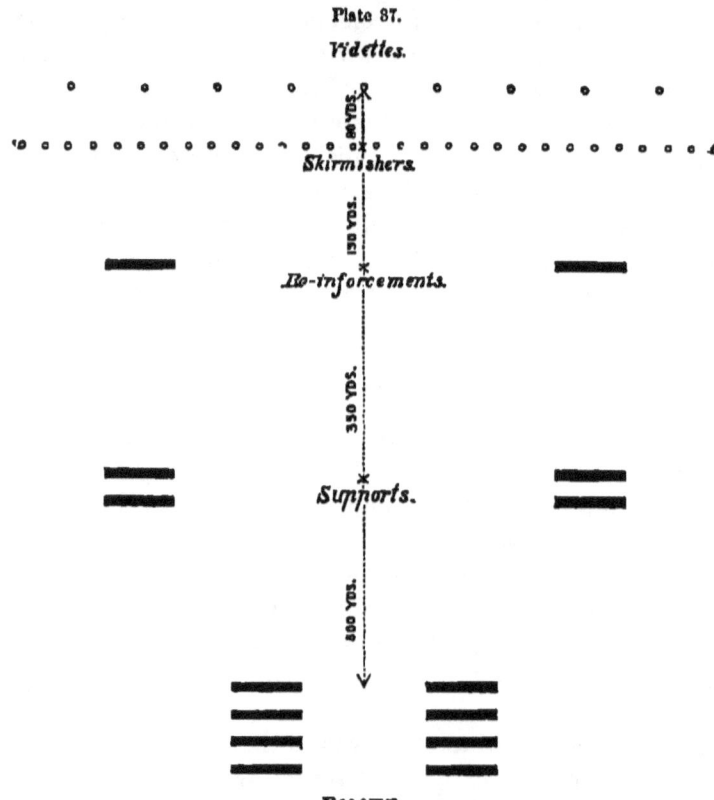

commander carefully instructs the captains as to the object to be attacked, and the method of attack, and then detaches two companies, which immediately take the order of combat prescribed for a company.

The skirmishers deployed by these companies form the

skirmishers of the battalion; their reënforcements form the line of reënforcements of the battalion, and their supports the line of supports.

The reserve is composed of the remaining two companies, or one-half of the battalion, and is kept united as long as possible at a distance of about 500 yards from the supports. In its movements it takes any formation that may best enable it to cover itself from the enemy's fire.

Plate 37 represents a battalion in the normal order of combat. The distances given are the maximum. When the ground is broken the distances may be diminished, but, in order that the different fractions may not engage too precipitately in the action, the minimum depth of the battalion should not be less than 500 yards.

In the normal order of combat for the defensive, the distance from the skirmishers to the reënforcements is about 100 yards; from reënforcements to the supports 100 yards, and from the supports to the reserve 300 yards.

METHOD OF ATTACK WITH A BATTALION.

The object to be kept steadily in view with the breech-loading tactics is to shake the *morale* of the enemy by securing in every stage of the advance a preponderating fire, at the same time advancing in such small fractions, up to the moment of the final rush or assault, as to reduce the casualties to the lowest limit.

To accomplish this object the battalion forms in the order of combat at 2,000 yards from the enemy's artillery. In this order, with videttes in front of the undeployed squads, the battalion moves forward to within 800 yards of the enemy's skirmishers, when their fire becoming dangerous, the squads deploy as skirmishers in rear of the videttes.

During the advance up to this moment the videttes, accompanied if necessary by an officer, designate the positions that may be successively occupied to advantage; the points from which fire can be opened with success, and with least exposure; also the spaces over which the troops should move either with caution, or with rapidity. They approach under cover as near as possible to the enemy's position, and at all times keep the battalion commander informed of everything transpiring within their view.

At 800 yards the videttes open fire, and at 600 yards are reënforced by the skirmishers, when the whole line joins in the action. At this stage only one section, or one-fourth of each of the two leading companies, has become engaged.

The line now darts forward from cover to cover, the captains causing the sections as reënforcements to move forward in squads or all at once, according to the necessity of the case. If the entire section of either company move forward, the supports close to 150 yards, or one section may close to that distance while the remaining section holds itself farther to the rear.

As the opposition of the enemy grows stronger, and the necessity of increasing the fire before each succeeding rush becomes more apparent, the supports approach the line, availing themselves of every cover. The supports are never sent forward to the line, except either in squads or sections, in order that each unit may be kept together as long as possible. The units move up to the line either in open or close order, the latter order being preferable when intensity of fire is desired.

The two reserve companies conform to the movements of the supports, gradually diminishing their distance, and finally taking the positions of the supports, when the latter move forward to replace the reënforcements.

Up to the time that the supports replace the reënforcements only one-half of the line of combat of the leading companies has become engaged, and not till it becomes impossible to make any further advance is the remaining half of the line of combat, composed of the two sections in support, ordered into action.

All of the movements thus far described, by means of which the battalion has advanced from 2,000 yards to within from 200 to 300 yards of the enemy, are simply considered as the "*preparation for the attack.*"

The impulse necessary to induce the skirmishers to advance from one position to another has been given by reënforcing them successively by squads and sections, until all of the two leading companies have become engaged. But the most difficult part of the work still remains; the skirmishers have been reënforced until they have attained nearly the strength of a line in single rank, and yet the enemy resists, and covers every inch of the intervening space with a deadly fire.

To overcome this resistance is the object of the *attack*, which is preceded for a few moments by a rapid fire from the entire line of combat. One company of the reserve then moves forward in line (closed ranks), when, as it joins the skirmishers, they fix bayonets, the drums beat the charge, the officers cheer the men, and all, shouting "Forward!" make a rush for the enemy's works.

If the distance be too great to carry the position at a single bound, the line of combat, reënforced by a company from the reserve, gains ground by short rushes, keeping up a rapid fire, until the line arrives within 50 or 100 paces of the enemy.

The second company of reserve, the last of the battalion, is now ordered into the line, and the charge is executed as before.

The second company of the reserve is kept as long as possible in rear so as to be ready to repulse any counter-attack of the enemy, also to form a support for the skirmishers should they be driven back. In any event it is only ordered into action at the last instant, when it is replaced by a company sent forward from a battalion of the second line, which then assumes all of the duties of a reserve company.

If the attack succeed, dispositions are at once made against a counter-attack. To this end the line of combat pursues the enemy to a favorable position from which it can open fire, while the reserve companies are rallied, and in close order move forward so as to again support the skirmishers. The cavalry also at this juncture may be employed to pursue the enemy, or by its presence prevent him from taking the offensive.

If the attack fail, or if the position be lost by a counter-attack, the battalion of the second line already prepared deploys, and by its resistance gives the skirmishers time to rally and take position in rear. The second battalion, now in front, may resume the attack or remain on the defensive, according to the state of the enemy.

DEFENSIVE.

The normal order of combat on the defensive is the same as for the offensive, except that the distances between the skirmishers, reënforcements, and other portions, are diminished.

The defense is begun by the videttes, who resist as long as possible without interfering with the fire of the skirmishers, who, as the enemy approaches, are successively strengthened by squads and sections from the reënforcements and the supports.

As on the offensive, the reserve replaces the supports, and supports the reënforcements. The squads and sections are conducted to the line at the points most threatened, and fire by volley or by file at the subdivisions of the enemy in line or in mass.

The movements are so combined as to resist each successive advance of the enemy by an increasing fire. The reserve must therefore join the skirmishers before the final assault; and in close order fires by volley or file, according to the enemy's movements.

A passive defense is forbidden as being fatal to the *morale* of the troops; battalion commanders are therefore directed, whenever practicable, to take the offensive, and the most favorable moment is that just preceding the final attack.

The counter-attack is generally made by directing a subdivision against an exposed flank of the enemy, while the line of defense in his front rapidly increases its fire. If the counter-attack succeed, the whole line of defense charges with the bayonet, and seeks to drive the enemy as far as possible.

If compelled to abandon the line of defense, the battalion of the second line deploys, and, when the skirmishers of the leading battalion have passed to the rear, endeavors to take the offensive and regain the position that has been lost.

Whenever a battalion fights separately the general dispositions are the same as when operating in connection with other battalions, the principal difference being an increased front, and the consequent necessity of so posting the fractions as to give prompt assistance to the part of the skirmish-line most threatened.

DISPOSITIONS AGAINST CAVALRY.

Any formation, with breech-loaders, against cavalry, is regarded as good, provided the men can bring their fire to bear at good range.

The "column against cavalry" executed by each company column is the most usual formation.

To form the column, the front section halts; the fourth closes up to the third, halts, and faces to the rear; the intervals between the first and second, and second and third sections are filled by files designated from the second and third sections, which wheel to the right and left.

If the battalion be in battalion column, or line of company columns, the companies, if there be time, are first posted in echelon, and then form columns against cavalry.

A battalion in line, if surprised, breaks a crotchet to the rear, and receives the charge in line.

COMPANY COLUMN IN ITALY, AUSTRIA, AND RUSSIA.

The company column in Italy, Austria, and Russia, as in France, varies so slightly from the German, from which it was derived, that its formation and use need not be described.

Plate 38 represents a regiment of the Russian Guard in the order of combat at the manœuvres near Krasnoé Selo in August, 1876.

The distances between the first battalion and the other battalions, at first well regulated, gradually diminished until the company columns, and even the battalion in mass, without deploying, were found immediately in rear of the skirmish-line.

At the manœuvres near Peterhoff, at one stage of the attack, a portion of the offensive party was formed in four lines of battle; the leading line fired into the company columns, and columns in mass, of the retreating enemy at a distance of 50 yards.

Plate 38.

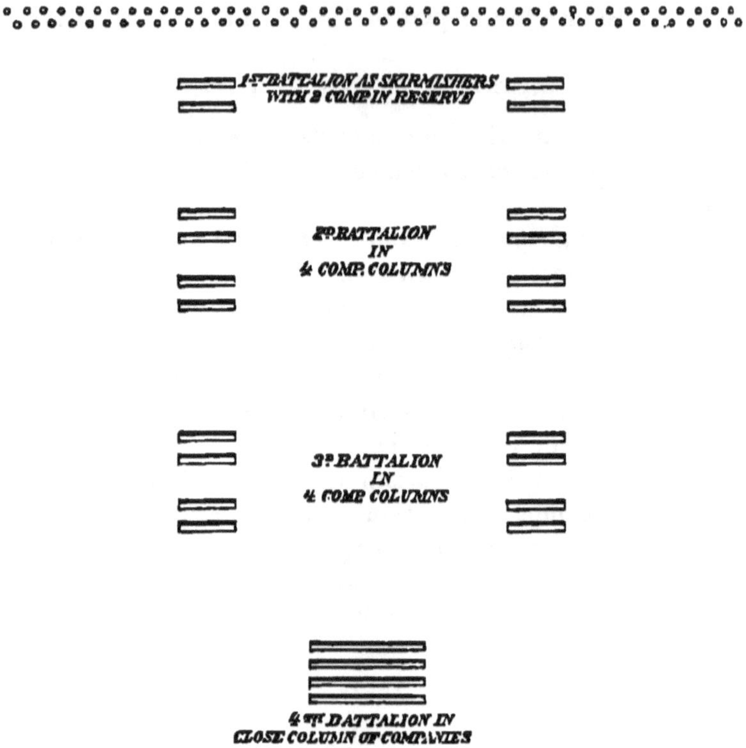

1ST BATTALION AS SKIRMISHERS WITH 2 COMP IN RESERVE

2D BATTALION IN 4 COMP. COLUMNS

3D BATTALION IN 4 COMP COLUMNS

4TH BATTALION IN CLOSE COLUMN OF COMPANIES

Plate 39.

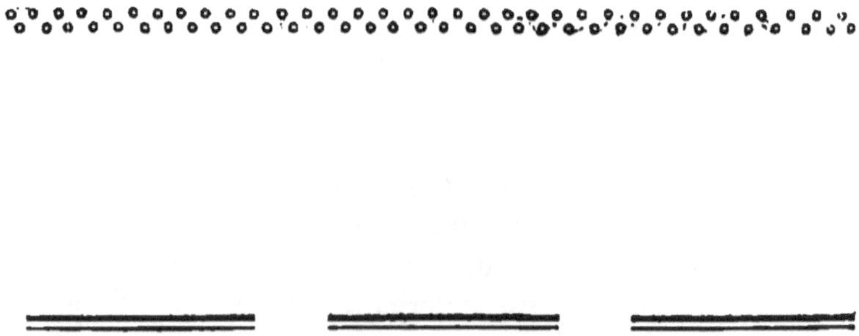

Plate 39 represents the formation of a regiment of the line

RUSSIAN SKIRMISHING FORMATIONS.   305

of three battalions, of five companies each, as seen at the Camp of Instruction at Moscow in 1876. The three battalions are in line, each covered by its fifth company as skirmishers.

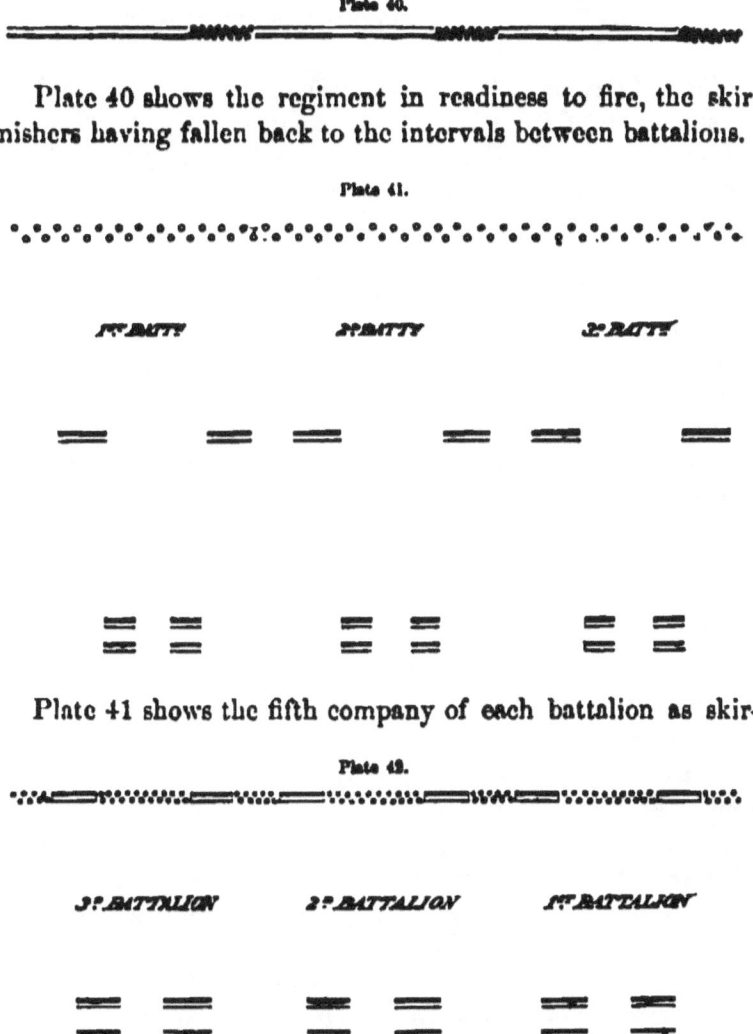

Plate 40 shows the regiment in readiness to fire, the skirmishers having fallen back to the intervals between battalions.

Plate 41 shows the fifth company of each battalion as skirmishers; the first and fourth in support, in line; the second and third in company column of two platoons each.

Plate 42 represents the skirmishers reënforced by the advance of the first and fourth companies.

Plate 43.

Plate 43 represents the skirmishers further reënforced by the second and third companies in company column, which on arriving on the line close up in four ranks; the first and second ranks fire kneeling, the third and fourth standing.

ENGLISH SKIRMISHING.

By the English tactics, skirmishers, in the School of the Battalion, may be deployed either from column, or from line.

The columns principally used are:

The "quarter column," or column of companies formed by ployment, or by wheeling and closing in mass.

The "half-battalion column," formed by ploying the companies of each wing in mass in rear of either flank company.

The "double column," formed by ploying the companies in rear of the two centre companies.

The principles of the deployment are illustrated in the following plates:

Plate 44 represents the deployment of a battalion of ten companies from "quarter column." The first company deploys from its centre; the second prolongs the line to the right; the third to the left; the fourth, fifth, and sixth companies are posted as supports; the remaining four companies, in column, are held in reserve.

Plate 45 represents the deployment of a battalion of six companies from "quarter column." The first company deploys to the right; the second prolongs the line to the right; the third and fourth act as supports; while the fifth and sixth, in column, act as reserve.

ENGLISH SKIRMISHING.

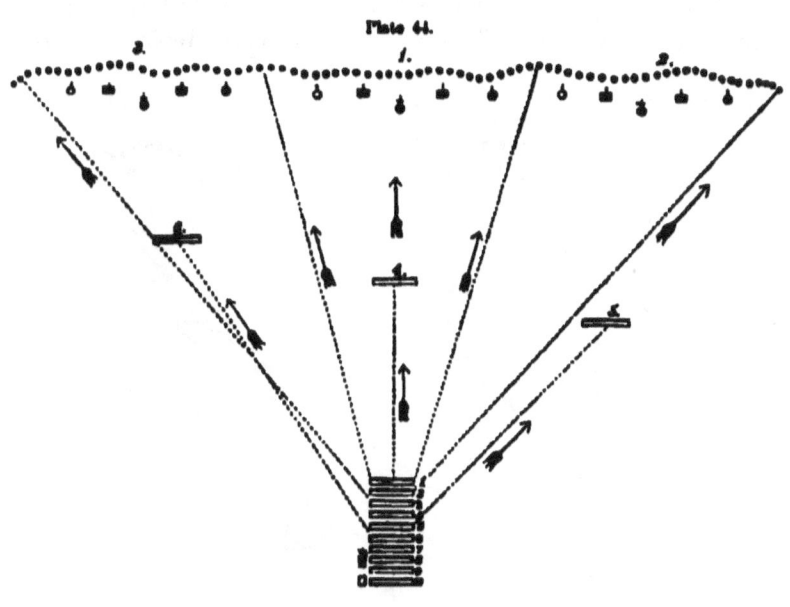

Plate 44.

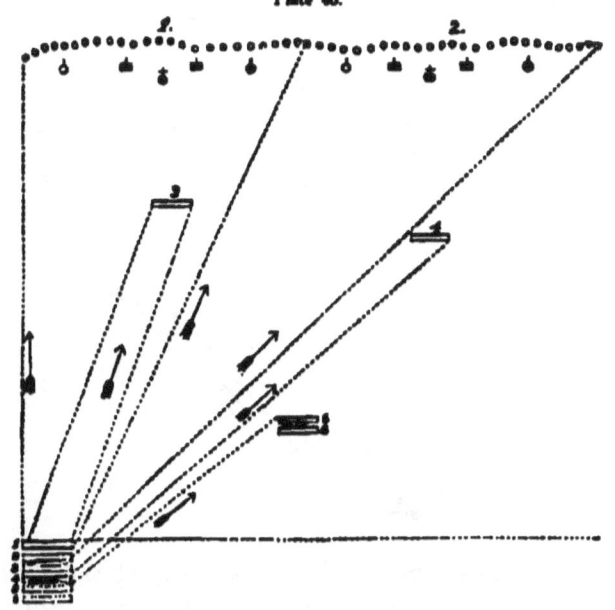

Plate 45.

308   INFANTRY TACTICS.

Plate 46 represents the deployment of a battalion of eight companies from line. The second company deploys to the

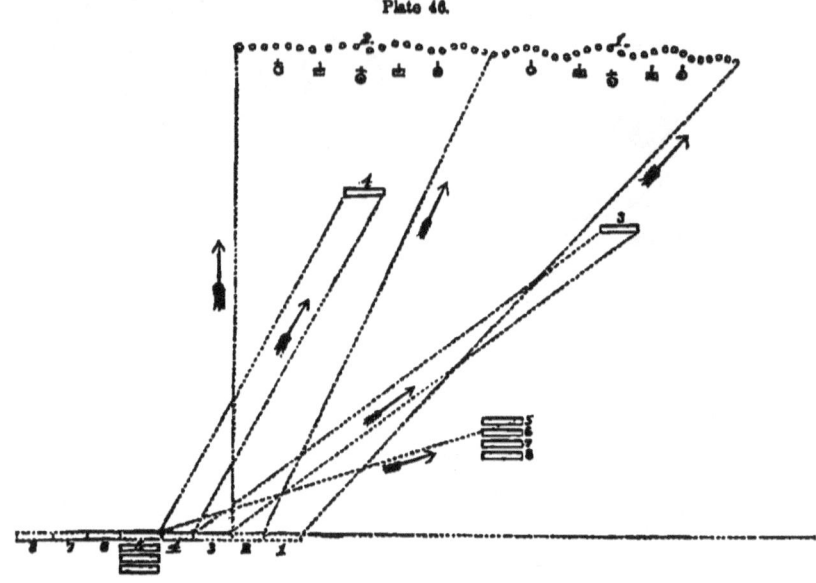

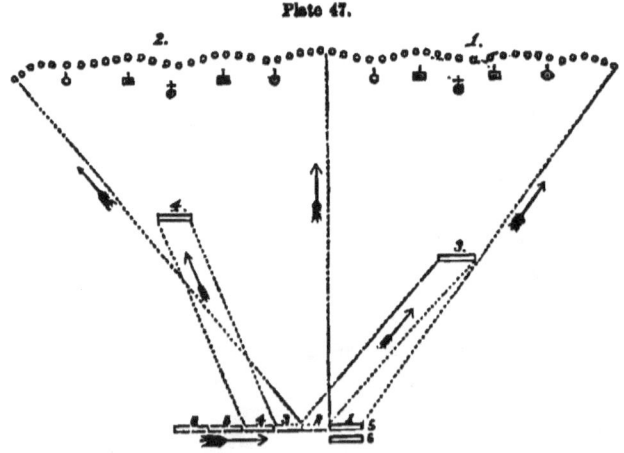

right; the first prolongs the line to the right; the third and fourth are posted in support; the remaining companies ploy

ENGLISH SKIRMISHING. 309

into a half-battalion column, in rear of the fifth, and are conducted in column to their place in reserve.

Plate 47 represents the deployment of a battalion of six companies from line. The first company deploys to the right; the second prolongs the line to the left; the third and fourth move

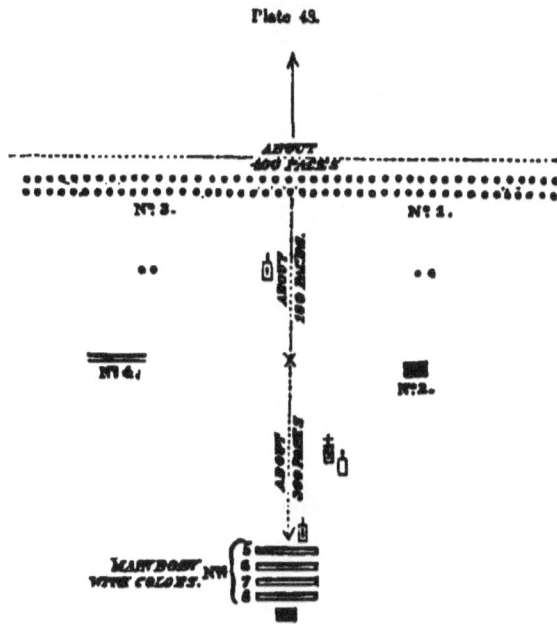

Plate 48.

to their positions in support; the fifth and sixth, in column, act as reserve.

Plate 48 represents a battalion of eight companies in fighting formation.

Plates 49, 50, and 51, represent the successive changes of formation while advancing to a position within 150 or 200 yards of the enemy. The final attack is made by the advance of the entire battalion in one general line.

Plate 52 represents the order of combat of a division of infantry, composed of two brigades of three battalions each, at the Camp of Instruction at Delhi, India, in 1876.

In the formation, the leading battalion of each brigade, which constitutes the line of combat, is arranged in three lines.

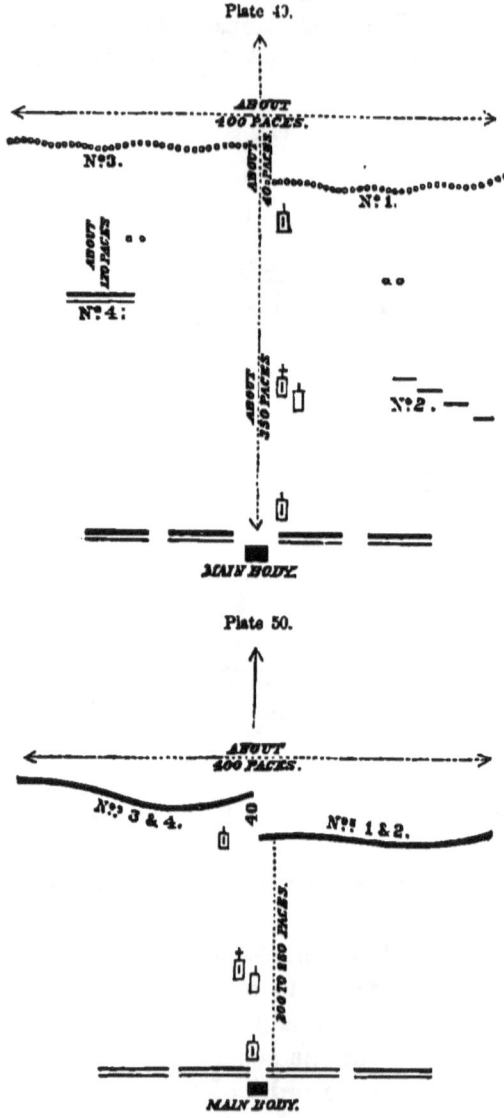

The first and second lines are each formed by two companies,

ENGLISH SKIRMISHING. 311

deployed as skirmishers, with a distance between them of 200 yards. The third line, which constitutes the supports, is formed

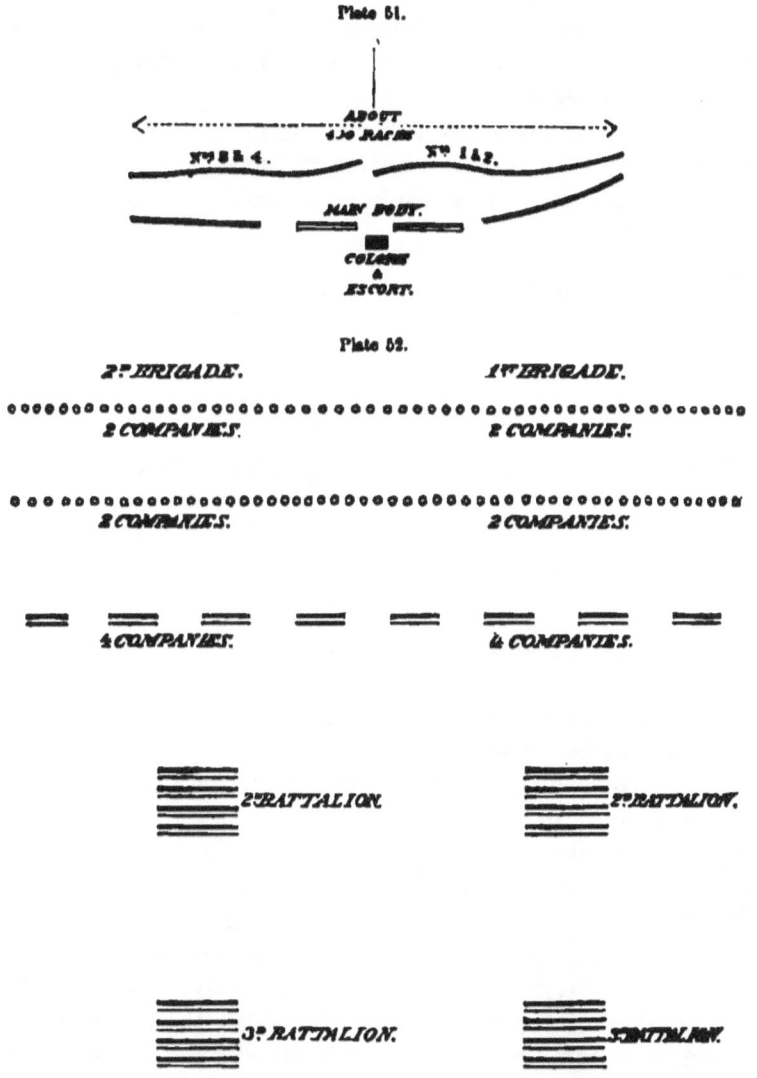

by the four remaining companies of the battalion, which are posted in line with intervals, at a distance of about 200 yards from the second line.

The second and third battalions are formed in column of double companies, the distances between them and the line of combat varying with the nature of the ground.

Plate 53 represents the formation of a brigade for an attack on the villages of Badlee Serai and Azadpore during the manœuvres near Delhi in 1876.

The formation consisted of two heavy lines of skirmishers, supported by two battalions in line of battle.

In the English system, as in the German, ground is gained

Plate 53.

by a series of rushes, usually preceded by reënforcing the skirmish-line and increasing the fire.

The disposition of the supports shows that quarter, half, or full companies can be sent to a flank, or to any part of the line, while the arrangement of the rear battalions in line, and double column of companies ready for deployment, shows that the deployed line is still adhered to as the best and safest formation to stem retreat when the skirmishers are forced back.

Our own system of skirmishing, like the English, is adapted to a battalion of ten companies. The skirmishers may be deployed both from line and from column, and are posted in one or two lines, with supports in one or in two lines in the rear.

The unit of "four" corresponds with the "section" of the German, and "squad" of the French tactics.

The system also provides a single rank, which can be used offensively or defensively, and also a deployment by numbers, whereby, if necessary, eight successive lines of skirmishers may be advanced from a battalion in line, thus enabling the entire battalion to advance in skirmishing order.

Three of these lines of skirmishers, and even four, may advance, leaving the battalion still in line ready to support the skirmishers if successful, or to receive them if repulsed.

Plate 54 illustrates this method of deployment:

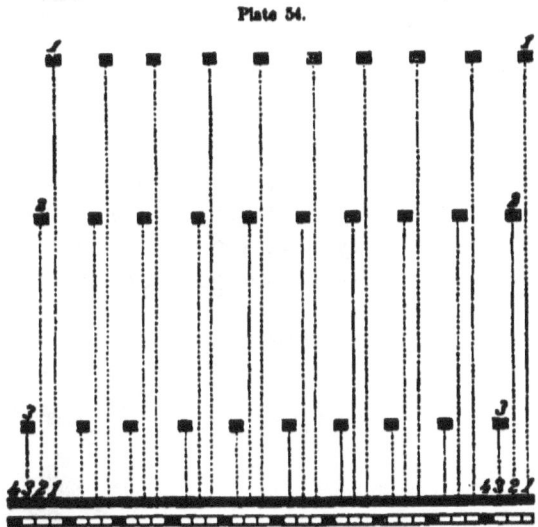

Plate 54.

GENERAL REMARKS ON THE OPEN ORDER OF FIGHTING.

If the method of fighting in open order be cursorily examined, it will be observed that the real attack is only made after the skirmishers have been reënforced to such a degree as to form a line of battle.

It will be further observed that, as the company column is generally disintegrated on arriving within 600 yards of the enemy, it is in reality less an essential feature of the open order, than a necessity resulting from the organization of large companies, the subdivision of which for manœuvres is indispensable. Once divided into two, or four divisions or sections, the company column follows naturally, the same as the battalion in mass in the evolutions of a brigade.

With a battalion of eight or ten companies, subdivisions may be dispensed with, and, so long as this organization is retained

Plate 55.

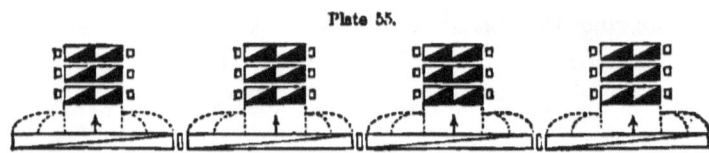

in England and America, the company column will not therefore become a necessity; but, should we adopt the regimental system of three battalions, of four companies each, all of the advantages claimed for the company column can be secured by adopting the double column of fours for each company.

This formation, already employed in our "Cavalry Tactics," par. 839, is equally applicable to large and small companies; is

Plate 56.

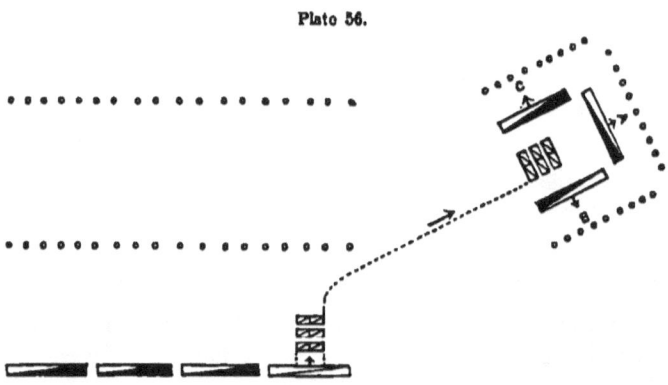

better adapted to our topography than the company column, and is also susceptible of more simple and varied application.

Plate 55 represents a battalion of four companies formed in line of double columns.

Plate 56 represents a battalion with two lines of skirmishers deployed by numbers; the lines *A*, *B*, and *C*, show the posi-

GENERAL REMARKS ON SKIRMISHING. 315

tions that may be occupied by a company, according to its deployment from the double column to the front, to and on the right or to and on the left.

The theoretical use of the company column has been sufficiently described; but how far it will be modified by future wars has yet to be determined. It is possible that for battalions of the first line on the offensive it may supersede the line of battle, but on the defensive, particularly in a country like ours, where rifle-pits can be constructed in a few minutes, its use in preference to a deployed line would invite disaster.

In all the later campaigns of the war the history of our tactical movements could be frequently traced by the lines of abandoned trenches, which were often provided with abatis and head-logs, underneath which were horizontal loop-holes for musketry. A line, even a single rank, unshaken by fire while moving into position, could calmly await behind them the approach of the enemy's skirmishers, and bid defiance to the successive fractions sent to their support.

In such cases, the general system adopted was to press up the skirmishers toward the enemy's works, seek a position for fresh troops so near that an attack would give promise of success, and then charge in one or more lines.

By the German system the charge is practically made in line; only, however, after the courage of the men has been gradually exhausted by repeated rushes, and exposure to the enemy's fire.

The feature of the open order of fighting which should engage our most serious attention is the subdivision of the battalions and companies into constituent parts, or fractions, each one of which must have its appropriate commander.

In the new system the major assumes the functions of a brigade commander; a captain requires the knowledge and skill of a colonel; a lieutenant performs the duty of a captain; a sergeant takes the place of a lieutenant, and a corporal, no longer required to simply fire his musket, takes command of a squad or section.

To all of these grades latitude is given in the management

of their commands under fire, and hence an error of judgment in any one may initiate a movement that may lose a battle.

In Europe the success of the company column is acknowledged to depend on *good captains*, and, that they may be supported throughout, the Governments not only thoroughly train the commanders of each squad, but, having trained them, they offer to their non-commissioned officers special inducements to remain in the service.

The fact that the Continental powers find it necessary to train each officer, and non-commissioned officer, for his special duty, should impress us with the importance of providing in time of war at least one trained officer to command every company and battalion.

CONCLUSIONS.

The true object to be kept in view in studying European military organization is to present those features which are common to all armies, and to indicate those which we should adopt as indispensable to the vigorous, successful, and humane prosecution of our future wars.

These features, or general principles, may be briefly stated *en résumé* as follows:

1. To enable a nation to put forth, in the hour of danger, its greatest military strength, every citizen, in consideration of the protection extended to his life and property, is held to owe military service to his government.

2. Every nation maintains a regular army, which constitutes the chief bulwark in case of invasion, and almost the sole instrument for waging wars of aggression.

3. For the purpose of equalizing the burdens of military service, and of facilitating the rapid equipment and mobilization of troops, each country is divided into military districts, to which are permanently assigned army corps, divisions, brigades, regiments, and battalions, which draw from the districts all of their recruits, both in peace and in war.

4. The army is maintained on two distinct footings—one of peace, the other of war.

5. The relative size of the army, on the peace and war footings, is determined by political considerations, and the financial

resources of the country. As a rule, the army on the peace-footing is about one-half as large as on the war-footing.

6. The army on the peace-footing is but a school of training to prepare officers and men for efficient service in time of war.

7. The term of military service is so divided that those men who happen to be drafted shall serve from three to four years with the colors; then pass into reserve from four to five years —subject at any moment to be recalled to the colors; then into an army of the second line, called "Landwehr," "militia mobile," or "army territoriale;" and, lastly, into a body as yet unorganized, termed "Landsturm," "militia territoriale," or "reserve of the army territoriale." The total length of military service varies in different countries from twelve to twenty years, and usually begins with the twenty-first year of age.

8. By requiring men, after serving from three to four years with the colors, to remain from four to five years subject to recall to the ranks, the Government forms a reserve of trained soldiers, by means of which it can raise the army immediately to the war-footing, and still have a supply of disciplined men to fill the vacancies occasioned by battle and disease.

9. In addition to the reserve of trained soldiers, who may not be able to fill all the vacancies occasioned by a prolonged war, there is maintained, as in Germany, and Italy, a second body of men, termed the "ersatz reserve," whose training has been limited to two or more months.

10. Officers of reserve, or complement, are provided in time of peace, who, in time of war, join the army, and serve to raise the number of officers to the war standard.

11. To support the regular army, and, when necessary, to reënforce it, the Landwehr, composed of troops of all arms, is organized into an army of the second line. This army is largely made up of soldiers who have previously been trained with the colors, and is officered by former officers of the army, or by officers specially educated for their position.

12. Every regiment of infantry, artillery, cavalry, and engineers, has a depot, which, in time of war, receives, drills, and forwards to the regiment, the men called in from the reserve.

13. The time required to make an efficient cavalry-man is so great that the cavalry is maintained continually on the war-footing.

14. No officers are commissioned in the army without either graduating at a military school, or by promotion from the ranks, after pursuing a professional course of study, followed by a qualifying examination.

15. A War Academy is specially created to educate officers in the art of war, and to prepare them for the staff, and to hold high command.

16. The general staff, corresponding to our Adjutant-General's Department, which demands the highest professional training, and the widest experience, of any staff department in the army, is organized in such a manner that the officers constantly pass from the line to the staff, and the reverse. They thus keep in sympathy with the troops, know their wants and fighting qualities, and, furthermore, know how to manœuvre them in nearly every emergency that may arise.

17. To enable the Government to profit by the best talent in the army, rapid promotion, either by entering the staff corps or by selection, is provided for all officers who manifest decided zeal and professional ability.

18. To enable the Government to know the qualifications of its officers, either annual or biennial reports are required from commanding officers, showing the zeal, aptitude, special qualifications, and personal character, of every subordinate under their command. These reports are not secret or confidential. On the contrary, when a commanding officer reports adversely upon an officer, the latter is notified, in order that he may amend his conduct. In Austria the officer has a right, and in every other country should have the right, to know what his record is at the War Department.

19. Officers are maintained for the sole benefit of the Government. If, therefore, an officer is ignorant or incompetent, the Government, by means of personal reports, and special examinations, can stop his promotion, and thus prevent injury to

the service, which directly increases with the size of his command.

20. To keep regiments, batteries, and squadrons, up to their fighting strength, detached service is avoided by setting aside in each organization the number of non-combatants known to be necessary, such as artificers, teamsters, etc., who are never counted in the fighting strength. The evil of detached service is further avoided by the complete organization, on an independent footing, of the different staff departments, and administrative services, and especially by separate organization of artillery and general military trains.

21. The *morale* of troops in the field is maintained by constantly filling the vacancies occasioned by death and disease, partly by men who have formerly served with the colors, and partly by recruits who have had more or less military instruction at depots, and camps of instruction.

22. The Government increases its chances of success, and promotes economy, by keeping the battalions in the field up to their war strength. The old soldiers teach the new, while officers already accustomed to battle know how to lead their troops into action with the least loss of life, and the best assurance of victory.

23. Only when the troops of the regular army become depleted, or outnumbered, does the Government call out the army of the second line, which, with special foresight, has been organized, and is led to battle by officers, many of whom have had service in the regular army, in both peace and war.

24. Discipline is principally maintained by granting to commanding officers of every grade, and even to non-commissioned officers, the power to inflict, within certain limits, summary punishment for all minor offenses.

As the reward of the application of these principles, Prussia, in 1866, was enabled to dictate terms of peace to Austria, after a short campaign of six weeks; while, in 1870, between the 15th of July and the 1st of September, Germany mobilized her forces, crossed the frontier, overwhelmed a great army, forced it to seek the shelter of its fortresses, securely invested it, captured an Emperor, at the head of a relieving army, and destroyed what was supposed to be the strongest military empire on the globe.

In the Austro-Prussian War, the Prussian loss in killed, and died of wounds and of disease, was 10,877; in the Franco-German War, the total German losses were 40,881.

If we now compare our military policy during the first century of the Republic with the present military policy of European nations, we shall find that the difference lies principally in this—that, while they prosecute their wars exclusively with trained armies, completely organized in all of their parts, and led by officers specially educated, we have begun, and have prosecuted, most of our wars with raw troops, whose officers have had to be educated in the expensive school of war. As the result of this policy, the duration of our wars has been as follows:

War of the Revolution	7 years.
War of 1812	2½ "
War with Mexico	2 "
War of the Rebellion	4 "

The total number of men called out in these different wars was as follows:

War of the Revolution.

Continentals	231,771
Militia	164,087
Total	395,858

War of 1812.

Regulars	38,186
Militia	458,463
Volunteers	10,110
Rangers	3,049
Total	509,808

War with Mexico.

Regulars	26,922
Volunteers	73,532
Total	100,454

War of the Rebellion.

Regulars	46,679
Volunteers and militia	2,637,080
Total	2,683,759

The figures for the Revolution are taken from the report of the Secretary of War, made to Congress in 1790, in which, for want of accurate returns, the estimate for the militia is conjectural.

The figures for the War of 1812 are taken from the records of the Third Auditor's office, which show that the total number of militia, volunteers, and rangers, who were regularly discharged amounted to 471,622. The strength of the regular army is taken from the return for September, 1814, when it numbered 38,186, and, therefore, falls below the total number called out.

The figures for the war with Mexico were furnished by the adjutant-general to Congress.

Those for the Rebellion are taken from the report of the provost-marshal-general for 1865. According to the figures of the adjutant-general, the number of volunteers of all classes who enlisted between April 12, 1861, and April 19, 1865, and were regularly discharged, was 2,234,421, their average service being twenty-eight and seven-tenths months.

In the War of the Rebellion, our losses in killed, and died of wounds and disease, according to the report of the surgeon-general, were 304,369. The losses of the Confederates, as nearly as can be determined, were between 200,000 and 250,000 men, making the total number of citizens who perished in the war exceed half a million.

In order to diminish the disparity in the loss of life, due to the difference between our military policy and the military policy of Europe, two plans suggest themselves, either of which, if matured in time of peace, and adhered to in time of war, will enable us to prosecute our future campaigns with economy and dispatch.

The first plan is to so organize, localize, and nationalize the regular army that, by the mere process of filling its cadres, it may be expanded to such proportions as to enable it, without other aid, to bring our wars to a speedy conclusion.

The second plan is to prosecute our future wars with volunteer infantry, supported by the regular artillery and cavalry, apportioning the officers of the regular army among the volunteers in such a manner that all of the staff departments, and, if possible, all of the companies, battalions, brigades, and higher organizations, shall be trained and commanded by officers of military education and experience.

Both of these plans, to be efficacious, must rest on the same foundation, viz.:

1. The declaration, that every able-bodied male citizen, between certain ages, owes his country military service—a principle thoroughly republican in its nature, as it classifies in the same category, and exposes to the same hardships, the rich and the poor, the professional and non-professional, the skilled and unskilled, the educated and uneducated.

2. The division of the country into military districts and sub-districts, apportioning to them certain military organizations, whose cadres shall be recruited within the limits assigned.

3. The abandonment by the Government of all payment of bounties, relying upon its right to draft men into the service whenever a district fails to furnish its quota.

4. The assumption by the Government of the recruitment of its armies through the medium of the Provost-Marshal-General's Department, as was done by both Governments toward the close of the late war.

5. The inauguration of all of the machinery for enrolling and drafting, the moment war is declared.

6. The organization of regiments in all arms of service, as in Europe, with depots representing them in the districts to

which they belong, upon which depots requisitions shall be made by regimental commanders whenever vacancies are to be filled. It should be the duty of each depot to receive, arm, equip, and train all the recruits who volunteer, or are drafted, and to forward them to their regiments; also, whenever recruits are wanted, or men desert, to notify the provost-marshal of the district that the quota is deficient, in order that the number may be immediately supplied by volunteering, or drafting.

7. All commissions to be issued by the President, apportioning the extra appointments among the States, or military districts, according to the number of troops furnished.

8. All commissions in the expanded organization to be provisional for the war; one-third of the promotions to be reserved for distinguished skill and gallantry in battle, and to be made only on the recommendation of military commanders in the field, or upon the report of boards specially appointed to investigate the act of skill, or gallantry.

9. Promotion of all officers, after expansion, to be made on two lists—one being that of the regular arm of service, or staff department, to which the officer belongs; the second being the provisional list in the arm of service to which he is apportioned. Each officer, on the contraction of the army, to return to duty with the rank attained in the regular list. One-third of the promotions in the regular list to be regarded as original vacancies, to be filled by selection from the provisional list, no officer on the regular list being advanced more than one grade at a time; all promotions to the grade of second-lieutenant in the regular list to be made from cadets graduating from the Military Academy, and from lieutenants on the provisional list.

Neither of the above plans can be successfully executed, nor can any other plan be devised for prosecuting our wars with economy of life and treasure, without special legislation looking to the increased efficiency, and radical reorganization of the army.

THE STAFF.

The chief object to be kept in view in the proposed reorganization is that the army in time of peace shall be simply a training-school to prepare officers for staff duty, and to hold high command; and to this end it is indispensable that an interchangeable relation be established between the staff and the line.

The permanent officers of the different staff departments should be limited to the grades of major and above, all of the captains and lieutenants being so many *supernumerary* officers of the line, detailed from two to four years, with a legal provision that, after each detail, the officer serve with the troops, either in his own or another arm of service, for a period at least equal to one-half of the time he was detached.

To insure the success of the principle of detail, the first condition must be that the officers needed for staff duty *shall be supernumerary*, or in excess of the number required to fill all the regiments of the line to their complement. It was in consequence of the effort to economize in the staff at the expense of the line, that the otherwise excellent law of 1821 proved a failure.

It will be remembered that by this law the Ordnance Department was merged with the Artillery, and made to consist of four supernumerary captains, and such other officers as might be necessary, who were to be detached from the artillery.

In the Quartermaster's Department, the ten assistant quartermasters were to be detailed from the line, with an extra compensation of twenty dollars per month. In the Commissary Department, the chief was the only permanent officer; the assistant commissaries, limited to fifty, were all officers of the line, who were given an extra compensation, varying from ten to twenty dollars per month. The officers detailed in the Quartermaster's and Commissary Departments were required to do duty, when necessary, in both departments.

The number of vacancies made in the line by the execution of the law (as many as thirty officers of artillery being required in the Ordnance Department) was alone sufficient to insure a fatal result. All of the reports from the chiefs of staff departments, in addition to urging a permanent organization, dwelt upon the evils of detached service. The absence, too, of so many officers from their regiments, caused dissatisfaction in the line, and as companies were sometimes entirely stripped of their officers, repeated applications had to be made for their return to duty. This produced a reaction in favor of permanent staff corps, and accordingly the Ordnance Department was reëstablished in 1832, and the Quartermaster's Department in 1838. The change in the two departments was coincident with the Black-Hawk and Florida Wars, the latter of which was so destructive of life as to require that every officer on staff duty, who could be spared, be returned to his regiment. In the Commissary Department the principle of detail was continued till 1866.

The failure of the law of 1821, it will be perceived, was partly due to the want of a certain number of permanent officers in each staff corps, but more especially to that provision by which the staff could only be made efficient at the expense of the line.

Should we decide to reorganize our staff departments so that each shall be composed partly of permanent officers, and partly of supernumerary officers of the line, detailed for a term of years, we may assure ourselves that we are making no rash experiment by recalling the facts previously stated, viz.: That in India all of the officers in the Adjutant-General's Department, Quartermaster-General's Department, Ordnance Department, all brigade majors, fort adjutants, personal staff officers, and garrison instructors, are detailed for a period usually limited to five years; that in England all officers in the Adjutant-General's Department and Quartermaster-General's Department are detailed for the same period; that in Austria all of the officers of the Adjutant-General's Department belong to the line of the army in which they receive their promotion; and that in Italy, Germany, and Russia, no officer, even after receiving a permanent appointment in the staff, is exempt from service with the troops.

To the War Academy, and to the principle of requiring every officer of the staff to serve with troops in the line, before each following promotion, is ascribed the brilliant success achieved by the German staff in the Austro-Prussian, and Franco-German Wars.

PERSONAL REPORTS.

To secure the success of the principle of staff detail, the selection of officers for staff duty, like the promotions by selection in foreign services, should be based upon a system of personal reports.

These reports should be made annually by post commanders, and should set forth in full the military and moral character of their officers, stating their zeal and aptitude for the profession, attention to duty, and qualifications for any special employment.

In the navy, the system of personal reports is applied with admirable success. This enables the department to know the character and qualifications of its officers, and furnishes a basis for the selection of officers for all of the varied and important duties that can be committed to their charge.

But in the army no such system exists, and, as a consequence, officers who evade the performance of duty, and are alike ignorant of tactics and regulations, are too frequently detailed on detached service, while the officer who faithfully performs his duty may be left to perpetual banishment on the frontier.

These personal reports should be forwarded through regimental and department commanders for indorsement, and transmitted to a bureau in the office of the General of the Army, where, being systematized and arranged, the Government could ascertain the qualifications of every officer in the service.

By making a rule that no officer shall be detailed from the troops whose conduct has been unsatisfactory to his commanders, the principle of detail would effect a revolution in the army, and would offer a career which every officer of merit could pursue with zeal and ambition.

ADJUTANT-GENERAL'S DEPARTMENT.

The chief object of the Adjutant-General's Department, as administered in Europe, is to aid in the control and direction of armies; and so important is this mission, as we have already seen, that every great nation has established a War Academy for the education of its generals, and the instruction of the staff officers, who are to advise and assist them.

The corner-stone of the European staff system is the War Academy, and next in importance is the constant interchange between the staff and the line.

This interchange enlarges the experience of staff officers, keeps them in sympathy with the troops, enables them to know their wants, to be familiar with their discipline, to know the reliance that can be placed upon them for attack and defense, and finally enables them, by occupying successive grades in the line, to prepare themselves for the high commands, which are the certain rewards of superior skill and ability.

The War Academy, and the staff and the line, thus constitute the school of instruction for all of the great commanders of Europe, no less than for the staff officers whose province it is to assist them.

To qualify staff officers for this trust, their employment, in time of peace, is made to conform as nearly as possible to their occupation in war. The adjutant-general of a division, instead of engrossing himself with the routine of papers, devotes his time to studying strategy, grand tactics, military history, and the movements of armies.

The chief of staff of a corps necessarily devotes some of his time during peace to the papers and business he must submit to his general; but, in time of war, all work in the office is devolved upon adjutants, and aides-de-camp, who are detailed from the line, while the chief of staff occupies himself in the management and direction of the troops, in the study of maps, and in the collection of such military, geographical, and statistical information as may be useful to his commander. In battle, he sends a staff officer to each division commander, accompanied by orderlies, who bring back reports of the progress of the fighting.

The aim of the staff officer, in peace and in war, is to qualify himself for the discharge of his duty in battle. And, with this idea paramount in his mind, he looks upon the drudgery of official routine with little less than contempt.

The strength of this feeling in the German army is forcibly illustrated by the remark of an officer, greatly distinguished as the chief of staff of a corps in the battles around Metz, who, on being asked by me if, during the war, he attended to the paper-work of his office, made the reply, "No! I preferred to sleep." In explanation, he added that he would not suffer himself to become entangled in work which inferior officers could perform equally well, lest he might neglect the higher mission of assisting and directing the movements of troops.

This theory of the true employment of a staff officer finds its origin at Berlin, where the chief of staff of the army, assisted by able subordinates, elaborates the orders for mobilization and concentration, and prepares plans of campaign, which, carried speedily into execution, have won for his Government imperishable renown.

That these plans of campaign were based on no guess-work we have ample proof in the fact that the able officer in charge of the section for collecting military statistics in reference to France, reported 250,000 men as the largest force she could assemble on her frontier within two weeks after a declaration of war.

The exactness of this estimate, confirmed by subsequent events, enabled the famous chief of staff, General von Moltke, to make all of his preparations; and, when war was declared, having no further duties at Berlin, he distributed the officers of the general staff to the various armies, when all locked up their desks, and repaired to the field, to take part in the military achievements which astonished the world.

To make possible such results we must abandon our system, and consolidating the Adjutant-General's and Inspector-General's Departments, we should adopt an organization like the following:

The Adjutant-General's Department, in time of peace, to consist of—

1 General,
6 Colonels,
6 Lieutenant-colonels,
12 Majors,
12 Captains.

The grades above captain to be permanent, each major being required to serve a term of three years in the line before being promoted to lieutenant-colonel, his place during the interval to be filled by a major from the line. The grade of captain to be filled by the detail of captains from the line for the period of two years, during which time they should learn to perform the office-work at the headquarters of our different military divisions, and departments.

Promotions to major to be limited to those officers who have served two years on detail in the department; to be selected by competitive examination, or by the simpler method of selection, from the number of such officers as have received the special certificate of the adjutant-general, approved by the General of the Army, setting forth that these officers while serving in the department have merited the special approbation of their superiors.

The above organization is based on the consideration that, as in all modern armies, the Adjutant-General's Department should be divided into several sections or bureaux:

The first section should conduct general correspondence, and be the common medium for the Secretary of War, and the General-in-Chief, to communicate their orders and instructions to the army.

The second and third sections, as now practically organized, should be under the Secretary of War, for the purpose of examining and correcting the rolls and returns of the army, and to assist him in the discharge of the ministerial duties of his office.

In addition to these sections there should be three others, under the General of the Army:

The first of these sections should be charged with the collection of information and statistics relating to all foreign armies, but especially in reference to Mexico, Canada, and Cuba.

ADJUTANT-GENERAL'S DEPARTMENT.

The duties of the second section should be to write the military history of our wars, both Indian and civilized, thereby enabling our future officers to become familiar with the peculiarities of American fighting.

The third section should be charged with the arrangement of the individual history of the officers of the army, based upon the personal reports, and the part they have taken in campaigns and battles.

The establishment of a statistical section would enable the General of the Army to have statements in readiness showing the exact military resources of our neighbors, upon which calculations could be based as to the number of troops required for any given campaign.

The number of officers given in the proposed organization is based upon the present division of the country into the three geographical divisions, and ten departments, each of which requires a permanent officer as chief of staff; and, further, upon the assumption that from one to two permanent officers will be required to superintend each section, and the sub-sections, into which they may be divided.

In time of peace the chiefs of staff of military departments (mostly majors) should be encouraged to study the art of war; to instruct the captains on detail in both the practical and theoretical duties of a staff officer; and, when not engaged in this labor, they should be sent to inspect the troops of the department, or division, thereby keeping themselves and their generals informed as to the discipline, instruction, and condition, of their commands.

By thus emancipating themselves from the routine of paper-work, this system, and this only, will enable us in future wars to provide competent chiefs of staff, who have been so sadly needed in all of our past wars.

The distribution above contemplated requires—

1 Adjutant-general,
6 Colonels, chiefs of section,
3 Lieutenant-colonels, assistant chiefs of section,
3 Lieutenant-colonels, chiefs of staff, military divisions,

2 Majors, assistant chiefs of section,

10 Majors, chiefs of staff, military departments,

12 Captains, assistant adjutant-generals, under instruction at division and department headquarters.

Comparing this organization with the number of officers now in the Adjutant-General's and Inspector-General's Departments, which is as follows—1 general, 6 colonels, 5 lieutenant-colonels, and 12 majors—we need for the inauguration of the new system the addition of but 1 lieutenant-colonel, and 12 captains.

In time of war, the Adjutant-General's Department should consist provisionally of the necessary number of officers for bureau-work at Washington, and an additional number for the field, at the rate of—

1 Major, chief of staff, and 1 captain for each brigade,

1 Lieutenant-colonel, chief of staff, and 2 captains for each division,

1 Colonel, chief of staff, 1 lieutenant-colonel, and 3 captains for each corps,

1 General, chief of staff, with the necessary number of field-officers and captains for each army.

The chief of staff of every command should be an officer who has been trained in the Adjutant-General's Department; and the same, in an army of small numbers, should apply to the other staff officers; but, in case of a great war, the captains might be appointed from among officers whose general education specially qualifies them for the duties of such a position.

Under this organization, the chiefs of staff of corps, and armies, would be enabled to devote themselves to the study of maps, and to the collection of such geographical and statistical information as would enable them to assist in directing the movements of troops; while their assistants would perform the work of adjutant-generals, inspector-generals, and mustering officers, done heretofore by officers of separate departments.

The value of this unity of action the first war could not fail to demonstrate.

QUARTERMASTER'S DEPARTMENT.

This department, as at present organized by law, consists of—

- 1 Brigadier-general,
- 6 Colonels,
- 10 Lieutenant-colonels,
- 12 Majors,
- 30 Captains.

To reorganize the department on the principle of detail, the law need only prescribe that the 30 captains shall be distributed as so many supernumeraries to the infantry, artillery, and cavalry; the 30 captaincies in future to be filled by captains, or first-lieutenants, detailed from the line for the period of four years.

The promotions to the grade of major should be made on the same principles as in the Adjutant-General's Department.

In time of war, the department should be provisionally increased by the addition of the necessary number of officers: the chief quartermasters of corps and armies, and those in command of all of the great depots to be officers who have been trained in the department; all captains in great wars to be appointed from civil life.

SUBSISTENCE DEPARTMENT.

This department to consist of the same number of officers as at present, viz.:

- 1 Brigadier-general,
- 2 Colonels,
- 3 Lieutenant-colonels,
- 8 Majors, and
- 12 Captains.

The grades of major and above to be permanent; the captains to be distributed as supernumeraries in the line, the captaincies afterward to be filled by detail from the line for the period of four years. Promotion to major to be by selection from the officers who have been on detail, or trained in the department.

In time of war, a sufficient number of officers to be provisionally appointed to perform bureau, depot, and field duty. All chief commissaries to be appointed from officers of experience, in the department; division and brigade commissaries to be appointed from civil life.

PAY DEPARTMENT.

As reorganized on the principle of detail, this department should consist of—

    1 Brigadier-general,
    6 Colonels,
    6 Lieutenant-colonels,
    12 Majors,
    30 Captains.

The grades of major and above to be permanent; no promotions to be made to the grade of major till the number is reduced below twelve; the captains to be supernumeraries, detailed from the captains and first-lieutenants of the line for the period of four years.

Promotions to the grade of major to be made by selection from the captains who have been detailed in the department.

The war organization to consist provisionally of the necessary number of officers; all chief paymasters to be selected from officers trained in the department; all field paymasters to be appointed from civil life.

SIGNAL CORPS.

This corps should consist of—

    1 Colonel as chief, and
    20 Lieutenants.

The lieutenants should be detailed from the line for a period not exceeding four years. In time of war, the department should consist provisionally of the necessary number of officers of all grades, those in the grade of major and above to be selected from officers who have been trained in the corps.

ARTILLERY AND ORDNANCE.

These corps to be merged, with a chief having the grade of brigadier-general.

The artillery to consist of the same number of officers and men as at present, organized into a corps; or retaining the present regimental formation, with lineal promotion.

The Ordnance Department to consist, under the chief of artillery and ordnance, of—

    5 Colonels,
    5 Lieutenant-colonels,
    10 Majors,
    15 Captains, and
    15 First-lieutenants.

The grades of major and above to be permanent; the captains, and lieutenants, to be supernumerary officers of artillery, detailed for the period of four years.

Promotions to the grade of major to be made by selection from the captains who have been detailed in the department.

In time of war, the necessary number of officers to be provisionally added for service at arsenals, the duties of ordnance-officers in the field being performed under the direction of the chiefs of artillery of armies, corps, and divisions.

ENGINEERS.

This corps should consist, as at present, of—

    1 Chief of engineers, with rank of brigadier-general,
    6 Colonels,
    12 Lieutenant-colonels,
    24 Majors,
    30 Captains,
    26 First-lieutenants, and
    10 Second-lieutenants.

The grades of captain and above to be permanent. First and second lieutenants to be supernumeraries of the line, detailed for a period of four years.

Promotions to the grade of captain to be made by competitive examination prescribed by the chief of engineers, the examinations to be held every four years, and to be open to all first-lieutenants who have been detailed in the department.

RESULTS OF A SYSTEM OF STAFF DETAIL.

If Congress, in its wisdom, should see fit to inaugurate this system, giving it a trial for eight years, we would have, at the end of that period—

  48 Captains, trained as assistant adjutant-generals,
  60 Captains, trained as assistant quartermasters,
  24 Captains, trained as commissaries of subsistence,
  60 Captains, trained as paymasters,
  40 First-lieutenants, trained as signal-officers,
  30 Captains, trained as ordnance-officers,
  30 First-lieutenants, trained as ordnance-officers,
  52 First-lieutenants, trained as engineers,
  20 Second-lieutenants, trained as engineers,

Making a total, in eight years, of 364 officers in the line who would have received an education in the staff.

DETACHED SERVICE.

But still greater results can be attained if Congress, in addition, will limit the period for which captains, and lieutenants, can be absent from company duty.

For want of such a system a second staff, nearly permanent, has sprung up in our army, composed of officers on signal-duty, aides-de-camp, and other officers on various kinds of detached service, some of whom have never joined their companies.

Besides these positions, there are others in the service which afford to the occupants rare opportunities for acquiring professional information, such as the command of a light battery, regimental adjutant, and regimental quartermaster, in which the tenure of appointment is indefinite, and often extends from ten to fifteen years.

Were the law to limit the appointment of the 29 aides-de-camp, 5 light-battery commanders, 40 regimental adjutants, and 40 regimental quartermasters, to four years, we would have at the end of the next eight years, including the present incumbents—

87 Officers, trained as aides-de-camp,
15 Captains, trained as light-battery commanders,
120 Lieutenants, trained as regimental adjutants, and
120 Lieutenants, trained as regimental quartermasters.

Applying the same limit, we would have, in addition to the above, nearly as many officers who would have had experience as instructors at the Military Academy, and professors of science and tactics at various colleges.

If to these officers we add the number trained under the proposed system of staff detail, we could soon boast, India not excepted, that our officers possess the most varied experience of any army in the world.

Such a system, based upon personal reports, would soon break up any tendency to idleness and dissipation, and would give to every officer of zeal and ability the opportunity to perfect himself in nearly every branch of his profession.

In war, officers of such varied experience would adapt themselves either to regulars, or volunteers, and if placed in high commands would give us results that must forever be impossible so long as we adhere to a military system which has been abandoned by every nation in Europe.

INFANTRY.

In determining the organization of the line of the army, wisdom forbids that we should ignore the strength and military resources of our neighbors. Keeping in remembrance that under the system of mixed troops we employed more than 100,000 men in the Mexican War, and a half-million of men in the War of 1812; that Spain has already sent out more than 160,000 men to suppress the Cuban insurrection, prudence suggests that, independent of reserves, our peace establishment should be capable of expansion to at least 150,000 men.

To obtain this result, the peace organization of the infantry should consist of the present 25 regiments, formed in 2 battalions of 4 companies each, with the 2 remaining companies as a regimental depot.

The field, staff, and non-commissioned staff of a regiment, on the peace-footing, should be as follows:

RANK.	Officers.	Men.	DEPOT. Officers.	DEPOT. Men.
Colonel	1	..	..	..
Lieutenant-colonel (battalion-commander)	1	..	..	..
Senior major	1	..	..	..
Junior major	..	..	1	..
Regimental adjutant (captain)	1	..	..	..
Regimental quartermaster (captain)	1	..	..	..
Battalion adjutants (first-lieutenants)	2	..	..	..
Battalion quartermasters (first-lieutenants)	2	..	..	..
Regimental sergeant-major	..	1	..	..
Regimental quartermaster-sergeant	..	1	..	..
Battalion sergeant-majors	..	2	..	..
Battalion quartermaster-sergeants	..	2	..	..
Total	9	6	1	..
Aggregate	10	6	..	..

Company on a Peace-footing.

RANK.	Officers.	Men.	Total.
Captain	1	..	1
First-lieutenant	1	..	1
Second-lieutenant	1	..	1
First-sergeant	..	1	1
Sergeants	..	4	4
Corporals	..	4	4
Musicians	..	2	2
Artificers	..	2	2
Wagoner	..	1	1
Privates	..	40	40
Aggregate	3	54	57

Battalion on the Peace-footing.

RANK.	Officers.	Men.	Total.
Field-officer (commandant)	1	..	1
Adjutant	1	..	1
Quartermaster	1	..	1
Sergeant-major	..	1	1
Quartermaster-sergeant	..	1	1
Captains	4	..	4
First-lieutenants	4	..	4
Second-lieutenants	4	..	4
First-sergeants	..	4	4
Sergeants	..	16	16
Corporals	..	16	16
Musicians	..	8	8
Artificers	..	8	8
Wagoners	..	4	4
Privates	..	160	160
Aggregate	15	218	233

INFANTRY.

Depot-Company on Peace-footing.

RANK.	Officers.	Men.	Total.
Captain	1	..	1
First-lieutenant	1	..	1
Second-lieutenant	1	..	1
First-sergeant	..	1	1
Sergeants	..	4	4
Corporals	..	4	4
Musicians	..	2	2
Aggregate	3	11	14

Depot on the Peace-footing.

RANK.	Officers.	Men.	Total.
Field-officer (commandant)	1	..	1
Captains	2	..	2
First-lieutenants	2	..	2
Second-lieutenants	2	..	2
First-sergeants	..	2	2
Sergeants	..	8	8
Corporals	..	8	8
Musicians	..	4	4
Aggregate	7	22	29

The following table shows the organization of a regiment of two battalions, with its depot-cadre, on a peace-footing:

RANK.	FIELD, STAFF, AND TWO BATTALIONS.		DEPOT.		TOTAL.		AGGREGATE.
	Officers.	Men.	Officers.	Men.	Officers.	Men.	
Colonel	1	..	..	..	1	..	1
Lieutenant-colonel	1	..	..	..	1	..	1
Majors	1	..	1	..	2	..	2
Regimental adjutant	1	..	..	..	1	..	1
Regimental quartermaster	1	..	..	..	1	..	1
Battalion-adjutants	2	..	..	..	2	..	2
Battalion-quartermasters	2	..	..	..	2	..	2
Regimental sergeant-major	..	1	..	..	..	1	1
Regimental quartermaster-serg't	..	1	..	..	..	1	1
Battalion sergeant-majors	..	2	..	..	..	2	2
Battalion quartermaster-sergeants	..	2	..	..	..	2	2
Captains	8	..	2	..	10	..	10
First-lieutenants	8	..	2	..	10	..	10
Second-lieutenants	8	..	2	..	10	..	10
First-sergeants	..	8	..	2	..	10	10
Sergeants	..	32	..	8	..	40	40
Corporals	..	32	..	8	..	40	40
Musicians	..	16	..	4	..	20	20
Artificers	..	16	..	..	..	16	16
Wagoners	..	8	..	..	..	8	8
Privates	..	320	..	..	..	320	320
Total	33	438	7	22	40	460	500

Aggregate, 25 regiments on peace-footing, 12,500.

The number of privates in each depot-company would average a little less than 40, and would depend upon the number of men required to keep each of the battalions of the regiments up to their authorized strength of 218 enlisted men.

WAR ORGANIZATION OF INFANTRY.

As the infantry is more easily improvised, and made efficient, than artillery and cavalry, it is in this arm of the service that the principle of expansion should find its widest application.

On the war-footing, each regiment of infantry should, therefore, consist of two, three, or four battalions, and a depot, according as the army is to be raised to 50,000, 75,000, or 100,000 men.

The following table shows the field, staff, and non-commissioned staff, required for a regiment on a war-footing of two battalions.

By adding 1 lieutenant-colonel, 1 major, 1 adjutant, 1 quartermaster, 1 sergeant-major, and 1 quartermaster-sergeant for each additional battalion, it will likewise represent the field staff and non-commissioned staff for a regiment of three and four battalions:

RANK.	2 BATTALIONS.		DEPOT.		TOTAL.		Aggregate.
	Officers.	Men.	Officers.	Men.	Officers.	Men.	
Colonel..........................	1	..	..	..	1	..	1
Lieutenant-colonels	2	..	..	..	2	..	2
Majors..........................	2	..	1	..	3	..	3
Regimental adjutant (captain)....	1	..	..	..	1	..	1
Regimental quartermaster (capt.).	1	..	..	..	1	..	1
Battalion adjutants................	2	..	1	..	3	..	3
Battalion quartermasters.........	2	..	1	..	3	..	3
Regimental sergeant-major.......	..	1	..	..	..	1	1
Regimental quartermaster-serg't..	..	1	..	..	..	1	1
Battalion sergeant-majors	..	2	..	1	..	3	3
Battalion quartermaster-sergeants.	..	2	..	1	..	3	3
	11	6	3	2	14	8	22
	3 Battalions.						
	15	8	3	2	18	10	28
	4 Battalions.						
	19	10	3	2	22	12	34

Company on a War-footing.

RANK.	Officers.	Men.	Total.
Captain	1	..	1
First-lieutenants	2	..	2
Second-lieutenants	2	..	2
First-sergeant	..	1	1
Sergeants	..	12	12
Corporals	..	24	24
Musicians	..	2	2
Artificers	..	2	2
Clerk	..	1	1
Privates	..	200	200
Aggregate	5	242	247

The sergeants and corporals are arranged on the basis of one corporal to each set of fours, and one sergeant to every two sets of fours, or one to every eight and sixteen men respectively.

Battalion on a War-footing.

RANK.	Officers.	Men.	Total.
Lieutenant-colonel	1	..	1
Major	1	..	1
Adjutant	1	..	1
Quartermaster	1	..	1
Sergeant-major	..	1	1
Quartermaster-sergeant	..	1	1
Clerks	..	4	4
Captains	4	..	4
First-lieutenants	8	..	8
Second-lieutenants	8	..	8
First-sergeants	..	4	4
Sergeants	..	48	48
Corporals	..	96	96
Musicians	..	8	8
Artificers	..	8	8
Clerks	..	4	4
Privates	..	800	800
Aggregate	24	974	998

The allowance of two field-officers to each battalion is based upon the known moral superiority which rank carries with it; upon the great loss of life in these grades, as established in our late and more recent wars; and also the demands for detached service, which constantly occur in campaign.

Depot Company on War-footing.

RANK.	Officers.	Men.	Total.
Captain	1	..	1
First-lieutenant	2	..	2
Second-lieutenant	2	..	2
First-sergeant	..	1	1
Sergeants	..	12	12
Corporals	..	12	12
Musicians	..	2	2
Aggregate	5	27	32

The number of officers and men is based upon the demand for instructors for the raw recruits. The recruits, or privates, who would be attached to each company until sent to the field, would probably vary from 100 to 300.

Depot on a War-footing.

RANK.	Officers.	Men.	Total.
Field-officer	1	..	1
Adjutant	1	..	1
Quartermaster	1	..	1
Sergeant-major	..	1	1
Quartermaster-sergeant	..	1	1
Captains	2	..	2
First-lieutenants	4	..	4
Second-lieutenants	4	..	4
First-sergeants	..	2	2
Sergeants	..	24	24
Corporals	..	24	24
Musicians	..	4	4
Aggregate	13	56	69

The following table shows the strength of a regiment with its depot, on a war-footing of two, three, and four battalions:

REGIMENT.	2 BATTALIONS.			3 BATTALIONS.			4 BATTALIONS.		
	Officers.	Men.	Total.	Officers.	Men.	Total.	Officers.	Men.	Total.
Regimental and battalion field, staff, and non-commissioned staff, including 6 clerks for regimental headquarters and 4 for each battalion headquarters	11	20	31	15	26	41	19	32	51
Eight companies	40	1,936	1,976	..	....	....	....	....	....
Twelve companies	..	....	....	60	2,904	2,964	....	....	....
Sixteen companies	..	....	....	..	....	....	80	3,872	3,952
	51	1,956	2,007	75	2,930	3,005	99	3,904	4,003
DEPOT.									
Field, staff, and non-commis'd staff	3	2	5	3	2	5	3	2	5
Two companies	10	54	64	10	54	64	10	54	64
Aggregate	64	2,012	2,076	88	2,986	3,074	112	3,960	4,072

The aggregate field strength of the present twenty-five regiments, raised to the war-footing, would therefore be for—

Two battalions........................ 50,175
Three battalions....................... 75,075
Four battalions........................ 100,075

OFFICERS FOR THE WAR-FOOTING.

Deducting the number of officers the infantry would lose by promotion in the expanded war organization of the staff, we could send every company into action, on the basis of 50,000, with at least two officers of military experience to train and command it. Expanded to 75,000, and to 100,000 if necessary, we could still furnish an experienced captain to each company, and by a system of lineal promotion, and by promotion by selection, the command of companies could be confided to trained officers till the lieutenants appointed from civil life would be able to replace them.

COMPLEMENTARY OFFICERS.

The extra lieutenants required to raise the infantry companies to the war standard, should, as far as practicable, be selected in time of peace, and, as in other countries, their names should be borne on the Army Register below the grade of second-lieutenant.

There are several classes from which we can draw such supply:

The first class embraces all non-commissioned officers of the army, who, on quitting the service, can pass a special examination to be prescribed for officers of complement; their appointments to be distributed at large.

The second class embraces such graduates as have pursued the course of military instruction at colleges where officers of the army are detailed as professors of tactics, at an expense to the Government on account of their salaries of about $20,000 to $30,000 per annum.

The utilization of this expense by the Government, it is more than probable, would supply us with a class of officers such as we have never seen in our army during any past war; and being assigned to the regiments whose depots are within their several States, their appointment would tend to nationalize the army in the same manner as the present system of appointing cadets to the Military Academy.

The third class embraces the graduates of Military Academies, like those of Pennsylvania, Virginia, and Vermont, assigned as above.

The fourth class embraces such officers of the national guard, or militia, as can pass the prescribed examination; their appointments being assigned as already explained for the graduates of colleges, and Military Academies.

Not till such a system is adopted will an American army ever be able to show its prowess, nor will we be able to avert the extravagance, and bloodshed, which inhere in our system.

CAVALRY.

Keeping in mind the fact that the 60,000 to 80,000 cavalry maintained from the beginning to the end of the rebellion, did not become really efficient till the battle of Beverly Ford, in 1863, after it had been trained for nearly two years; that the expense of supporting it is doubly if not trebly as expensive as infantry—we ought from our own experience to follow the example of European nations, and as far as practicable maintain our future cavalry either on a war-footing, or else on a basis capable of such expansion as to meet quickly the demands of war.

PEACE-FOOTING OF CAVALRY.

Adopting the model presented for the infantry, each of the ten regiments of cavalry should be organized into three battalions, and a depot; one battalion to consist of four companies, the other battalions of three companies each; the remaining two companies forming the depot, to be stationed in the State whence the regiment is to draw its men and horses.

Already having five field-officers available for the command of each battalion and depot, as also a regimental adjutant and quartermaster, the only extra officers required for the peace-footing are three battalion adjutants, and three battalion quartermasters.

If we ultimately fix the enlisted strength of the ten companies which constitute the battalions at sixty-two men, the same as allowed by Congress after the reduction in 1842, the strength of each regiment would be as follows:

RANK.	Officers.	Men.	Total.
Field and staff...	13	...	13
Non-commissioned staff................................	..	8	8
Three battalions (10 companies)....................	30	620	650
Depot (2 companies).....................................	6	22	28
Aggregate...	49	650	699

Aggregate ten regiments, 6,990.

WAR ORGANIZATION OF THE CAVALRY.

In this organization, the enlisted men should be increased to 100 per company, including 1 first-sergeant, 6 sergeants, and 8 corporals; the officers should consist of 1 captain, 2 first-lieutenants, and 1 second-lieutenant.

By adding an extra company to the two battalions of three companies each, the strength of a regiment, on the war-footing, would be according to the following table:

RANK.	Officers.	Men.	Total.
Field and staff...	13	....	13
Non-commissioned staff................................	..	8	8
Regimental and battalion clerks....................	..	18	18
Three battalions (12 companies)....................	48	1,200	1,248
Depot (2 companies).....................................	8	50	58
Aggregate...	69	1,256	1,325

Total ten regiments, 13,250.

This force of 13,250 we could send into the field with two trained officers to lead every company. Further, by adding two more companies to each battalion, an organization permitted by the tactics, we could increase our cavalry to 19,490, and still have a regular officer at the head of every company.

This force would exceed by more than 3,500 the number of

cavalry led by Sheridan at Five Forks, and by more than 7,000 the number led by Wilson from the Tennessee to the Ocmulgee, although at that time we had more than 85,000 cavalry on our rolls.

The officers of this force, both regular and complementary, should be provided as explained for the infantry, the provisional list being kept at the War Department in a state of constant readiness for a battalion organization of either four, or six companies.

PEACE ORGANIZATION OF THE ARTILLERY.

The immense expense of the matériel of artillery, and the professional training necessary to make artillery formidable, require that this arm of the service, even more than the cavalry, should be maintained on a basis capable of immediate expansion.

It should therefore consist of the present number of batteries, organized into a corps, or of the five existing regiments, organized into three battalions of three batteries each, with two batteries as a depot; the light battery being assigned to one of the three battalions.

If to the present number of officers we add three battalion adjutants, and quartermasters; fix the enlisted strength of each battery at 1 first-sergeant, 4 sergeants, 4 corporals, 2 artificers, 2 musicians, and 42 privates, which is but one greater than allowed by the law of 1842; and allow each light battery an enlisted strength of 1 first-sergeant, 6 sergeants, 4 corporals, 2 musicians, 2 artificers, 1 wagoner, and 64 privates, the same as was allowed before the last order for reduction, the peace organization of a regiment would be as follows:

REGIMENT.	Officers.	Men.	Total.
Field and staff	13	...	13
Non-commissioned staff	...	9	9
Three battalions (9 companies)	36	495	531
Light battery	5	80	85
Depot (2 companies)	8	22	80
Total	62	605	667
Aggregate five regiments	310	3,025	3,335

On the assumption that the Artillery and Ordnance should be consolidated under a common chief, the Ordnance Department being composed of a sufficient number of permanent officers, to insure the uniform operation of the department, the depots of the several regiments of artillery should be located at the great arsenals where they would not only be able to protect the Government property, but would also find at hand the facilities and means for instructing recruits in the use and manœuvres of all the guns employed in the service.

A still better organization of the artillery would be to make one battalion in each regiment to consist of two light batteries; the remaining two battalions to consist of four batteries each. This would increase the aggregate enlisted strength of the five regiments only 125 men.

With this organization, limiting the service of a light battery to two years, every battery in each regiment could serve as light artillery every ten years.

WAR ORGANIZATION OF THE ARTILLERY.

While it is the function of the artillery in every country to provide batteries for the field, and for the attack and defense of fortified places, our attention in time of war should be concentrated almost exclusively on the light artillery, which, by its precision and steadiness, should be able to inspire confidence in the other arms of service; and particularly should this be our purpose so long as it is, our policy to rely at first on raw troops.

Allowing as a liberal calculation four guns to a thousand men, if we add 13,000, the proposed war strength of our cavalry, to 50,000, 75,000, and 100,000, representing the war strength of the infantry on the three different footings, the three armies of 63,000, 88,000, and 113,000 would require 42, 58, and 75 batteries respectively.

The batteries for the first army could be instantly furnished by mounting forty-two batteries, while by increasing the enlisted strength of each of the remaining eight batteries to 250 men, there would be a battalion of 1,000 men available as heavy artillery for each of the two corps, into which the army would be divided.

To provide for the second and third armies, organized into two and three corps, the artillery should be increased by dividing, and converting, as many of the existing batteries as necessary into two batteries each. This would give nearly two trained officers to each battery, besides a nucleus of experienced non-commissioned officers and privates, whose example would soon convert new recruits into veteran soldiers.

By this method thirty batteries would form the fifty-eight light batteries required for the second army; the remaining twenty batteries, increased to 250 men each, would form five battalions of 1,000 men, available as heavy artillery, either for service in the field, or for the defense of our sea-coast fortifications.

For the third army thirty-eight batteries would form the seventy-five light batteries, while by converting the remaining twelve batteries into two batteries of 250 men each, we would have six battalions of 1,000 men each, available as before for service in the field, or for fortress-defense.

Without stopping to enumerate the organizations of trains, but simply allowing to each army 1 brigadier-general, as chief of artillery, with 6 staff officers; two or three extra colonels specially selected as chiefs of artillery of corps; one half as many lieutenant-colonels as there are battalions, the remaining battalions to be commanded by majors; further, allowing to each chief of artillery of a corps a staff consisting of 1 adjutant, 1 aide-de-camp, 1 quartermaster, and 1 ordnance-officer—an adjutant and quartermaster likewise being allowed to each battalion—the approximate strength of the artillery on the three different war-footings would be as follows:

Artillery for an Army of 63,000 Men.

RANK.	Officers.	Men.	Total.
Chief of artillery (brigadier-general)	1	....	1
Staff	6	....	6
Clerks	....	12	12
Colonels of regiments	5	....	5
Colonels, corps chiefs of artillery	2	....	2

ARTILLERY.

RANK.	Officers.	Men.	Total.
COMMANDANTS OF BATTALIONS AND DEPOTS.			
Lieutenant-colonels...	10	....	10
Majors...	10	....	10
STAFF.			
Regimental...	10	....	10
Corps...	8	....	8
Battalion and depot...	40	....	40
NON-COMMISSIONED STAFF.			
Regimental...	...	10	10
Corps...	...	4	4
Battalion and depot...	...	40	40
CLERKS.			
Regimental...	...	20	20
Battalion...	...	60	60
FIELD-ARTILLERY.			
12 Battalions, 42 batteries (light and horse).......................	210	6,342	6,552
HEAVY ARTILLERY.			
2 Battalions (8 companies)..	40	2,000	2,040
Depots (10 companies)...	50	210	260
Aggregate...	392	8,708	9,100

Artillery for an Army of 88,000 Men.

RANK.	Officers.	Men.	Aggregate.
Chief of artillery (brigadier-general).............................	1	....	1
Staff...	6	....	6
Clerks..	....	12	12
Colonels of regiments...	5	....	5
Colonels, corps chiefs of artillery.................................	2	....	2
COMMANDANTS OF BATTALIONS AND DEPOTS.			
Lieutenant-colonels...	15	....	15
Majors...	15	....	15
STAFF.			
Regimental...	10	....	10
Corps...	8	....	8
Battalion and depot...	60	....	60
NON-COMMISSIONED STAFF.			
Regimental...	....	10	10
Corps...	....	4	4
Battalion and depot...	....	60	60
CLERKS.			
Regimental...	....	20	20
Battalion...	....	60	60
FIELD-ARTILLERY.			
15 Battalions, 60 batteries (light and horse).......................	300	9,600	9,900
HEAVY ARTILLERY.			
5 Battalions (20 companies)...	100	5,000	5,100
	522	14,796	15,318

Artillery for an Army of 113,000 Men.

RANK.	Officers.	Men.	Aggregate.
Chief of artillery (brigadier-general)	1	....	1
Staff	6	....	6
Clerks	....	12	12
Colonels of regiments	5	....	5
Colonels, corps chiefs of artillery	3	....	3
COMMANDANTS OF BATTALIONS AND DEPOTS.			
Lieutenant-colonels	18	....	18
Majors	17	....	17
STAFF.			
Regimental	10	....	10
Corps	12	....	12
Battalion and depot	70	....	70
NON-COMMISSIONED STAFF.			
Regimental	....	10	10
Corps	....	6	6
Battalion, and depot	....	70	70
CLERKS.			
Regimental	....	80	80
Battalion	....	100	100
FIELD-ARTILLERY.			
19 Battalions (76 batteries, light and horse)	880	11,470	11,850
HEAVY ARTILLERY.			
6 Battalions (24 companies)	120	6,000	6,120
	642	17,699	18,840

To officer efficiently this force of artillery, all regular officers should be advanced on the provisional list, the vacancies at the bottom being filled by graduates of the Military Academy; by promotion of deserving non-commissioned officers of the army; and as far as practicable by graduates of military universities and colleges.

RECAPITULATION OF THE INFANTRY, CAVALRY, AND ARTILLERY, ON THE FOOTING OF PEACE AND OF WAR.

Peace-footing.

ARM OF SERVICE.	Regiments.	Battalions.	Depots.	Officers.	Men.	Aggregate.
Infantry	25	50	25	1,000	11,500	12,500
Cavalry	10	80	10	490	6,500	6,990
Artillery	5	15	5	310	3,025	3,335
	40	95	40	1,800	21,025	22,825

RECAPITULATION.

War-footing—First Basis.

ARM OF SERVICE.	Regiments.	Battalions.	Depots.	Officers.	Men.	Aggregate.
Infantry..........	25	50	25	1,500	50,300	51,900
Cavalry..........	10	30	10	690	12,561	13,250
Artillery.........	5	15	5	392	8,708	9,100
	40	95	40	2,592	71,569	74,250

War-footing—Second Basis.

ARM OF SERVICE.	Regiments.	Battalions.	Depots.	Officers.	Men.	Aggregate.
Infantry..........	25	75	25	2,200	74,630	76,850
Cavalry..........	10	30	10	690	12,560	13,250
Artillery.........	5	20	5	522	14,796	15,316
	40	125	40	3,412	102,006	105,418

War-footing—Third Basis.

ARM OF SERVICE.	Regiments.	Battalions.	Depots.	Officers.	Men.	Aggregate.
Infantry..........	25	100	25	2,800	99,000	101,800
Cavalry..........	10	48 [1]	10	960	18,560	19,490
Artillery.........	5	25	5	642	17,698	18,340
	40	173	40	4,372	135,258	139,680

If to the number 139,630 be added the staff departments, military trains, signal corps, ambulance corps, etc., each of which should have its special organization, the total strength of the army would considerably exceed 150,000.

In addition, by increasing the number of privates in the 80 depot companies to 300 each, there would be 20,000 men receiving instruction, who would be available to fill vacancies.

A comparison of our present inexpensive organization with the proposed peace establishment shows that we can effect the transformation by the addition of 210 officers to the 1,589 already existing, while the number of enlisted men as compared with the number 23,135, now allowed to the three arms of service, can be reduced by 2,110.

But dispensing with the battalion adjutants and quarter-

---

[1] Six companies to each battalion.

masters—a measure that would be unwise considering the value of trained officers in war—the number of additional officers can be reduced to the twenty-five majors required to place the field-officers of infantry on the same footing as the artillery and cavalry. The additional cost, however, of the 210 officers, would be more than compensated by saving the pay of 2,110 enlisted men, and would thus make the reorganization a measure of economy.

If the expansive system be adopted, and the President be authorized within certain limits to increase the enlisted strength of the army, we can vary the war-footing anywhere from the peace establishment of 22,825 to 139,630, by simply increasing the privates of the companies, or any part of them, between the limits fixed for peace and for war.

The exact strength of the companies, and the number of troops required in any international emergency, should be left to the calculation of the officers in the Bureau of Military Statistics, under the General of the Army, who thus, at any moment, would be prepared to report to the Secretary of War the number of the enemy's troops to be overcome, and the organization best adapted to accomplish that object.

However great may be the advantages of the proposed organization, we must not overlook the fact that the success of the three and four battalion systems wholly depends upon its connection with a depot, territorial recruitment, and, in case of necessity, obligatory military service.

The two-battalion system was adopted in all arms of service in 1811, but the first law after the declaration of war in 1812, reduced the regiments of infantry from two battalions to one. For want of recruits, too, the new regular regiments of three battalions each, authorized at the beginning of the late war, could not be raised, while in 1864 nearly all of the three-battalion regiments of heavy artillery were consolidated as soon as the vacancies occasioned by field-service could no longer be filled.

From this experience we may, therefore, conclude that, if we adopt the three-battalion organization in peace, we shall have to abandon it in time of war, unless in connection with it we establish a depot, and a system of recruitment which shall insure a steady supply of reserve troops.

LINEAL PROMOTION.

An important feature of an expansive peace organization should be lineal promotion in each arm of the service.

The opposition to such promotion is based upon the supposed destruction of regimental *esprit de corps;* but the development of this feeling requires that the companies of a regiment shall serve together, and, what is more important still, that the regiment shall be excited to emulation by serving with others in the same brigade, or division. These conditions, which always exist in war, cannot exist with us in time of peace, because of the small size of our army, and the vast extent of our territory. Furthermore, desirable as it may be to cultivate this regimental feeling, it may be entirely absorbed in the pride and satisfaction of belonging, as in the German army, to the "corps of officers."

But whatever advantage may be claimed on the side of *esprit de corps*, it is more than counterbalanced by confining an officer from twenty to thirty years to the same regiment, whereby, if he remain continually with it, his knowledge of the army may be limited to the few associates he met on joining the service.

The present system likewise produces great inequality, if not injustice, as in some regiments officers are well up in the list of first-lieutenants, who received their appointments within the last two or three years, while other officers, entering the army eight or nine years before them, are still second-lieutenants.

Aside from the personal aspects of the case, lineal promotion is to be desired as the means of enlarging an officer's experience, and of keeping up his interest in his profession—a result which may be procured by adopting a system that may require him to serve as second-lieutenant of one regiment in Texas; as first-lieutenant of another in Oregon; as captain of another in Arizona; as major of another in New York; as lieutenant-colonel of another in Kansas; as colonel of another in Georgia.

This variety of service, extended knowledge of the geography of the country, enlarged acquaintance with the officers of the army, and association with the people of different States and sections, could not fail to inure to the advantage of the Government.

Again, lineal promotion is to be desired as a stepping-stone to examination for promotion, as thereby an officer who fails to pass his examination can be held at the head of the list, while others, more meritorious, can be advanced above him. Already colonels, lieutenant-colonels, majors, and captains, are on the same general list for promotion; and, as it belongs to these officers to maintain the tone and dignity of the service, all that is needed is to add to the list the first and second lieutenants.

If this be accomplished, all officers in future wars, whether they receive provisional commissions in the expanded organization, or remain in the regiments not raised to the war-footing, will receive a due share of promotion. It will also enable us to discard the brevet, and, by reserving not to exceed one-third of the promotions for selection for distinguished skill and gallantry in battle, we can secure to brave and skillful officers the same substantial reward as is now guaranteed to officers of our navy, and to officers of nearly all foreign armies.

EXAMINATION FOR PROMOTION.

This principle already exists in the medical corps, the corps of engineers, and ordnance.

By the laws applicable to the engineers and ordinance, no officer below the rank of field-officer can be promoted to a higher grade without being "examined and approved" by a board of three officers senior to him in rank. If the officer fail at the examination, his promotion is suspended for a year, when he is again reëxamined. In case of failure on reëxamination, the law prescribes that the officer "shall be dismissed from the service."

In the navy the law is still more explicit, and better adapted to protect both the interest of the Government, and the officers concerned.

Its first and second provisions prescribe that, except in case of wounds received in the line of his duty, no officer shall be promoted in the active list of the navy "until he has been examined by a board of naval surgeons, and pronounced physically qualified to perform all his duties at sea."

Another section prescribes that "no line officer below the grade of commodore, and no officer not of the line, shall be promoted to a higher grade in the active list of the navy *until his mental, moral, and professional fitness* to perform all of his duties at sea have been established to the satisfaction of a board of examining officers appointed by the President."

By another section of the law the examining board must consist of three members senior in rank to the officer to be examined. The board is also authorized to take testimony, the witnesses being examined under oath, and "to examine all matter on the files and records of the Navy Department relating to any officer whose case may be considered by them."

The officer who is to be examined is also authorized to be present before the board, and to submit a sworn statement of his case.

At the conclusion of the examination, the report of the board; all of the testimony; and the information relative to the officer on file at the Navy Department, which is based on an excellent system of personal reports, are forwarded to the President for his approval, or disapproval.

If qualified for promotion, the board reports as follows:

"We hereby certify that —— —— has the mental, moral, and professional qualifications to perform efficiently all the duties, both at sea and on shore, of the grade to which he is to be promoted, and recommend him for promotion."

If the officer fail, he is suspended for a year with *corresponding loss of date*, when, in case of failure on reëxamination, he is dropped from the service.

Another excellent section prescribes that—

"Any officer of the navy may, by and with the advice and consent of the Senate, be advanced, not exceeding thirty numbers in rank, for *eminent and conspicuous conduct in battle, or extraordinary heroism.*"

The law of the navy which has done so much to elevate and

improve this branch of the public service, deserves all the more consideration from the fact that it was passed in 1864, after three years of war had demonstrated to the satisfaction of the people and Congress that ignorant, incompetent, and dissipated officers, should no longer jeopardize the interests of the Government by obstructing the promotion of others better qualified to command.

In the application of such a law to the line of the army, the following recommendations are submitted:

1. That every second-lieutenant be examined at the expiration of five years from the date of his appointment; that his examination be conducted by a general board appointed by the President; or, if the expense of mileage, and loss of time, be deemed objectionable, then the boards to be appointed in each department either by, or on the recommendation of, the department commander.

2. That all records, or personal reports, relative to the officer be submitted to the board, with a further personal report signed by a board of one field-officer and two captains of the regiment to which the officer belongs, certifying as to the "mental, moral, and professional qualifications" of the officer as evinced during his five years' probation.

3. That the examination of the officer in the tactics of his arm, in regulations, interior economy of a company, and military law, the proceedings and practice of courts-martial, be in writing; and that the officer be required to demonstrate before the board his ability to drill a squad, a platoon, and company, in all the movements prescribed for his arm of the service.

4. That all first-lieutenants before promotion shall be examined, so far as personal reports and reports from a board of the officers of their regiments are concerned, in the same manner as second-lieutenants; and that, in addition, all first-lieutenants of artillery be required to pass, in writing, an examination in the course of study pursued at the Artillery School; or, in lieu thereof, show a certificate from the staff of the school that they have satisfactorily passed such examination at the conclusion of their course of study when students at the school.

The practical examination should consist in manœuvring all of the guns in service; ability to drill a light battery; and, in infantry, to drill a battalion, both in close order and as skirmishers.

For first-lieutenants of cavalry and infantry the theoretical examination, so long as they are not provided with a course of instruction like that pursued at the Artillery School, should be modified according to the few advantages for professional improvement which they now possess. Their practical examination should embrace all of the movements of a company and battalion prescribed in the tactics of their arms.

5. That captains be subjected in regard to mental and moral qualifications to the same scrutiny as lieutenants, and that their further examination be mostly of a practical character, extending to the manœuvres of a battalion and regiment, and also to outpost duty, and combinations of the three arms of service.

6. That all of the proceedings of the examining board, with copies of personal reports, be forwarded to the President for his approval.

7. That in case a second-lieutenant fails in the examination, his name be dropped from the rolls of the army.

8. That if a first-lieutenant fail in moral qualifications, his name be dropped from the rolls of the army; but, if he fail on the theoretical or practical examination, that his promotion be stopped for a year, with loss in date of commission, when, if he fail on reëxamination, he be dropped from the service.

9. That if a captain fail in moral qualifications, he be dropped from the service; while, if he fail on the theoretical or practical examination, his promotion be stopped for a year with loss in date of commission; if he fail on reëxamination, that he be held at the head of the list of captains, till, on serving twenty or twenty-five years, he can be retired on half or three-quarters pay.

The first of the foregoing recommendations is based on the fact that the military and moral character of young officers generally develops within the period of five years. If, during this period of probation, a second-lieutenant shows inattention or indifference to duty, and particularly if he shows an inclination to drunkenness, or gambling, he should, in the interest of the Government, be dismissed from the service.

The second recommendation, in giving a first-lieutenant a another chance for promotion, except in case of moral disqualifications, recognizes the justice of not turning an officer adrift in the world to begin a civil career after the years of greatest hope and ambition have been spent in Government service.

The third recommendation would enable boards to stop the promotion of officers whose moral qualifications are unobjectionable, but who, for lack of practical talent, frequently obstruct, if they do not stop, the instruction of their commands.

DISCIPLINE.

In no country should the military code be prepared with greater care than in our own; yet, adhering to articles of war passed in 1806, nearly three-quarters of a century ago, the officers of our army are constantly compelled to resort to arbitrary punishments, while those of other countries can administer military justice in exact conformity with law.

In India, Italy, Russia, Austria, and other countries, the minor punishments, which, in our army, can only be inflicted by regimental, garrison, and field-officers' courts, can be imposed by all regimental and battalion commanders; while others, still smaller in degree, can be administered by captains, lieutenants, and even non-commissioned officers.

The objection to our system is that it is practicable only at regimental headquarters, and at large posts, where either a field-officer is available; or the presence of a surgeon, a quartermaster, or a hospital-steward, is sufficient to convert the garrison into a "mixed" command.

If a captain with his company be on detached service, and absent from all superior authority for months, the only legal punishment he can inflict is confinement. As this cripples the command, and enables the culprit to escape military duty, besides being no adequate punishment for the many minor offenses that are continually committed, the captain finds that either his authority and the discipline of his company must be relaxed, or else that he must take punishment into his own hands. Confronted on one side by a law giving him no authority, and on the other by the law of necessity, which frequently will brook no delay, he is compelled to choose the lesser evil, and therefore administers summary punishment.

The defect of the law was so conspicuous during the Revolution that Washington, on the 3d of February, 1781, wrote to the President of Congress:

"There is one evil, however, which I shall particularize, resulting from the imperfection of our regulations in this respect. It is the increase of arbitrary punishments. Officers, finding discipline cannot be maintained by a regular course of proceeding, are tempted to use their own discretion, which sometimes occasions excesses, to correct which the interests of discipline will not permit much rigor. Prompt and arbitrary punishments are not to be avoided in an army; but the necessity for them will be more or less in proportion as the military laws have more or less vigor."

Notwithstanding the evils of arbitrary punishments, they have, for want of a modification of the law, been continued as a necessity up to the present moment, and in war have been more often the rule than the exception.

During the rebellion there was scarcely a regiment in which corporal punishment, in some form, was not daily administered. And this arose from no desire to violate the law, but from a necessity, to which many of our representatives in Congress can testify.

Even the expedient of the field-officer's court failed of its object; for, when troops were on marches, there was no time to take evidence, and make out proceedings. When, therefore, stragglers and marauders returned to their regiments, the colonels adopted the sure and expeditious process of pronouncing a punishment, which, being brief in its character, allowed the offender to be restored speedily to duty.

But, in addition to the impracticability of the present system, it operates with no uniformity. At the same post one garrison court-martial may sentence a man for drunkenness to a fine of two dollars; another court, the day after, and for the same offense, may inflict imprisonment on bread-and-water, and loss of a month's pay.

All of these irregularities can be corrected by a law fixing the limits within which minor punishments can be inflicted by all commanders of regiments, battalions, companies, and detachments.

By this method the commanding officer, like a police-judge, can hold his court every morning, hear the evidence, and pronounce sentence, which, as in the English and other armies, on being entered upon a defaulters' book, becomes a part of the history of each offender.

The cheerfulness with which our officers and men within the past year have endured hunger and cold, have performed marches unprecedented in length, and have fought a well-armed foe often ten times their number, affords conclusive proof that the discipline of our troops is not surpassed by that of any other army. But this only furnishes an additional reason for enabling our officers in future to regulate their authority in strict conformity with law.

MILITARY EDUCATION.

If we consider the sole object of our Military Academy to be the qualification of officers to receive commissions in the army, we may justly claim that our system of preparatory training is superior to that in any other country; and the reason for this superiority may be made to appear by a very brief comparison.

In Germany, a member of the Cadet Corps, after six to seven years of study, pursues the mathematical studies taught to the cadet at our Academy in his first year.

In France, the course of study at St.-Cyr for officers of infantry and cavalry is but two years; in Russia, three years; in Austria, four years; in England, one year; at West Point, it is four years.

At the École Polytechnique, the most celebrated in Europe, where there is scarcely any military training and discipline, the cadets pursue only the same scientific subjects as are taught at West Point.

As to thoroughness of instruction, the general practice on the Continent is for the professor to deliver lectures to entire classes, numbering often a hundred or more; after which the cadets are questioned by interrogators once or twice a week, perhaps not oftener than once in two weeks. In such cases the cadet is frequently told when he will be questioned, and also the particular subject on which he will be questioned.

At West Point, on the contrary, in the important subjects like mathematics, analytical mechanics, astronomy, and engineering, the classes are divided into sections of ten to twelve cadets, and these sections, under the supervision of the professor, are each in charge of an instructor, who devotes an hour and a half to its recitations daily, Sundays only excepted. By this division into sections, which is the sole secret of the thorough mental training at West Point, the cadet recites from four to six times per week, while the foreign cadet may escape weeks at a time.

At West Point the standard of examination is so high that from thirty to fifty per cent. of the different classes fail to graduate; abroad, the demand for officers is so great that rarely more than three or four per cent. fail.

But it is not alone for its scholastic thoroughness that our Academy is renowned throughout the world. The secret of its success is found in the law of 1812, which prescribed that the cadets shall "be trained and taught all the duties of a private, non-commissioned officer, and officer."

Combining this practical with the theoretical course, we have been able, at our Academy, to train officers equally for engineers, for ordnance, for infantry, for artillery and cavalry, and have given the cadets such a competent knowledge of all the arms of service that in the late war they were transferred from one arm to another, frequently serving in all three, with a success and distinction that challenged foreign admiration.

In all of the academies abroad for educating officers of infantry and cavalry, little or no effort is made to teach them anything pertaining to the science of artillery, or engineering; much less are they taught the tactics and evolutions of other arms.

At West Point the practical education of a cadet begins as an infantry-soldier, and he is successively carried through every school to that of the brigade, serving progressively as private, non-commissioned officer, and officer. In cavalry he begins with the School of the Trooper, and in the course of three years is carried through the Schools of the Platoon, and Company, until he learns all of the duties from private to lieutenant, both mounted and dismounted. In artillery he begins as a cannoneer, and successively learns all of the duties from private to chief of platoon in both light and horse artillery; not only that, but, on going into heavy artillery, he is made familiar with the loading, firing, and manœuvres of all kinds of heavy ordnance, from an 8-inch mortar to a 15-inch gun.

The cadets, who each year are inspected by their congressional patrons, perform before them a variety of military manœuvres in engineering, and all arms of the service, which is nowhere approached, or even attempted, in Europe.

This peculiarity of the Academy has been studied by all foreign officers visiting West Point, who have frequently reported to their governments the admirable advantages of combined instruction for all arms.

So well are these advantages understood that we can point with pride to our Academy as the model adopted by the French commission for the education of officers of the modern army of Japan.

But, notwithstanding the superior preparatory education we have secured to a portion of our officers, we have not as yet, except in the artillery, provided for them the means for acquiring a theoretical and practical knowledge of the higher duties of their profession.

Abroad, it is the universal theory that the art of war should be studied only after an officer has arrived at full manhood, and therefore most governments have established post-graduate institutions for nearly all arms of service, where meritorious officers, from whatever sphere they may enter the army, may study strategy, grand tactics, and all the sciences connected with modern war.

These institutions for the training of the staff are known as war academies, war schools, and staff colleges; for the artillery and engineers and cavalry they are known generally as schools of application, or as advanced artillery and engineer courses.

Our first approach to this system of post-graduate education was made in 1867 by the General of the Army, when by General Order No. 99, of November 13th, he established at Fort Monroe a school designated as the

"ARTILLERY SCHOOL OF THE UNITED STATES ARMY."

The school was organized with a staff consisting of 1 colonel, 1 lieutenant-colonel, and 1 major, 5 instructors, who are captains of the five companies which constitute the permanent garrison. The two first and two second lieutenants of these companies, which are selected from the five regiments of artillery, compose the class of officers under instruction.

Up to November 10, 1875, the course of theoretical and practical instruction was for one year; but by General Orders No. 92, from the War Department, of that date, the course was enlarged and extended to two years, to take effect in May, 1876.

The advantage of this institution to the artillery may be inferred from the nature of the course of instruction.

The theoretical course embraces, according to the programme, the study of—

Light Artillery.—Manual of the piece; service of mitrailleur; mechanical manœuvres; school of the battery dismounted; formation of battery mounted, including "to unpark" and "to park."

Heavy Artillery.—Service and mechanical manœuvres of guns, howitzers, and mortars; methods of constructing and laying platforms; construction and use of hydraulic and other jacks, gun-lifts, sling-carts, trucks, cradles, gins, and all implements used therewith; use of pulleys, and methods of knotting, splicing, and lashing ropes.

Science of Artillery.—Gunpowder and other military explosives; projectiles, cannon, small-arms; gunnery; loading, pointing, discharging; kinds of fire; effects of fire and projectiles; manner of determining time of flight and range of projectiles; description of velocimeters and densimeters; method of inspecting cannon; employment of artillery in war; war-rockets; electricity; telegraphy, as far as artillery necessities require; signaling, and defensive torpedoes.

Infantry.—School of the company; school of the battalion, and ceremonies.

Mathematics.—Algebra to discussion of quadratics involving but one unknown quantity; geometry (plane), to embrace regular polygons, and measurement of the circle; trigonometry (plane).

Engineering.—Mensuration; permanent fortification; surveying and leveling; military bridges; military reconnaissance; description of surveying, plotting, and drawing instruments; castramentation.

Law.—Military law and courts-martial; international law; constitutional law, and Constitution of the United States.

History and Strategy.—Universal history; operations of war; military logistics.

The course of practical exercises comprises—

Artillery.—Drill; target-practice; mechanical manœuvres; laying platforms; inspection of cannon, projectiles, and powder; determination of ranges, velocities, and pressures; duty of the laboratory; use of electric telegraphy (as far as it relates to artillery), and signal-apparatus; preparation of written essays.

Infantry.—Drill.

Engineering.—Tracing and profiling field-work; construction of siege-batteries, and cover for field-guns; surveying and leveling; use of sextant and telemeters; military reconnaissance and mapping; preparation of written essays.

History and Strategy.—Preparation of written essays.

Official Papers.

The details of the practical exercises are as follows, viz.:

Artillery.—Drill of the field-battery, dismounted; "service of the piece" of each kind in use in the land-service of the United States; target-practice with the same; use of mortar-wagon, sling-carts, trucks, cradle, skids, blocks, railway-trucks, and movable track for transporting artillery; use of gins, and gin as shears; of

Laidley's gun-lift; of hydraulic and other jacks; and generally of all machines and appliances employed for artillery purposes, and of the various methods of combining and applying them in any operation required in placing or removing the armament of permanent or field works; use of pulleys and of knottings, splicings, and lashings of ropes, applicable to artillery operations; use of instruments for determining velocity, pressure, time of flight, and range of projectiles; analysis of gunpowder; use of densimeter; inspection of cannon and projectiles; fabrication of rockets, time-fuses, quick and slow match; determination of muzzle velocities of cannon; application of formula to gunnery; methods of discharging cannon by means of electricity, under various conditions; use of chronoscope and chronograph; charging, planting, and exploding defensive torpedoes; discharging cannon by electricity; signal and electric telegraphing; linear drawings of such artillery machines and implements as do not appear in the artillery course of studies (these drawings to be executed rapidly and freely, but still with accuracy to scale); and preparation and public reading of written essays.

Infantry.—Drill in bayonet-exercise; school of the company and battalion, and practice of ceremonies.

Engineering.—Method of laying out camps; tracing and profiling field-works; construction of siege-batteries and cover for field-guns; construction of earthen magazines, bomb-proofs, and traverses; surveying and leveling; use of sextant and telemeters; military reconnaissance and mapping; and preparation and public reading of written essays.

History and Strategy.—The preparation and public reading of written essays.

Official Papers.—Making-out of muster-rolls; inventory and inspection reports; monthly company returns; return of ordnance and ordnance-stores; clothing receipt-roll, and records of target-practice.

The system of instruction when perfected so as to employ to the best advantage the increased time now allowed, will give our officers of artillery facilities for procuring a theoretical and practical knowledge of their arm not equaled in any army of Europe.

The time, too, devoted to history, strategy, law, and the art of war, will obviate, so far as the artillery is concerned, any necessity for a war academy.

INFANTRY AND CAVALRY SCHOOLS.

The success which has already attended the Artillery School suggests that we should establish schools, with similar constitution, for the infantry and cavalry—one to be located at Atlanta, and the other at Fort Leavenworth.

In order still further to increase the usefulness of the schools, at least two officers from each regiment should be permitted to attend the course of instruction; and to stimulate their zeal, those who distinguish themselves should be rewarded, after graduation, by detail in some of the staff departments. By establishing these schools, which will require no special appropriation, our system of military education will be made to comply with the most recent demands of military science.

MILITARY PROFESSORSHIPS.

Allusion has already been made to military colleges, as one means of providing officers of complement for an expansive organization; but as yet the country, except in a general way, has derived no benefit from the excellent law which permits the President to detail an officer of the army to act as president, superintendent, or professor, at any college " having capacity to educate, at the same time, not less than one hundred and fifty male students."

As these colleges are supposed to be located according to population throughout the United States, they can be made to provide officers of complement far superior in general attainments to those afforded by the system of volunteers for one year adopted in foreign countries. To this end, as the Government expends from twenty to thirty thousand dollars a year in providing the colleges with military professors, it ought to prescribe a uniform programme of theoretical and practical instruction, and to decline to furnish a professor unless the programme be accepted.

Having pursued this course of military instruction, such of the graduates as may volunteer, should have their names inscribed in the Army Register, to be borne there as officers of complement until they resign, or attain the age of thirty-five.

SUPERINTENDENT OF MILITARY EDUCATION.

In all foreign war departments there is a Bureau of Military Education, presided over by an officer styled the Superintendent, or Director of Military Education.

Through this bureau all of the business connected with the various military academies and schools is transacted.

Should such a bureau be established in our War Department, one of the duties of the chief, in addition to inspecting our army schools, should be to inspect the colleges to which military professors are attached.

NATIONAL VOLUNTEERS.

It has been the theory of our Government, from its foundation, to dispense, as far as possible, with a regular army, and to substitute in its place a well-organized militia, thus converting ourselves into an "armed nation."

The fact, however, that the active militia numbers but 90,000, and that the States, collectively, appropriate scarcely a million dollars for its support, while many make no appropriation whatever, affords conclusive evidence that the expectations based upon the militia cannot be realized, and that, if we would prosecute our national wars with dispatch, we must adopt an expansive organization.

But were such an organization actually adopted, the prepossession in favor of the use of volunteers is so strong in the popular mind as to endanger its being set aside at the first outbreak. In connection, therefore, with the adoption of any definite peace establishment, based on the expansive principle, the people must be led, as in all foreign countries, to regard the army as the only true field for the exercise of courage and patriotism.

And this can possibly be done by organizing, in connection with each of the twenty-five regimental depots for infantry, one or two battalions of *National Volunteers*, which in time of war we could unite with the two battalions of the regular regiment, giving us twenty-five regiments of four battalions each.

The battalions of national volunteers should be organized into four companies each, with three lieutenants to each company; all of the officers being appointed by the President. The captains, in view of the experience required to command a company of two hundred and fifty men, should be officers of the regular army, who would join their companies when war is declared.

In order to insure these battalions proper training and instruction, the commandants, and adjutants, should be selected from the regular officers serving at the depot.

In connection with the depot there should be provided armories for depositing arms, and drill-rooms for drilling both the volunteers, and regulars.

These battalions, in addition to the title of National Volunteers, should be designated in the Army Register as Third or Fourth Reserve Battalion (such) United States Infantry.

The adoption of this system would at once tend to nationalize and popularize our army. In case of war, the impulse of such men as could not find places in the two battalions of national volunteers, would be to enlist in the two battalions of the regular regiment. The whole regiment would thus become volunteers, would go forth with the sympathy of the entire community, and differ only from the volunteer regiments of the late war in having at the beginning trained officers to lead every company.

The first cost of establishing forty regimental depots, twenty-five of which to be adapted to the use of the national volunteers, would not exceed from ten to fifteen million dollars.

The maintenance of the two hundred companies, with a maximum of one hundred men to each, exclusive of arms and clothing, would be about six hundred thousand dollars per annum.

This estimate is based upon extra pay being allowed to the commandant and adjutant of each battalion; upon the requirement that there shall be an encampment of ten days each year, and also thirty drills in the armories; that in camp the officers shall receive four dollars, and the enlisted men two dollars, per day; and that for each drill in the armory each officer shall receive one dollar, and each enlisted man twenty-five cents.

By increasing this appropriation to one million dollars annually, additional companies could be formed in towns not occupied by the regimental depots, sufficient to raise this force on the peace-footing to 40,000 men.

The impossibility of forming a trained reserve as in Europe, and the certainty that the States cannot be relied upon to support a numerous and well-organized militia, even with the aid of the two hundred thousand dollars appropriated annually by the Government, should impress us with the importance of devising some method whereby both in peace and in war we may have a national force ready to increase, and support, our troops in the field.

During the late riots, had there been available from twenty-five to fifty battalions of national volunteers, commanded by regular officers, it is possible, and probable, that much of the bloodshed and loss of property might have been avoided.

In drawing my conclusions, I have not been influenced by convictions as to what plans may, or may not, be adopted; but recognizing, in the fullest degree, that our present geographical isolation happily relieves us from the necessity of maintaining a large standing army, I have sought to present the best system to meet the demands of judicious economy in peace, and to avert unnecessary extravagance, disaster, and bloodshed, in time of war.

Should we recoil before the small expenditures required to give us most of the advantages of an expansive peace establishment, we ought to bear in mind that in interest alone on our national debt, mostly accumulated as the fruit of an expensive military policy, we have paid in the last ten years more than eleven hundred and fifty millions of dollars.

The organization of national volunteers would give us in time of peace a regular army, a reserve, and the militia, and would enable us in time of war to prosecute our campaigns with vigor and economy, and with that regard for human life which becomes a free people.

EMORY UPTON,
Brevet Major-General U. S. Army.

LETTERS FROM ASIA.

In September, 1874, the General of the Army visited the Military Academy at West Point, and, while conversing upon his recent trip to Europe, and the Caucasus, suggested to me the advantage to the service of a military tour through Asia, which had been offered to him and another officer immediately after the Mexican War.

The object of the tour was to make military observations, which were to be submitted to the Government in an official report.

While traveling in Asia I kept a journal, or diary, in the form of letters to members of my family.

The letters were written with no idea of publication, and make no pretension to novelty, or to a graphic description of the many objects and scenes in the Eastern world which might interest the general reader. They simply convey a few impressions of the things which most interested me at the time, and are only given to the public in response to the requests of friends who have read them.

LETTERS FROM JAPAN.

YOKOHAMA, *August* 27, 1875.

WE left San Francisco on the 2d of August, 1875, on the steamer Great Republic, commanded by Captain Cobb. On the 26th, having scarcely encountered a ripple in our passage, we arrived off the shores of Japan.

You can imagine that the sight of land, after twenty-three days at sea, was a feast to the eyes.

As we approached the coast, mountains about three thousand feet high were on our right, while on our left expanded the never-ending Pacific.

The day was beautiful; Japanese junks, with their white sails, dotted the mouth of the bay, and, scudding before the wind in different directions, imparted an air of busy traffic to the scene. Some of them were propelled by oars, manned by strong, hearty fellows who, as we approached, gave us a lesson in economy, for the only clothing they wore was a breech-cloth at the loins.

In front of us as we steamed toward the entrance of the bay of Yedo was Fusi Yama, the sacred mountain of Japan. Its base was hidden by a bank of fog, while its summit, towering amid the clouds, stood out lofty and grand two miles and a half above the sea. As we proceeded up the bay the clouds disappeared, unfolding to us the graceful proportions of the mountain, which loomed up like an immense cone fourteen thousand feet high. The affection with which the volcano is cherished is shown by the fans, boxes, etc., which generally have "Fusi Yama" as the feature of their decorations.

To us was given the opportunity of witnessing one of the gorgeous sunsets of the East. To the right of Fusi Yama was a low range of mountains, capped by clouds tipped with gold. Between these and Fusi Yama the rays of the sun played upon a gauzy mist, making the entire mountain at one instant look like a mass of molten iron, at another like a beautiful amethyst, at another like an opal, after which it passed through the shades of light and dark blue, and finally blended with the darkness.

Our progress up the bay showed us we were among a busy people. The mountains were terraced from the bottom to the top, making every inch available for cultivation. All along the bay, villages, as at Naples, dotted the shore, twelve or more being visible at one time. At 7.30 we dropped anchor. In an instant the water was covered with small craft of all descriptions. Men-of-war sent their launches for the mail, while runners for the hotels thrust their cards thick and fast upon the travelers.

We were taken ashore in one of the small boats belonging to the agent of the Pacific Mail, and when we reached the wharf a new sensation awaited us. There were no noisy hackmen about, making the night hideous by their cries and cracking whips, but arranged in front of us was a line of large baby-carriages, with wheels about three feet high. Into these vehicles we stepped. A horse without harness grasped the thills, and, with a Chinese lantern dangling as a headlight, we started furiously up the street, the tawny legs of the swift Japanese giving us a speed that would have shamed an American hackman.

When we arrived at the International Hotel the modest sum of six cents was claimed by the man who had drawn us and our hand-bags a distance of fully half a mile. The *jin-rick-shah* is the modern conveyance of Japan. It is generally drawn by one man, but, when distances of forty to sixty miles are to be traversed in a day, a second man, throwing a cord over his shoulder, pulls tandem, or else pushes in rear. The seat is very comfortable, and, were it not for the fact that one's ease is purchased at the expense of a fellow-creature, no conveyance for short distances could be more desirable. The tariff is twelve cents per hour, which leaves no excuse for walking.

The weather is excessively hot. White is the prevailing color worn by the gentlemen, and is used even as full dress. It would be idle to describe a Japanese town; one must be seen to be appreciated. The people seem to be gay and light-hearted, the men all muscular and fleet of foot, while the women are small, graceful, and not without beauty.

YEDO, *August* 31, 1875.

We left Yokohama yesterday at 8.15 A. M., and arrived here at 9.15. After depositing our baggage, we went at once to call on Mr. Bingham, our minister, who is to procure us facilities for visiting objects of military interest. In the evening he came and drove us to the "Sheba," the burial-place of the Tycoons. The gateway is a lofty edifice, with a double roof, one above the other, after the manner of the pagoda. It is of wood, painted red, and is nearly two hundred years old. The tombs, six in number, are marvels in architecture; each consists of a series of buildings, one in rear of the other, crowned by the peculiar concave roofs of Eastern temples. Each edifice in the sunlight appears like a glittering mass of bronze and gold.

The ceilings are frescoed with gold, and the altars are literally covered with platings of the precious metal. Birds, dragons, and animals of all kinds, are delicately carved, and give an effect at once graceful and of surpassing beauty. In a room of one of the series of temples dedicated to the sixth Tycoon, one hundred varieties of flowers are carved in the panels of the ceiling, while one hundred kinds of birds nestle among the flowers; but, what is more remarkable, each panel is carved from a single piece of wood, through which the light plays as through a filigree of gold.

Photographs which I have purchased show the perfection of the art employed to do honor to the ashes of departed greatness.

It may be interesting to know how we pass our time, so I will give you a slight idea in the form of a journal.

To-day, Dr. Murray, Commissioner of Education, called and invited General Forsyth, Major Sanger, and myself, to spend a couple of days with him, which invitation we accepted. In going to his residence he drove us to the great temple of Asakusa. Passing through a gateway, a vast edifice in itself, we proceeded up a broad pavement, ascended the steps and entered the temple, which presented a vivid picture of the temple of Jerusalem when cleansed by the Saviour. There were the doves, the booths, the tables of the money-changers, and there was the treasury into which the people cast their gifts. The devotees having made their offerings, advanced to the altar, rang a bell to summon the god, prostrated themselves before the image of Buddha, uttered their prayers, loitered within the courts, and then departed. Near by was a wooden image of the God of Pain. Any one who was sick would go up to it, prostrate himself, say his prayers, touch the image on the spot corresponding to the seat of his malady, and then, rubbing the diseased parts, would rise, supposing the god would grant relief. The poor image, sans eyes, sans teeth, and sans nose, showed some of the prevailing diseases of the country.

After visiting the many side-shows which surrounded the temple, we drove through a magnificent park to Dr. Murray's, where Mrs. Murray received us with Eastern hospitality.

September 1st.—To-day Mr. Bingham drove us through the Hamogoten, or garden surrounding one of the Mikado's palaces. These grounds, which have been much extolled, consist of lakes and groves, but are not particularly beautiful. In the evening Mrs. Murray gave us a dinner, at which were present General Legendre, Mr. House, Mr. Mori, late Japanese minister at Washington, and General Yamada, who came to West Point at the time the Japanese embassy visited America.

September 2d.—Dr. Murray drove us to the agricultural farm established by General Capron, to show the Japanese modern agriculture. As they have fields which have yielded annual crops for the last fifteen hundred years, it is evident that they lack little in the art of agriculture, and that all that can be done is to introduce labor-saving machines. In the evening Mr. Bingham entertained us at dinner, and at 11.15 P. M. we left for Yokohama.

September 3d.—At 6.30 A. M. we took jin-rick-shah for Kamakura and Daibutzu. The landscapes were picturesque and beautiful, and the journey across the country gave us a good opportunity of seeing Japanese farming. Rice is the principal crop, and, in terraces, arranged for flooding, is cultivated to the very hill-tops.

The Daibutzu is a mammoth image of Buddha in the state of "Nirvina," or serene happiness and contemplation. The statue is in bronze, and represents Buddha in a sitting posture, on a lotus-flower. It is forty-four feet high, eighty-seven and a half feet in circumference, face eight feet, eyes three feet, ears six feet long, thumbs three and a half feet in circumference, diameter through the knees thirty-four feet. The expression, true to its intention, represents the god in self-satisfied repose. Near by a polite priest receives gifts from the visitors.

On our way to and from the image, we walked up a few hills, and, with this exception, the two men, going at a dog-trot, drew each of us in our jin-rick-shahs not less than twenty-five miles. On finishing my toilet, after returning to the hotel, the first man who presented himself to draw me to the station for Yedo was one of the men who had been to Daibutzu. Seating myself in his jin-rick-shah, he started off at a brisk run, and did not slacken his pace till he reached the depot, a mile distant. For this service he would have been glad to receive ten cents, but on doubling the amount his expression surpassed even that of the great image.

September 4th.—In the afternoon, Mr. Stevens, Secretary of Legation, gave us a dinner at a Japanese tea-house. On our arrival we were asked to take off our shoes, which are never permitted to be worn in a Japanese house. In our stocking-feet we mounted to the second story, where mats being provided, we sat down *à la Turque.* Four beautiful singing and dancing girls welcomed us with a sweetness and grace peculiar to Japan. The "chow" then commenced with fish-soup, followed by fish boiled; fish raw (sometimes cut from the fish while alive); fish boiled, smothered in sweetmeats; then fish with sauce and chestnuts, with still other preparations of fish to the end of the dinner. Between, and during the courses, we had saki, the great beverage of Japan, distilled from rice. During the service the four girls played on an instrument like a banjo, and sang, making a squeaking noise through the nose and teeth. Two of them also danced very gracefully, the dance consisting simply of pantomime, graceful motions and positions. After the dinner, which lasted about three hours, jugglers entertained us with tricks of various kinds.

YEDO, *September* 8, 1873.

We are having a delightful time, never better. Socially, we are dined and tiffined (breakfasted) a little too much—a sure indication, however, of a large-hearted, generous hospitality. The country is beautiful, and every landscape is a solace to the eyes. The people are amiable, and so polite as to make us wish we could imitate their manners. The servants are the best. Houses are never locked, trunks are left open, jewelry and "curios" exposed, and yet nothing is stolen. It is rather startling to a foreigner in a hot day to see so many bare heads, bare arms, bare bodies, and bare legs, and, as one ordinarily judges of the density of a crowd by the upturned faces, this *sans-souci* exposure of the person gives to a street the appearance of being alive with human beings. You must not imagine that all the Japanese go about in this manner; many, and by far the greater majority, wear dresses and robes very becoming. The children especially seem to enjoy the liberty of dress; up to four and five years of age they run about without regard to appearance. On our way to the great image, they stood naked in rows on the sides of the streets, and continually saluted us with the welcome "Ohio, ohio!"

Indifference to the exposure of the person is most clearly shown in the national habit of bathing. At Yokohama we visited a public bath-house, and, by mistake or intention of the guide, were taken into a large compartment where women and children continued to bathe as if unconscious of our presence.

We would have been shocked at our intrusion had we not instantly observed men and boys bathing in an adjoining apartment, with only a railing for a partition.

STEAMER COSTA RICA, BETWEEN NAGASAKI AND SHANGHAI,
September 23, 1875.

On the 8th we were given a review of the troops at Yedo. It rained nearly all night, rendering it necessary to defer the ceremony till 9 A. M. On arriving at the Champ de Mars, we found four battalions of infantry belonging to the Imperial Guard, two battalions of non-commissioned officers belonging to the military school for non-commissioned officers, and two squadrons of cavalry. All these troops marched and manœuvred creditably.

The Minister of War received us at the review, and after it was over invited us to meet him at breakfast (tiffin) in the grounds belonging to the late Prince Meto.

From the review we went to the castle, where we found a school of instruction in practical engineering, for both officers and non-commissioned officers. Batteries, rifle-pits, redoubts, trous-de-loup, and everything pertaining to field-intrenchments, were constructed and explained in theory to the apt scholars who are to direct the modern sieges of Japan.

The castle consists of three or more walled inclosures, one rising within the other, the massive masonry of each commanding everything exterior to it. Each wall is surrounded by a wide moat filled with water, on which floats the lotus, now in blossom. The lotus is a magnificent flower, almost sacred to the Japanese, as you will see from its association with the colossal images of Buddha, which usually sit upon it.

The grounds of the inner castle, where formerly was the residence of the Tycoon, are superior to any I have yet seen; artificial cascades, ponds, and lakes; avenues of trees, hundreds of years old; groves of bamboo; a suspension-bridge spanning a moat eighty feet deep; picturesque edifices crowning the angles of the lofty walls, make up a variety of scenery of which no modern park can boast.

It is hoped that the Mikado will build his palace in these ancient grounds; if not, a few years will insure the demolition of the walls, and the destruction of the trees. In fact, much of their former grandeur has already disappeared, so great is the mania for tearing down everything reminding the people of the former government of the Tycoons.

From the castle we went to the artillery-grounds, to witness a review of three batteries; thence went to the arsenal, where we saw Japanese apprentices learning all the varieties of work in wood and iron necessary to make arms and munitions of war.

The buildings are in process of construction, but some are finished, and supplied with machinery. Already the wood-work of small-arms is manufactured at the arsenal, and Enfield muzzle-loaders are converted into Albini breech-loaders.

From the arsenal we went into the grounds of Prince Meto, which will be surrounded by the arsenal, and, through the good taste of the French officers, will be preserved in all their beauty.

Here, on the border of an artificial lake, we again met the Minister of War.

In a Japanese house, one hundred and eighty years old, a delicious French breakfast was served. The grounds, although very small, are so laid out as to give an idea of great extent. Winding walks, mounds, miniature lakes, brooks, falls, and temples, present a picture of beauty, and testify to the perfection attained in landscape-gardening.

On our return toward the hotel, we visited the barracks of the Imperial Guard. They are lofty brick buildings, inclosing a square court as large as the grass plain at West Point. The Japanese tidiness was again proved by the soldiers who luxuriate in warm baths.

On the 10th of September we visited the *Military Academy*, accompanied by the French officers. Two years have sufficed to construct the buildings and place the academy, modeled after West Point, in running order. We heard recitations in geometry and trigonometry, saw riding in the riding-hall, and were given a review of the corps of cadets, which was but six months old.

From the academy we went to the gymnasium and school of musketry, where were assembled officers and non-commissioned officers from every regiment in the empire, who, as soon as they learn the practical course, return to their regiments as instructors.

We saw them perform many gymnastics, and were well pleased with our observations. Japan, beyond doubt, will be the first power in the East. She has gone too far forward to recede. The railroad, telegraph, and steamboat, are uniting her people, while on every hand there is a manifestation of increasing knowledge and power, which gives an earnest of what she will do in the immediate future.

We left Yedo on the 10th, and at 4 P.M. sailed on the Golden Age for Hiôgo, or Kobe, where we arrived at 12 P.M. on the 12th.

We went ashore at 9 A.M. on the 13th, and without delay took the 11.30 train for Osaka, twenty-two miles distant. At 6 P.M. we took a boat for Kiyoto. The boat was poled by six men, three on a side, who, as they ran from front to rear on all-fours, pushing against their poles, looked like so many monkeys.

The twilight ride up the Yodogawa, through the heart of Osaka, gave us new views and many interesting scenes. Lights lined the shore, bridges at short intervals crossed the river, over which darted, like will-o-the-wisps, the fleet-footed jin-rick-shah men with their lanterns, while boats of every size and description moved up and down in unending succession. No sooner had we left the city than our boat approached the shore, when, splashing into the water, one after another, our boatmen forsook their poles, seized a rope, clambered up the steep bank, and, appearing on a tow-path, began to drag us up the stream.

We spent an almost sleepless night combating fleas and mosquitoes, and watching the movements of our boatmen.

At times, as they appeared and disappeared in the bushes, they looked like Indians seeking our scalps, but lively talk, and merry laughs, told plainly who were having the best of the night vigils. All night long they toiled, alternately poling and towing, until daylight, when we arrived at Fujimi, where we took jin-rickshahs, and, after a ride of seven miles through a continuous street, arrived at Kiyoto.

Until 1868, Kiyoto, for more than eleven hundred years, had been the capital of the Mikado, the spiritual Emperor of Japan. He represented a dynasty of twenty-five hundred years, and was regarded by his people with a reverence due to a god. At Yedo, for seven hundred years, the Tycoons, under the Mikado, had wielded the temporal power of the empire. The revolution of 1868 overthrew the Tycoons, and made the Mikado actual emperor of his country. He then moved his capital to Yedo.

Kiyoto is at the head of the Yodogawa Valley. Skirted on three sides by mountains, it basks in the sunshine of eternal spring. Grand old temples lift their venerable heads far above the trees, and in solemn stillness look down upon a city given to idolatry. Like all cities, its houses are mostly one and two stories high. Here and there is a "Godown," built fire-proof, into which people carry their treasures, when large conflagrations sweep over the city. It is expected in Japan that a city will be destroyed by fire about every fifteen years.

This would be discouraging in America, but here the houses are cheap and combustible, and are rebuilt almost as quickly as they burn down.

We visited several temples at Kiyoto. At one we saw worshipers kneeling, while in front of the altar two priests intoned the prayers, lighted the candles, and performed other ministrations. In another were one thousand images of Buddha, while in a third the bust of this deity was sixty feet high.

On the 15th we took horses and went to Lake Biva, eight miles off. Our route was along the Tokiado, or great road, which encircles the island of Nippon. We last saw it three hundred miles off near Yokohama. At Kiyoto, as near Yedo, it was a scene of busy life. We met carts, horses, and bulls, laden with heavy burdens, and vast numbers of men and women walking under large umbrellas. The women are particularly graceful and attractive. Their costume is a single garment, a loose, flowing robe, open in front, yet so secured by a broad sash as to conceal the person. The sash is tied behind the back, in a large bow six or eight inches wide. Sometimes they wear an underskirt of bright scarlet, the overskirt being looped up so as to reveal a brilliant combination of colors.

But to return to Lake Biva. It is a picturesque sheet of water, surrounded by mountains sloping gently to its shores, which are studded with villages and small cities. The country is amazingly fertile. Tea and rice are cultivated in terraces from the bottom to the tops of the hills and mountains, which look upon its placid waters. The lake was dotted over with small fishing-boats, while here and there a line of dark smoke pointed out the small steamers which ply as ferries from shore to shore.

As we stood in the court of a temple overlooking the scene, the familiar notes of the bugle fell upon our ears, and, turning to the left, we saw the handsome barracks of a regiment. Here, as on the banks of the Hudson, preparations for grim-visaged war resound from hill to hill.

We breakfasted in a tea-house on the shore of the lake, and, as elsewhere, had to remove our shoes, lest we should soil the spotless mats.

During our ride to and from the lake, bettos ran at full speed ahead of us, and cleared the way. There seemed to be no limit to their endurance, and when we returned they appeared as fresh as when we started.

We returned from Kiyoto to Osaka in a steamer, about as large as a teapot. The three first-class passengers occupied the front of the cabin, and were separated from the second-class by a string stretched from side to side. As the width of the partition did not materially affect our vision, we could see behind us a tangled mass of arms and legs, the bodies of our fellow travelers being twisted and contorted into all kinds of positions. One incident only marked our descent of the Yodogawa. The steamer in trying to land ran violently against the bank, crushing a small boat. Women, naked to the waist, forsook their work, and instantly lined the shore, wondering at the havoc we had made.

The steamer bounded off like a rubber ball, and finally, having transferred to another boat the one passenger who had caused the trouble, proceeded majestically down the river. The women, polite till the last, remained on the shore till we were lost to sight.

Friday and Saturday, the 17th and 18th, we spent at Osaka, visiting the castle, and inspecting the troops.

The castle is a vast mass of masonry, nearly one hundred feet high, the three inclosures, as at Yedo, rising one above the other. From the top of the inner castle a magnificent view of the Yodogawa Valley is obtained, extending nearly to Kioto toward the north, and to the sea toward the south.

Osaka is the headquarters of the fourth military district, in which three regiments, of two battalions each, are stationed, one regiment being at Lake Biva. The troops were drilled before us in the French tactics, and did very creditably.

Tuesday morning, at three o'clock, we started on the steamer Costa Rica for Shanghai.

The sail to Nagasaki through the Inland Sea was the most beautiful I have ever seen. The sea is two hundred and eighty miles long, and from four to twelve miles broad. Its shores are bounded by mountains from one thousand to seven thousand feet high, while the sea is studded with rocks and islands, sometimes two thousand to three thousand feet above its level. The conical shape prevails among the islands, many of them resembling in grace of outline the sacred Fusi Yama. Some of the peaks are covered with a fringe of trees, others with a crown of verdure, while the slope descends in cultivated terraces to the base, where nestle the thatched roofs of villages and hamlets.

In the distance we could see castles perched on rocks, looking down menacingly upon the cities at their feet. But the sea cannot be described. Overspread by an Italian sky, it combines and surpasses the Hudson with its Highlands, the St. Lawrence with its thousand isles, and Lake George with its mountain-peaks. As the steamer glided through the tortuous channels, each turn of the wheel gave fresh delight, yet shadowed with regret that the fleeting scenes of beauty were every moment becoming themes of recollection. Anticipation, enjoyment, remembrance of ever-varying, ever-changing views—such was our voyage on the Inland Sea.

Nagasaki was the first place we made after leaving Hiogo. Picturesque, encircled by mountains two thousand feet high, it appeared a fitting haven after the beauties of our voyage. As we approached its entrance, we passed Papenburg Rock, from the summit of which, about two hundred years ago, four thousand Christians were thrown into the sea. A few miles from Nagasaki is a boiling spring, in which it is said thousands were put to death.

At Nagasaki, September 23d, we left the Land of the Rising Sun.

To-day we are on the Yellow Sea, and to-morrow morning shall be at Shanghai. From San Francisco to the present moment, a glass placed on the edge of a table would not have been disturbed by the gentle billows, which have borne us up, and caressed the bows of our floating palaces.

LETTERS FROM CHINA.

STEAMER SHING-KING, GULF OF PEE-CHE-LEE,
October 1, 1875.

My last letter closed with our arrival at Shanghai. The coast of China, off the mouth of the Yang-tse River, is like that of the Mississippi, low, flat, and monotonous, with a vegetation verging on the semi-tropical. Shanghai is on the Hwang-pu, about twelve miles from the Yang-tse. It is one of the treaty ports to which foreigners are admitted, hence its importance. From the deck of the steamer, as we ascended the Hwang-pu, we could overlook the adjoining fields covered with rich crops.

On the left bank of the river the Chinese are throwing up long lines of batteries, as if to intimidate the foreigners by threatening their communications. The approach to Shanghai is impressive. Tall massive buildings lift their heads far above the trees, and look out upon the river teeming with life. Here are English, French, German, American, and Japanese steamers and sailing-vessels, discharging and receiving their cargoes, giving occupation to innumerable *sampans* and lighters, which ply between the vessels and wharves. Each sampan has two large eyes painted on the bows, and these are held responsible that no collisions occur. The Chinese junk is a great, clumsy structure, with square bows and stern, both pointing heavenward. As in the small sculls, eyes are painted on the bows two or more feet in diameter. Above the town these junks are anchored in lines parallel to each other, presenting to the eye a sea of masts. The European part of Shanghai is beautiful. The architecture is that of the Italian villa, modified and combined with porticoes and piazzas. The great business-houses are on the Bund, a broad street with buildings only on the inland side, overlooking the harbor. Here the merchant princes have established themselves in Oriental splendor.

The dwellings of these merchants are generally by the side of their places of business, and are palatial in their appointments, due in part, perhaps, to the fact that, in former times, when there were no hotels, they had to entertain all travelers. The night of my arrival, having letters to Russell & Co., I was invited to dine. As in Japan, the real breakfast is at twelve, the dinner is served at eight, and consists generally of seven or eight courses.

The Chinese part of Shanghai is densely crowded. The streets are packed with human beings all clad in blue. In Japan, the jinrick-shah amused us; here it competes with the wheelbarrow. This vehicle is impelled by a man who supports most of its weight by means of a strap passing over the shoulders. If wheeling one Chinaman, who always sits on one side instead of in the rear of the wheel, he cants the barrow till the centre of gravity of the human freight is above the track of the wheel, and, distorting his lips and shoulders to preserve the equilibrium, pushes his load laboriously along. The lazy Chinaman who rides at the expense of his fellowman, spreads his fan, protects his face from the sun, and looks like a contented monkey. I have seen as many as three on the wheelbarrow, giving the poor man all he could do to stand under his load. The Chinese women are taller and stouter than the pretty Japanese. They dress their hair much in the same style, and are fond of gaudy head-ornaments. I saw but one woman with tiny feet, who hobbled along the street, a victim of the inexorable laws of fashion.

We left Shanghai at 2 A. M. on the 27th for Peking, and yesterday stopped two hours at Che-fu, where Dr. Nevius resides. I went ashore, but found, to my regret, that he was on a missionary tour in the interior. The town is a desolate one, streets narrow, gutters filthy, and reeking with blue mud; the men dirty, ill-dressed, and squalid. In buying a curio, I dropped my purse; the gold and silver coins jingled on the pavement, but no one in the crowded street sought to molest me, or take what was not his own. I gathered up the pieces, hurried from the scene, and, thankful for a breath of pure air, returned to the ship.

PEKING, *October* 5, 1875.

My last letter was written on the gulf of Pee-che-lee, *en route* to Tien-tsin, where we arrived on Saturday morning, October 2d.

Tien-tsin is a city of about four hundred thousand inhabitants, one-half of whom reside outside of the walls. The houses are mostly of mud; the streets are unpaved, narrow, filthy, and redolent of bad odors. To one who has seen the worst streets of New York, a comparison therewith would convey but a slight idea of Tien-tsin. Squalid men and women, half-famished dogs gnawing offal from the butcher-shops and the kitchen, hogs wallowing in the gutters, and rooting up their malarious contents, carts, wheelbarrows, mules and donkeys—*voilà* Tien-tsin! The city, in 1870, acquired an unenviable reputation through the massacre of the French missionaries.

We left Tien-tsin on the morning of the 3d on ponies for Peking, distant eighty miles. The country throughout is a level plain, interspersed here and there with groves of trees. The Peiho frequently overflows its banks, and then for miles the country becomes a vast lake. The same thing happens along the Hoang-ho and Yang-tse. The deposit of these three rivers has compelled the sea to recede until forty-five thousand square miles have been added to the territory of China, an area almost equal to the State of New York. The waters of the Yellow Sea hold clay and alluvium in suspension, the deposit of which annually increases the shoal water, and gradually advances the low, thread-like line of the encroaching coast.

In many respects, the country which we traversed resembles the prairies of Illinois, even to its cornfields; but here the poverty is apparent, from the fact that the corn-stalks are dug up for fuel. The villages are all composed of mud-huts, roof and wall alike, which in floods and heavy rains often wash down and disappear. In going through one of the villages, a member of our party sought to change a silver dollar. He was told it was too large a coin to circulate in that town, and retired with his ideas of Chinese wealth essentially modified.

The roads, with time, have become sunken below the surface of the fields, and frequently look like canals. The covered cart is the principal vehicle. It is drawn by one or two mules, in the latter case driven tandem. With cushions, and good roads, it is quite comfortable, but with bad roads it becomes an engine of torture. Our hotel at night was a curiosity. We rode into a square court, inclosed by low, one-story buildings. In the centre the mules were hitched, and around them the carts were parked. When we were shown into our room we found it had a clay floor. At one end was a stone platform, about two feet high, on which to place our beds. This platform is usually heated at night, giving one the novel sensation of sleeping on an oven.

On the 4th we resumed our march at 5 A. M., sending the carts off at 3.30. All day the country was like that already described. At 5 P. M. we came to the walls of the famous city of Kublai Khan. They are between fifty and sixty feet broad at the top, with square bastions like buttresses projecting as flank defenses on the exterior side. On the top is a crenelated parapet-wall, behind which archers discharged their arrows in olden times, but which would now serve as a defense for riflemen. There is also an inner parapet-wall adapted to use against the city. Over the gate which we approached there was a lofty, imposing structure, crowned by a double roof. The effect of these massive Tartar walls, so like the defenses of Babylon and Nineveh, was somewhat diminished by the sight of a poor mule, struggling and floundering in a great mud-hole in the middle of the main highway leading to one of the gates of the city. Through the gate, by which we entered as through a funnel, lines of carts, mules, donkeys, camels, coolies, and lastly dusty travelers, eagerly pressed into the city. Within the walls no marble palaces greeted our vision. We were only in the Chinese city, which is separated from the Tartar city by another great wall, with gates more formidable than those we had already passed. Finally, we entered the Tartar city, and, tired out with our two days' ride of eighty miles, were glad to find rest at a forlorn hotel, where we soon received an invitation from our minister, Mr. Avery, tendering us the hospitality of the legation.

The city is not much of an improvement on Tien-tsin. There are no pavements nor sidewalks. The dust is insufferable, and the water, coming from the wells sunk in the ruins of centuries, is so hardened with lime as to be intolerable either for drinking or washing. This deprivation of itself is sufficient to make it a sacrifice to live in Peking. The city is well laid out on a square plan with broad avenues, but the buildings consort badly with the grand plans of the founder. They are mostly one story high, and built of a grayish brick. The fronts of many of the stores are covered with gilded filigree-work, which soon tarnishes and turns black. The people are badly clad, some with cotton, others with silk, others with sheep-skins. Many of them appear half naked, and all are very dirty.

October 5th.—We went to see the white elephants, presented to the emperor as tribute from the King of Burmah. On our return a walk on the wall gave us a good view of the palaces of the Forbidden City, and also of the mountains to the north and west of Peking.

October 6th.—We called with Mr. Avery upon the English, German, Russian, French, and Spanish ministers. In the afternoon we went to the Hall of the Astronomers, and the Temple of Confucius; also the Lama Temple, containing a standing image of Buddha seventy feet high.

October 7th.—We visited the Temple of Heaven, where the emperor worships once a year, and also the Altar of Heaven, where he offers an annual sacrifice.

October 8th.—Breakfasted with Mr. Holcombe, a missionary, now interpreter and Acting Secretary of Legation, and attended prayers in a Chinese chapel. The Chinese sang "Am I a soldier of the Cross?" to the tune of "Arlington."

At 3 P. M. we were received by Prince Kung, and the Tsungli Yamen, or cabinet, composed of all the ministers of the different departments. On arriving at the Foreign Department we rode through a large door, into a small court, where we dismounted. We then passed into another court, where four of the ministers welcomed us by folding and shaking their own hands. They led us into a third court, where Prince Kung, the regent, received us, shaking his own hands, like the others. This ceremony over, we entered a room in which there was a round table, covered with fruits and confectionery. Plain, square, cushioned stools were provided for seats. Prince Kung, the son and brother of an emperor, and uncle of two emperors, took the head of the table, having four ministers on his right. Mr. Avery sat at the left of the prince, then came myself, Forsyth, Sanger, and Mr. Holcombe, Acting Secretary of Legation. The interview began by Mr. Avery, who told the prince in the usual form that he hoped he was well, etc. The prince immediately asked where we had come from, and what we thought of China. The conversation took a wide range, military, among other matters, being discussed. He was particularly anxious that we should see Li Hung Chang, the viceroy, or governor-general, of the province of Chihli, and generalissimo of the forces. The Secretary of War was the jolly member of the board, and continually proposed healths which were drunk with saki. During the interview the fruits and confections gradually disappeared. The prince was in good-humor, and laughed repeatedly. His health being offered by one of the party broke up the *séance*, when, accompanying us into the court where he had welcomed us, he shook his hands and retired. The ministers saw us to our horses, and, after we had mounted, bowed and returned to their offices. We were all much pleased by the manifest cordiality of the reception, which Mr. Avery said he had never seen equaled.

October 10th.—Mr. Avery received notice that Li Hung Chang would call upon him, and our commission, at 10 o'clock. At 10.30 he came in a chair borne by coolies, preceded and followed by footmen. He is a man of fine stature and personal appearance, and strode into the legation like a king. In China all official visits are accompanied by refreshments, so Mr. Avery had a large table covered with fruits and sweetmeats. The viceroy was in excellent humor, and prolonged his call an hour and a half. As generalissimo of the forces of the empire he was inquisitive about military affairs; admitted the feeble condition of China, the necessity of a military academy, and the organization of a large army. With him, therefore, as with Prince Kung, we enlarged upon the fine military organization of Japan as the surest way to stimulate them to action.

October 11th.—Mounted on ponies, and accompanied by Mr. and Mrs. Avery, who rode in mule-litters, we started for the Great Wall; and, carrying all our provisions and bedding with us, spent the night at Nankow. The next morning we started on mules and donkeys at 7, and arrived at the Great Wall at 11 A. M.

The wall is from fifteen to thirty feet high, fifteen feet wide at the top, with towers here and there as places of refuge. The facing of the wall is of hewed granite; the coping, covering, exterior crenelated parapet, interior parapet, and the towers, are of brick. We climbed two towers perched on the tops of rugged peaks, and from these could see the wall stretching away across hills and valleys along sharp rugged crests, appearing and disappearing over the highest mountains, as if nothing in Nature could daunt the intrepidity of its founders.

It is only when one asks how without gunpowder the hewed granite could be procured, and considers the cost of transportation, that an idea can be formed of the immense expense an empire was willing to incur to raise an inanimate barrier against the barbarians who finally subdued it. Had the same amount of money been spent in building a few fortresses, and in perfecting military organization, it is more than probable that to-day the Tartars would not govern a nation superior to them in all of the elements of civilization.

After inspecting the wall, we picked our way back through the rugged pass, which was obstructed by hundreds of camels going and returning from Mongolia; spent the night at Nankow, and the next day went to the Ming Tombs. These monuments, eleven in number, commemorate the reigns of the ablest monarchs China has ever had. They are too grand to be described in few words, so I will pass over them. On leaving the tombs we passed along the avenue famed for the double row of statues, life-size, of elephants, camels, horses, lions, etc.

On approaching them the mules became frightened and upset the litters, but fortunately Mr. and Mrs. Avery had got out to walk, and thus escaped injury.

The next day, October 13th, we returned to Peking, visiting *en route* the grounds and ruins of Wan Shushan, the summer-palace of the emperors, which was burned in revenge by the allies after the capture of Peking.

On the 16th of October, the date of our departure from Peking, we witnessed the funeral of the late emperor. His remains were carried in a catafalque covered with rich yellow silk, borne on the shoulders of one hundred and twenty-eight men. Behind was another catafalque, containing the remains of the empress who, from grief it was supposed, had committed suicide.

The procession, with the usual accompaniment of banners, was composed of all the officers of state, civil and military; of cavalry armed with the bow and arrow; and of many thousand coolies following and flanking the column with provisions and camp-equipage for their august masters. All along the route from the capital to the tomb dense crowds of people looked upon the ceremony, and were repeatedly driven back by the guards, who flanked the column. At Tung-Chow, where we saw the procession, we dined with Mr. Sheffield, an American missionary, and then took boats for Tien-tsin.

I am sure, could any one visit the modest household of this preacher of the gospel, he would not join in the accusation against the missionaries that they make themselves comfortable; nor would he begrudge these worthy people the possession of a single spot reminding them of the land they have forsaken.

On the 18th we arrived at Tien-tsin, and at once went on board the steamer Shing-King, where Captain Hawes gave us a warm welcome.

SHANGHAI, *Sunday, October* 24, 1875.

My last finished with our arrival at Tien-tsin on the 18th. This brick and mud city is the capital of the province of Chihli, of which Li Hung Chang, one of the ablest men in the empire, is viceroy or governor-general. The only object of military interest is the arsenal, built by an Englishman named Meddows. It is inclosed by an earthen wall or parapet for defense, and occupies a mile square. At present only Remington cartridges, powder, and shells, for cannon of different calibre, are manufactured, but machinery for Remington rifles is being erected. In visiting any official in China, you are invited into a room simply furnished with round and square tables, stools, or mats, and are then invited to take tea, which is always clear and of rare flavor. This ceremony completed, you can proceed to business. After our inspection of the arsenal, we were invited to dine with the quartermaster-general of the viceroy. Putting ourselves in full dress, and accompanied by Mr. Pethick, vice-consul, as interpreter, we entered the walled city, and arrived at his *yamen* about 4 P. M. The furniture of the dining-room was the same as I have already described, all the dishes being served on a round table, without a table-cloth. We were provided both with chopsticks and knives and forks, but the dinner was exclusively Chinese. The courses were so many, and the dishes so numerous, that I cannot do better than give you the bill-of-fare of a dinner we ordered at a Chinese restaurant at Peking, as the most faithful approach I can make to a description:

1st Course.—Tea.

2d Course.—Fruits and sweetmeats, viz.: lotus-seed fried; water-melon seed; green dates; prunes; apples dried in honey; English walnuts; fresh apples; pears and grapes.—This course remained on the table throughout the dinner.

3d Course.—Shrimps; Mongolia ham, boiled and served in thin slices; chicken; wine made of rice. The wine is served hot, in small glasses. Each time the servant passes it, if any remains in the glasses, it is poured back into the common reservoir, and again poured back into the glasses. This is another instance of Chinese economy.

4th Course.—Pickled eggs; pickled lotus-root. Skin of ducks' feet boiled; pickled sea-weed. The eggs are buried for years in clay and salt, and undergo a species of decomposition, making them, when exhumed, resemble a dark, gelatinous substance. In Chinese cookery articles are always pickled in salt, never in vinegar.

5th Course.—This course was preceded by changing our paper napkins, and consisted of plovers' eggs, stewed with sharks' fins, and curdled milk (delicious); duck; kidneys; sea-weed jelly, and bamboo-shoots.

6th Course.—Fish-sinew soup; mushroom and water-chestnut stew; stewed fish; tripe; stewed prawns; chicken stewed in jelly.

7th Course.—Duck smothered in jelly (delicious); jelly *pâté;* fluid fat-meat hash.

8th Course.—Skin of ducks' feet stew; stewed mushrooms; stewed snails. (We bound ourselves to taste of every dish.)

9th Course.—Fish smothered in vinegar and jelly (good).

10th Course.—Meat dumplings; onion omelette.

11th Course.—Vermicelli-soup.

12th Course.—Stewed chicken; vegetable soup with hashed meat balls; pork smothered in flour.

13th Course.—Rice-soup; boiled rice; bullocks' blood thickened; salt pickles.

14th Course.—We go to another table, and are served with tea and cigars.

The dishes are generally brought on in small bowls, one or more at a time. Each guest dips his chopsticks into the common dish, and eats directly from it, or transfers what he wants to a small saucer, provided for the purpose.

The dinner with the quartermaster-general was interspersed with conversation on guns, cannon, tactics, army organization, etc.

The saki, as harmless as boiled milk, flowed freely. Our amiable host proposed healths often, and after each one showed us the bottom of his glass. When we arose from dinner it was quite dark. Four soldiers with lanterns lighted us home, running swiftly before our horses. As we came into the street an enterprising reporter of a Chinese paper sought to interview us, and, I have no doubt, gave an amusing description of the foreign visitors.

This dinner was only preliminary to another. At 8 o'clock we dined with Captain Fyffe, and the officers of the United States steamer Monocacy. These naval heroes were rather forlorn over the prospect of being frozen up for three months in the Peiho. Since the Tien-tsin massacres foreign gunboats stay at Tien-tsin summer and winter.

October 30th.—We left Tien-tsin at 8 A. M., and arrived at the Taku forts at the mouth of the river at 2 P. M. Here we went ashore to inspect the fortifications. Word had preceded us, so when we arrived everything was in readiness. Flags floated upon the parapets of all the forts, while at the wharf, and along the route to the quarters of the commanding general, no less than a hundred banners floated from the staffs, supported by faithful soldiers of the empire.

"Terrible as an army with banners," was our first impression—nevertheless, without palpitation, we landed, rolled ourselves into carts, and proceeded along the line of troops.

A battalion of ten companies was paraded, the companies presenting arms successively as we passed. On approaching the sally-port, a salute of three guns, the highest in the empire, was fired. Troops without arms were arrayed in line in front of the general's quarters, who came out, shook his own hands, then shook ours, and invited us to enter his quarters. Having been served with tea, we went to see the fort, which is of mud, or clay, made hard by pounding. Three or four Krupp guns, mounted on cavaliers, overlook all the other guns of the fort. A German, Mr. Le Myer, instructs the Chinese in the use of these monsters. It was in front of these forts, clumsy as they appear, that three or four English gunboats were sunk years ago. An attack from the sea-front was also bloodily repulsed. On another occasion these forts were taken from the rear, which the Chinese regard as a very cowardly proceeding. After looking at the fort we had taken our seats for another Chinese dinner, but the whistle of the steamer brought our visit to a close. We went back amid the display of banners, the roar of cannon, and the clangor of trumpets.

Throughout our visit we have been treated courteously by all of the authorities. Prince Kung and the foreign ministers received us three days after our arrival. The viceroy, Li Hung Chang, called on us at the American legation, and sent his secretary, who goes as associate minister to England, to receive us at the arsenal and the forts. From this you can see that our official experience has been delightful.

STEAMER KASHGAR, *November* 13, 1875.

To-day finds us *en route* from Hong-Kong to Singapore; and, as at sea we have plenty of time, I must take up the thread of our travels, which was interrupted at Shanghai. On October 26th I went up the Yang-tse River as far as Chinkiang, one hundred and fifty miles from the mouth. At this point the Grand Canal crosses the river, making Chinkiang a great commercial centre. The river is muddy like the Mississippi, and at some points is ten miles wide. At Chinkiang there is little of interest, except an iron pagoda, claimed to be seventeen hundred years old. I saw a few troops, dirty and ragged, armed with the old smooth-bore musket. The hills around the city are covered with the graves of the soldiers killed in the Taiping rebellion. A conical mound about three feet high marks each resting-spot. On the side of a sunken road, one of the coffins projected. Upon it the surviving friends sometimes place rice for the deceased. After his spirit is refreshed, beggars, and even dogs, eat what is left. I returned to Shanghai on the 28th, and on the 29th took the beautiful steamer Ava, of the French Messagerie, for Hong-Kong, where we arrived Monday, the 1st, at 6 A. M. The voyage was pleasant, though somewhat rough. For the first time, since leaving San Francisco, we were compelled to use racks at the table. On November 1st we visited our consul, Mr. Bailey, and arranged to call upon the governor, and General Colborne, commanding the forces. The governor was too ill to receive us, but we had a pleasant interview with the general, who invited us to tiffin the next day—a pleasant occasion, at which we met several officers of the Eightieth Regiment. Wednesday, November 3d, we took the steamer for Canton, arriving there at 3 P. M. Mr. Geary gave me a letter to his house at Canton, where all three of us were entertained by Mr. Talbot.

November 4th.—We visited in the morning several curio-shops, where no end of beautiful objects were presented for purchase. The china-shops were particularly fascinating. In the afternoon we visited the arsenal, and saw them making guns of varied descriptions, among them breech-loading Spencer and Remington rifles, six or more feet long, with a calibre of one inch. On visiting the house of the superintendent, we saw for an instant his three wives, who were gaudily painted. He offered us wine, and seemed pleased that we had come to admire his works.

On our return we visited the Honan Temple, where, among other things, they keep sacred pigs, so fat that they can scarcely walk. In one of the priest's rooms was a sewing-machine, an evidence that foreign improvements are gradually being introduced.

November 5th.—We visited the house of a wealthy Chinese merchant. It was very large, and had many reception-rooms, most of them being furnished with black-wood, marble-top tables, and chairs. The partitions were frequently of carved wood and stained glass. The ladies' apartment we were not permitted to see. From the house we went to the military examinations, which consisted of tests in archery.

The Temple of Horrors is another place of interest. It is open to the people, who are permitted to see the different forms of punishment administered in the empire. The figures are life-size.

One represented a man being sawed in two from head to foot. He stands bound between planks, one in front, another in rear; two men with a cross-cut saw then begin at the top of the skull, and probably kill their victim at the first or second stroke.

Another represents a man on his face receiving the bamboo. Three hundred blows usually paralyze the lower limbs, and generally prove fatal.

A third figure represents beheading, quick and painless.

A fourth represents a man sitting under a red-hot bell, which is lowered over him, thus roasting him alive.

A fifth is a figure boiling in a caldron of hot water or oil.

A sixth is the figure of a man whose bones are being broken by a weight repeatedly falling upon him.

Another punishment, not represented, is cutting a man to pieces by inches, and consists of cutting out small pieces of flesh from time to time, from different parts of the body, until the man dies.

Such are some of the cruelties still practised under Confucian civilization.

From the temple we went to a prison, where we saw poor, half-starved creatures, covered with sores and vermin, who may languish for years before being tried; and thence went to a court and witnessed a trial. The prisoner, bound with chains, kneeled before three judges, and, with face bowed to the ground, not daring to look at his accusers, answered the questions put to him. He was accused of stabbing, which he admitted; had he not done so, it is probable that he would have been whipped till he confessed. The knife he used was produced, and looked at by his judges, who made a report to the prefect, by whom sentence was pronounced.

These were some of the things we saw at Canton, which we left on the 6th, arriving at Hong-Kong at 3 P. M.

LETTERS FROM INDIA.

POINT DE GALLE, CEYLON, *November* 25, 1875.

WE left Hong-Kong November 11th, on the steamer Kashgar, and arrived at Singapore on the 16th. The situation of the city near the extreme southern point of Asia, within two degrees of the equator, makes it a great distributing point from which steamers proceed to Hong-Kong, the Philippine Islands, Java, Australia, Calcutta, and Ceylon. Being a focal point for business, it is no less so for races. There you have the ubiquitous Chinese, the ruddy-faced Englishman, the copper-colored Malay, the swarthy Hindoo, the olive-colored Portuguese, and many other nationalities. The government is English, the architecture European, modified to suit the tropics. The weather is not so hot as it is many degrees to the north. Longer nights and frequent showers cool the air, and make the climate habitable for men of all nations.

You need only glance at the map to see the far-reaching—you might say overreaching—foresight of the English Government. Recognizing the vast wealth of the East, and the importance of opening up all of Asia for her manufactures, she has seized every strategic point commanding the channel of commerce from Western Europe to Eastern Asia. Gibraltar, Malta, Aden, Perim, commanding the only channel at the mouth of the Red Sea; Ceylon, Penang, Singapore, and Hong-Kong—are all in her possession.

Wherever there is a strait, she lays her iron grasp upon it. Her acquisition of Perim was interesting. A French naval commander, it is said, was sent to seize it in the name of his government. Being invited to dine on board a vessel in an English squadron, he indiscreetly revealed his mission, when an officer at the table recollected to have forgotten something, excused himself, and, while the Frenchman was regaled with wine, dispatched a ship to capture the barren rock, the importance of which had not before occurred to them. When the Frenchman arrived he found the cross of St. George floating over the coveted prize, and with it the command of the Red Sea, and the Suez Canal, had passed into the hands of his hereditary enemies.

With all their diplomacy, one cannot fail to admire English pluck and enterprise. In the East her foundations are of granite. At every seaport her government or consular buildings loom up as emblems of her mighty power. The heathen look upon them and tremble; while Europeans and Americans are made to feel that, however great may be their countries, in Asia they must take a subordinate position.

We left Singapore at 4 P. M. on the 17th, sailed through the straits of Malacca, and arrived at Penang at 10 A. M. on the 19th. It is a city of about 60,000, mostly natives and Chinese. We drove through tropical scenery to a waterfall about 400 feet high, the only object of interest in the place. The celebrated Banca tin-mines are near Penang. The Hindoos at Penang are the handsomest men in figure we have yet seen. Tall, erect, lithe, clean-climbed, they are models of symmetry and action.

We sailed from Penang on the 20th, about 9 P. M., and on the 21st, in the bay of Bengal, crossed the antipodes of Willowbrook and Batavia. The bay was as placid as a lake, but the weather was hot, compelling us to sleep on deck. We arrived here yesterday, the 24th, and in a drive to Waka Walla, the only point of interest, passed the banana, the cocoanut, the nutmeg, the cinnamon, the clove, and other fragrant trees, which reminded us that we were in the land of spices.

DELHI, *December* 10, 1875.

From Ceylon we sailed to Bombay, where the only special object of interest I visited was the Hospital for Lepers. But the form of leprosy was not that as "white as snow" described in the Scriptures; it appeared rather to be a decomposition of animal tissue, resulting in loss of the fingers and toes, and even of the hands and feet. Nothing but the desire to see so ancient a disease tempted me to look upon these hopeless unfortunates.

December 2d.—We lunched with Sir Philip Woodhouse, Governor of the Bombay Presidency, and at 6.30 P. M. left for Delhi.

Providing ourselves with wraps and pillows, we passed a comfortable night in the compartment-cars, which are so arranged as to give each passenger a lounge to himself. The morning of the 3d we found ourselves on the great plains of India, over which we have already traveled two thousand miles.

The country is entirely different from what I had anticipated. Far from being tropical in its vegetation, over the route we have traveled (*via* Allahabad), it resembles the plains of Illinois. Here and there groups of trees, looking like the live-oak of the South, diversify the landscape, and give to the country the appearance of a vast park. A small portion of the soil is cultivated, and, but for the censuses carefully taken by the English Government, we could not believe that India possesses a population of more than two hundred millions. Even the valley of the Ganges is sparsely settled, its mud-villages appearing at great distances from each other. After two days' ride in the cars we arrived on the evening of the 4th at Lucknow, famous for its siege during the mutiny of 1857. We spent Sunday the 5th at Lucknow, and on the 6th visited the Memorial Garden, and Church, at Cawnpore. In the garden is a statue of the Angel of Mercy placed over the well, into which were cast the remains of about two hundred and fifty women and children who were massacred by the mutineers.

Leaving Cawnpore at 2.30 P. M., we arrived at Agra at 11.30 P. M. On the morning of the 7th we visited the fort, which is by far the grandest mass of masonry I have ever seen. Its walls, built of red sandstone, are seventy feet high, and are flanked with circular bastions, giving it a contour of grace, strength, and grandeur. Within its inclosure are the palaces of the Mogul emperors, also the celebrated Pearl Mosque. From the fort we drove to the Taj-Mahal, a tomb of white marble built by the Emperor Shah Jehan in memory of his wife. It stands on the banks of the Jumna, so beautiful in design and proportion as to excite the admiration of the world. In traveling in the East, no less than in Europe, one sees that all of the noblest works of art have been inspired by religion and love.

In the afternoon of the 7th we drove over to Futtehpore

Sikree, a distance of twenty-one miles, where we spent the night amid the ruins of the city founded by the great Akbar. On the 8th we returned to Agra, visiting *en route* the tomb of Akbar, saw again the Taj by moonlight, and left at 10 P. M. for Delhi.

On arriving at Allygur I left Forsyth and Sanger, who continued on to Delhi, while I went to Moradabad to see Miss ———, and deliver to her the presents sent to her by her mother and friends. She is doing a noble work as a medical missionary, has her dispensary in the city, and visits all the sick women who send for her. On my way back I stopped an hour at Chundowsee, where the Methodist Mission was holding its annual conference. Mr. Parker met me at the depot, and drove me to the camp where services were just closing. In a large tent were gathered about seventy converted Hindoos and Mohammedans, of whom thirty-five were ministers. After service I went to Mr. Parker's tent, and was warmly welcomed by all the members of the mission, ladies and gentlemen. Their zeal and devotion, and the success which is attending them in establishing schools, circulating the Scriptures, and especially in forming a native ministry, afford encouraging evidence that Christianity is steadily advancing in India.

Leaving Chundowsee at 9.20 I arrived here this morning at 7.30.

DELHI, *December* 17, 1875.

Upon arriving at Delhi on the morning of the 7th, Major Sanger was dispatched to Lord Napier's headquarters with the letter of General Sherman, to ascertain at what hour we could call and pay our respects. The message was answered by Captain Kennedy, who came to our hotel, and invited us to dine with Lord Napier in the evening. We found him in camp, most comfortably established, bright fires crackling on the hearths, the tents being furnished with sofas and easy-chairs. Ladies lent their graceful presence, making us feel that we were in a palace rather than a camp. Lord Napier is a splendid soldier, and a man of most easy and affable manners. The dinner was served as nicely as in permanent quarters.

The next day we were invited to accompany the "Chief," as the staff officers designate their commander, to a review of a division of infantry. The appearance of the men was excellent. British and native infantry stood side by side, the latter emulating the precision and steadiness of their white comrades. The marching, both in quick and double time, was exceedingly good; while the alternation of the helmet and turban imparted peculiar interest to the scene. This review, short as it was, showed us the perfection of English discipline, which I have always admired. The men in ranks stood firm, and would no more have raised a hand than a cadet at inspection. After the review we witnessed a supposed attack of a village, according to the Prussian system. The skirmishers went forward in successive lines, rushing from position to position, as if thus, under the fire of an enemy, they could be made to obey every impulse of their leaders.

Sunday, 12th.—I attended morning and evening service at St. James's church. The observance of the Sabbath is a noticeable feature in the English army. There is no Sunday-morning inspection, neither morning nor evening parade. Instead of these military exercises, there is a church parade, attended by all of the men. The members of different denominations are then marched to their several churches; after which, the only duty of the day is attendance at roll-call.

Notwithstanding this absence of display, discipline of the highest type prevails—so high, in fact, that a second holiday per week (Thursday) does not seem to impair it.

Monday, December 13th.—Attended a review of the division of artillery at Bussunt. The distance from Delhi to Bussunt is ten miles, which we drove in a carriage, with the understanding that horses would be supplied us on our arrival. But here one of those *contre-temps* occurred which often lose battles. Both our own horses, and those of Lord Napier, had gone astray, having gone to Bussai instead of Bussunt. We, however, pushed forward, and on arriving at the grounds were supplied with another mount. The artillery consisted of eleven batteries, both horse and mounted; and, what was more novel still, there was an elephant-battery. These huge beasts dragged along the forty-pounder siege-guns like so many toys. But the objection to them is, that no persuasion can make them stand fire; so, behind each gun follow nine or ten yoke of oxen, which replace the two elephants on approaching the field of battle. This of course doubles the expense, and should suggest the discontinuance of so needless a luxury. After the review, a mimic artillery-duel took place, half of the batteries being assigned to a defensive position, while the other half attacked.

Tuesday, December 14th.—We left Delhi at 4.20 P. M. on an expedition to the Himalayas. At 11 P. M. we arrived at Saharunpoor, where our party of five took carriages for Rajpore. These *garries*, as they are called, are arranged so that the traveler can extend himself to his full length, enabling him, as the roads are smooth, to get a good sleep. After much vociferation, and a firm refusal on our part to pay in advance the expenses of a round-trip to Rajpore and return, our procession consisting of an omnibus containing General Forsyth and Major Sanger, and three garries, in which Mr. Gillette, of England, Mr. Cryder, of New York, and myself were esconced, began to move.

As we had but two days to go to the mountains and back, it was important to reach Rajpore by 7 A. M. Our first difficulty was, that each relay of ponies was bulky. After much coaxing, whipping, pushing, and shouting, the obstinate creatures, from standing stock-still, would break into a full gallop. With each burst of enthusiasm from the ponies, we cherished the hope of arriving at Rajpore at daylight, but were doomed to disappointment. Toward morning I heard confusion of tongues, and, looking out of my garry, perceived that the ponies had disappeared, and that I was being drawn up the mountain by coolies. In some of the other garries, oxen had been substituted. This was not so bad, for, by means of twisting their tails and tickling their backs, these little bullocks can be made to trot four or five miles an hour. Daylight found us out of temper and fifteen miles from Rajpore, but in front of us was the beautiful valley of the Doon, with its groves of bamboo, orchards of banana, and fields of tea. Beyond was a range of hills, 7,000 feet high, covered with patches of white, which we took to be snow, but afterward found to be the villages of Mussoorie and Landour. In the presence of so much beauty our better feelings prevailed, and we traveled joyfully onward to Rajpore, arriving there at noon. Here we breakfasted, and, taking ponies, immediately set out for Landour. The road, which was well made but very steep, zigzagged up the mountain along the edge of precipices and around bold headlands, offering us a succession of enchanting views. With each elevation the scene changed. Behind us was the valley of the Doon, with its streams looking like threads of silver winding across the plain; still farther was the range of hills a thousand feet high, separating the valley from the great plains beyond; above were the lofty peaks we must crown before the grand view would burst upon us. Our ponies pushed on bravely. In seven miles they were to climb six thousand feet, equal to the height of Mount Washington.

At 4 P. M. we arrived at Mussoorie and Landour. Here, after taking refreshments, the proprietor of the hotel kindly offered to be our guide. Following him, we threaded the tortuous streets of the villages, until he brought us to a crest, whence, without preparation, the whole range burst into view. We were chained to the spot. At our feet was a valley, almost a chasm, thousands of feet deep; and twenty miles away rose the peaks of the Himalayas nestling in the clouds. Clad in white, reposing in solitude and grandeur, they stood before us the mighty witnesses of Him whose power is infinite and whose ways are past finding out. Reverently, I could not but feel "the heavens declare the glory of God, and the firmament showeth his handiwork."

After the startling emotions of the first view had subsided, we proceeded to the highest peak in Landour (7,300 feet) to witness the sunset. Behind us, toward the setting sun, were the great plains, enveloped in purple mist, in which the waters of the Jumna sparkled like the fire of an opal. Below us were the white bungalows of English residents, who seek health in the hills, perched on the peaks, and half concealed by the spreading trees, which added their verdure to the charm. To the eastward, extending sixty or eighty miles, stood the mighty monarchs, bathed in pinkish light, up whose flanks the lengthening shadows crept, until the peaks and fleecy clouds alone caught the last rays of departing day.

The next afternoon, on our departure from Saharunpoor, sixty miles from the range, we had our last view. From that distance the mountains loomed up among the clouds, enabling us to realize their great height of five miles above the sea.

Friday, 17th.—We witnessed a grand cavalry review of thirteen regiments. They marched past first at a walk, in column of squadrons, then countermarched and passed at a trot. After which, they deployed into line and swept by at a gallop. The turban and the helmet; the elephants, with purple caparison, bearing spectators; the camels grazing in the distance; the ruins of Delhi—gave us a combination of Oriental and Occidental scenes to be found only in India.

Saturday, 18th.—We left Delhi at 11 A. M., and arrived at Calcutta on Monday, the 20th.

General Litchfield, United States consul-general, met us at the depot, and we are now enjoying his generous hospitality.

CALCUTTA, *December* 28, 1875.

Everything here is in excitement in anticipation of the visit of the Prince of Wales. The evening of our arrival we attended a Hindoo reception given by two *nawabs*. It did not differ from a European reception, except that there were some native singers, who, sitting on the floor, entertained us with a succession of plaintive nasal sounds not at all agreeable to the ear.

On the 22d we lunched at Government House. After lunch we were presented to his Excellency the viceroy, Lord Northbrook. He is an exceedingly affable man, a ready talker, and, belonging to a business family—the Barings, of London—showed himself *au courant* with affairs, whether civil, military, or commercial.

He soon decided our future plans. The unsettled condition of Afghanistan bars that route, while, were we able to go to Kashgar, the passes would not be open before May or June. The only route now open is that through Persia. The viceroy told us we should have invitations to all the ceremonies in honor of the Prince of Wales, and that if any failed to reach us it would be purely accidental. The interview lasted about half an hour, and I need not say we retired well pleased with the ruler of nearly two hundred and fifty millions of people.

From Government House we drove to the residence of the lieutenant-governor of Bengal, Sir Richard Temple, who rules sixty-three millions of people. Even colonels of the army, as civil commissioners, rule as many as five millions, equal in number to the population of the State of New York. Such are the capacities of the civil and military service in India.

December 22d.—We visited Fort William, and inspected the armory and barracks. The latter are the best in India, and show what care the Government takes of its soldiers. The men perform military duty only. The policing is done by coolies, the cooking is done by coolies, and, when the tired soldier seeks his rest at the end of the day, a coolie works his *punka*, and fans him to sleep. In hot weather, screens are hung before the doors of the quarters, and these are kept wet by coolies. The rapid evaporation of the water cools the temperature within sufficiently to make life endurable.

While on the subject of coolies, I may as well speak of servants generally. At one house where we dined, twenty-four were employed. Of these, six found occupation in and about the kitchen, and a large number about the stables, one to each horse.

At another house thirty-nine servants, all men, constituted the domestic household. This horde was not fed by the employer. Each received about three dollars per month, and provided for himself.

The evening of the 22d we dined at Government House. The viceroy gave me the seat on his right, and throughout the dinner entertained me with conversation on every variety of subject. After dinner the company ascended to the drawing-rooms, and there we saw the viceroy receive several of the maharajas. These chiefs came into the room in gorgeous robes, their turbans glittering with diamonds. It was Europe and Asia again face to face. The native princes displayed their plumage like peacocks; the ruler of India, attired in a plain black suit, moved among them as modestly as his humblest guest.

December 23d.—In the afternoon we went to the landing to witness the reception of the Prince of Wales. As on the evening before, the native chiefs were the special objects of attention. Attired in their richest apparel, they stood resplendent, glittering in the sun. Patiala wore a turban which alone was valued at half a million dollars. About his head were festooned strings of diamonds; among them, those formerly belonging to the Empress Eugénie. Any one of the precious ornaments he so lavishly displayed would have been a modest fortune. Pearls and emeralds also decked his clothes, enabling him to stand from head to foot a monument of Oriental splendor.

Other chiefs emulated, but did not surpass Patiala. Some had their robes embroidered in gold, others in pearl and turquoise. Above their heads glistened sprays of diamonds, while here and there huge solitaires twinkled like the stars. Among the chiefs stood one of commanding stature, gorgeous in his robes, but, Naaman-like, a leper.

At 4.30 P. M. the prince left his ship under a royal salute from the fleet. On reaching the wharf an address was presented, to which he replied. He was then conducted to the platform, where the native princes and other dignitaries were presented, after which he immediately left for Government House. Thousands of people turned out to welcome him. After he had gone, Patiala and his friends staid upon the platform, and with evident satisfaction permitted the people, as many as liked, to gaze upon a sight that will never be repeated. On retiring from the landing, at his request, I was presented to the Maharajah of Cashmere, who invited us to visit him at his capital.

In connection with this display, another scene deeply impressed me. A native woman fainted, and, as the throng passed by, I saw a frail girl bending over her, administering restoratives, whom I recognized as Miss W——, a young missionary from Brooklyn.

December 24th.—The city was illuminated in honor of the Prince of Wales. From the Maidan, a great park, the public buildings and private residences were revealed in outline, making Calcutta, indeed, appear the City of Palaces. For miles the streets were a blaze of light. On each side wire was stretched like telegraph-lines, from which, at intervals of six or eight inches, were hung small white and colored glasses, filled with oil and floating wicks. Other wires, similarly prepared, hung in festoons from those already described. The carriages thus moved through an avenue of light. Here and there triumphal arches spanned the streets; while illuminated trees, gateways, and other devices, increased the effect. All along the line, the streets were packed with people clad in white. Some of them stood on distant house-steps, and looked like spectres unmoved by the display. Mohammedan and Hindoo gazed calmly upon the small procession of Europeans who, like conquerors, enjoyed the scene. No mark of enthusiasm was shown. We passed quietly through the flickering light, and, after a drive of five miles, returned to the home of our consul.

DELHI, *January* 9, 1876.

On Monday, the 27th of December, we were invited to a garden-party at Sir Richard Temple's, to meet the Prince of Wales. There were about a thousand people present, who walked up and down the grounds, the scene reminding me of the Saturday afternoon promenades on the plain of West Point. There was a band in attendance, and a dance by native men and women. The grounds were beautifully illuminated. During the afternoon Sir Richard Temple presented me to the prince, who charmed us all by his affable manners.

In the evening there was a ball at Government House, attended by at least fifteen hundred people. The prince opened the ball with Miss Baring, daughter of the viceroy, and in their set, and the sets adjoining, were all the dignitaries of the Government, from the viceroy down. The dancing could not be complimented—too much hopping, even in the waltz, to be graceful.

At 3 P. M. on the 28th we attended the levee of the Prince of Wales. The crush was about the same as at Washington at the President's reception, and differed from it only in this—that the prince, standing on a slightly-raised dais, bowed to each visitor, instead of offering his hand. In the evening the natives gave a *fête* at Belgatchie, consisting of singing, dancing, and fireworks. All of the distance from Government House to the *fête*, four miles, was illuminated as on the 24th.

December 29th.—We were invited to dine at Government House. The guests were received by an aide-de-camp in waiting, in full dress. After all had assembled, the viceroy and his daughter came in at one door, and were presented to the guests.

A few minutes after, the prince came in by another entrance, preceded by the lords of his suite. As he passed, he bowed to some, and gave his hand to others, among them myself. He then gave his arm to Miss Baring, and at once went to the table. The dinner was served on silver throughout; sixty-two servants, one to each plate, stood motionless behind the guests, while as many more served the courses. After dinner the company ascended to the drawing-rooms, where the prince received the maharajas.

On the 1st of January, the finest ceremony of the series occurred. It was the investiture of the Grand Star of India. The Prince of Wales opened the chapter, and conferred the order G. S. I. on several native chiefs. The assemblage was exceedingly brilliant. By the prince's special direction we were given seats among the members of his suite. Luncheon at Government House on the 1st finished the series of entertainments.

We left Calcutta on the evening of the 2d, and arrived at Benares on the evening of the 3d. The sacred city of the Hindoos is wholly given to idolatry. Their gods, however, seem to be more spiritual than those of the Chinese, inasmuch as the offering is more frequently flowers than food.

The view of the city from the Ganges is imposing, but within all is dilapidation and squalor. Every morning the Hindoos are expected to bathe in the Ganges, and in vast crowds throng the river-bank. The women walk in without undressing, and, on coming out, change the wet for dry clothing in so dexterous a manner as to avoid the slightest exposure.

At one point of the river our boat put in shore, where we beheld a peculiar sight. Two large fires were burning, each made of wood nicely corded. At a slight distance several natives were squatted in a semicircle, evidently enjoying the heat on so crisp a morning. Immediately in front others were bathing with careless indifference.

The guide pointed to the fires, and told us each was a funeral-pyre. We were witnessing unconsciously the cremation of two Hindoos, whose dearest object in life is to have their ashes mingled with the sacred waters of the Ganges. We left Benares on the evening of the 4th, and reached Delhi on the evening of the 5th.

On the 8th we witnessed a review of all the troops at Delhi: cavalry, infantry, and artillery, native and European, presented a superb appearance. The infantry passed in quick time; the cavalry and artillery passed at a walk, trot, and gallop. There was not the slightest check in the marching, nor apparently a single fault in manœuvre. In riding around the lines, the chargers of Lord Napier and a maharajah collided while leaping a ditch, causing Lord Napier to fall, and break his collar-bone, but, concealing his injury, he remained on the field till the review was over.

RAWUL PINDEE, *January* 20, 1876.

January 11*th*.—In the morning, the prince made his entry into Delhi. From the railway-station to his camp, a distance of four miles, the road was lined with troops on both sides, but the Oriental feature of his entry was reserved near his camp, where he passed through an avenue of twenty-two elephants brilliantly caparisoned. The embroidery on the housings of these immense beasts was of heaviest gold, and nearly two feet wide.

In the afternoon we attended a reception given by the prince, at his camp, to the officers of the army at Delhi, and in the evening were invited to a reception in his honor, given by Lord Napier at army headquarters. On both occasions the array of uniforms was exceedingly brilliant.

Wednesday, 12th.—The great review, for which the troops had been preparing a long time, took place. It was a superb spectacle, resembling the reviews we saw before going to Calcutta. We rode around the lines in the suite, and, as before, had a fine opportunity to witness the steadiness of the troops, both native and European.

The prince was mounted on a black stallion, which stood like a statue while the cavalry, in helmets and turbans, swept furiously past; but unmoved as was the horse, when the elephant-battery came shuffling along, and the huge beasts threw up their trunks, as a royal salute, the *rider* could not suppress a broad smile at their act of civility.

After the review, colors were presented to two regiments, which, during the mutiny, signalized their loyalty to the Government.

In the evening a ball was given in the Dewan Khass, at the fort. This was the Hall of Audience, built by the Mogul emperors, where used to be the "Peacock Throne," so famous for its costliness and elegance. The edifice is of white marble, and consists simply of a massive roof, supported by parallel rows of square and rectangular columns, heavily gilded, and inlaid with precious stones. The effect is one of great richness, and so enchanted was the emperor that, in the central arcade, he had placed the inscription mentioned in "Lalla Rookh," "If there is a paradise upon earth it is this, it is this!" Could he have looked through the mists of centuries, and seen the future King of England dancing in his marble halls, no doubt, like Belshazzar, his face would have blanched and his knees smote together.

Thursday, 13th.—The troops to act on the offensive in the manœuvres moved out eighteen miles on the Kurnaul Road. Having been invited, I went out with them provided for a two days' campaign, and was the guest of Colonel Watson, commanding the cavalry. The manœuvres were limited to six hours on each of the two following days.

Friday, 14th.—The troops moved promptly forward. Making a

mountain of a mole-hill, a canal about twelve feet wide was regarded as formidable an obstacle as a great river. So the cavalry started off at a trot, and gallop, for six or eight miles, to seize bridges which the enemy did not care to destroy. The infantry, without much opposition, moved straight down the road to within seven miles of Delhi.

An exploit which was regarded as particularly brilliant on the part of the offensive, was to mount eighty infantry on the caissons of the artillery, and to send them at a fast trot to the bridge over the canal eight miles in advance of the camp of the army. In the same situation we would have sent a company of cavalry, which, in the event of opposition, would have dismounted and fought on foot, and would have thought no more of it. In India, however, few officers appreciate the true use of cavalry, so infantry had to be mounted on artillery-carriages for an exploit which legitimately belonged to cavalry.

Saturday, 15th.—The battle raged along the whole line. The cavalry of the right wing crossed over to the left, joined that of the left wing, and, without scouts or skirmishers, advanced in mass to within fifteen hundred yards of two of the enemy's batteries, when, the latter opening fire, an umpire rode up and declared fifty per cent. of the cavalry killed or wounded. This unexpected decision finished the cavalry for the day.

The infantry advance was no less unfortunate. The leading brigade, in order of battle, moved straight down the road toward a small village, held as an outpost by the enemy. The commander marched his brigade mostly in double time, neglected several opportunities to turn the enemy's flank, but finally took the village in consequence of a flanking force sent in farther to his right. The enemy then fell back a few hundred yards to Azadpore, which was his main position. Without reconnoitring, the pursuing force fell upon this position with all its might and main, and, as the enemy was so posted as to bring two lines of fire upon him, one being above the other, his attack was soon badly repulsed; and again an inexorable umpire declared nearly half of the troops *hors de combat.*

A force trying to turn the enemy's right centre, moved so as to be enfiladed by the enemy's artillery on the heights near Delhi, and, when it got into position, was met in the same stern manner by two lines of fire.

Farther to the right another division found itself in a flat, open field, with walled inclosures, strongly held, staring it in the face. These the commander wisely refrained from attacking. The enemy's left, facing the canal, could easily have been turned; but moving in straight lines is so much simpler that the generals, as has frequently occurred in all wars, took not only the easiest but the shortest route to inevitable defeat.

Between the infantry at Azadpore and the cavalry there was an interval of nearly two miles. The infantry being repulsed, had the enemy advanced nothing could have saved the offensive army from destruction, as the cavalry was beyond reach, and could not have come to the support of his hard-pressed infantry.

At the conclusion of the manœuvres, I rode back to the city, where I found General Forsyth and Major Sanger. On Friday, the first day of the manœuvres, we were invited to dine with the Prince of Wales at his camp; but, as I was with the offensive, they went alone. During the manœuvres, they rode in his suite, and also lunched with him. But this was not all. In order to show his consideration for us as American officers, he gave an extra dinner, to which we were invited, on which occasion he gave me the seat on his right.

As we entered his tent he came forward with a smile, and remarked, "Caught you at last." During the evening he was very affable; spoke with gratification of his visit to America, and of the friendly relations between the two countries; and, when we took our leave, gave each of us a print of himself and the princess.

Monday, the 18th, we paid our parting calls; and in the evening started for Peshawar. Tuesday at three we arrived at Lahore, and at six arrived at Wizirabad, where we took carriages for Goojrat. Wednesday we skirted the Himalayas, and this morning at 3 A. M. (January 20th) arrived here, where we are compelled to lie over a day for want of conveyance. We are now in the Punjab (Five Rivers—Sutlej, Ravee, Chenab, Jhelum, and Indus). It is a beautiful country, well watered, but in summer terrifically hot.

RAWUL PINDEE, *January* 27, 1876.

We left Rawul Pindee, by a government conveyance, at 8 A. M., on the 21st, and arrived at 4.30 P. M. at Attock, which is at the junction of the Indus and Cabul Rivers. The two streams unite in a large plain, apparently with the view of forcing their way through a range of hills which crosses the Indus immediately below the junction. A Mussulman fort, built by Akbar, dominates the rivers, and in its day was a formidable obstacle to barbarian invasions.

Continuing our journey, we arrived at Peshawar at 3 A. M. on the 22d. After breakfast we called upon Colonel Yorke, who received us very kindly. In the afternoon he turned out the Twentieth Punjab Infantry, and the Fourteenth Native Infantry, for our inspection and review. These men are mostly recruited in the vicinity, and many of them are wild Afghans, who, in their love for fighting, make no distinction between their own people and other hostile tribes.

Sunday we attended the garrison church, and walked through the old native city. The latter resembled many of the cities we saw in China, except that the inhabitants were more squalid in appearance. If you could see the mud-houses of the Hindoos, without windows or furniture, filled with smoke and filth, you would realize that poverty is unknown in America. In these wretched huts many men live who are quite wealthy, not having learned that it is unnecessary to conceal their wealth from their English masters, as they were wont to do under their native rulers.

Monday, 24th.—Major Omaney organized for us an expedition to the Khyber Pass. Accompanied by him and several English officers, we proceeded to Jumrood, the frontier post of the English, thirteen miles from Peshawar, where we were met by one hundred and fifty armed Afghans from across the border.

Half-clad in sheep-skins, wearing the turban, and armed with matchlocks, swords, pistols, and knives, a worse-looking set of cut-throats it is difficult to imagine. A general discharge of fire-arms from the parapet of the old fort of Jumrood signalized our approach. Here we took horses, and with our murderous-looking escort started for the pass, two miles off. We all thought how easy it would be for these fellows to close the pass and turn upon us; and our confidence was not increased by the sight of a murdered Afghan, whose grave was being dug by the road-side, and whose murderer, in retaliation, had bitten the dust before our return.

Such is their life. Claiming to be descendants of the "lost tribes of Israel," they mercilessly enforce the law, "Eye for an eye, and tooth for a tooth." If a man is shot or stabbed, his friends hunt down the murderer like a wild beast.

These are the characteristics of the many tribes to whose tender mercies we would have committed ourselves, had we endeavored to cross Afghanistan against the counsel of the viceroy. They acknowledge no law, and are as independent of the Emir of Cabul as they are of the English. The latter they have been taught to fear, hence they rarely make forays upon the villages under English protection; but between each other, village against village, and family against family, are often arrayed in deadly hostility. In their faces there is no gleam of compassion, and they look as if to fire at a man from ambush, or to stab him in the dark, would be the greatest of secret pleasures. As we rode in the midst of the rabble we could see old men, and even boys of twelve and thirteen, bearing the deadliest weapons. From the cradle to the grave, war and bloodshed appear to be their occupation; and even in cultivating the soil they never quit their weapons, lest every bush conceal an enemy.

The entrance to the pass was like a gateway between two cliffs, about one thousand feet high. Inside we ascended the gravelly bed of a dry stream, and then, taking a fine road, constructed by the English in 1841, we penetrated about three miles and a half, when the civil commissioner thought he had gone as far as was prudent. The mountains were treeless and verdureless, resembling those about Salt Lake.

On our return to Jumrood an excellent lunch awaited us, after which our Afghan friends amused us with feats of marksmanship. They proved that, with the old flint-lock musket, a bottle could readily be hit at one hundred and fifty yards. The day was a most pleasant one, and in interest was worthy of being classed with the day we visited the Nankow Pass, and the Great Wall of China.

Tuesday, 25th.—The whole garrison, consisting of two British and four native regiments of infantry, two native cavalry regiments, and three batteries of artillery, was turned out for review. The blending of uniforms and colors I have already described at Delhi; but here the picturesqueness was increased by the proximity of the mountains which, like a horseshoe, almost encircled us.

Above and beyond the troops were the Hindoo Koosh, fifteen

thousand feet high, completely covered with snow; while, in the gardens at our backs, could be culled the sweet lemon, and roses, almost in full bloom.

Peshawar lies almost in the centre of a plain, fifty by sixty miles square; and, being nearly surrounded by mountains, is one of the hottest and most unhealthy places in India. British regiments are required to remain in it but one year. The Seventeenth Regiment, seven hundred strong, have all had chills and fever except eight men, and over three hundred were sick at one time.

Alexander wintered in the valley of Peshawar, then covered with forests, and the home of the rhinoceros. It was also in the devastating path of Tamerlane. To-day, under the English, it knows more peace and prosperity than in all the ages since Alexander.

We left Peshawar on Wednesday, the 26th, at 9 A. M.; stopped at Attock, where we "tiffined" with officers of the artillery, and resuming our journey arrived here, where for want of horses we are again detained. We shall, however, get off to-morrow, and then shall make our way almost directly to Bombay.

BOMBAY, *February* 6, 1876.

We left Rawul Pindee at 12 P. M. on the 27th of January, and arrived at Wizirabad at 6 P. M. on the 28th. From there it was our intention to go to Jumoo, to visit the Maharajah of Cashmere, who invited us at Calcutta; but a telegram apprised us that we could not go beyond Sealkote, in consequence of the cholera which had broken out at the capital. We therefore reluctantly set our faces toward Bombay, stopping over a few hours at Lahore and Allahabad.

The latter city is at the junction of the Ganges and Jumna, both sacred rivers among the Hindoos. On the day of our visit there was a religious festival, when, according to custom, everybody is expected to bathe at the junction of the rivers. Immense crowds of men, women, and children, lined the shores; while going to and from the city were streams of people, some believing they had washed away their sins, others hurrying to secure absolution. Those who had bathed had to walk back in a blazing sun amid clouds of dust, yet to their ignorant minds they were free from pollution, and returned on their way rejoicing.

From Allahabad to Bombay we had a pleasant ride. The Begum of Bhopal, whom we saw at Calcutta with a large number of retainers, traveled in our train. At Jubbulpoor she was received with military honors, and in a palanquin disappeared from our view.

The stations on the line of railroad from Bombay to Jubbulpoor are models of beauty. They are literally embowered in vines and flowers; and so pleasing is the effect upon the parched and dusty travelers that the company gives a prize to the station-master who presents the finest display.

We arrived at Bombay at 11.45 on the 29th, two months to a day from the time we left it, and are delighted with a tour that has been but a succession of pleasures. Everywhere we have been treated with special consideration as Americans, and every avenue of information has been freely thrown open. We have been permitted to see the great work England is doing in educating and fitting a people for freedom. Railroads, telegraphs, churches, and schools, are sure pledges of a bright future for India, and we cannot leave without hoping that England may preserve her sway till, in the order of Providence, she shall have accomplished the mission she was called to perform.

LETTERS FROM PERSIA.

BUNDER ABBAS, PERSIA, *February* 20, 1876.

WE left Bombay, Friday, February 11th, at 6 P. M., on the steamer Umbala, for Bushire.

Monday, the 14th, we arrived at Kurrachee. The city contains about seventy thousand people, and lies in a low, flat plain, about twenty miles from the mouth of the Indus. The country back of the city is almost barren; yet, within, irrigation produces fine crops, and shows that only water is required to make the desert beautiful as a garden. Behind the city there is a range of verdureless hills, rising to eight hundred or a thousand feet. The harbor contained no less than eight steamers the morning we arrived, and we were naturally puzzled as to the reason for such a commercial appearance. It lies, however, in the fact that the port is the outlet for the valley of the Indus, which is navigable as far up as Moultan.

Tuesday, at 11 A. M., we sailed for Muscat, where we arrived on the morning of the 18th. The harbor is a small bay, protected on each side by precipitous rocks from three to five hundred feet high, which are crowned with castles bristling with cannon.

The city lies at the head of the bay, as in the neck of a funnel, and looks more like a place in Europe, in the middle ages, than the capital of an Oriental despot. The front of the city, and also the castles, were built by the Portuguese, when it was in their possession, who lost the city in a general massacre resulting, it is said, from the effort of the ruler to marry a native woman in defiance of the precepts of her religion.

Squeezed between barren, broiling rocks, on which the eye seeks in vain for verdure, the city claims geographically the benefit of both a tropical and temperate climate. It lies on the tropic of Cancer—an imaginary line which assumes a painful reality when, in summer, the torrid winds, sweeping across it, keep the thermometer at 108° night and day.

The only place of interest, as in most Asiatic towns, is the bazaar in which the tradesmen expose for sale the few wares and curiosities of the country.

We brought letters to Colonel Miles, the political agent of Great Britain, who received us kindly and invited us to lunch. But the great object of interest was our visit to the Sultan, or Imaum. On expressing a desire to pay our respects, the colonel sent a note to the palace, receiving in reply an appointment for 2 P. M. At that hour we proceeded through a narrow alley to the palace, which we approached from the rear. As the door was thrown open, an Arabian lion glared at us from his cage on the left. A couple of horses stood on our right, while in front about a dozen ragamuffins, with knives, and arms of the oddest pattern, awaited to do us military honor.

On entering the court, his majesty sent his regrets that, in consequence of lameness, he was not able to receive us at the foot of the stairs. This flattering explanation having been interpreted, we mounted the rickety stairway, and at the top were met by the Sultan, who shook us cordially by the hand, and motioned us into an adjoining room. The furniture of the room was very simple, consisting of a green covered table in the centre, a sofa, and some chairs, arranged with military precision against the walls.

The Sultan wore a turban, a gray gown extending from his head to his feet, a white under-garment richly embroidered, and sandals which exposed his well-shaped bare feet.

His face is said to be the handsomest in Asia, but this I think an exaggeration, or at least a compliment to kingly vanity. He was, however, fine-looking, with a high forehead, arched eyebrows, aquiline nose, firm mouth, and patriarchal beard. A feeling of sadness seemed to overspread his countenance, which could be accounted for by his meditation on the lives of his predecessors, most of whom have died by violence ; or by reflecting on his own experience, which has not been devoid of danger.

Only a few weeks since he was compelled to flee to Persia; was reinstated through the kind offices of England, and again finds himself tottering on his throne, not knowing what moment some bloodthirsty wretch may dispatch him.

The conversation was not very edifying. We told him we had come from America, and, having learned accidentally that morning that we had a treaty with the Imaum of Muscat, we expressed the hope that the relations of the two countries might remain cordial. He then began to inquire about India, the Franco-German War, and particularly the war between the Khedive of Egypt and his brother the Sultan of Zanzibar. We told him that the armies of the Khedive had been repulsed. He said, for a great man with a great many soldiers, to attack a small man with a few soldiers, was mean and cowardly, and, as this accorded with our ideas as soldiers, we gave a formal assent.

During the course of the interview refreshments were served. The first consisted of a confection looking like cocoanut-candy, then followed coffee, after which the servant brought in four very large glasses filled with a transparent sweet fluid like sherbet. Politeness only requires one to take a sip; but some persons, thinking this would not be a suitable appreciation of hospitality, have been known to drink the entire glass, and have been very sick for their pains.

After removing the sherbet, the servant returned with a large server on which was a very small vial. For an instant I was puzzled, but recollecting that we were in the land of cassia, myrrh, and frankincense, a fortunate intuition suggested an Arabian perfume, so, placing the end of my finger in the neck of the vial, I wet it, and immediately stroked my mustache. The delicious odor of attar of roses soon filled the room, and, enveloped in perfume, we thanked his majesty for his kind reception, and took our departure.

We left Muscat Friday, at 7 P. M., and arrived here at 9 A. M. this morning (20th). At this port Alexander was met by his fleet about 325 B. C. The country has the same sterile aspect as at Muscat. The mountains a few miles in the interior rise to ten thousand feet, and are now capped with snow.

Shiraz, Persia, *March* 6, 1876.

From Bunder Abbas we went to Linjah, where we arrived at 1 P. M. on the 21st of February. The town is a squalid-looking place, scarcely distinguishable from the gray coast-line, and from the clay-colored mountains rising in the rear. We called on the sheik, and afterward visited the wells, and saw where he had walled in, and left to die, a thief, who had stolen one of his horses. This is not an uncommon punishment in Persia. They frequently compel the culprit to build his own tomb, which is just large enough for him to stand inside, and then placing him in it, head downward, pour it full of liquid lime. Death in this manner is almost instantaneous. The feet are allowed to project, where they remain as a terror to evil-doers, until they drop off from decay.

Another punishment, inflicted for minor offenses, is beating the bottom of the feet with sticks. This is done so mercilessly in some instances as to beat off the toes, and leave the offender a cripple for months.

The only European at Linjah was the agent of the British India Steamship Company, whom we took on board, a wretched sufferer from rheumatic fever. From Linjah we went to Bahrein in Arabia, where we arrived at 1 P. M. on the 23d. The town is on an island, and is celebrated for its pearl-fisheries. We endeavored to buy a few pearls, but found that during the fishing-season experts from the jewelers at Bombay had purchased the valuable ones, and sent them to India and Europe.

We left Bahrein on the morning of the 24th, and, sailing almost due north, reached Bushire at 10 A. M. on the 25th. Captain Campbell, commander of the British gunboat, came on board to call on us, and sent us ashore in his boat. We thence proceeded on horseback to the British residency, where we were delightfully received and entertained by Colonel and Mrs. Ross. This brave little woman has followed her husband to all his stations on the Persian Gulf, and wherever he has been has made him a home that has been admired by all who have had the good fortune to visit them.

The city lies on a flat peninsula of sand, and from the sea presents an imposing appearance; but a nearer approach, like that of Muscat, dispels the illusion, for it is built of rubble-stone and mud, with streets so narrow as to be easily roofed over, thus excluding the sun. We remained at Bushire Saturday and Sunday, completing our outfit for the long journey of more than a thousand miles on horseback. All superfluous baggage had to be sent off to Naples.

My kit, when made up, consisted of an undress uniform, a dark winter suit, half a dozen collars, half a dozen handkerchiefs, one change of under-clothing, half a dozen stockings, and a folding dressing-case. These articles are wrapped in several parcels, and are carried in saddle-bags made of Persian carpet, which are slung over the horse's back in rear of the saddle. The bedding consists of one comforter, a pillow, and a tick, which is filled with chopped straw at each station.

Our riding-suit is made of dust-colored corduroy. The coat is a short plaited frock, full of pockets; trousers cut tight like riding-breeches; leggings to the knee, and shoes, are made of brown leather. This suit, which we all wear, has been admired as the best traveling-dress that has been seen in Persia. All of the above outfit, after leaving Shiraz, is to be carried on the horses we ride.

For the trip to Shiraz we took three horses and six mules. The Persian saddle which we rejected, having English saddles of our own, covers the horse from his shoulders to his hips; the skirts are four inches thick, and the hideous, unsightly thing weighs not less than sixty pounds. To carry these three saddles, used as pack-saddles, required an extra mule. Our entire train consisted of three horses and six mules. The route at times not having been free from robbers, we each carried a carbine and revolver.

All of our arrangements having been completed, we took leave of Colonel and Mrs. Ross, and at 11.30 A. M on the 28th of February commenced our march. Several gentlemen escorted us a short distance out of the city, and Dr. Andreas, of the German scientific expedition, at our invitation, accompanied us to our first halting-place.

The road from Bushire, for about fifteen miles, is through sand, overflowed by the sea at high tide. The next few miles the land is flat, with here and there a patch of barley. With this exception, the only vegetation is a low sage-bush, which half covers the soil, and gives the ground a gray, mottled appearance. The date-palm appears here and there, wherever water is found. It being quite hot, the air rose tremblingly from the plain, giving rise to mirage, not so dazzling as to people the waste with villages and groves; yet, apparently, we saw lakes where no water existed, while the black tops of the date-palms seemed to stand trunkless, suspended above the horizon.

The first night we spent at Ahmadi in a handsome caravansary. These structures take the place of hotels throughout Asia, and in Persia are built by rich extortioners, who thus hope to smooth their way heavenward. They are built in the form of a square, usually one story high, and are entered through a pointed arched gateway. In the centre of the court is a raised platform, about three feet high, upon which saddles and packs are deposited. Facing the court on all four sides are a number of arched recesses, with an aperture at the back of each leading into a dark room. These rooms, to which the arched recesses serve as parlors, are the only accommodation the traveler can hope for. In the centre of each is a hole in the floor, about the size and depth of a hat. This serves for a fireplace, and, as there is no chimney, the smoke rises to the blackened ceiling, and thence descends to plague the eyes and noses of the occupants. If no felt has been provided by the traveler to cover the aperture for the door, he must sleep in communication with the open air, no matter how cold.

In the angles stabling is provided for the animals. The best caravansaries usually have a room over the arched gateway, and also above the centres of the other sides. Even with this advantage there is no approach to luxury; yet the Persian who, doubtless, has never seen anything better, looks upon them as the perfection of rest for the traveler.

We were most fortunate in securing a servant who speaks a little English. He had just made the trip from Teheran with Mr. and Mrs. Arnold, of London, whom we met at Bunder Abbas. Without him we would have been in a sorry plight, as not another servant was to be found in Bushire. His mess-kit is so small as to be carried in a pair of saddle-bags, and yet, with the small fire before described, he manages in a few minutes to gives us an omelette, or a stew, to which no reasonable man can object. The night of the 29th we stopped at Dáliki, near the foot of the mountains. A short distance from the village we passed several sulphur and naphtha springs.

March 1*st.*—We clambered up the mountain-paths to the plain Konartakteh, eighteen hundred feet above the sea, thence still higher to the plain of Kamaraj, twenty-nine hundred feet above the sea. The mountains consisted simply of the upturned edges of stratified rock, the inclination of the strata being 45°, while the broken faces were frequently almost vertical. Near the summit of the pass, or *kotal*, leading to Kamaraj, we saw vast quantities of gypsum. The mountains were all treeless, but small patches of grass were here and there visible.

March 2d.--We left Kamaraj at 6 A. M., and spent the night at Kazeroon. When about three miles from the city we were met by the governor and a large body of horsemen, who escorted us to the governor's house. As we approached his gate a man struck off the head of a lamb, and, holding it up, exclaimed, "Welcome in the name of the Prophet!"

On our way in we were entertained with feats of horsemanship. Two men caracoled backward and forward across the road, leaping ditches and hedges, and firing their guns and pistols at each other. All this time the *calaon*, or pipe, about two and a half feet high, was kept circulating. Being in a complimentary frame of mind, I admired the governor's horse. He immediately gave him to me, and insisted on my taking him, but that was impossible, which, I half suspected, he knew before making the generous offer. On entering his house breakfast was served in a room overlooking the court. It consisted first of sweetmeats, which were delicious; then melons and fruits; and, lastly, chickens, game, and meats. The cooking was good, and far superior to that of China and Japan.

At the breakfast there was present Sayed Mahomet, a descendant of the Prophet. Like the descendants of Confucius, those of the Prophet are highly honored, and are insured a comfortable living. The one before us must have stood six feet four in his stockings. When sitting his beard reached to his girdle. On his head he wore a green turban, the sign of his lineage. With a high forehead, arched eyebrows, aquiline nose, and flowing beard, he lacked only the frost of age to make him the perfect type of the patriarch.

When breakfast was finished, the governor escorted us to a house in a large orange-grove, where we were allowed to refresh ourselves, after which tea was served in the garden. Toward evening we returned to the governor's house, where we dined. After dinner, which did not differ much from the breakfast, we went back to our quarters in the grove, and at daylight were off for Shiraz.

Two steep *kotals* brought us to the plain of Dashtiarjan, nearly six thousand six hundred feet above the sea. The night we spent at the telegraph-office. As I have already written you, the Anglo-Indian telegraph runs along the entire route from Bushire to Teheran. It is splendidly constructed, with cast-iron poles. Every forty or fifty miles there is a telegraph-office, and an operator who speaks English. At these offices we were kindly received and hospitably entertained. All along our line of march we had only to look at the telegraph-line, to remind us of the civilization to which we were hastening. In mountain-passes, where the poles were perched on dizzy heights, and the wires spanned gracefully the intervening chasms; or on the plains, where for miles the poles could be seen growing shorter and shorter, till lost in a point of the horizon, we felt that we were not alone, and that our mute companion, though silent to us, was transmitting messages to hundreds of people in Europe, Asia, and even distant America.

We left Dashtiarjan at 5.55 A. M. on the 4th, and arrived at Shiraz at 6 P. M. Mr. Walker, the superintendent of the telegraph, came out to meet us, and made us very comfortable at his house. The pleasure of our visit was increased on account of his having a brother, Captain Fergus Walker, in the First Infantry.

Shiraz lies in a valley about forty miles long and twelve broad. Around the city the soil is well cultivated, but nearly nine-tenths of the land is suffered to lie idle. We called on the governor, who is a brother-in-law of the Shah, and had a particularly pleasant interview, as he spoke French fluently, enabling us to dispense with an interpreter.

The only objects of curiosity at Shiraz are the tombs of the great poets Saadi and Hafiz. We were also shown a stream, about two feet wide, which the former has made immortal. These three objects, and a walk through the bazaar, constituted all of our sightseeing at Shiraz.

TEHERAN, *March* 19, 1876.

We left Shiraz on Monday the 6th at 3 P. M., on chapar-horses for Ispahan, and passed the night in a chapar-khanah at Zirgan. Mr. Walker and several friends accompanied us a few miles on our road, and then left us to our new experience in Persian travel. There are no railroads, as you well know, in Persia; nor have we seen a wheeled vehicle of any description from Bushire to Teheran. As a substitute, there are lines of post-horses established on all the main routes centring at the capital.

The distance between stations is from sixteen to twenty-eight miles. At each station there are from three to five chapar-horses, and such horses as are only to be met in Persia. Foundered, ring-boned, and spavined, they often start off on three legs; but, on warming to their work, they gradually get the use of the fourth, and then, breaking into an ambling gait, canter almost without a stop from one station to another. It hardly does to speak of their backs. The hard, inflexible Persian saddle, which looks like the roof of a small house, has made them so sore that it is far preferable to ride them in winter than summer. To the above defects must be added another which involves some peril to the rider, and that is, that they are knee-sprung and frequently stumble. Each one of us got a fall—horse and rider tumbling into a heap—yet we all escaped without a bruise or a scratch.

The stations are called chapar-khanahs, and are built exclusively of mud. In form they are like the caravansaries, with the exception that they have small, round towers at the angles, and that there is a single room over the arched gateway for the accommodation of travelers.

As you enter this room, through an aperture for a door, which has to be stopped with a felt or a blanket, the view of its mud floor, mud walls, and mud ceiling, is nowise cheering or encouraging. Presently the servant appears with a light, spreads your bedding, and then brings in a soup, and some kind of a stew, which he calls your dinner. After you have eaten it—sitting cross-legged like a Turk—the only resource left is sleep.

Our cook was remarkable for the variety of uses to which he could apply the few articles composing our kit, a quality we had overlooked until one day we discovered that the soup had been served in our wash-basins! Fortunately our appetites had been appeased, but from that time we requested him to exert his ingenuity in other directions.

From Zirgan we went to the ruins of Persepolis, the ancient capital of the empire. The city was situated at the junction of five fertile valleys, and was surrounded with snow-capped mountains.

The ruins consist of the lower stories of the palaces of Darius and Xerxes, the Hall of Xerxes, and the propylæa of Xerxes. They stand on three terraces of different elevations, the walls supporting the terraces being about fifty feet high. The outside walls, which face the plain, are composed of large blocks of limestone, which required no little engineering skill to place one above the other. From the top of the walls the terraces extend back three or four hundred yards to the mountains, which rise precipitously in the rear. A broad, double staircase, up which our horses clambered, leads from the plain to the terraces. On the inner walls of the staircases, processions of men and beasts are sculptured in bass-relief; also in the gateway and on the sides of the doors of the palaces combats between men and beasts are represented in the same manner.

In the propylæa of Xerxes, beneath one of the huge winged lions, carved in large letters, was the name "Stanley—New York Herald." The names of British embassadors, and many other visitors, are also written or carved conspicuously on the columns of the different edifices. The grandest building must have been the Hall of Xerxes, which consisted of a massive roof supported by seventy-two columns, each seventy feet high and six feet in diameter.

Alexander visited Persepolis, and it is supposed burned its palaces. Behind the ruins, excavated in solid rock, are several tombs. The tomb of Darius is said to be at Nakh-i-Rustam. It consists of a Greek cross, sculptured in the face of a vertical cliff about two hundred feet high. In the centre of the cross a door leads into a gallery excavated parallel to the horizontal arm. From the inner face of the gallery, if like the one we entered at Persepolis, three arched recesses are excavated, each of which contains two graves sunk beneath the floor. Above the door, on the horizontal arm, there are two tiers of human figures in bass-relief. At the top of the vertical arm there is a figure of the sun, and below it an altar of fire. Standing in front of the altar, a bow in his hand, the king adores the source of light and heat. To-day in Teheran the fire-worshipers render the sun the same homage as in the days of Cyrus. Neither Christianity, nor astronomy, nor the persecuting power of Mohammedanism, has sufficed to turn them from their ignorant worship. They move among the Persians probably the only true descendants of the people who lived twenty-four centuries ago when the empire was at the zenith of its power.

Leaving Persepolis and Nakh-i-Rustam we passed on to Saidan, where we spent the night.

Wednesday, 8th.—We proceeded to Dehbid. On our way we passed the tomb of Cyrus. It stands in a large plain about six thousand feet above the sea, surrounded by low mountains. The tomb, which looks like a small, one-story rectangular house, with massive roof and eaves, rests on a pyramidal pedestal, the steps of which are composed of blocks of marble nine feet long and three feet high. Around the base of the pyramid are fragments of columns which probably supported a stone roof above the tomb. Notwithstanding this edifice has disappeared, the elements for centuries have beaten in vain against the mausoleum of the great king. His sarcophagus is gone, his ashes are scattered to the winds, but his sepulchre still stands, almost the only monument of the greatness of his reign.

Near by is a solitary column about fifty feet high, and a high wall, the end of a hall, the only remains of the city of Passargardæ. Among the many visitors to the tomb of Cyrus was Alexander. Unlike visitors at Persepolis, he did not inscribe his name thereon, but wrote it in blood from the gulf of Issus to the valley of the Indus.

Leaving Dehbid at 6 A. M., we spent the night of the 9th at Abadeh, the night of the 10th at Kumesheh, and arrived at Ispahan at 3.30 P. M. on the 11th, where we were the guests of Mr. Bruce, an English missionary. This brave man has had a hard time among the Armenians and Mussulmans. Four times he has been shot at, but still continues to work in the hope of success.

Ispahan lies in a large plain, with mountains rising in every direction. The soil is cultivated exclusively by irrigation, not only by artificial streams brought along the surface of the ground, but by subterranean streams brought from the mountains miles away.

To dig one of these streams, they sink a well near the base of the mountains till they find a spring of living water large enough to supply a stream three or four feet wide and a foot in depth. The first well is sometimes as many as three hundred feet deep. Having found water, they sink other wells, about every hundred feet, along the line of the proposed stream, the bottoms of which are on the same level as the first. A channel is then dug from the bottom of one well to another until, as the wells gradually decrease in depth, the water is brought to the surface miles from the source. On leaving Ispahan we followed one of these *connauts*, as they are called, for forty miles.

As soon as the water is brought to the surface it is conducted in ditches to the small fields, varying in size from one hundred to one thousand or two thousand square feet. For the purpose of being flooded, the fields are separated from each other by a raised furrow about a foot high. It is only after seeing the immense labor the poor people of Persia have to perform before receiving a grain from the soil, that one can appreciate the blessing of living in a country of rains and fruitful seasons.

At Ispahan we called upon the governor, who, although the eldest son of the Shah, is not the heir to the throne, as he was not born of a princess. The heir is Governor of Tabriz, but is now in Teheran, where he has come to pay his respects to the Shah, on the opening of the New Year.

From Ispahan we came through to Teheran in four days, stopping the first night (13th) at Soh. The 14th we crossed the pass of Kohrud, eight thousand eight hundred feet above the sea. Notwithstanding the elevation and snow, we suffered more from the heat, and reflection of the sun, than on any day since leaving Bushire. The night of the 14th we spent at Kashan. The night of the 15th at Pul-i-dilak; and on the 16th, at 5.30, arrived at the British legation in Teheran.

The last two days from Ispahan we rode one hundred and sixty miles; on the other days we averaged from fifty to seventy.

The country from Bushire to Teheran is the most arid I have ever seen, and the poverty of the people passes description. During the famine of 1871–'72 one-fifth of the population—more than a million souls, perished from starvation. In some villages and districts every man and beast perished. The people were so hungry that, when dogs were shot in the streets, they tore them to pieces and devoured their flesh raw. Even in Teheran the dead were allowed to decay in the streets. In some places children fell victims to the hunger of their parents.

On our way to Shiraz I visited a village. It consisted of a low stone shed, inclosing a court about one hundred feet square. In the centre of the court was a huge pile of manure, and several stagnant pools of discolored water. The rooms which faced the court were not more than ten feet square, and were without beds, windows, or floors. The people sleep on felts and skins, spread on the ground, and, to make up as much as possible for the want of fire, they bring their sheep and calves into their rooms to avail themselves of their animal heat. In the stalls I have described, which we would not use for the meanest of domestic animals, were crowded together one hundred and fifty men, women, and children, the picture of misery, filth, and despair.

This village was but one of many we passed along our route. We saw several which had been completely depopulated by the famine. Ruin everywhere prevailed. Even a large portion of Ispahan, which two hundred years ago was a city of several hundred thousand people, was a heap of rubbish and deserted walls. Most of the houses, including the roofs, are built of mud mixed with straw.

In cities like Shiraz and Ispahan the bazaars are built of brick, the streets being completely arched over, so that when one approaches the city he enters a tunnel, and emerges at a point several hundred yards away. On each side of the street, within the arcade, every article of merchandise is exposed to the best advantage. The salesmen sit cross-legged awaiting customers. If so fortunate as to be driving a bargain, a fierce discussion at once ensues, in which everybody is free to participate. Between the booths, an incessant crowd of people, horses, mules, camels, and donkeys, move up and down, but never in a hurry. The measured sound of bells, swinging slowly from one side to the other beneath the necks of camels, tells of the arrival of caravans from distant parts of the empire.

No heavy stages or express-wagons are seen lumbering through the streets. As you crowd your way along, with perhaps the Mohammedans cursing you, and the camels gazing at you with their meaningless brown eyes, you feel that you are in a strange land in the far East.

In the days of Ahasuerus, Haman asked for the extermination of the Jews, and the king granted his request. Queen Esther, at the peril of her life, begged for her people; and, when Haman had met his fate, the king sent orders to the Jews to defend themselves. He could not revoke his first law, but the second gave courage to the Jews, and when assailed they slew five hundred people within the palace. To-day, the Shah could sport in the same manner with the lives of his people. Here, as in China, monarchy and absolutism culminate, and corruption is the order of the day. Even the Shah takes bribes, and when he wishes to extort money he announces a visit to some distant province, in order that the governors and officials may buy him off, rather than incur the expense of entertaining him. When he travels, his soldiers, like a swarm of locusts, devour the sustenance of the people.

Governorships are bought and sold; and, when the revenue is not forthcoming, the people are squeezed till they yield the last farthing.

TEHERAN, *March* 25, 1876.

It was our intention, when we arrived on the 16th, to leave on the 20th. Mr. Thompson, who desired that we might have the pleasure of meeting the society of Teheran, has given two dinners, to which were invited many of the Europeans in the city. Nearly every European in Teheran holds some official position, either at one of the legations, or in connection with the Anglo-Indian telegraph, which belongs to the Government. At the first dinner were present the *chargés d'affaires* of Russia and France, and some of the instructors of the Shah's army. At the second dinner the Austrian and Turkish ministers were present, and we also had the pleasure of meeting Mr. and Mrs. Bassett, and Mr. Potter, of the American mission, who are highly esteemed by all of the European residents.

The 21st of March is the New-Year's-day of the Persians, and, like the custom in Europe and America, the Shah celebrates the occasion by giving a public reception. Being under the protection of the English minister, we were invited to accompany the diplomatic corps.

At twelve o'clock the various legations assembled in an upper room of the palace, where they were received by the prime-minister, who wore a scarlet uniform, heavily embroidered with gold. The uniforms of the various members of the legations were scarcely less brilliant, their breasts being covered with sparkling crosses and decorations, arranged in double and triple rows. In this room tea and coffee were served, and the tall *calaon*, or Persian pipe, made several revolutions, as many as desired smoking it one after the other.

By an article in all of the treaties, at every interview with the Shah, the foreign representatives have to wear galoches, or over shoes, which are removed just before entering his presence. It is a partial concession to Persian custom, which requires everybody to remove his shoes before stepping on a carpet.

The Shah having signified his readiness to receive the diplomatic corps, galoches were resumed, when, descending from the room before described, the procession moved through two courts into a large garden, overlooked by the hall of audience. If the Shah had presented himself at the window, he would have been saluted, but, as he did not show himself, galoches were removed, and everybody began to ascend the high steps of the Persian stairs. At the top was a door immediately leading into the Shah's presence. On entering it, all saluted; advanced half-way, saluted again; and, finally, a third time on arriving near his majesty's person. The ministers then arranged themselves in first line.

Count Dubsky, the Austrian minister, who is the dean of the corps, made a short address in French, in the translation of which his Oriental secretary completely broke down. The Shah relieved the awkwardness by immediately entering into conversation with the ministers, asking them how they were, if their sovereigns were well, and several other commonplace questions.

During this exchange of civilities I had ample opportunity to examine the Shah's dress. He wore a dark, almost black coat and trousers, and black cap. On his coat were six horizontal and two vertical rows of diamonds, each row containing not less than nine or ten solitaires as large as the ball of one's thumb. There were also two vertical rows of rubies, each ruby being not less than an inch and a half long. His epaulets, including the pendent part, ordinarily made of gold bullion, and the scabbard of his sword, were completely studded with diamonds, and presented a mass of white light. Over his shoulders he wore a blue sash, on which, near the centre of his breast, a star of diamonds, three inches in diameter, sparkled like an immense cluster. A spray of diamonds on his plain black cap completed his apparel. Behind him was the seat of the celebrated Peacock Throne of Delhi, which was captured by Nadir Shah, and sent to Teheran, about one hundred and fifty years ago. It was thickly studded with precious stones, but was at such a distance that I could not distinguish them.

From the survey of so much magnificence my attention was attracted by the voice of Mr. Thompson, who, addressing his majesty in Persian, said he had the honor to present three American officers, and then introduced us severally by name. The Shah, who held a pair of gold spectacles in his hand, leveled them upon us. He asked us when we arrived; if the soldiers of Japan wore the European uniform; if China had an army; and if General Grant were our President. His conversation, which the diplomatic corps regarded as very gracious, did not long interrupt my survey of the surroundings.

The room was Eurasian in appearance. The floor was inlaid, and European paintings decorated the walls and columns. The ceiling was highly painted, after the manner so common in Asia.

When the Shah signified that the audience was at an end, every one saluted, and then, with more or less dexterity, retreated backward, stopping and saluting twice as at the beginning.

We had deferred our departure from Teheran one day in order to witness this ceremony; and, well out of the Shah's presence, were happy in the thought that the morrow would see us on our way to Constantinople. But, as we were about to descend the stairs, the prime-minister came to me, and, addressing me in French, told me that his majesty desired us to stay and witness the manœuvres that would take place the following week. As it would have been a breach of etiquette not to comply, I promptly accepted the invitation; and so, contrary to our wishes, we found ourselves detained for another week. But we cannot complain. Everybody in Teheran has contributed to the pleasure of our visit, and spared no pains to give us agreeable entertainments.

After the reception was over for the diplomatic corps, we were conducted to a room where we could see the grand salam, or public reception. As the Shah took his seat on a throne facing a large court, the bands struck up, and the guns thundered a salute. The oldest prince then read an address, to which the Shah replied, and then followed a poem. Afterward there was a distribution of money to the people, who crowded the court—a silver piece of the value of a penny being given to each person as a souvenir of the occasion. The Shah, having smoked the calaon, came down from the throne, walked off in state, and disappeared amid the clangor of trumpets, and the strains of martial music. The salam being over, we returned to the legation.

On the 22d of March, M. de Belloy, the French *chargé d'af-*

faires, gave a breakfast in one of the Shah's gardens near Reh, after which we had some coursing. We caught only four of the seven hares that were started. Mounted on a good horse, I enjoyed the chase, but my sympathies were always with the hare, and I secretly rejoiced whenever he escaped.

On the 23d, while we were at dinner, Mr. Thompson received notice, through an aide-de-camp, that the Shah desired to give us a private audience the next day at twelve o'clock. We accordingly went, and found his majesty promenading in the large garden in front of the hall of audience. Dr. Tholozan, his French physician, accompanied us as interpreter.

Having made the usual salutations, the Shah began an ejaculatory and inquisitive conversation, lasting at least an hour. He asked us where we were from; the population of New York and Washington; when our presidential election would take place; the extent of our railroads; the size of our army; and the time it took us to go to Japan. All this, however, was preliminary to the real object of the interview, which was to acquire information about American fire-arms. In regard to them he showed great interest, and well he might; for, when in Europe, more than forty thousand breech-loaders were palmed off on him which were perfectly worthless.

He brought out a Henry-Martini, and showed us its action. We regretted not having our arms with us, but I told him we had a revolver at the legation, and that I would be happy to present it to him, which he accepted. During the conversation he strolled through the garden, charging us with a great number of commissions—among them, the expression of his regrets that our Government was not in diplomatic relations with him; to write Roach & Co., of Chester, Pennsylvania, asking the cost of a vessel that would serve for peace and for war; also to write the Colts, of Hartford, Smith & Wesson, of Springfield, and the Remingtons, to ascertain their prices for Gatling guns, revolvers, and carbines.

All this may amount to nothing, but I have been told that the revolver, which has been tried in the presence of the Shah, pleased him so highly that he has resolved to order several thousand for his officers and non-commissioned officers. The interview was very pleasant. The Shah laid aside all reserve, and laughed and chatted freely. He wore a plain, dark uniform, with no other ornamentation than a sword and sword-belt, covered with diamonds. The contrast between the public and private reception was so marked that we all returned charmed with our visit.

TIFLIS, *April* 15, 1876.

On the 28th of March we attended the manœuvres and reviews of the garrison at Teheran. The troops were formed on the race-course, about two miles west of the city, the infantry in front, the artillery distributed along the line, and the irregular cavalry in the rear. As we had delayed our departure a week to witness the review, and had been specially invited by the Shah, we were told that no pains would be spared to impress us with the efficiency and appearance of the Persian army.

The Persian troops owe all of their knowledge of the military art to the presence of five or six European instructors. The senior of these, General Andrini, an Italian, presided at the manœuvres. The infantry was formed in four ranks, of which the first and second fired kneeling, the third and fourth standing.

The principal manœuvre consisted in advancing a line of skirmishers, supported by a line of battle in double rank, behind which, at intervals of forty or fifty yards, were posted a number of companies, also formed in double rank. When the fire became too severe for the skirmishers, they fell back to the line of battle, which fired kneeling; the companies in rear advanced to the line, and, pouring their fire over the heads of the men in front, gave the finishing stroke to an already staggering enemy. On the left, the irregular cavalry, which knew nothing of line or column, charged in swarms, firing at full speed, and raising a great cloud of dust.

We witnessed the review from the grand stand, where, previous to his arrival, the Shah kept everybody waiting for two or three hours. Several of the ladies of the harem, closely veiled, and attended by eunuchs, were present to witness the display. After the Shah had ridden along the lines, he came up in front, and asked if the American officers were present, and, being assured that they were, the troops began to march past.

The irregular cavalry marched in squads of five and six, and, when in front of the Shah, nodded, as a salute. After passing the stand, the troops broke ranks, and straggled back to the city, mingling with the throngs that were returning from the sight.

At the conclusion of the review, we took leave of the Shah, whose ruling thought was the fire-arms, of which he spoke at the private audience. He asked if we had written to the parties, and, when we told him we had, he seemed much pleased.

On the 29th we took leave of Mr. Thompson, and the good people at the legation, and, accompanied for some miles by several gentlemen of the city, we started for Tabriz, distant three hundred and fifty miles, which we rode in five days. The first half of the distance the horses were the worst we had had in Persia. But, being forced to ride them, we had this consolation—that, with the English saddle, the poor beasts suffered less than they had for weeks with the Persian engines of torture. The last half of the distance the horses were excellent, and we made the stages with comfort. In crossing the Kaflan Pass, about eighty miles from Tabriz, we saw, for the first time, crops raised by the rains instead of irrigation.

Tabriz is in a fertile valley, and contains about one hundred thousand inhabitants. It is like all other Persian cities—built of mud and brick, without a single edifice to attract attention. We stopped with Mr. Easton, an American missionary, who came on with us to Tiflis. The mission consists of himself and wife, and a Miss Jewett, but he has come on to Tiflis to meet other friends, who are on their way to join them. We staid at Tabriz but one day; called on the governor, and were invited to breakfast and shown great kindness by the French consul.

On the 5th, at 5.30 P. M., we started for Tiflis, and on the 6th, at about the same hour, arrived at Julfa, the frontier of Persia. Our last day's ride was eighty miles, or a distance greater than from Syracuse to Rochester, while the average during our eleven hundred miles ride was between fifty and sixty per day.

Our food consisted principally of boiled eggs, tea, milk, honey, boiled chicken, and Persian bread. The latter is unleavened, and is baked in the shape of long, thin slabs. The Persians do not know the use of the knife and fork, and instead eat with the thumb and first two fingers.

At Julfa we crossed the Araxes, the boundary between Persia and Russia. On the one side stood the cheerless chapar-khanah, with its mud walls and floors; on the other stood the Russian post-station, the first modern stone building we had seen since leaving Bombay. We had enjoyed our ride through Persia, we had seen its misery and decay, and were glad enough to be once more under the protection of a progressive nation.

At Julfa a four-seated, covered carriage awaited us, which had been sent from Tiflis. Bidding adieu to chapar-horses, we entered our carriage, and on the morning of the 7th continued our way to Tiflis.

The first village of interest on our route was Nakh-i-chewan, where, according to tradition, Noah descended from Ararat. Tradition likewise points to his tomb. It is situated in an Armenian cemetery, is built of brick, and octagonal in shape. A flight of stairs leads down to a vault, supported by a pillar in the centre, at the base of which there is a small fireplace. Here Armenians come on picnics, cook their food, and, after the feast, as a matter of devotion, break their plates, and destroy everything that remains.

All the next day we traveled in the direction of Mount Ararat, and toward evening crossed the Araxes, and spent the night at a Cossack post near its base. This station looked as lonely and forlorn as a post in Arizona. On presenting ourselves, we at once experienced all of the inconveniences of being among a people with whom we could not speak, or communicate. I tried French in vain. We were first taken to the adjutant, who was seated at a table in the open air, drinking a cup of tea. This sphinx-like individual, although told by our conductor that we were American officers, kept his seat, gave us no salutation, and, when he found we could not communicate with him in his native tongue, sent us on to the doctor, but with no better success. Sanger now came to the front, and, by a happy accident, discovered that the armorer was a German, whom he made to understand that we wished to stay all night, and the next morning make a partial ascent of the mountain. This sub-officer at once conducted us to the sutler's store, where, as at all posts, we found a crowd of soldiers, some of whom were playing billiards. They immediately laid down their cues, and retired, when, being sorry to interrupt their amusement, we spread our comforters and pillows, and installed ourselves in the billiard-room for the night.

The next morning we mounted Cossack horses, and began the ascent; but the rain almost immediately obscured the greater part of the mountain, so, on approaching within a few hundred feet of the snow-line, we relinquished the attempt. Ararat, like Vesuvius and 'Fusi Yama, is a volcanic mountain, rising like a graceful cone from the midst of a large plain. Its height is seventeen thousand feet. On its southeastern slope stands Little Ararat, also a perfect cone, eleven thousand feet high. A graceful curve connects the bases of the cones, which were wrapped in their snowy mantle. Little Ararat frequently stood out in all its beauty; but far above its head Great Ararat veiled itself in the mystery of the clouds. Only once, by moonlight, did we see the summit. For a hundred miles we skirted its base, hoping the sun would dispel the storms that enveloped its form, but in vain. On looking back from the last point whence it was visible, we could only see black, surging clouds.

Descending the slope in the rain, we returned to the Cossack post, and, recrossing the Araxes, arrived at Erivan on the evening of the 9th. The next day we began to climb the mountains, passed a picturesque lake five thousand feet above the sea, traveled all night, and arrived at Tiflis at 5.30 P.M. on the 11th, exactly two months from Bombay.

Tiflis contains about one hundred and twenty thousand inhabitants, and lies in a fertile valley, the waters of which flow into the Caspian. It is the capital of the Caucasus, of which the Grand-duke Michael is governor. It was here that General Sherman terminated his travels to the eastward, which suggested the tour we have just completed.

BLACK SEA, *April* 30, 1876.

On Saturday, the 15th of April, while at Tiflis, we were presented to the grand-duke. He received us very cordially, spoke English well, and kindly showed us over his palace.

After the presentation we visited the military school for officers, the model company of infantry, composed of soldiers from every regiment in the Caucasus, and also the Military Club. In the evening we were invited to attend the services at the cathedral, which consisted mostly of processions, chants, and incense. In recognition of the resurrection, the occasion is made one of joy, and is attended by all of the officers in full dress. The priests never shave or cut their hair, which hangs some distance down the back, giving them when old a patriarchal appearance.

Conspicuous above all of the congregation was the Grand-duke

Michael—a tall, handsome man, beside whom stood his son, seventeen years old, still taller than his father. At the conclusion of the services the archbishop held in his arms a cross, which the members of the congregation successively kissed. They then kissed the archbishop three times, twice on the left cheek and once on the right. The three kisses were typical of the Trinity. The grand-duke was the first to perform this ceremony; after which he took his stand near one of the large pilasters of the church; when, after kissing the cross and the archbishop, his generals successively approached, kissed him, and were kissed in return. This custom, strange as it may seem, is the usual one in Russia. At the railway-stations it is common to see men kiss as affectionately as husband and wife.

On Easter-Sunday we were invited to a reception and lunch at the palace, at which were present most of the dignitaries of church and state.

Easter-Monday we dined at the palace. The dinner was charming, due, in a large degree, to the presence of six children who, with the exception of an infant, constituted the whole family. The grand-duchess, a lovely woman, looked with affection and pride upon her family, and especially upon a beautiful daughter of sixteen, who will soon grace the courts of Europe.

From Tiflis there are two ways of reaching Constantinople; one *via* Poti and the Black Sea; the other *via* Vladi-Kavkas, the Crimea, and thence by the Black Sea. As the latter route would permit us to pass through the country of the Cossacks, and at the same time cross the Caucasus, we chose it, and left Tiflis on the morning of the 18th.

The road from Tiflis to Vladi-Kavkas, in construction and for scenery, is one of the grandest in the world. It is macadamized throughout; and, as it zigzags up the mountains along the edges of steep precipices, it gives a succession of magnificent views. It crowns the summit at an elevation of eight thousand feet. Here we found the snow on each side of the road from fifteen to twenty feet deep. The road had been dug out through huge drifts that stood up like perpendicular walls on each side.

The night of the 18th we spent at Kasbeck, at the foot of Mount Kasbeck, sixteen thousand feet high. The next morning for a moment we saw its lofty peak, which was quickly enveloped by surging clouds. The descent was through a pass unequaled in Europe. The walls on each side rose almost perpendicularly to a height of two or three thousand feet, reminding us of the great chasm of the Yosemite. The road in many places was hewed out of the solid rock, and was full of picturesque turns and surprises.

At the end of the pass we came out of a magnificent gateway, and before us lay the great steppes of Russia as smooth and as fertile as the prairies of Illinois. I had never before fully understood the meaning of steppes. I had supposed them to be rather elevated, desolate tracts, across which the wind howled piteously, and where the cold in winter was of arctic fierceness. But here all was explained in a moment.

From Vladi-Kavkas, where we took the railroad, on the 20th, to Rostoff, thence to Losovai and Simferopol in the Crimea, a distance of six hundred miles, the country was exactly like the plains of Illinois, Kansas, and Iowa. Sparsely populated, hundreds and thousands of square miles, which have never been cultivated, invite the immigrant as in our own great West. It only needs their labor to make Southern Russia one of the most fertile and populous countries in the world.

At Vladi-Kavkas we visited the military school, and also witnessed feats of horsemanship by the Cossacks. They are certainly wonderful riders, far excelling anything we saw in India and Persia. A skirmish-line made their horses lie down, fired from behind them, and, when the enemy charged, they rose, mounted, and disappeared like the wind. They also threw themselves out of their saddles, simulated the rescue of wounded comrades, and, hanging by one leg over the horse's back, scraped the ground for a hundred yards, the horses moving at full speed.

After the riding, the governor, with whom we dined, invited us back to his palace, where the Cossacks entertained us with dancing and music.

After a short stay at Vladi-Kavkas we again took the cars. The road, built by government subsidy for military purposes, has already developed the country, and villages are springing up along the line, the same as in America. We reached Rostoff on the 21st, at 9 A. M., and left at 4 P. M. Mr. Martin, an Englishman who is our consular agent, gave us a cordial reception. His warehouses and yards were filled with steam-thrashers, ploughs, American horse-rakes, and other agricultural implements, showing that the spirit of improvement has already taken hold of the people.

The city is at the mouth of the Don, and has grown so rapidly as to gain for it the nickname Chicago. With a great fertile country at its back, it certainly has a fine future. The Don, where we crossed it, was five miles wide. Below the railroad it expands and forms the head of the Sea of Azof.

At one point the Don and the Volga are but a few miles apart. A canal across the isthmus would enable Rostoff to become a port of the Caspian Sea.

Leaving Rostoff on the 21st, we arrived at Sevastopol on the 23d. Here we reached the traveled routes of Europe, and, as the rest of our journey will be through countries too well known to need description, here must end this series of letters.

INDEX.

	PAGE
AGGRESSIVE power of England	268
Armies:	
Austria	161
China	13
England	250
France	225
Germany	191
India	33
Italy	98
Japan	1
Persia	88
Russia	146
Armies (strength of):	
Austria	161–2
China	19
England	250
France	225–6
Germany	191–2
India	33–4
Italy	98
Japan	8
Russia	147
Army territoriale (France)	235
Arms (Persia)	91
Artillery (strength of):	
Austria	161–2
China	16
England	250
France	226
Germany	191–2
India	3–34
Italy	98
Japan	8, 10
Persia	91
Russia	147
United States (proposed)	346–50
Administrative corps (Italy)	100
Bannermen (China)	17
Battalion (organization of):	
Austria	163
England	251
France	228
Germany	193
Italy	102
Japan	9, 10
United States (proposed peace-footing)	338
United States (proposed war-footing)	341
Battalion formations (German)	260–4
Battalions of instruction (Italy)	120
Barracks:	
India	68
Japan	11
Bazaar (India)	59
British army (India)	65
Bersaglieri (Italy)	104

INDEX

	PAGE
Brigade:	
Austria	166
England	251
France	231
Germany	194
Italy	105
Russia	150
Cavalry (strength of):	
Austria	161–2
China	15
France	225
England	250
Germany	191–2
India	33–4
Italy	98
Japan	8, 10
Persia	90
Russia	147
United States (proposed)	344–6
Civil and military authorities (India)	51
Company (organization of):	
Austria	163
France	228
Germany	193
Italy	101
Japan	10
Russia	149
United States (proposed peace-footing)	338
United States (proposed war-footing)	341
Conclusions	317–70
Corps:	
Austria	166
England	252
France	231
Germany	195
Italy	105
Russia	150
Company column:	
French	287–91
German	271–75

	PAGE
Austria	303
Italy	303
Russia	303
Deployment of a battalion as skirmishers:	
English	306–12
French	297
German	275
Russian	304–6
Deployment of company column as skirmishers:	
French	293
German	274
Deployment by numbers (United States)	313
Detached service (United States)	336
Detail (staff):	
Austria	189
England	255
Germany	218–19
Italy	140
India	43
United States (results of)	336–7
Depot:	
Austria	161–5
England	254
France	228, 230
Germany	199–201
Italy	103
United States (peace-footing)	339
" " (war-footing)	342
Discipline:	
Austria	181
China	21
Germany	224
India	61, 77
Russia	159
United States	358
Distribution of troops (India)	81
Division:	
Austria	166
England	252
France	231

INDEX. 443

	PAGE
Germany	194
Italy	105
Russia	150

Examinations for:
  Bengal staff corps ... 38
  Native languages (India) ... 41
Examination for promotion:
  Austria ... 183–9
  England ... 267
  United States ... 354
"Ersatz" reserve:
  Austria ... 167
  Germany ... 199
  Italy ... 109

French company column ... 287–91
Furlough-list:
  Germany ... 199
  India ... 47

Garrison instruction (India) ... 40
General list (India) ... 36
General officers (France) ... 226
General remarks:
  China ... 29
  India ... 75
  Persia ... 93
  Tactics ... 313
German company column ... 271–8
Governor-generals (China) ... 26

Honors (China) ... 24
Hospitals:
  India ... 72
  Japan ... 11

Infantry:
  Austria ... 162
  China ... 15
  England ... 250
  France ... 226–31
  Germany ... 192

	PAGE
India (native)	54
" (British)	63
Italy	101
Japan	9
Persia	88
Russia	149
United States	337–43

Infantry tactics ... 270
Invasion of India ... 84

Jäger battalions, German ... 285

Landwehr:
  Austria ... 168
  Germany ... 201
Landsturm (Germany) ... 203
Languages (native) ... 41
Lineal promotion (United States) .. 353–4

Military districts (Italy) ... 106
Military education (United States) 360–66
Military professorships (United
  States) ... 366
Militia (England) ... 254
Militia reserve (England) ... 254
Militia mobile (Italy) ... 112
Militia territoriale (Italy) ... 114
Movable columns (India) ... 63

National volunteers ... 367
Non-commissioned officers:
  Germany ... 204
  Italy ... 123
  India (native) ... 57
  Russia ... 151

Officers:
  Army territoriale (France) ... 237
  India (European) ... 34
  " (native) ... 56
  Persia ... 89
  Reserve (complement) United
    States ... 343

INDEX.

	PAGE
Officers:	
Reserve (France)	236
" (Germany)	198
" (Italy)	116
Landwehr (Germany)	202
Militia mobile (Italy)	114
Old cadre-list (India)	37
Pay:	
India (staff)	45
" (native regiment)	57
" (British regiment)	74
Persia	92
Personal reports:	
Austria	183–7
England	256
United States	327
Promotion:	
Austria	183–9
England	267
Germany	223
India	46
Italy	142
Russia	158
Probation staff (India)	43
Punishments:	
Austria	181
China	23
Germany	224
India	61
Russia	159
United States	358–60
Recruitment:	
Austria	166
England	252
France	232
Germany	196
Italy	108–12
Regiments (organization of):	
Austria	164–5
England	250
France	228–30
Germany	194

	PAGE
India { British	65
{ Native	54
Italy	102
Japan	9
Persia	89
Russia	150
United States:	
Infantry { Peace-footing	339
{ War-footing	342
Cavalry { Peace-footing	345
{ War-footing	345
Artillery	346
Recreation (India)	67
Reserve:	
England	253
Germany	197
Reserve (obligations of):	
Germany	202
Retirement (India)	46
Rewards (India)	59
Schools (men):	
Austria	169–70
Germany	203–4
Italy	117–18
School of Musketry and Gymnastics:	
Japan	5
Schools (non-commissioned officers):	
Austria	170–2
Germany	204–5
Italy	119–22
Japan	5
Schools (officers):	
Application (artillery and engineers, Austria)	177–8
" (artillery and engineers, France)	247
" (artillery and engineers, Italy)	134
" (artillery, United States)	363–65
Cadet Corps (Germany)	209–211

INDEX. 445

	PAGE
Central infantry and cavalry (Austria)	180–1
Infantry and cavalry (United States)	366
Military Academy (infantry and cavalry, Austria)	174
Military Academy (artillery and engineers, England)	260–3
Military Academy (artillery and engineers, Italy)	133
Military Academy (infantry, cavalry, artillery, and engineers, Japan)	3
Military Academy (infantry, cavalry, artillery, and engineers, United States)	360
Military Technical Academy (artillery and engineers), Austria	176
Military College (preparatory), Austria	172
Military Colleges (preparatory), Italy	128
Military College (infantry and cavalry), England	256–60
Military Schools (infantry and cavalry), Italy	131
Military Schools (infantry and cavalry), France	240
Military Schools (artillery and engineers), Russia	155–6
Military Schools (infantry and cavalry), Russia	151–4
Military Technical School (preparatory), Austria	173
Normal School (infantry), Italy	134
" " (cavalry) "	136
Prytanée Militaire (preparatory), France	239
Polytechnic (artillery and engineers), France	243
Staff College (England)	263–6
Staff (application), France	248
War Academy (staff), Austria	179

	PAGE
War Academy (staff), France	249
" " " Germany	213–18
" " " Italy	136
" " " Russia	157
War Schools, Germany	208
Skirmishing:	
French	292–303
German	274–80
English	306–12
Russian	308–6
United States	312–15
Staff:	
Austria	189–90
England	255
France	237–8
Germany	218
Italy	90
Japan	8
United States:	
Adjutant-General's Department	327–32
Engineers	335
Ordnance	335
Pay Department	334
Quartermaster's Department	338
Subsistence Department	333
Signal Corps	334
Staff Corps:	
Bengal	37
India	36
Staff probation (India)	43*
Sundays (India)	68
Superintendent of Military Education	367
Supplies:	
China	24
India	64
Tactics:	
China	20
Infantry	270
Japan	12
Tenure of staff appointments (India)	43

	PAGE		PAGE
Territorial commands:		Volunteers:	
England	254	England	253
France	232	Italy	115
Germany	195	Volunteers for one year:	
Italy	105	Germany	205
Russia	151	Italy	115
Transportation:		United States (national)	367
China	25		
India	62	War Department:	
		China	13
Unemployed list (India)	37	Japan	6
Variety of service (India)	48	Yeoman cavalry (England)	254

THE END.

www.ingramcontent.com/pod-product-compliance
Lightning Source LLC
Chambersburg PA
CBHW031957300426
44117CB00008B/805